The
Baseball
Business

James Edward Miller

THE BASEBALL BUSINESS

Pursuing Pennants and Profits in Baltimore

The University of North Carolina Press

Chapel Hill and London

© 1990 The University of North Carolina Press
All rights reserved
Manufactured in the United States of America

The paper in this book meets the guidelines for
permanence and durability of the Committee on
Production Guidelines for Book Longevity of the
Council on Library Resources.

94 93 92 91   5 4 3 2

Library of Congress Cataloging-in-Publication Data
Miller, James Edward.
    The baseball business : pursuing pennants and
profits in Baltimore / by James Edward Miller.
        p.   cm.
    Includes bibliographical references.
    ISBN 0-8078-1876-3 (alk. paper)
    ISBN 0-8078-4323-7 (pbk.: alk. paper)
    1. Baseball—Maryland—Baltimore—Finance—
Case studies.
    2. Baseball—Economic aspects—Maryland—
Baltimore—Case studies.
    I. Title.
    GV880.M55   1990
    338.4'7796357'64097526—dc20   89-36996
                                                CIP

Design by April Leidig-Higgins

Contents

A section of photographs will be found
beginning on page 157.

Preface

In a rare moment of grammatical clarity and simplicity, the New York Yankees' famed manager Casey Stengel once remarked, "Baseball's business." Professional sports have become an important part of the entertainment business and a significant factor in the nation's economy. Not only do millions of spectators pay anywhere from five dollars to more than five hundred dollars per head to see professional sports in person, the public appetite for athletic entertainment has opened the way to multimillion dollar television contracts for promoters, lucrative personal endorsement agreements and enormous salaries for successful athletes, and the utilization of millions in tax revenues to provide new stadiums and services for owners and fans. Sports is business, and professional baseball, which occupies center stage for more than six months of the athletic year, is a central element in athletics for profit.

In a November 1983 essay, Roger Angell, the *New Yorker*'s resident baseball sage, pronounced the Baltimore Orioles "the dominant American League team of our time." During the previous quarter-century, the Baltimore team had been the major leagues' most consistent winner. Between 1966 and 1983, the team participated in seven American League championship series and six World Series. The thirty years during which Baltimore consolidated this dominant position were also an era of radical change within the baseball industry.

This study focuses on six aspects of the business of baseball: (1) the changing relationship between the major and minor leagues; (2) marketing, especially by means of television; (3) the evolution of one club's management from community ownership to one-man control; (4) organized baseball's increasingly complex and costly labor relations; (5) the peculiar partnership of for-profit sports teams with local governments, particularly the utilization of tax dollars to construct public stadiums; and (6) baseball's treatment of its most significant minority, blacks, as it is manifested on the field, in the front office, and in marketing.

The Baltimore club is a useful vehicle for studying the changes that have taken place in the baseball industry since the 1950s. St. Louis owner Bill Veeck's 1953 decision to move his franchise to Baltimore was one of the first significant responses by major league baseball to its postwar difficulties, and the move ushered in an era of franchise shifts and expansion. The Orioles built their highly successful farm system at a time when minor league baseball was undergoing a series of fundamental changes. During the 1970s, the club struggled to deal with serious personnel losses brought about by the introduction of "free agency" in the labor market. Later, it made a major and disastrous investment in free agent players in an effort to maintain its competitiveness. The relationship between the club and the city's political and business elites has always been close, and the effort to attract and maintain major league baseball in Baltimore has been a critical part of the city's attempt to refurbish its image and attract new industries. The nearly twenty-year debate over replacing Memorial Stadium with a more modern facility is a case study of the often-difficult relationship between sports enterprises and state and municipal governments. Working in a limited market area, the Orioles have frequently been a pioneer in developing new techniques to attract paid attendance. Under the leadership of Edward Bennett Williams, the club was very successful at utilizing up-to-date sales methods, including cable television technology, to maintain its profitability despite a series of mediocre teams. Finally, and regrettably, Baltimore's handling of racial issues has frequently mirrored the general pattern of baseball discrimination.

The book is organized into an introduction, three parts, and an epilogue. The Introduction provides an overview of major league baseball at the beginning of the 1950s. Part 1, Community Baseball (Chapters 1–5), traces the development of the Baltimore Orioles from their establishment in 1953 to the 1965 season, emphasizing the changing relationship between the major and minor leagues, the painfully slow process of racial integration in baseball and in the community, and the struggle within the Baltimore board of directors over the personalities and policies needed to build a winning and profitable team.

Part 2, The Hoffberger Years (Chapters 6–11), looks at team management as the Orioles became a marketing arm of a larger corporation. During this period, which extends from 1965 to 1979, the Orioles won their first World Series, in 1966, and achieved their greatest sustained success, dominating baseball from 1969 to 1971 and the American League East from 1973 to 1975. In spite of these successes, the club's financial position became increasingly perilous as a result of low attendance and the onset of a revolution in labor-management relations. By the mid-1970s, owner Jerold Hoffberger was actively seeking to sell the club. The book chronicles these negotiations and the efforts of Baltimore civic groups to retain a major league franchise, as well as the growing involvement of the state of Maryland in efforts to meet the demands of the city's major professional sports franchises for a new stadium.

The Williams Era, 1979–88, is the subject of the book's third part (Chapters 12–14). Unprecedented success in marketing baseball accompanied the gradual collapse of the Orioles on the field. This section explores the decline of the Orioles once-proud minor league system and the struggle over control of baseball operations that followed successive poor seasons. It discusses the marketing techniques that Williams employed to turn the Orioles into a profitable regional franchise. The Williams years saw the struggle between labor and management reach new depths of bitterness, and the book looks at the issues that divided the two sides. It also analyzes the events that led Maryland's political leadership finally to approve a costly and controversial plan for the construction of two new stadiums in Baltimore.

Shortly before his death, Edward Bennett Williams reorganized his club's management in an effort to rebuild the Orioles into a consistent winner. The ultimate success or failure of this effort and the club's continued profitability hinged on his choice of a management team and on the ability of organized baseball to adapt to serious changes in its most important economic and political relationships. The Epilogue examines the current state of baseball's complex relationships with the media, local government, and its own unions, and the renewed efforts of blacks to win equal treatment.

Historians venturing to study contemporary sports are naturally concerned with both the paucity of solid studies and the problems of finding adequate documentation. A few excellent studies have helped to inform and guide my own research: David Voigt's *American Baseball*, Jules Tygiel's superb *Baseball's Great Experiment*, Kevin Kerrane's *Dollar Sign on the Muscle*, Roger Kahn's *Good Enough to Dream*, Benjamin Rader's *In Its Own Image*, and Murray Polner's *Branch Rickey*. Among dozens of memoirs, those of Bowie Kuhn, Earl Weaver, Bill Veeck, Frank Robinson, and Curt Flood were particularly helpful. Regrettably, Lee MacPhail's memoirs appeared too late for use in this volume.

The other problem facing the historian of professional baseball is the quality and quantity of sources. Like most historians, I have a strong prejudice for written primary sources. Baltimore records repositories—the City Archives, the Maryland Historical Society, and the Pratt Library—provided some useful materials, as did the Maryland State Archives in Annapolis. However, the best collections, particularly on issues that affected the entire sport, were located at the National Baseball Library in Cooperstown, New York, and the National Archives and the Library of Congress in Washington. Librarians at the University of Rochester and the University of Michigan provided assistance with the papers of former senators Kenneth Keating and Philip Hart. Congressional hearings were another excellent source. I am very conscious of the debt I owe to archivists and librarians at all these institutions for their assistance.

I supplemented the written record with interviews. I am very grateful to Hank Peters, Harry Dalton, the late Jim McLaughlin, Brooks Robinson, Lee MacPhail, the Hon. Frank Horton, and the late Jack Dunn, who without exception were gracious with their time and frank in their discussion.

Finally, I have relied heavily on the sporting press. *The Sporting News*, which until the 1970s functioned as a trade newspaper, and Baltimore newspapers—the *Sun*, *Evening Sun*, and *News Post* and its successor, the *News American*—provided increasingly sophisticated coverage of baseball's business side. Since the departure of the Senators in 1971, the *Washington Post* has offered first-class coverage of the Orioles' on- and off-the-field activities. The press in Rochester and San Antonio aided my efforts to understand the travails and triumphs of minor league baseball. The *New York Times*, *Sports Illustrated*, and, more recently, *Baseball America* and *USA Today* are helpful in treating the broader issues confronting baseball during the past four decades.

As a young man I passionately followed two rival major league teams, the Orioles and the Washington Senators. Their contrasting fates gave birth to the question that lies at the heart of this book: Why were the Orioles so successful and the Senators so woebegone? In the last five years, this question has returned in a new form as the Orioles moved from mediocrity to collapse. Fynnette Eaton turned the question into a book by introducing me first to Earl Weaver's entertaining memoirs and then to Jules Tygiel's study. Weaver's book started me thinking about the business side of baseball. Tygiel showed me that the topic could be dealt with in a serious manner. Fynnette, Eric Edelman, and Ted Weir patiently read the manuscript and offered helpful suggestions. The book is dedicated to Fynnette, who inspired it, with gratitude.

The
Baseball
Business

Introduction
A Very Peculiar Business

Rep. Celler: You mean baseball is a business, an industry? Mr. Wrigley: It is a very peculiar business, but it is a business.
—House Judiciary Committee Hearings, 1951

During the summer and fall of 1951 the Judiciary Committee of the U.S. House of Representatives held a most unusual series of hearings. The subject of their antitrust investigation was organized baseball, the industry that played America's "national game" for a profit. Congressmen listened intently to a parade of witnesses from one-time career minor league players to former major league stars like Ty Cobb, as well as many of the sport's most influential executives. These witnesses provided the most comprehensive picture of the baseball business ever available to outsiders. While giving respectful attention to the reminiscences of the game's former stars, the congressmen sharply questioned baseball executives and their lawyers about the sport's labor policies and its failure to increase the number of major league teams. The hearings uncovered evidence that professional baseball was in deep trouble. Committee chairman Emanuel Celler of New York noted that a number of lawsuits filed against the sport had challenged the legality of the basic elements of professional baseball's organization: its labor policies, its franchising methods, its player development system, and its geographic distribution.[1]

The Horsehide Cartel

During most of the first half of the twentieth century professional baseball was a relatively stable industry. Organized baseball was a vertically integrated monopoly. Control of the sport rested with the owners of the sixteen major league teams. In 1903 the National League had formally recognized the major league status of the upstart American League, and the two "big leagues" signed an agreement with the organized minor leagues defining their relationship. The 1903 pact divided the market, established firm controls over player salaries, and set up rules to limit competition for talent, allocate franchises, and regularize relations with the minor leagues. While the number of their supporting minor leagues fluctuated, the teams that composed the two major leagues remained constant, firmly installed in the major urban areas of the northeastern United States. They possessed a large pool of cheap talent and benefited from the development of improved transportation and communications technology. Additionally, after 1922, organized baseball enjoyed immunity from antitrust prosecution.

The sixteen independent major league clubs were simultaneously business partners and competitors. They cooperated by creating a general set of operating rules, by working out common playing schedules, by eliminating competition for players within organized baseball, by preventing the formation of rival "major" leagues, and by taking actions that would maintain public faith in the sport's integrity. The last issue became particularly important after the Black Sox scandal in which Chicago players cooperated with gamblers to fix the 1919 World Series. To reassure the public that the game was honest, the owners created the office of commissioner of baseball.

While the commissioner's primary function was guaranteeing that professional baseball remained free from the influence of gamblers, he also promoted cooperation between the leagues by arbitrating their disputes, handling aspects of major league–minor league relations, and serving as a final arbitrator in labor relations issues.

Cooperation between teams and the rival leagues rested on common rules for player acquisition, scheduling, division of attendance income, labor relations, and publicity. Each league had a unique set of rules that further defined the relationship among its member franchises. The leagues elected their own presidents, individuals who possessed limited authority over issues involving the league's specific rules. The league presidents also controlled the hiring and terms of employment of umpires.

Competition between the clubs and leagues extended beyond the playing field. Professional baseball franchises engaged in a no-holds-barred struggle for top amateur talent. Clubs operating in the same city battled for attendance. Each team jealously guarded its territorial rights and those of its minor league subsidiaries.

The major leagues operated by consensus. Changes in the rules governing the sport usually occurred only when organized baseball faced a crisis. Effective long-term planning was rare, particularly when it involved interleague cooperation.

The sixteen American and National League clubs played on a circuit of ten cities whose geographic boundaries were marked by Washington to the southeast, St. Louis to the southwest, Chicago to the northwest, and Boston to the northeast. Major league baseball's organization reflected the larger social and economical realities of the United States at the turn of the century. The wealth and population of industrial America, as well as its best transportation systems, were concentrated in the Northeast. The location of all of its teams in this relatively compact and most economically developed region of the country was a key factor enabling major league baseball to cope with the damaging impact of two world wars and the Great Depression.

Baseball, particularly the major leagues, profited from the development of technology. A first-class rail passenger system connected the major cities of the northeastern quadrant, making it possible for teams to travel swiftly and economically. Radio enjoyed a rapid development during the 1920s, and in the 1930s it became a major factor in marketing professional baseball.

In addition to taking advantage of a superior location and the ability to utilize key technology, major league baseball firmly controlled its large talent pool. Approximately 3,000 Little League, 9,000 high school, 650 college, and 16,000 American Legion teams were playing amateur baseball in 1950, together with 8,000 semiprofessional squads whose players received some financial compensation. Professional baseball acquired its prospects from this pool. It trained and evaluated them in a nationwide system of minor leagues that developed the skills of aspiring major leaguers while offering local entrepreneurs the opportunity to make a profit. The lower minor leagues (Classes D and C) played an exciting, if not always highly skilled, brand of baseball in small-town America. First year professional ballplayers reported to the lower minor leagues for their initial training and development. If a player's skills improved, he could advance to higher-paying and more challenging Class B and A ball in larger towns and eventually to the higher minors (AA or AAA), clubs that played in some of the largest cities of the United States and Canada. Through outright ownership or "working agreements" with teams at all levels, the major league clubs held effective control of the minor league system.

Major league control subtly changed the nature of the minor leagues. Initially, the minors were independent, profit-making, local business enterprises offering entertainment. Minor league owners' objectives were winning games, filling the stands, and selling talented prospects when the season concluded. Major league clubs, by contrast, placed primary emphasis at the minor league level on player development, even at the cost of winning. Still, the ability of major league clubs to provide top young players and cash subsidies attracted many minor league owners to participate in their development programs by signing working agreements with them. Independent minor league owners fought the trend toward major league control without success. As winning and entertaining local fans took a back seat to player development during the 1940s, the possibility of making a profit in the minor leagues eroded.[2]

In 1950 approximately 8,000 men were playing minor league baseball, a ratio of twenty-four minor league prospects for each major league roster spot. Throughout a player's career his wage-earning ability was limited. The minor leagues enacted salary caps. The competition created by the large number of prospects trying to achieve the same goal of playing on a major league team depressed each player's bargaining power even if he achieved big league status. Most important, a "reserve clause" bound the athlete to play for the team holding his contractual rights for as long as he remained in professional baseball. Very few of the players who finally won a coveted spot on a major league roster earned more than a middle-class wage. In 1951 Ford Frick, the president of the National League, admitted that the average player often received less pay than a "skilled workman."[3] A 1952 congressional study found that in real dollars the salaries of players in the lower minor leagues were less than they had been in 1929 and that salaries in the higher minors had not kept pace with those in other U.S. industries. Baseball was seasonal employment for most players, who normally sought winter jobs to supplement their summer income. The players sacrificed educational possibilities that could have given them later wage-earning power. Baseball's commissioner, Albert "Happy" Chandler, a flamboyant, loquacious former U.S. senator from Kentucky, frankly admitted that few of the many players signed by baseball scouts would be able to make a career as professional athletes: "They lose an opportunity to get an education and they can not play ball. The competition is too tough. Pretty soon they are out of baseball and have no education, . . . and they are gone."[4]

Major league control over its economic environment was solidified by a 1922 Supreme Court ruling (the Federal League case—259 US 200) that baseball was not a form of interstate commerce and thus not subject to antitrust laws. Exemption from prosecution under antitrust law gave baseball a unique status. It became a self-regulating cartel that devised rules of conduct ("baseball law") for its member teams. The major leagues wrote the rules, for example, that covered their relationship with the minor leagues.

The reserve clause, territorial rights, and the minor league draft were the key elements in baseball's system of self-regulation for profit. The reserve clause enabled all the member clubs of organized baseball to control the terms of employment of their respective players. Strictly enforced rules against "tampering" prevented one club from raiding the roster of another to hire away top players. Territorial rights prohibited one team from shifting into the playing area of another squad without league approval and monetary compensation. Finally, an annual draft of minor league players ensured that qualified prospects would advance up the ladder toward the majors—but on terms that favored the interests of the big leagues. The major leagues set low fixed prices on the drafted players to encourage minor league owners to sell their best players and top box office attractions rather than risk losing them in the less profitable draft.[5]

Operating within this self-regulated system, organized baseball survived the economic dislocation created by the two world wars and the Great Depression. In the immediate aftermath of World War II, it enjoyed a period of unprecedented growth. Major league attendance reached 21,250,000 in 1948, double its prewar peak. The number of minor leagues grew from twelve in 1945 to forty-two in 1946 and to fifty-nine in 1949. By the latter year, 454 minor league teams were in operation. "Professional baseball," a 1946 major league steering committee report proudly stated, "is BIG BUSINESS—a $100,000,000 industry—actively engaged in providing the American public with its greatest, and next to the movies, its cheapest entertainment buy."[6]

Caught in a Rundown

By 1950, however, the men who ran organized baseball at all levels were aware that their industry faced a major crisis. Major and minor league attendance levels peaked in 1948 and 1949 respectively and then declined sharply. Numerous minor league teams went bankrupt and the minor league system shrank. A new form of communications technology, television, offered additional revenue but simultaneously threatened to undercut live attendance, baseball's chief source of income. The players started to demand costly improvements in their working conditions. Racial integration began in 1946 and briefly thrust organized baseball into the forefront of a major struggle for social change. The advantages that came from playing in the major cities of the eastern United States began to vanish as the demographic contours of American society shifted radically. In 1903, the area encompassed by the ten cities that made up baseball's circuit had included two-thirds of the nation's population as well as its greatest concentration of wealth. Movement away from these cities, already underway before World War II, accelerated after V-J Day. By 1950 a major population shift to the Sunbelt of the South and West was fully underway. A growing number of Americans who chose to remain in the northeastern quadrant abandoned the city for the suburbs. The major U.S. cities had become unwilling hosts to large urban ghettos where poverty, crime, and racial tensions flourished. An increasing number of major league teams played baseball in aging stadiums in the centers of decaying cities, drastically reducing their ability to attract paying customers.[7]

Changing U.S. demographic patterns brought with them a strong political challenge to the structure of major league baseball. During the 1951 Celler committee hearings, representatives of the major leagues sought to convince Congress to enact legislation that would end court assaults on their exemption from antitrust law. Republican congressman Patrick Hillings of Los Angeles pressed the sport's leaders to expand to the West Coast or assist the Pacific Coast League in becoming a third major league. One or both houses of Congress held hearings into some aspect of the sport in 1951, 1953, 1954, 1957, 1958, 1959, and 1960 as they sought to put pressure on baseball to expand, to improve the situation of the minor leagues, or to bend to constituent desires for increased television or radio coverage. House Judiciary Committee chairman Emanuel Celler, a harsh critic of organized baseball, advocated that Congress strip the sport of its special legal status. Hillings agreed, labeling organized baseball the "horsehide cartel."[8]

Paralleling demographic changes were alterations in the leisure patterns of Americans. The automobile facilitated and encouraged their search for new sources of entertainment. Major league teams were poorly prepared to capitalize on the growing use of cars to seek leisure, as aging central city major league stadiums had little parking. The introduction of air-conditioning in homes, restaurants, bars, theaters, and other places of recreation reduced the attraction of minor league night baseball. Television offered an alternate form of entertainment. Other professional and amateur sports grew in popularity and challenged baseball for a share of the entertainment dollar and for athletic talent.[9]

The One-Eyed Monster

In the spring of 1953, two of baseball's elder statesmen, Branch Rickey and Clark Griffith, singled out television as the source of baseball's postwar problems. Radio, Rickey stated, created a desire to see baseball in person. Television fulfilled that need. Both men agreed that television was cutting badly into attendance at minor league games and was responsible for the decline in the number of minor leagues. Rickey believed that the answer to baseball's television problem lay in getting control of TV broadcasting, limiting it, and pooling television income.[10]

Those who shared Rickey and Griffith's opinion could already point to a number of examples of what they saw as the deleterious impact of television on baseball at both major and minor league levels. Spokesmen for the minor leagues complained that the Jersey City and Newark teams of the International League (IL) moved as a result of competition from the televised New York Yankees games. Boston Braves owner Lou Perini claimed that television caused the massive drop in attendance that led him to transfer his team to Milwaukee in 1953.[11]

Actually, television was an unlikely culprit in any of these specific cases.

Proximity to New York's three major league teams and direct competition with major league night baseball had more to do with the International League's troubles than television did. Perini's difficulties resulted more from the Braves' poor field performance and competition with the American League Red Sox franchise than from television. Although TV was clearly of great importance for baseball's future, television broadcasting was still in a formative stage in the early 1950s. Local broadcasting of baseball games had begun in 1946. In 1949 the National Broadcasting Company (NBC) put together the first limited "network" to telecast a World Series along the East Coast. In 1950 only 12 percent of U.S. households had televisions. As late as 1953 only a dozen TV stations were regularly broadcasting baseball. Baseball's conservatism, the same impulse that caused it to resist broadcasting games over radio for many years, led a number of owners to suspect the new technology of creating problems that, in fact, had deeper roots.[12]

Sports and television were natural partners. Television, especially in the early days of live broadcasting, desperately needed sporting events to utilize air time and attract sponsors. Rerun syndication to cover programming gaps was years away, so the networks and local stations filled the airwaves with all forms of sports, including boxing, wrestling, bowling, and roller derby. Baseball was especially attractive since it filled up the summer months when the networks supplied fewer programs to local affiliates. Baseball, for its part, needed television as a source of revenue and a marketing tool.[13]

The real issue was the degree of control organized baseball would be able to exert over television. Shortly after the end of World War II, baseball took its first step toward control by enacting what was called Rule 1d. This baseball law prohibited clubs from broadcasting into another major or minor league team's territory and prevented a visiting team from broadcasting from the home club's stadium without permission. Organized baseball showed its determination to control television and radio rights by killing the Liberty Broadcasting System. Established in 1947, LBS was the first effort to create a national radio sports broadcasting network. Its founders planned to re-create major league games rather than broadcast them live. The Liberty System put together a 400-station network. The owners of LBS realized that the fate of their initiative rested on winning organized baseball's cooperation. The major leagues responded by invoking Rule 1d to prohibit the Liberty System from broadcasting re-creations of their games in minor league territories. National League attorney Louis Carroll told a House committee that organized baseball quashed the Liberty System in order to firmly establish the principle that it enjoyed absolute control over broadcasting rights.[14]

In 1950 the Department of Justice warned organized baseball that Rule 1d violated antitrust law. Fearful of an avalanche of private and government lawsuits, the major leagues modified 1d in 1950 and again in 1952. The 1952 revision stripped the minor leagues of the rule's protection.[15]

The major leagues could afford to abandon Rule 1d. By 1952 they had experienced the positive effects of televised games. In the summer of 1952 the New York Yankees circularized the other teams of the American League to ascertain the effects of TV on their attendance. The responses were favorable. The baseball-television relationship needed fine tuning but the clubs agreed that it was profitable and would continue. Combined major league income from television agreements reached $3.3 million in 1951. The big leagues netted an additional $1 million annually from a five-year pact for broadcasting rights to the World Series and the All-Star Game.[16] Even some minor league officials believed that television's impact on their operations was not all bad. In 1953 Earl Mann of the Atlanta Crackers (Class AA), after experimenting with televising his team's games, stated that the minor leagues would have to learn how to turn TV into a marketing tool.[17]

By 1953 the major leagues were firmly committed to television. Organized baseball began discussing a Saturday afternoon national "game of the week" with the new DuMont network in the winter of 1952–53. NBC put together a 125-station network for the 1953 World Series. Fifteen of sixteen major league clubs had television contracts. The purchase of television sets, as well as the creation of local stations and their inclusion in broadcasting networks, accelerated nationwide. By 1956, 34.9 million U.S. homes had a TV set. Looking over the "baseball bonanza," *Television Age* defined it as a "jackpot" for both telecasters and the major leagues but added ominously that this mutually profitable arrangement had "an uncertain future."[18]

Two factors clouded the future of baseball's marriage to television. Organized baseball's antitrust exemption was under challenge in the Supreme Court. In the 1953 suit *Toolson v. New York Yankees* (346 US 356), a former player argued that by entering into contractual arrangements with television, professional baseball was engaging in interstate commerce. Organized baseball was wary of concluding a national TV contract until the Court ruled on this suit. Commissioner Frick declined to talk about a pooling of TV rights, leaving each club to make its own deal with the national networks. The minor leagues mustered support in Congress to convert the 1950 version of Rule 1d into law. Minor league owners believed that protection against competition from televised major league games would permit them to operate at a profit. Senator Edwin Johnson (D.-Colo.), the powerful senior minority member of the Senate Interstate and Foreign Commerce Committee and president of the Western League (Class A), introduced legislation to legalize 1d. Johnson warned that television was destroying the minor leagues and arranged hearings to put pressure on the major leagues to end the game of the week plan and back his legislation.[19]

The major leagues and their spokesman, Commissioner Frick, reluctantly fell into line and tepidly supported Johnson's bill. Frick, who in 1951 hearings had stressed the major leagues' desire to work out their deals with television free from federal supervision, now indicated that they would be willing to sacrifice some profit to assist the foundering minor leagues.[20]

The major leagues were saved from the painful sacrifice of revenue by their allies in the television industry. The TV lobby proved stronger than minor league baseball, mustering enough senators to table the Johnson bill. At the same time, Toolson's court challenge failed. Shortly before the end of 1953, in the case *United States* v. *the National Football League*, a federal district court in Philadelphia ruled that the NFL (and by implication organized baseball) had the right to black out its home games. The road appeared open for the major leagues to establish firm control over their TV rights.[21]

Minor League Woes

While the minor league owners were mistaken in pinpointing television as the primary cause of their difficulties, they were correct in claiming that minor league baseball was in serious trouble. At the root of the minor leagues' difficulties were the same factors affecting major league baseball: changing demographic patterns, the impact of the automobile on U.S. leisure patterns, and the challenge of other forms of recreation. Additionally, the nation was supersaturated with minor league baseball clubs. The small businessmen who acquired minor league franchises in the wake of World War II were counting on a return to the leisure patterns that had prevailed in the Depression era. Minor league baseball shared in the profits as overall U.S. spending on leisure rose dramatically in the immediate postwar years. But this spending quickly leveled off, and it began to drop in 1947. The baby boom, combined with the availability of previously scarce consumer goods and new housing, reined in spending on entertainment. Meanwhile, the number of minor league clubs bidding for the reduced entertainment dollar continued to increase.[22]

The major leagues had encouraged small businessmen to invest in minor league clubs. During the 1930s most major league teams watched the success of Branch Rickey's farm system with envy. Operating under the theory of producing quality from quantity, Rickey signed large numbers of amateur players and assigned them to minor league clubs under the control of the St. Louis Cardinals. His system produced both championship major league baseball and a tidy profit through the sale of excess talent. The New York Yankees imitated Rickey in the 1930s. During the war Rickey moved to Brooklyn and set about building a farm system that eventually outstripped St. Louis's in size and productivity.[23]

As soon as the war was over, the other major league teams followed suit, either buying minor league clubs or forming working agreements with them. In 1951 the major leagues owned 73 teams, the majority in the higher minors

(Classes A, AA, and AAA), and had working agreements with another 136 clubs. By 1953 even the nearly bankrupt St. Louis Browns had a thirteen-team system. Baseball men soon discovered that most of the advantages of large farm systems vanished when everyone had one. Top talent was in finite supply, and intense competition to sign the best prospects touched off a "bonus war." Clubs shelled out huge sums to sign unproven youngsters to professional contracts. Most of these "bonus babies" were spectacular flops. Moreover, the major league clubs soon found that they had to finance too many of their farm clubs. As a result, the boom in acquiring farm clubs was followed by a move toward streamlining. In February 1947 the Cincinnati Reds announced that they would reduce their farm system to eight or ten clubs and concentrate their resources on scouting and signing top prospects. The Reds noted that it was easy to find places to develop the talent they had signed. In fact, even with a reduced farm system, the Reds would have to stock their farms with a large number of players "without major league potentialities. The greater the number of clubs, the larger the number of that type of player."[24]

The reduction in the size of farm systems was a key element in under-cutting minor league operators. The major leagues simultaneously limited the ability of independent operators to field competitive teams. Immediately after the war, the minors were flooded with aging or marginal talent that had wartime major league experience. After 1947 a number of very talented but older players from the Negro leagues joined minor league clubs—Luke Easter, Piper Davis, Ray Dandridge, Dan Bankhead, and Sam Jethroe, among them. From the viewpoint of the major league clubs, farm teams that utilized a large number of veteran players, particularly aging Negro league stars or former major leaguers, were frustrating the objective of a minor league system: developing new talent. Taking advantage of their control of the various committees dealing with major league–minor league relations and the trustworthy votes of their farm clubs, the majors imposed rules that severely limited the number of veteran players at all levels of the minor leagues.[25]

The introduction of these rules injured independent minor league owners in two ways. First, in an era of bonus wars, independent owners were simply unable to compete for top young talent that inevitably ended up playing for competing major league farm clubs. Simultaneously, they lost the right to hire enough veteran players to stay competitive. Losing teams meant low attendance and large financial losses for their owners. Finally, independent minor league teams traditionally made their profit by selling their best prospects to the major league teams or their farm clubs. Without top talent to sell to the major leagues, the independent owner lost his ability to make a profit.[26]

To compound these problems, shifting population and leisure patterns were undercutting the lower minor leagues. As more Americans moved out of small towns, fewer communities possessed the financial resources and fan base needed to support a minor league team. The automobile and cheap fuel encouraged fans in smaller towns to drive to larger cities to see the superior play of higher minor league or big league games. Towns that tried to save their local teams found that the costs of minor league baseball were prohibitive. Limited markets, high travel costs, inadequate publicity, and rising maintenance costs for parks and equipment inevitably drove small-town America out of the baseball business.[27]

Against this background two other major league actions acted as catalysts for the crisis of minor league baseball. The decision by the big league clubs to play an increasing number of games at night placed them in direct competition with the minors, which traditionally played after dark. The televising of these night games was a second serious blow to the minors. Major league night games drew 50 percent better attendance than daylight games. The audiences for televised night games were twice as large as those for daytime contests. A 1950 study of the impact of TV on the entertainment patterns of fans living in cities with minor league teams found that given the option of attending minor league night baseball or watching a major league night game, 53 percent would stay at home in front of the television.[28]

The minor leagues appealed to Congress for legislative relief from the impact of television and organized to demand that the major leagues provide relief as well. In October 1953 the representatives of twenty-three minor leagues met in Dallas to coordinate their strategy. They demanded a radical revision of the major league–minor league agreement, including the introduction of an unrestricted draft that would break down major league control of the minors and the provision of protection against television broadcasts of major league games. Representatives of the minor leagues pressed their views before Congress and at the annual winter meetings of baseball executives.[29]

While moderately sympathetic to the plight of minor league operators, the major league owners were unwilling to upset arrangements that worked for their benefit. Commissioner Frick rejected minor league claims for compensation for losses due to the impact of major league television and radio broadcasts, asserting that it would violate antitrust law. Lee MacPhail, then a senior official in the New York Yankees farm system, recalled that major league policy was to do what was necessary to keep enough clubs operating to continue the production of major league prospects. The major leagues, MacPhail added, simply could not afford to subsidize the bloated minor league system of the early postwar years.[30]

The Players

The rapid contraction of the minor league system had little effect on the wage scale of either major or minor league players. The large pool of athletes eager to enter the major leagues continued to assist owners' efforts to keep salaries low throughout organized baseball. The major leagues, however, had a brief and, from the owners' viewpoint, frightening encounter with unionization immediately after World War II.

The attempt by Boston attorney Robert Murphy to organize the players in 1946 was but one in an intermittent series of efforts to build a players union that dated back to the 1880s. The owners repeatedly bought off the players with salary raises and other concessions to undercut support for a union. In 1946 the owners followed the same strategy. The key player demands were for a pension fund, a minimum salary, and spring training expense money. Management agreed to these demands and also permitted the members of each team to elect "player representatives" who would relay player complaints to management. The player representatives in turn elected an American and a National League player representative to serve as their spokesmen in dealings with the owners as a group. Murphy's effort collapsed. The player representatives accepted their narrowly defined responsibilities: they could present specific player grievances to management, which would then consider and adjudicate these requests but would not negotiate with the players.[31]

The 1946 arrangement appears to have satisfied both sides. The players were genuinely pleased with the concessions they won. Throughout the 1940s and 1950s most players supported the continuation of the reserve system and opposed the idea of unionization. American League player representative Fred Hutchinson probably expressed the majority's view when he told the Celler committee in 1951 that the reserve clause was "necessary" and that he and his fellow ballplayers were "well satisfied" with their relationship with the club owners. Indeed, most of the players, young men with middle-class ambitions and values, appear to have been satisfied with their salaries, the pension plan, and other benefits and seem willingly to have accepted the rules imposed by management. Quite a few publicly stated that they were thrilled to have the chance to play the game they loved and be paid for doing it.[32]

The owners were pleased to have avoided what Commissioner Chandler called the "evil" of unionization. They had displayed their horror of unions in 1945 when Chandler encouraged major league umpires to form an association. American League president Will Harridge promptly fired umpire Ernest Stewart for acting as Chandler's contact with the other umpires and rejected Chandler's efforts to reinstate Stewart. Chandler's support for an umpires association was one of the factors that ultimately led to his ouster as commissioner in 1951.[33]

The owners' uneasiness about unionization was reinforced in 1949 when a U.S. court of appeals upheld a suit by Danny Gardella against organized baseball. Gardella had been blacklisted for jumping from the New York Giants to play for higher pay in a new Mexican "major" league. In its ruling, the court stated that baseball should be subjected to antitrust law and added that the reserve clause was of questionable legality. Rather than take a weak case to the Supreme Court and face the end of its treasured immunity from prosecution, organized baseball rescinded its blacklisting of ex-Mexican League players and settled out of court with Gardella. In 1951 Chandler frankly told the Celler committee that the end of the reserve clause would mean a massive increase in player salaries. "Do you not think that Ted Williams would like to have something come up where he would be a free agent? They would bid on him. There is no telling how much he would get."[34] Fortunately for management, young players, nurturing dreams of stardom and fearful of a short career, were too committed to individualism and too preoccupied with playing the game to mount a serious challenge to the reserve clause.

Concern about player challenges to the reserve clause played a powerful role in the major league owners' decision to set up a pension fund. Both the owners and the players contributed to this fund. A decade after the fund was established, pitcher Jim Brosnan explained the psychological satisfaction that players derived from the pension plan: even after a defeat a player could tell himself, "Well, at least it's one more day in the pension plan."[35] Establishing the fund ended the threat of unionization for nearly two decades. In 1949, when the fund was incapable of meeting its obligations, Chandler negotiated a five-year deal for broadcast rights to the World Series and the All-Star Game with the Gillette Company and assigned the annual $1 million payment to the pension fund. The owners accepted Chandler's action, although they recognized that he had created a potentially dangerous precedent by agreeing to share broadcasting income with the players. The pension fund was critical to maintaining labor peace. The Brooklyn Dodgers' powerful owner, Walter O'Malley, beat a quick retreat after publicly suggesting that the owners might abolish the pension fund when the five-year deal with Gillette expired.[36]

Owner fear of unionization laid the groundwork for eventual labor-management conflict. In the summer of 1953 the two league player representatives, Allie Reynolds and Ralph Kiner, presented the owners with a list of requests for changes, including raising the minimum salary from $5,000 to $8,000. The owners rejected these requests. The players responded by hiring a lawyer, J. Norman Lewis, as their adviser. Major league administrators, led by Commissioner Frick, initially allowed Lewis to attend talks along with the player representatives in his advisory capacity. In December 1953, however, they suddenly barred Lewis from a meeting called to discuss the pension fund. Frick stated that the owners refused to recognize Lewis's right to act as a bargaining agent for the players. The players refused to meet with Frick and set up the Major League Baseball Players Association. A compromise permitted Lewis to attend meetings on the pension issue, and in April 1954 a new pension agreement established a joint committee to administer the fund. The Players Association survived without a role in labor-management relations until another outside adviser uncorked its potential in 1966.[37]

Realignment or Expansion?

The owners were able to satisfy labor through compromises that maintained their control over wages, but they had less success in dealing with rising political pressures for the extension of major league baseball outside the established circuit. The owners' control over the assignment of major league franchises was a central element in their monopoly. Twice in the twentieth century, in 1915 and again in 1946, the major leagues defeated efforts to set up rival big leagues. Any expansion of the two existing major leagues would involve questions of profit, an increased competition for player talent, and difficult interleague negotiations over territorial rights. The owners preferred to avoid these tough issues, but were eventually unable to do so. The strongest pressure for expansion came from the West Coast. Los Angeles and San Francisco were mushrooming and felt that they merited recognition as major league cities. Representative Celler expressed the frustration of many large U.S. cities when he told major league executives that his committee did not favor any specific solution to expanding baseball but that organized baseball ought to "get going" on some solution that would broaden the geographic distribution of the game.[38]

Economic reality compounded political pressures to force a change in the organization of major league baseball. Los Angeles, Minneapolis, San Francisco, and Dallas, for example, none of which had a major league team, were all larger markets than some of the cities hosting major league baseball. At the same time, in cities with more than one major league club, three teams—the St. Louis Browns, the Boston Braves, and the Philadelphia Athletics—were losing money and attendance to their intracity rivals.

Baseball had four options. First, the major leagues could give the Pacific Coast League (PCL) a special classification, suspend the draft, and permit it to build up its talent to major league levels. A second possibility would be to form a special classification league out of PCL and other minor league teams in major cities and grant this new league freedom from the draft until it was competitive. A third alternative was to add two or more teams to each of the existing major leagues. Finally, organized baseball could achieve the goal of increasing the number of cities with major league teams by moving some of its financially weaker franchises out of cities that already had two teams.[39]

Major league owners were dissatisfied with all of these proposed alternatives. Granting an exemption from the draft to higher major league teams was the sort of precedent the majors wanted to avoid for fear of its impact on their future relations with the minor leagues. Creating a major league out of the PCL or a mix of PCL and other larger minor league cities would close off choice territories to possible moves by existing major league teams. Few minor league cities had stadiums with adequate seating for a major league club. Expansion or realignment was also complicated by mutual suspicions between the two leagues. Neither wanted its competitor to take the best available markets. Ultimately, a number of the owners were simply reluctant to take any sort of dynamic action. Crusty old Clark Griffith of the Washington Senators best exemplified this outlook when he told the Celler committee that while Milwaukee was a possible site for expansion, "California is entirely out of the major league circuit."[40]

Throughout the early 1950s the major leagues continued to temporize over what action to take. The weaker franchises exhausted their options and began quietly to lobby for permission to move. Finally, in December 1952, the two leagues modified their rules to limit each league's ability to block relocation by the teams of the other league. The American League changed its rules to require that only six of eight teams needed to agree in order to permit a franchise move. The owners of the Braves, Browns, and Athletics quietly began scouting for new homes.

Civic Support

The key element in the search for a new home was the availability of a major league stadium: a facility with adequate playing dimensions, a large seating capacity, and big parking lots. Prior to World War II almost all major league franchises constructed their own facilities. By 1950, however, the costs of site acquisition and construction were too great for most teams to consider. The era of public financing of professional sports had begun. City governments faced the difficult question of whether to invest millions of tax dollars in the construction of stadiums to hold or attract major league baseball and football. Complicating this decision was the unwillingness of the sports leagues to commit themselves to a given city until a facility was at least under construction.[41]

In 1953 only two cities without major league teams had stadiums that met the requirements of big league baseball. Milwaukee, a city that was actively campaigning to acquire a major league team, had constructed a new 50,000-seat facility with parking for 11,000 cars. Baltimore had a modern stadium capable of quick and relatively inexpensive expansion to a 50,000-seat capacity. The most attractive West Coast sites, Los Angeles and San Francisco, had small, older, minor league parks that required replacement. Both Baltimore and Milwaukee had AAA minor league franchises and strong attendance records. Thus, two cities on the fringes of baseball's traditional circuit possessed the best credentials for franchise transfer. In the winter of 1952–53 the Braves and Browns were eyeing Milwaukee as a new home. Braves owner Lou Perini had a critical advantage: he owned Milwaukee's minor league franchise and territorial rights.

Black and White Together?

In selecting sites for baseball, owners appear to have assumed correctly that the game attracted all social and ethnic groups. Baseball fans represented a cross section of the U.S. population. While each team drew its attendance from a slightly different pool that reflected the nature of the local economy, the limited statistical data on fans shows that baseball was not exclusively or even predominantly a game for blue-collar males. In 1954 the Baltimore Orioles conducted a survey of their attendance base. It showed that nearly 42 percent came from white-collar professions against approximately 25 percent from blue-collar occupations. Of the Orioles fans surveyed, 66 percent had completed high school and 28 percent held college degrees. Only 5.3 percent of the individuals attending baseball games in Baltimore had less than a high school education. While women constituted a small part of attendance at Orioles games, they traditionally formed a large part of the broadcasting audience. Baseball had been attempting to attract women since the nineteenth century with some success.[42]

Another group had been attending baseball games in record numbers in the immediate postwar years: blacks. Between 1947 and 1950, as overall major league attendance fell, black attendance rose. Blacks wanted to see their new stars, particularly Jackie Robinson. The movement for black political and social rights began to gain momentum in the late 1940s. Organized baseball unwittingly provided an arena for the civil rights movement. The maneuvering that led to the restructuring of organized baseball took place as an American social revolution gained momentum. Black Americans began to move boldly to claim the rights guaranteed them under the Constitution. After initially attempting to avoid involvement in civil rights issues, organized baseball later sought to avoid the effects of the reform movement. Deep-seated racial prejudice combined with concern over the economic impact of integration to keep organized baseball a Jim Crow sport until 1946. Thereafter, baseball executives grudgingly permitted a few black athletes of superior talent to play at the major league level. Four hundred roster slots existed in the big leagues. By 1950, four years after Jackie Robinson broke baseball's color barrier, nine blacks were playing in the major leagues. Unspoken agreements put limits on the number of blacks playing on most major league teams. Racial prejudice also limited the number of black prospects recruited into the minor leagues.[43]

In spite of club owners' claims that baseball had mastered its problems, racial issues continued to play an important role in organized baseball over the next three decades. Initially, black civil rights activists tried to utilize baseball as a wedge to further their objective of opening public accommodations throughout the United States. After this goal was achieved, with a late and somewhat reluctant contribution from organized baseball, black athletes still had to break down the remaining barriers to their participation in management. Black fans frequently faced harassment as they sought to attend games. After first flooding major league stadiums as fans went to see their heroes, black attendance fell off dramatically. The major leagues made no effort to win them back. The owners were apparently convinced that rising black attendance would drive away white fans.[44]

Declining black attendance after 1950 contributed to a worsening of baseball's economic problems. In the spring of 1953 economic difficulties forced two owners to act to save their franchises from bankruptcy by means of relocation. The Braves' move to Milwaukee and the Browns' shift to Baltimore enabled these teams to meet their immediate and specific troubles. However, neither of the two teams could escape baseball's major problems: reducing the cost of minor league player development, managing television's potential impact on attendance, responding to growing political pressure for expansion, and dealing with race issues and with potential labor discontent. Baseball was entering a new era, and Baltimore would be deeply involved in the dramatic changes it would bring.

1   Community Baseball

1 How Veeck Was Wrecked

Veeck . . . told stories about how poorly the Browns in St. Louis drew: One day he asked someone to come to a Browns game. The person said, "What time does it start?" Veeck replied, "What time's convenient?"
—Ira Berkow, *New York Times*, 4 January 1986

I would say the St. Louis Browns are in very difficult financial circumstances, and a drowning man clutches at a straw.
—Ford Frick, 1951

On 15 March 1953 a beaming Mayor Thomas D'Alesandro, Jr., appeared alongside the smiling owner of the St. Louis Browns, Bill Veeck, at a press conference announcing that major league baseball would return to Baltimore after a half-century absence. The city's newspapers and business community celebrated a major achievement for civic pride and private profit. Baltimore's claims to status as a big league city had been reaffirmed. Within forty-eight hours, joy turned to bitterness as American League owners vetoed the proposed franchise shift. Baltimore civic leaders and fans would wait anxiously another six months before the city won its major league team. Veeck's actions, however, triggered the first change in the structure of major league baseball since 1903, ushering in a new and contentious era of franchise moves and expansion.

St. Louis Blues

The St. Louis Browns of the American League were baseball's byword for futility and mediocrity. In fifty-two years, the team won one American League championship (but went on to lose the World Series). It finished second twice, sixth eleven times, seventh twelve times, and last ten times. Attendance at Browns games reflected this on-the-field record: it was consistently the lowest in the American League after 1926. Even the team's one great success was tarnished. The 1944 American League champion Browns were simply the best of the weak. Wartime call-ups had stripped baseball of most of its star players by 1944. The Browns won with a group of journeymen and career minor league players. The following year, the regulars began to return, and the Browns slid back toward their accustomed home in the second division.

Bad management was at the root of bad field performance. The team had moved to St. Louis from Milwaukee in 1902. Robert Hedges, who owned the team at the time, was a successful promoter who managed to turn a profit without winning a pennant. In an effort to improve both the team's league standings and its profitability, in 1913 Hedges hired a young ex-professional ballplayer and college coach, Branch Rickey, to rebuild the club. Rickey was a pietistic Protestant businessman with a sharp eye for baseball talent and a genius for cost-effective innovation. He built up the club's links with minor league operators and began to recruit talent on college campuses and sandlots.

Rickey had just begun his building effort when Hedges sold out to Philip Ball, a tough, hard-drinking St. Louis businessman. Frictions quickly developed between the owner and his Bible-quoting, teetotaler general manager. Rickey took his talents to the rival St. Louis Cardinals after the 1916 season. Within a decade Rickey made the Cardinals a consistent pennant contender and the major box office draw in St. Louis. Ball's Browns, benefiting from Rickey's player acquisitions, especially Hall of Fame first baseman George Sisler, played decent baseball until 1925. Anticipating success, Ball had expanded the seating capacity of Sportsman's Park, a facility he owned and rented to the Cardinals. In 1926 the Cardinals won the National League pennant and the Browns began their descent to the bottom of the American League. Ball took heavy financial losses trying to rebuild the club and maintain the park until his death in 1933. The Cardinals drew the big crowds and accompanying profits.

By the time Ball died, St. Louis's inability to support two major league clubs was evident. The city had been among the smaller major league sites in 1902. By 1920 it was the smallest major league city, with a population of approximately 476,000. Boston, the next smallest city to host two clubs, had a population of 886,000. Washington was struggling to support one club with 507,000 people. While St. Louis continued to grow, its population expansion in absolute terms was smaller than that of any other major league city and a number of minor league cities. The onset of the Great Depression cut heavily into both the Browns' and the Cardinals' profits. Recognizing that a franchise shift was inevitable, Sam Breadon, the Cardinals' owner, sought American League permission to play in rapidly expanding Detroit during the early 1930s, but the American League blocked a move into its territories. Then Breadon reconsidered as his profits mounted. He could wait out the Browns.[1]

Ball's death deprived the Browns of their one remaining resource: a rich owner willing to take financial losses. The executors of Ball's estate refused to put more capital into a losing business. In 1934 the club finished sixth, drew only 115,305 fans, and lost over $54,000. The next year it finished seventh and drew 80,922 spectators.[2]

In 1936 the executors sold the club to a combine headed by Donald Barnes and the De Witt brothers. By selling stock in the Browns, the new owners raised $100,000 to pay for the club. The American League loaned them an additional $50,000 to complete the deal. Bill De Witt, one of Rickey's former assistants, soon experienced the perils of running a baseball club with insufficient financing. In the first four years under new management, the Browns lost over $100,000 each year. De Witt's objectives were sound: hiring scouts, building a farm system, and acquiring some major league quality players from other teams. He simply lacked the financial resources to achieve his goals.[3] De Witt ruefully admitted to one interviewer: "The Browns had a hell of a time because the Cardinals were so popular and the Browns couldn't do a damn thing. We didn't have any attendance money to build up the ball club with. Most of the other clubs had players in the minors that were better than some of the players we had on the Browns."[4]

By 1941 the club's financial picture was so bad that senior partner Barnes attempted to arrange a franchise shift to Los Angeles. That city's establishment was eager to host the Browns and put together a strong syndicate to purchase stock in the team. Barnes and De Witt worked out the practical logistics of a move. American League owners discussed the plan at their December 1941 meeting. The owners took no decision. They were worried about scheduling and transportation problems. As it turned out, the Japanese attack on Pearl Harbor killed the idea. Wartime controls on fuel and transportation made any move westward impractical. Even without the war, American League owners would have resisted franchise relocation. League president William Harridge recalled their concerns about scheduling and transportation costs and added that Los Angeles was unlikely to have supported a "tail end ball club."[5]

The Browns struggled on. In 1942 the club found a financial angel. St. Louis businessman Richard Muckerman invested $300,000 in return for a vice presidency. In 1944 the club won its only American League championship and outdrew the mighty Cardinals for the first time in twenty years. However, the Browns' attendance was fifth in the American League, and the team lost the World Series to the rival Cardinals.

Barnes sold out to Muckerman in 1945. The new owner retained De Witt as his business manager. Meanwhile, the club again began declining in the standings. After finishing third in 1945, the Browns dropped to seventh in 1946 and last in 1948. Attendance followed suit. After reaching a postwar high of 526,435 in 1946, it plummeted to 270,939 in 1949, just as the rest of major league baseball was enjoying unprecedented attendance growth.[6]

Muckerman invested heavily in improving Sportsman's Park, upgrading the minor league system, and building new training facilities in Florida. In 1947 the Browns became the second American League team to sign and suit up black players in an unsuccessful attempt to improve performance on the field and attract a new group of fans. In 1948 Muckerman bailed out, selling the club to the De Witt brothers. An American League loan of $300,000 enabled the De Witts to meet the first payment on the Browns.[7]

The De Witts inherited a ball club without a sufficient fan base, a strong minor league system, or adequate financial reserves. Their plight was obvious. A few years later, during the 1951 House hearings on baseball, Representative Kenneth Keating of New York asked Ford Frick the question that was on many observers' minds: "What is going to happen to the Browns?" Frick had no answer. As usual, he spoke for organized baseball.[8]

Surprisingly, the American League loaned money to the Browns and accepted the financial losses that accrued from fielding the noncompetitive St. Louis club in nearly empty stadiums. The league owners were unwilling to interfere in the operations of another franchise because of the precedent it would create. They shelved and never revived the Barnes–De Witt plan to move the club, the obvious solution to the problem. Commissioner Chandler believed that the underlying cause was the owners' desire to maintain the status quo. Related factors may have been minor league reluctance to surrender one of its choice franchises and major league concern that moving the team would encourage the creation of a rival "outlaw" big league. Another problem was the reaction of the National League to an American League franchise move. The owners apparently had decided that resolution of the St. Louis problem would have to await an agreement by both leagues on a general realignment of the sport.[9]

Meanwhile, the De Witt brothers continued taking a financial beating and putting bad baseball clubs on the field. They managed to avoid bankruptcy by utilizing a traditional minor league strategy: selling off their best players. Bill Veeck, who later had the dubious privilege of running the Browns, recalled that "anytime you dealt with St. Louis it was understood that you were going to contribute a certain amount [of cash] toward the upkeep."[10] By paying cash and trading off their journeymen for the Browns' few quality athletes, the other major league teams undercut the St. Louis club's already limited competitiveness. The Browns' owners paid for their shortsighted strategy in lowered income. The Browns had the league's lowest attendance in twenty-eight of the forty-one years between 1910 and 1950. Overall they contributed an average 4 percent of total league attendance against the 12.5 percent they might have been expected to provide.[11]

American League loans and subsidization by fellow owners were two key elements in continuing the Browns' precarious survival in St. Louis. Two other factors were a large minor league system and the lowest salary scale in baseball. Pitcher Al Widmar initially refused to report to the Browns from the

AAA Baltimore Orioles because he would have had to accept a $2,000 pay cut to play in the major leagues. In 1950 the Browns had the smallest payroll in the major leagues. The club's median salary of $7,000 was $3,000 below that paid by the next lowest-paying club and less than half that of the mighty New York Yankees.[12]

The Browns farm system was "respectable" according to its longtime director, Jim McLaughlin, but had a hard time competing for talent with more attractive clubs like the Yankees. The Yankees' annual spending on scouting, signing, and developing players was twice the Browns' total budget. The farm system contributed to the Browns' survival by recruiting a few top prospects for sale and trades. The minor league operation, however, was poorly financed and managed to keep going by "breaking baseball law":

> Under the theory . . . of farm systems the major league club paid the minor league club X number of dollars to . . . develop its players. The Browns . . . because they didn't have sufficient money, could not afford a large farm system, so we started something in which we got teams that had a hard time getting a working agreement . . . and we said we'll put players in there if you pay us X number of dollars if you finish first, second, on a graduated scale. . . . If they finished below fourth they didn't pay us anything. . . . [That] let us finance a farm system.[13]

Enter Veeck

By the spring of 1951 the De Witt brothers were searching for a buyer for the Browns. They began negotiations with Bill Veeck, the energetic and charming thirty-seven-year-old former owner of the Cleveland Indians.

A gregarious, impatient, and talkative man, with a keen intellect, Veeck was one of the youngest owners in baseball and the most iconoclastic. Veeck literally grew up with the sport. His father was president of the Chicago Cubs during the 1920s. Veeck began his career as an office boy for the Cubs, worked his way up the career ladder, and in 1941 purchased a minor league franchise in Milwaukee. He lost a leg while on military duty in the South Pacific during World War II. Recurrent problems with the leg forced Veeck into long hospital stays for the rest of his life but never slowed his drive or his sense of fun. Veeck idealized the game he had known in the 1930s because it gave him the maximum opportunity to utilize his talent for improvisation. He viewed the growth of major league control over the minors and the intrusion of the television networks with distaste since they destroyed opportunities to innovate and raised the costs of owning a team.

Veeck was a promotional genius and a keen judge of athletic talent who had shown his ability to rebuild franchises quickly at Milwaukee and Cleveland.

He was also chronically underfinanced. This last trait, he cheerfully admitted, defeated his efforts to turn the Browns into a profitable franchise.[14]

Veeck acquired the Browns in the middle of the 1951 season. He characterized them as "the worst looking collection of ballplayers I've ever seen." Nevertheless, Veeck was convinced that he could build a winner and, more important, that he could beat the Cardinals in a battle for attendance by combining improved play with skillful marketing. Veeck's ability to realize his plans was directly linked to his ability to spend in acquiring better players.[15]

Financing difficulties delayed Veeck's purchase of the Browns. In order to take advantage of special tax breaks, Veeck insisted that his syndicate had to hold 75 percent of the Browns' stock. He had a hard time buying up enough Browns stock to reach that goal since the shares were in the hands of over 1,400 stockholders. Finally, with the aid of St. Louis stockbroker Mark Steinberg, Veeck collected 79.9 percent of the outstanding shares and on 5 July 1951 assumed control of the club. By the time the deal was closed, Veeck had borrowed so heavily that he had exhausted his credit. "I was not in a position either to sell any of my stock or to borrow against . . . it. I couldn't borrow on the ball park either; it was already heavily mortgaged."[16]

Once in control of the club, Veeck unleashed a torrent of promotions to draw fans to the park. In his most famous stunt, he sent a midget into one game to pinch hit. Veeck had a group of fans manage the club at another game. He invented bat day, buying a shipment of bats from a bankrupt firm and giving them away to paying customers. He hired former Cardinals stars Rogers Hornsby and Marty Marion to manage the club. Veeck traded players at an astounding rate in search of a few who could lift the club out of last place. He toured the St. Louis area and surrounding counties, speaking to any groups willing to listen, in an effort to build interest in the club.[17]

More aggressive promotions followed in 1952, and although the club's performance was only marginally better than it had been in 1951, Veeck managed to attract 518,796 paying customers, the fifth highest attendance in club history. He capitalized on the natural rivalry with the Cardinals, baiting Cardinals owner Fred Saigh. Veeck made no secret of his objective: running the Cardinals out of St. Louis. He enjoyed two potential advantages. First, Saigh was under indictment for income tax fraud. More important, the Cardinals had dropped out of pennant contention after a 1946 World Series appearance. Gradually, the National League club was exhausting Rickey's legacy of superior players. Nevertheless, Veeck faced an uphill battle. The Cardinals continued to play better baseball than the Browns, and they had their large minor league system and a radio network that Veeck admitted was "vastly superior." Veeck recognized that St. Louis could not support two teams and that he would have to win the battle for attendance or move. During the 1952 season he quietly contacted individual American League owners to obtain their support for a move in the event his battle with the Cardinals went badly.[18]

At the December 1952 winter meeting of baseball executives in Phoenix, Veeck sought assistance from his fellow American League owners in the battle for control of St. Louis while simultaneously taking preliminary steps to move his franchise. He informed the other owners that the Browns might have to leave St. Louis before the next season and that he would present them with his plans at a spring meeting in Tampa. Veeck then rashly undercut his position by offering a set of proposals designed to make the league more competitive and, not incidentally, provide the Browns with the players and cash needed to turn them into a pennant contender. Veeck's plans for an unrestricted draft of minor league players would have negated the advantages of farm systems for his major league rivals and increased the independence of minor league operators. His proposal to pool television revenues and divide them equally, if accepted, would have seriously cut into the profit margins of teams in larger cities. He also wanted to change the formulas dividing gate receipts to increase the visiting club's share of the take. The Yankees vetoed Veeck's plans, believing they were aimed at destroying New York's predominant position both on the field and within the American League leadership.[19]

Veeck compounded his error by confronting the Yankees and other big-city teams from an extremely weak power base. He announced that teams that were unwilling to share their broadcast revenues could not telecast their home games with the Browns. Veeck claimed that televising his team's road games cut down on its share of the box office and thus further reduced his already limited income. The argument was valid because the Browns had very limited drawing power, especially away from St. Louis, even without competing against television.[20]

But Veeck had chosen the wrong enemies and the wrong issue. The New York, Cleveland, and Boston franchises responded by refusing to permit either the broadcast or telecast of their games with the Browns, effectively cutting Veeck off from both TV and radio revenues for forty-four games. The same three clubs also announced that they would use their scheduling latitude to force the Browns to play eight extra day games rather than the more profitable night contests. The Detroit club supported the Yankees, Indians, and Red Sox, pointedly underlining Veeck's isolation.[21]

The fight over television rights revealed how tenuous Veeck's position was. He was deeply in debt. The Browns had no 1953 television contract and only a limited radio network. Combined sales of radio and television rights produced only $22,000 in income for the 1952 Browns. Falstaff Brewery was willing to sponsor Browns TV broadcasts for 1953, but St. Louis's only station was unwilling to air them. Another station would begin broadcasting in the late spring and was ready to pick up the Browns, but it offered the same rights payment for twenty-two games that Veeck had received for six the previous year. Meanwhile, in his effort to compete with the Cardinals, Veeck was acquiring new and more expensive player contracts and, ironically, publicizing these deals on television. He entered the 1953 season with increased overhead and was totally reliant on his team's still-limited box office pull and the Cardinals' rent payments at Sportsman's Park to make a profit.[22]

Veeck appealed to baseball's new commissioner, Ford Frick, to force the other league owners to share their television income. Unfortunately, he had already alienated the commissioner by opposing his election. Frick declined to intervene, telling Veeck to work out his problems with the other owners. American League president Will Harridge then upheld the right of other clubs to refuse to play night games with the Browns.[23]

In February 1953 Veeck's position received the final blow. Saigh was convicted on the charges of income tax fraud and sold the Cardinals to millionaire brewer August Busch. Busch's motives for acquiring the Cardinals were a mix of civic pride and business calculation. He would save the franchise for St. Louis and simultaneously acquire a subsidiary that could promote his beer. Busch's first move was to seek a television outlet for marketing both his team and his beer. Veeck recognized that he could not compete with the wealthy Busch and decided to move the Browns. He immediately paid the price for a winter of antagonizing the other American League owners.[24]

Tampa

Once he determined to move, Veeck began casting about for a site. He quickly ruled out Los Angeles because it lacked a suitable stadium. In any case, Veeck's real desire was to return to Milwaukee, the scene of one of his greatest franchise building successes. Veeck discovered that he had been outfoxed by the National League owners. That league had been laying the groundwork for a westward move since 1947. Brooklyn's owner, Walter O'Malley, had his eye on Los Angeles as a future home for his Dodgers and wanted to shift the league's axis westward as a first step toward his eventual move to the Pacific Coast. He supported the 1952 rules change that gave each league control over franchise realignment. Phil Wrigley of the Cubs owned the PCL's Los Angeles franchise and was ready to cooperate with O'Malley. Wrigley wanted to stay in profitable Chicago but was quite happy to ensure that the National League would be first to play on the West Coast. He recognized that setting up teams on the Pacific Coast would increase the entire league's profits. By exercising his territorial rights, Wrigley kept the American League out of Los Angeles until O'Malley could arrange a franchise shift to the Far West. Wrigley then traded minor league franchises with the Dodgers. Boston's Lou Perini meanwhile quietly rounded up the support of other National League owners for a move to Milwaukee, where he owned the minor league franchise.[25]

Perini kept his plans secret. Veeck's were known to the National League owners. He had contacted Perini about moving the Browns to Milwaukee and had also informed the Cardinals' new owner of his intentions, offering to sell Sportsman's Park. Perini refused to sell Veeck his rights to Milwaukee, and news of the Browns' proposed move to that city leaked to the press.[26]

Perini's refusal to sell left Veeck with only one suitable site, Baltimore. Its minor league team was independently owned, and the city government and business establishment were actively seeking a major league team. Jack Dunn, the owner of the International League Baltimore Orioles (AAA), had only one condition for permitting Veeck to move into his territory: stock in the franchise. Moreover, Dunn preferred bringing an American League team into the city. Veeck always favored having local interests involved in the financing of any club he owned, and, in any case, he desperately needed a fresh infusion of cash in his operation. In the fall of 1952 he quietly contacted Dunn to discuss a move. Negotiations resumed in February 1953. In subsequent conversations with his attorney, Dunn referred to the chain-smoking Veeck by the code name "Ashtray" in order to keep their discussions secret. The two men agreed that Dunn would get stock in the transferred club and Veeck would acquire and dispose of the minor league Orioles.[27]

While he negotiated an agreement with Dunn on territorial rights, Veeck started dealing with the city government over the terms of a stadium contract. He had held exploratory talks with city leaders during the summer and fall of 1952. Veeck's chief contact was mayor Thomas D'Alesandro, Jr. A small man with blue eyes and a thin moustache, D'Alesandro, a former New Deal congressman, was a classic ward-heeling politician. A colorful extrovert, skilled at working crowds, he built a strong base of support through close attention to constituent needs and with large public works programs. During D'Alesandro's three terms as mayor, Baltimore built new schools and roads, public housing, a major airport, and, of course, Memorial Stadium. D'Alesandro possessed a strong sense of civic pride. He wanted to bring baseball to the city to show that Baltimore was a big league town. Veeck and D'Alesandro swiftly moved toward an agreement. The city pledged to add a second deck to the stadium, bringing its seating capacity up to 50,000, offered liberal lease terms, and agreed to set up temporary seating for 13,000 during the 1953 season.[28]

In order to give Baltimore a greater stake in the team and acquire badly needed operating cash, Veeck was simultaneously dealing with a group of local businessmen organized by Clarence Miles. A lawyer, banker, and businessman, Miles came from one of the state's most distinguished families. His brother was the state treasurer, and he himself had been active in Democratic politics since the 1930s, becoming an important powerbroker. Miles first became aware of the possibility that the Browns would move in December 1952 during a visit to Chicago. After organizing a group of investors, he got in touch with Veeck. The Miles group was ready to buy up to 20 percent of the team's stock.[29]

When the major league owners convened in Tampa on 11 March 1953, Veeck believed he had done everything necessary to ensure a move to Baltimore. The press broke the news of the proposed move on 12 March. Initial league reaction was generally favorable. Washington Senators owner Clark Griffith told reporters, "It will be great for baseball." Griffith noted that he had a television contract with a Baltimore station that had to be settled to his satisfaction but added soothingly, "That is only a minor problem." Jerold Hoffberger, owner of Baltimore's National Brewery, offered to pay Griffith $350,000 to cover his television losses. Privately, American League owners were assuring Veeck of their support.[30]

American League opposition waited quietly while other interests began to attack the proposed move publicly. In telegrams to Commissioner Frick and American League owners, St. Louis mayor Joseph Darst threatened a legal battle to retain the team. George Trautman, the president of the National Association of minor leagues, denounced the proposed move, pointing out that it would disrupt the operations of the International League on the eve of a new season. Criticism began to arise from other sources, including two of the three clubs with territorial interests in Baltimore. Robert Carpenter, president of the Philadelphia Phillies of the National League, called Veeck's proposed move "asinine." Frick expressed irritation over the suddenness of the proposed transfer. More important, two American League club spokesmen suddenly indicated opposition. Arthur Ehlers, the general manager of the Philadelphia Athletics, stated that he favored the move but would prefer local owners to Veeck. Dan Topping, part owner and president of the Yankees, indicated his club would support a move only if "certain conditions are met."[31] Topping did not state what these "conditions" were.

Veeck and Mayor D'Alesandro presented their plans for a franchise shift to the American League owners on 16 March. They quickly discovered that the Yankees had put together a coalition to block Veeck. Both Washington and Philadelphia reversed their public positions, indicating their concern that a Baltimore club would oversaturate the market area. Opponents took up the minors' complaint about the last minute timing of the move. They brought up other complications: the threat of lawsuits, scheduling problems, television arrangements, and the move's impact on ticket sales. Veeck's critics noted his cloudy financial picture and questioned his ability to pay the costs of a move. By a vote of six to two the American League owners rejected Veeck's bid to move. They then voted to establish a watchdog committee of four clubs, including Veeck opponents New York, Boston, and Detroit, to oversee St. Louis's finances and advise the league on a suitable site for the club.[32]

While all of the factors cited by opponents played a role in blocking a move to Baltimore, the central motivation behind American League action was the determination of a clique of owners to drive Veeck out of organized baseball. Del Webb of the Yankees put together the opposition that included Washington, Boston, Detroit, Philadelphia, and Cleveland. Philadelphia's Ehlers publicly laid out the objective of these owners even before the vote: permitting a franchise move in exchange for Veeck's agreement to sell out. They were ready to force Veeck into bankruptcy to achieve their objective.[33]

Veeck, although beaten, was unwilling to relinquish control of the Browns. Burning his bridges, he lambasted his tormenters: "I've been the victim of duplicity of conduct by lying club owners. The vote against me was silly or malicious and I prefer to regard it as malicious."[34] He returned to St. Louis to face angry fans and the prospect of bankruptcy. American League president Will Harridge tried to make the best of a public relations fiasco by assuring Browns fans that improved attendance would preserve the franchise for St. Louis. Veeck insisted that he would attempt to move the Browns again as soon as the 1953 season ended.

Striking a Bargain

Veeck's defeat at Tampa stimulated the formation of a Baltimore syndicate with adequate assets to buy control of the Browns. A group of Baltimore businessmen led by Lawrence Lockwood offered to meet Veeck's reported $2.4 million selling price on 17 March. Veeck declined, reiterating his unwillingness to "peddle the club."[35] While the Lockwood bid proved ephemeral, Mayor D'Alesandro encouraged Clarence Miles's efforts to expand the financial base of his syndicate of local businessmen. Baltimore's civic pride was aroused by rejection. Its desire for major league status was whetted by assurances from both major and minor league officials that they would support the city's bid after the 1953 season. *Evening Sun* sports editor Paul Menton commented that after the Tampa fiasco Veeck's surrender of ownership was "only a question of time." He urged the city's leaders to draw the obvious lesson from St. Louis's plight and insist on local control in order to ensure a long life for major league baseball in Baltimore.[36]

The city's October 1953 bid was greatly aided by the success of the National League's shift of the Braves to Milwaukee. While American League owners fought over Veeck's plans, their National League rivals unanimously granted Perini's request. The Braves attracted over 1.8 million fans in their first season in Milwaukee, proving that franchise realignment would be profitable for the major leagues and ending any possibility that the Browns would remain in St. Louis. "Baseball," the industry's trade newspaper, *The Sporting News*, commented, "may be a 'peculiar business' . . . but is undeniably a business . . . and as such it cannot long defy the laws of economics." When the American League met in October 1953, the only questions were where the Browns would move and who would own the franchise.[37]

The political leadership and business community of Baltimore strengthened their syndicate to ensure that the American League would choose Baltimore. Business leaders, convinced that major league baseball "would be a development of great importance to our economic and community progress and a proper and overdue recognition of our city's national stature," urged D'Alesandro to continue his pursuit of the St. Louis franchise. Baltimore's breweries took a leading role, pledging financial backing while publicly competing in displaying their support for the city's effort to acquire the Browns. The mayor promised to use congressional leverage and legal action to achieve Baltimore's goal. The city underlined its seriousness by opening bidding for the construction of a second tier for Memorial Stadium. In order to generate publicity for Baltimore's claim to major league status, D'Alesandro led groups to St. Louis to watch the Browns play.[38]

While D'Alesandro publicized his city's continuing interest in the Browns, Miles put together the financing. Miles had long-term ambitions to run for political office and recognized that the prestige acquired by bringing a major league team to Baltimore would aid his eventual bid.[39] Miles was "absolutely shocked" by the American League's rejection of Veeck's March 1953 effort to move the Browns to Baltimore. Once he realized that Veeck was unlikely to survive as an owner, Miles broadened his syndicate and his objectives. He planned to acquire controlling interest in the club. Miles's group could count on the city's major breweries for a large share of its financing.[40]

Meanwhile, Veeck staved off bankruptcy in St. Louis. He concluded an agreement with Busch for the sale of Sportsman's Park for $1.1 million. During the 1953 season he sold off his better players to cover mounting debts. Browns general manager Rudie Schaffer announced that the team would drop promotional activities and would decline to cooperate with St. Louis groups trying to retain the franchise. Veeck also signed an agreement with Falstaff Brewery to telecast games on a station in nearby Belleville, Illinois. In spite of these economies, Veeck ended the 1953 season with losses that he claimed totaled $1 million. Fans stayed away from the Browns games. Seasonal attendance dropped by half, and a demoralized Browns team plunged into last place, losing one hundred games.[41]

Veeck resisted the temptation to utilize the threat of congressional action against his American League opponents. When told that two Maryland congressmen were demanding a probe of the league's rejection of his bid to move, Veeck angrily told reporters that he wanted the two men to "keep out of our affairs." He declined to sue the league. In spite of the stinging rebuke his fellow owners had delivered, Veeck was unwilling to take actions that might undermine baseball's monopoly structure. On issues relating to economic organization, such as labor relations, television rights, and farm systems, Veeck's outlook was fundamentally conservative. His 1952 proposals for reorganizing baseball were aimed at restoring the game's prewar structure.[42]

Veeck's fellow owners reluctantly faced the need for innovative structural changes in the game. In July 1953 they met to discuss the Browns' future. Del Webb dominated the meeting. He insisted that the American League must follow the example of the National and begin a westward expansion. Webb championed a move by the Browns to Kansas City. The Yankees owner's motives were hardly altruistic. Kansas City was a New York AAA farm club. A move to that city would mean financial compensation for his club and the shift of its AAA farm club to a lucrative market in Denver. Moreover, Kansas City's municipal government was preparing to purchase the local stadium from the Yankees and finance a major expansion of its seating. Webb's construction company was bidding for the job. His subsequent enthusiasm for moving the Browns to Los Angeles was influenced by that city's need for a new stadium and perhaps by a desire to acquire the franchise for himself. Nevertheless, Webb proved to be correct when he argued that moving the Browns east would only increase the difficulties of two existing second division American League clubs, Washington and Philadelphia. A relatively restricted market became oversaturated. The Athletics moved to Kansas City within a year, and for nearly twenty years Washington and Baltimore struggled to make a profit. Moreover, by failing to expand to California in the 1950s, the American League entered the lucrative West Coast market much later than the National League and only after the latter had appropriated the best sites.[43]

American League owners concluded their meeting without making any commitment on the Browns' future. A majority preferred to wait until Veeck was ready to sell out. They privately and subtly communicated this decision to Veeck.[44]

Commenting on the inconclusive results of the meeting, *The Sporting News* observed: "It is evident that the baseball map is heaving like a turbulent ocean. Within the next few years it probably will bear only token resemblance to the design established 50 years ago." Noting that a number of growing cities with minor league clubs were bidding for major league franchises, it concluded: "If all these ambitions . . . are allowed to reach realization in a haphazard way, the result obviously will be chaos, not only for the majors but for the minors as well."[45] The warning was prophetic.

In the specific and pressing case of the Browns, the American League's owners failed to establish any sensible strategy for realignment. Rumors swirled in regard to the Browns' next home. Veeck remained intent on Baltimore for practical reasons. He denied press reports and speculation that he would move to Los Angeles, Montreal, Toronto, or Kansas City, insisting that their stadiums were inadequate. However, he declined to commit himself publicly to Baltimore.[46]

On 16 September 1953 Veeck met with the American League watchdog committee to outline his 1954 plans. Veeck announced that he would once again seek league approval for a move to Baltimore and introduced Miles as a spokesman for local financial interests. The committee gave Veeck its permission to move from St. Louis but deferred a decision on the new site. Both Veeck and Miles appeared pleased to have won league approval for a move. Miles and Veeck's Chicago financial backers discussed the purchase of stock by the Baltimore group. Once again, Veeck and his Baltimore allies appeared to be on the verge of a smooth transition of the franchise to its new home.[47]

This illusion shattered quickly. Representatives of the Washington and Philadelphia clubs began to criticize Veeck's plans to the press, noting that Baltimore's new stadium would have nearly twice the seating capacity of their parks and publicly complaining of the impact of the new club on their television markets. Dan Topping, the co-owner of the Yankees, indicated that other cities might offer better sites for realignment, while Del Webb openly championed Los Angeles as an alternative to Baltimore.[48]

Veeck defended his choice. Jerold Hoffberger again attempted to purchase the Griffith family's support by offering a deal on television sponsorship. This time the president of National Brewery agreed to continue sponsoring the Senators through the 1955 season and to arrange a $300,000 compensation for Griffith to cover the loss of his air rights in Baltimore. Meanwhile Veeck and Miles came to an agreement that would give Baltimore investors 40 percent of the club's stock and a majority of six on the team's eleven-man board of directors. Miles would become chairman of the board while Veeck remained president. The club would purchase Baltimore's minor league franchise and compensate the International League for shifting the Orioles to another city. The major league team would sell stock to Jack Dunn and give him a five-year personal contract.[49]

On 23 September a representative of the American League inspected Memorial Stadium and approved it as a site for major league play. Two days later St. Louis stockholders joined with Veeck's syndicate to overwhelmingly approve the move to Baltimore. Everything, the Baltimore *Sun* nervously remarked, appeared set, but the support of at least three clubs was still in doubt as Veeck met with his fellow league owners on 27 September 1953.[50]

Once more, Veeck, D'Alesandro, and Miles presented the case for a move to Baltimore. After extended debate, the American League's owners blocked the proposal by a vote of four to four. Boston, Cleveland, and Philadelphia joined New York in turning back Veeck's bid. A grinning Webb exited the eleven-hour meeting and announced the "doom" of Baltimore's hopes. A downcast D'Alesandro called the vote a "shattering blow" to his city.[51]

Baltimore's representatives quickly recovered their equilibrium and on the following day resumed their negotiations with the American League. American League president Harridge intervened to press the owners to break their deadlock and make a speedy decision on the Browns' future. Eventually, the various parties worked out a compromise. League leaders recognized that a West Coast move was too costly. Kansas City found little support. The Baltimore group's threat of legal and political action aimed at the reserve clause had its effect. Veeck, facing bankruptcy and receivership on 1 October, agreed to sell his syndicate's entire holdings to the Miles group. Zanvyl Krieger, a lawyer and the brother of the president of Gunther Brewery, speedily rounded up the additional money needed to meet Veeck's $2.4 million selling price. The Miles group acquired the AAA Orioles for $350,000 and agreed to pay a $48,749 indemnity to the International League for the loss of the Baltimore franchise. With Veeck out of baseball, his opponents were ready to welcome Baltimore into the major leagues. Webb agreed to support Baltimore in exchange for a modification in league rules that would permit expansion to ten teams and the establishment of franchises on the Pacific Coast. Philadelphia's general manager, Arthur Ehlers, a Baltimore native, swung the Athletics' vote in favor of the move.[52]

The deal was announced on 29 September. Veeck had $1 million in profit to soothe his battered ego and pay off his syndicate. Baltimore's business community was ecstatic. "No other event in years has given Baltimore as much national publicity," the city's Association of Commerce proclaimed. Local businessmen believed a major league baseball team would bring increased profits and improve the city's image. They eagerly awaited the opening of the 1954 season.[53]

For major league baseball, the franchise shifts of 1953 were the first concrete reaction to the serious economic, legal, and political problems it faced in the postwar era. This initial response was hasty and poorly coordinated, but it worked. The major leagues slowly regained control of their market by moving financially weak teams and selling franchise rights to eager groups in other major markets. The reorganization and expansion of the major leagues took place at the expense of the already hard-pressed minors. The minor leagues surrendered their best markets one after another. The contraction of minor league baseball continued throughout the 1950s under the twin impact of major league reorganization and the expansion of television. During this same period, the Baltimore franchise struggled on the field but created a model minor league system and learned how to harness television to its marketing objectives.

2 Trial and Error
Franchise Building

I don't know much about
the baseball business,
I'm a lawyer.
—Clarence Miles,
February 1954

This will be the first time
in five years I've started a
season without secretly
hoping to be fired. I knew
I wasn't stepping into a
bed of roses late in
1954. . . . But I hadn't
expected such chaos. . .
When I took over the
club . . . I was assured
there was no particular
hurry in producing a
winner. I later learned
this meant that everyone
was perfectly willing
to wait as long as
six months.
—Paul Richards, 1961

Bright sunshine replaced morning rain and a
crowd of nearly 500,000 persons lined the parade
route as the train bringing the Orioles to town
arrived at Baltimore's Mt. Royal Station on 15
April 1954. The players, dressed in their new uniforms, climbed into convertibles, and the parade
moved along a three-and-a-half-mile route toward Memorial Stadium. Bands, floats, and young
women dressed as Orioles and baseballs joined in
what *Life* pronounced the city's "biggest and most
exuberant demonstration since Civil War days." At
the still-unfinished stadium, Philadelphia's Connie Mack and Washington's Clark Griffith, the
two grand old men of baseball, joined American
League president Will Harridge in welcoming the
new team. Vice President Richard Nixon threw
out the first ball. The Orioles, led by fireballing
pitcher Bob Turley and scrappy catcher Clint
Courtney, completed a successful opening day by
beating Paul Richards's Chicago White Sox 3–1.
Major league baseball was back in Baltimore. The
auspicious beginning was the prologue to a six-
year struggle to turn the former Browns into a
contender.[1]

The Market

In 1950 Baltimore was the ninth largest city in the
United States, with a population of approximately
940,000 and a metropolitan area population of
1.5 million. It had a strong tradition of support for
its minor league franchise as well as a modern

stadium. The city had sufficient wealth to support professional sports. Baltimore's industrial base was strong. It was a major port and a center for shipbuilding and other heavy industries involving the manufacture or processing of steel, chemicals, plastics, electrical equipment, and fertilizers. The city's business and political leaders supported the new team; during his three terms (1947–59), Mayor Thomas D'Alesandro, Jr., came to the aid of the Orioles, as well as the Baltimore Colts of the National Football League (NFL), with favorable stadium contracts and improved services.[2]

Nevertheless, Baltimore was by no means an ideal place to establish a major league team. For one thing, its market area was extremely restricted. One former Orioles general manager described the situation:

> Our problem in those years . . . was that we had a very small market. You had metropolitan Baltimore. To the east . . . you had the Chesapeake Bay and an expensive bridge to get over and not that many people on the Eastern Shore. Directly north of you, you had the Phillies, and their influence comes clear down to Wilmington. . . . South of you, you've got Washington, and they take up half of the territory between Washington and Baltimore. To the west of you, you've got mountains. . . . Our best . . . area outside the Baltimore metropolitan area was a little slant up . . . into Harrisburg, Hagerstown, Carlisle, York . . . and you were fighting with Philadelphia and, if you got too far west, . . . with Pittsburgh.[3]

Only the departure of the Washington franchise for Texas in 1971 finally permitted the Orioles to build a large market.

The Orioles' problems extended beyond a restricted market area. The D'Alesandro years coincided with a gradual decay of Baltimore's tax base and a decline in its population. Middle-class and blue-collar whites moved out of the city into Baltimore County. Service industries and then manufacture followed them to the suburbs, creating communities that increasingly were self-contained. During World War II federal investment in new technologies and industries as well as in housing flowed to the Midwest and Far West. Shortly after the war a company financed by General Motors bought up Baltimore's privately owned public transportation system, replaced economically efficient street cars with more costly, polluting buses, and then sold the system to the city. Meanwhile, the rail commuter system was drastically cutting services, a victim of competition with the automobile.[4]

While white flight took hold, poor blacks were moving into the city. The number of blacks living in Baltimore rose from 230,000 (24 percent of the city's total population) in 1950 to approximately 403,000 (45 percent) by 1970. These new urban settlers were primarily from the farms and small towns of the South and of Maryland's Eastern Shore. A 1955 study found that 75 percent of them had less than ten years of education; and adjustment to city living proved difficult for many of them. The movement of whites out of the city accelerated. The suburbs erected barriers to keep blacks out. Even federal and local policies designed to assist the poor had negative effects. The welfare system consciously placed the poor, the old, the infirm, and women with dependent children in central city housing, increasing the burden on cities while hastening the flight of middle-class whites to the lower taxes of the suburbs. Between 1954 and 1965, Baltimore, like other American cities, helped to perpetuate its problems by a redevelopment strategy that demolished old, single-family housing, and concentrated the displaced poor with the other city poor in high-rise apartment buildings. The effect was not only to increase the concentration of the poor but also to encourage crime and vandalism and reinforce de facto segregation, since nearly 90 percent of the people in public housing were black. Due to a lack of public transportation, these individuals were generally without the mobility to find or maintain employment.[5]

Baltimore's overall population decline had important political consequences. The city's ability to dominate state politics vanished. In 1940, 47 percent of the state's population lived inside the city of Baltimore. By 1980 only 18 percent resided in the city, while 61 percent lived in the suburbs of Baltimore and neighboring Washington. Baltimore had to battle for a share of the state budget with the growing and economically more powerful suburbs.[6]

By the early 1950s city business and political leaders were aware that changes in Baltimore's population balance had seriously affected its economic viability, and they began seeking remedies. They saw major league professional sports as an attraction capable of bringing suburban money back into the city, particularly if combined with an aggressive effort to redevelop Baltimore's central business district. In 1955 Miles, Hoffberger, and a number of other wealthy Orioles stockholders helped to form the Greater Baltimore Committee. Miles served as the committee's first chairman, and Hoffberger as its treasurer. Committee objectives included making the port of Baltimore competitive, improving transportation facilities, and creating a revitalized downtown area to attract new business and rebuild the city's tax base. The effort was a long-term success, but during the 1950s and 1960s Baltimore struggled to maintain its city services in the face of growing unemployment, continued middle-class migration to the suburbs, and simmering racial tensions.[7]

Baltimore's shifting racial composition was key to its problems. The city's new immigrants were attracted initially by war jobs and city services. They faced the discrimination customary in mid-century U.S. cities: segregated schools, theaters, hotels, and restaurants and severe limitations in regard to employment opportunity and social mobility. "By and large," a 1955 report concluded, "Baltimore remains a racially segregated city, with the Negroes in the poorer jobs and the poorer housing." Baltimore's blacks organized politically and demanded recognition of their rights. A large and capable chapter of the National Association for the Advancement of Colored People (NAACP) took the lead in the struggle, aided by active church groups and by one of the nation's most influential black newspapers, the Baltimore *Afro-American*. Maryland's moderate political leadership was willing to make concessions, and the 1950s were marked by slow and limited progress toward racial equality.[8]

Baltimore's black leaders viewed the new baseball franchise with considerable suspicion. When Branch Rickey integrated the sport in 1946–47, black leaders had seen baseball as a useful vehicle for desegregating public accommodations such as hotels and restaurants. Club owners, however, had provided little support for black objectives. The men who owned sports teams wanted to make a profit, not a social revolution. When Bill Veeck, one of the sport's best-known opponents of segregation, announced he would bring the Browns to Baltimore, black leaders reacted ambivalently. The possibility of a Veeck-led club raised hopes that baseball might aid in breaking down racial barriers in Maryland. *Afro-American* sports columnist Sam Lacy commented that the city's business community could use Veeck's brand of "straight talk" on racial issues.[9] The Baltimore chapter of the NAACP took a less positive line. Racism in Baltimore extended to sports. White city fans had taunted Jackie Robinson mercilessly during his 1946 appearances as the first black minor league player. Blacks generally followed the Elite Giants of the Negro leagues rather than the AAA Orioles. Citing the city's history of racism and the continued segregation of its public facilities, the NAACP protested the proposed move. Lacy, who mirrored black ambivalence, commented that rewarding racism in a city that had a history of failed professional sports franchises made little sense. He questioned whether segregated Baltimore was ready for major league status.[10]

The team's new owners did little to alleviate black fears. The Orioles' first manager and general manager came from the segregated Philadelphia Athletics. The club's business manager had supported earlier efforts to ban blacks from baseball. One of the team's initial player actions was to release the only black on its major league roster, veteran relief pitcher and Negro league star Satchel Paige. When Maryland governor Theodore McKeldin asked Baltimore hotels to permit black players to use their facilities, the Orioles failed to lend public support to the governor's effort. Finally, after mounting a preseason publicity effort around its best black prospect, pitcher Jehosie Heard, the club discovered that Heard lacked major league credentials, so in June 1954 the Orioles sent their only black player back to the minor leagues. The team clearly suffered from comparison with the professional football Colts, who had a number of black stars.[11]

Racial prejudice may have influenced some of the team's initial actions. However, other factors were also involved. In the case of Paige, whose "official" age was forty-seven, team management was concerned about a high salary, a long history of weak self-discipline, and a poor 1953 performance that indicated that the years might finally be catching up with the future Hall of Famer. Blacks who trained with the 1954 Orioles reported that they were treated fairly. Most important, the team continued to recruit and promote black prospects within its farm system. Essentially, the club's attitude toward racial issues was indifference. Club policy, its first general manager stated, was to acquire anyone who could help the team win, not to make a "social statement."[12] The Orioles, and most other major league teams, declined to establish solid ties with black community leaders. Without a serious public relations program among blacks, the team cut itself off from a large potential base of fans. Major league baseball has persistently ignored blacks as a source of attendance. The motivations for what appears to be a consistent policy are undocumented but likely include prejudice, a fear of losing white fans, and concern about racial incidents.[13]

Putting Together a Management Team

Clarence Miles lead the initial effort to build a winning team in Baltimore. A small stockholder without any previous experience in sports management, Miles held the support of the business community and the team's board for nearly two years as a result of successfully negotiating the franchise transfer from St. Louis. Miles's first efforts to build a management team were unsuccessful, and the club's field performance, combined with his tendency to run the Orioles without consulting the majority stockholders, gradually sapped his support on the board of directors. Ultimately, Miles put together a management team capable of building a winning baseball club, but too late to save his position.

Bill Veeck resigned as club president on 2 October 1953. Bill De Witt once again took charge at St. Louis, assisted by general manager Rudie Schaffer and two representatives of the new owners, Jack Dunn and business manager Herbert Armstrong. A 14 October stockholders meeting elected Miles president of Baltimore Baseball, Inc., a company incorporated in Missouri to permit the new owners to take advantage of favorable depreciation rules for money-losing businesses in the U.S. tax code. Baltimore Baseball ran the club and its minor league subsidiaries. The Baltimore Orioles, Inc., a holding company for the St. Louis Browns stock purchased by the Miles cartel, controlled Baltimore Baseball. Its board of directors included most of the large stockholders in the new franchise and set broad policy. Miles, as president of Baltimore Baseball, was responsible for operating the club on a day-to-day basis.

The major decisions taken by the board on 14 October were to invest heavily in a minor league system, to pledge publicly that the Browns' policy of selling off talent had ended, to sell the team's broadcasting rights to stockholder Jerold Hoffberger's National Brewery, and to rid the club of Browns management. The board gave Miles a free hand to create a new management team.[14]

Miles permitted Schaffer and De Witt to remain with the club until they lined up new jobs. He fired manager Marty Marion for "defeatism" after Marion told a reporter that the Orioles would need years to build a contender. As a concession to maintaining continuity in club operations, Miles decided to retain the Browns' veteran minor league director, Jim McLaughlin. The new owners were determined to wipe out as many as possible of their team's associations with the Browns' dismal past. By chance, Miles saved a key to building a contending club by retaining the capable McLaughlin.[15]

The board balanced its decision to sell television and radio rights to Hoffberger's National Brewery with concessions to rival Gunther Brewery, the family business of stockholder Zanvyl Krieger. Gunther held the exclusive right to advertise on the Memorial Stadium scoreboard. The club permitted Gunther to print a letter from Miles to brewery president Abraham Krieger extolling his "invaluable" assistance in acquiring the franchise.[16]

Miles's initial choice for general manager was the colorful Frank Lane of the Chicago White Sox. Lane, known as "Trader Frank" for his endless player acquisitions, provided Miles with valuable advice during the October 1953 negotiations leading to the Browns' sale. Lane was willing to join the Orioles as general manager, but the White Sox insisted he honor an existing contract. Miles then turned to Arthur Ehlers. Baltimore-born Ehlers's support had helped swing a majority behind the city's franchise bid in October 1953. Moreover, Ehlers was a "baseball man," an insider who knew the mechanics of operating a franchise and was personally acquainted with the sport's key personalities.[17]

Unfortunately, Ehlers proved inadequate to the task of building the Baltimore franchise. He was a decent and cautious man who was reluctant to make major trades or to spend. Ehlers had worked for the financially hard-pressed Philadelphia Athletics. He was obsessed with making a profit for the club and never took advantage of the Orioles' main asset, the willingness of the club's owners to spend to build a winner. Similarly, Ehlers was reluctant to take the risk of trading any of the team's limited assets—like young pitchers Bob Turley, Ryne Duren, and Don Larsen—in an effort to improve the club's overall competitiveness. Ehlers may have been concerned that dealing away these players would appear to repeat the bad management practices of the Browns. He tried to improve the team by ridding it of a number of aging veterans and by exchanging journeymen with other teams. The 1954 Orioles were full of new faces, but in terms of athletic talent they were scarcely improved over the 1953 Browns. Ehlers's best trades were with the Athletics, whose personnel he knew well. Pitcher Joe Coleman, in particular, proved to be a superb acquisition for the 1954 Orioles. Ehlers also hired a number of Philadelphia's scouts and administrative personnel.[18]

Ehlers's major contributions were made in the winter of 1953–54 as he guided the team's initial marketing effort while slowly building its administration. Ehlers and Miles were able to capitalize on local enthusiasm to ensure the Orioles of a profitable first season.

Marketing considerations were key for both the Orioles and the American League. The league's leadership wanted impressive attendance figures to vindicate their decision to put another franchise on the East Coast. At the 29 October ceremony in which he turned the franchise charter over to Miles, American League president Harridge pointedly urged Baltimore to beat Milwaukee's so-called attendance miracle. The Orioles' new owners were equally hopeful of achieving attendance records, especially when they sold 1,600 season tickets in the first week after acquiring the team. Initially, the club limited its sales to season tickets, offering full- and part-season plans. In December 1953 individual tickets became available, and mail orders flooded the Orioles offices. By February 1954 the team had sold a total of 360,000 tickets for its inaugural season. To increase attendance, the club decided to play thirty-nine night games. To further build interest in the team, Orioles management played up Yankee opposition to the move to Baltimore and pledged to win "revenge" on the playing field. Baseball fever gripped the city. Fans recalled the Braves leap from seventh to second place in 1953 and hoped the Orioles would do the same.[19]

Meanwhile, the business community and political leadership were organizing to exploit the favorable national press coverage of the Orioles as part of their campaign to improve Baltimore's image. Mayor D'Alesandro put together a Baseball Celebration Committee composed of the city's elite to plan the festivities marking the return of major league baseball to Baltimore, and the city put up $10,000 to cover the costs of the celebration. It spent a further $2.5 million to complete the expansion of Memorial Stadium. The Association of Commerce happily noted that Baltimore was capturing "an amazing amount of favorable publicity—the kind that can't be bought"—from the Orioles. The *New Yorker*, *Life*, and *Newsweek* were among the national publications covering events in Baltimore. Association leaders reported that the arrival of the team had induced a number of firms to consider moving into Baltimore.[20]

The new franchise created part-time employment possibilities for about 500 Baltimore residents. In addition, the Orioles hired a number of administrative personnel and full-time scouts from the Baltimore area. Local businesses, particularly hotels, restaurants, and shops near the stadium, expected to cash in on the large crowds that the Orioles hoped to draw. Downtown merchants also counted on large profits. The Association of Commerce noted the widespread expectation that the Orioles would "help all aspects of the city's economy."[21]

By late March, advance sales of 600,000 assured the Orioles a good start, but continuing financial success for both the franchise and the business community rested upon the team's ability to win baseball games. Local enthusiasm grew when the Orioles posted a successful spring training record. Miles spoke of challenging the Yankees for the American League championship within three or four seasons. Even normally cautious manager Jimmy Dykes expressed confidence that the team would be respectable and finish in the middle of the standings.[22]

After a good start, the team began to slide toward the bottom of the American League. The Orioles' pitching and defense were adequate, but the club lacked offense. Memorial Stadium's cavernous outfield (450 feet to dead center, with 400-foot power alleys) frustrated the team's few genuine power hitters. Vic Wertz, one of the Orioles' home run threats, opened the season in a deep slump. The Orioles traded him to Cleveland, where Wertz regained his touch and helped the Indians to win a pennant. By June, Baltimore was out of the pennant race. Attendance slumped along with the team's play. The Orioles drew 119,747 to their first four home games, beating Milwaukee's 1953 record, and the club's management talked hopefully of reaching 2 million in paid attendance. By June they scaled back these goals considerably.[23]

Ehlers traded for offensive help, but power hitters were in short supply. The team squandered good pitching performances and lost thirty games by one run. A preseason deal in which Ehlers surrendered first baseman Roy Sievers for weak-hitting outfielder Gil Coan came back to haunt the Orioles general manager when Sievers blossomed into a home run hitter with the Washington Senators. In a desperate effort to improve the club, Ehlers signed eighteen-year-old pitching prospect Billy O'Dell for a reported $12,000 bonus and promised to acquire more young players to bolster the sagging club. In July the board of directors gave Dykes and Ehlers a vote of confidence.[24]

Frustration grew as the season wore on and defeats piled up. The business community's enthusiasm for the club shrank. The Orioles brought an estimated $5–8 million in trade into the city but failed to create the expected general business boom. Certain businesses did very well. The franchise made a sizable profit from admissions and the sales of its food and parking concessions. Various forms of public transportation made small gains, as did Baltimore's newspapers and hotels. Downtown merchants had little to show for their earlier hopes, however, since the stadium was located far from the city center. Restaurant owners complained that home games, and especially Sunday doubleheaders, actually hurt their business. Overall, *Business Week* reported, city merchants were "left out" of the profit taking.[25]

On 26 August 1954, following a fourteen-game losing streak, an angry Miles returned from his summer vacation in Maine to tell a press conference that no employee's contract was safe and to promise "drastic" changes. The next day he met with Dykes to discuss the club's problems. The Orioles manager laid out the realities of the baseball business for his boss:

> Clarence Miles asked me . . . what I thought about putting up a fence in center field. . . . I told him first, to get me some players who can hit 'em over the fence. . . . We need so much it's hard to know where to start. I also told Mr. Miles how hard it is to buy experienced ball players.
>
> I don't mean to look down my nose at money. It's nice to have it. This is the first team I've been with that could afford to pay Ted Williams' salary. . . . It's not easy, though, to improve yourself by trades. You have to give up good men to get good men in return.[26]

Dykes demanded a vote of confidence from Miles. The club president reacted by calling a meeting of the team's fourteen-man board of directors on 6 September. Meanwhile, he held talks with Chicago White Sox manager Paul Richards about taking control of the club. The board gave its full support to Miles. On 14 September Richards signed a three-year contract to serve as both manager and general manager of the Orioles. In announcing the change, Miles explained that Richards would "be relieved of the administrative functions usually undertaken by a general manager" in order to concentrate on building a contender and managing the club. Dykes and Ehlers would remain with the club until the season was completed, and then Richards would decide whether to keep them in other capacities.[27]

A tall, gaunt man with a leathery face and piercing eyes, the forty-five-year-old Richards was a tough, irascible, and ingenious baseball man with a well-earned reputation as one of the best field managers in the game. "He knew what made baseball tick," Brooks Robinson recalled.[28] Richards, however, had no administrative experience. Richards took the Baltimore job with the understanding that he would have full authority over player personnel. He retained Ehlers as his top assistant to smooth the transition and handle routine office management. After announcing "I'll have to tear up this club from top to bottom," Richards immediately set off on his first scouting trip.[29]

Home Grown by 1960

In March 1953 the Baltimore *Sun* shrewdly observed that the farm system would likely be at the center of the Orioles story for years to come. Browns manager Marty Marion told newsmen in October of that year that a minimum of five years of heavy investment in minor league development was the only way to produce a winner in Baltimore. Marion lost his job for this honest appraisal, but it proved to be remarkably accurate.[30]

Player development in the minor leagues was expensive. In addition to providing bonuses and salaries for the players, a major league club that wanted to be a contender had to hire a large number of full- and part-time scouts, aid at least some of its minor league affiliates with subsidies, and cover administrative costs such as travel, training programs, and office overhead. Between 1945 and 1950 the New York Yankees spent over $4 million on player development. They doubled their spending on minor league operations over the next 5 years. In 1954 the Philadelphia Phillies estimated that minor league costs took up one-third of their total budget.[31]

The Orioles spent $204,239 on player development in their first season, a reflection of Ehlers's cost-conscious management style. The owners, however, were ready to spend more and to take financial losses in order to build a winner. McLaughlin recalled: "They had interest in baseball. And . . . they had an interest in the community. . . . It really meant a lot to them for the Orioles, somehow, somewhere to become a contending and important club in the American League. And, although in the end it didn't cost any of them any money, and some of them made some money, they had a sort of civic pride. . . . They didn't want to do anything that would jeopardize the baseball franchise or the city of Baltimore."[32] In Richards, the Orioles' owners had the right man to help them spend their money.

In 1960 the Orioles' minor league development program produced a contender. The authors of this success were McLaughlin and Richards. Their joint achievement was the end product of a long and bitter personal battle. Richards and McLaughlin shared little in common except strength of character. They clashed from the first days of the Richards regime. The tall, thin, tart-tongued McLaughlin was the classic administrator: careful, organized, and intelligent, with a highly developed instinct for protecting his bureaucratic turf. Richards knew little of administrative procedure and never really understood or cared about the requirements of efficient management. He constantly interfered in McLaughlin's chain of command. Harry Dalton, McLaughlin's aide, recalled:

> Paul came in and they told him: build a ball club anyway you want. . . .
> Paul was not experienced in office procedures; he was a field man. It was
> a natural conflict. . . . Paul would pick up a phone and call one of our

scouts and give him an assignment and never bother to go through Jim [or] let Jim know what was going on. . . . Jim was a combative Irishman who had great pride in his department . . . and it just rubbed him the wrong way. If Paul had been a bit more steeped in administrative procedure it would have helped.[33]

Richards's major contribution was to take advantage of the club's chief resource: money. Richards spent. Jack Dunn, a close friend, smiled as he remembered, "Paul was the only man in baseball who had an unlimited budget and exceeded it."[34] Dalton added: "[Richards] jump started our spending program. When Paul came in . . . he went right after it in a hurry. And by the end of '55 I think the ownership realized they had a tiger by the tail. But, he had also shocked the whole organization into the fact that . . . you're going to have to be financially aggressive."[35]

McLaughlin's and Richards's contrasting styles were responses to two differing sources of pressure. McLaughlin needed to produce major league prospects. He stressed the patient knitting together of a competent scouting staff and the careful development of young talent. Richards was under tremendous pressure from the information media and the board of directors to field an improved major league club immediately. Full of self-confidence, Richards inadvertently added to this pressure by declaring at his first press conference in Baltimore, "I'm not thinking in terms of six years. I intend to see what can be done in six months." Richards was looking for players who could help the major league team immediately.[36]

McLaughlin proved the better judge of both baseball and administrative talent. By building a large, competent scouting staff and paying them well, McLaughlin created a "quality operation" with high morale. His scouts recruited the players who eventually turned the Orioles into a winner. He also sought out and hired good administrators and minor league managers. By introducing or developing ideas such as cross-checking scouts, regularized reporting forms, and scouting supervisors, McLaughlin made cash expenditures on talent as scientific as possible. Even with all these innovations, the Orioles made many mistakes in signing players, an indication of the difficulties major league clubs face in evaluating the athletic potential of young men just leaving high school.[37]

Richards, to his credit, kept McLaughlin on the club payroll and permitted him to develop talent. McLaughlin's operation benefited from Richards's openhanded spending. It permitted the farm system chief to hire more scouts and compete in signing more top prospects. Richards believed in Branch Rickey's theory of developing quality from quantity. He was ready to take risks, particularly if a young player appeared to have the tools to help the Orioles immediately. On 24 September 1954 Miles announced that the club had set up a special $250,000 fund to cover bonus signings. Within three weeks, Richards had spent $150,000. He quickly exceeded his budget for player signings. Acting as the club's chief scout, Richards roamed across the United States evaluating and signing prospects. He even left the Orioles during the regular season for short periods to look over prospects. By June 1955 the board of directors was concerned about the franchise's financial stability and made its first effort to rein in the free-spending general manager. Alarmed by his three-week $150,000 spending spree, the board instructed Richards to slow the pace of his bonus signings.[38]

Richards acted with equal boldness in restructuring the major league team. Asked about the team at his first press conference, Richards responded: "You mean the one coming or the one going?" In November 1954, less than two months after he joined the Orioles, Richards made one of the largest and most controversial player swaps in major league history. He sent pitchers Bob Turley and Don Larsen, together with shortstop Billy Hunter and some minor leaguers, to the Yankees for "an assortment of established . . . veterans and bright but untested rookies." The Yankees put a lock on the 1955 American League championship. Richards admitted the deal helped New York but added: "What concern is it of mine who wins the pennant? . . . I want to get the Orioles out of seventh place."[39]

Richards continued trading and signing prospects at a furious pace. Optimism again took hold among Orioles fans and the team's advance ticket sales for 1955 outpaced those for the preceding year. In April 1955, Ehlers estimated that the team needed only 400,000 paid admissions during the regular season to reach its financial break-even point.[40]

Unfortunately, Richards's first effort at building a team was unsuccessful. The young players he signed were not ready to help the major league club. Richards's revolving-door style of trading simply stocked the 1955 Orioles with a lot of marginal veterans. The Richards "youth movement" produced the oldest team in the major leagues, averaging 30.4 years by June 1955. By the end of the 1955 season fifty-four men had played for the Orioles, a team that finished last in batting, fielding, and slugging percentage. The Orioles remained in seventh place. The optimism of April turned sour, and season attendance dropped by over 200,000. Richards's administration, particularly his spending on bonuses, brought to a head opposition to Miles, which had been growing within the board of directors.[41]

Miles's one-man style of leadership and two years of bad baseball built up resentment among the businessmen who comprised the Orioles board. Jack Dunn commented: "Everyone wanted to run the club. . . . They were all powerful, successful men and sometimes powerful, successful men don't make a great team." The board's concern increased in July 1955 when the commissioner's office caught Richards violating the major league bonus rule. Commissioner Frick fined the club and its general manager $4,500 and declared pitcher Tom Borland a free agent after discovering that Richards had signed him to a large bonus and tried to hide the fact. This public embarrassment followed another widely reported major error in judgment by Richards, who paid a large bonus to pitcher Bruce Swango and then released him. The team was already stocked with five high-priced bonus players who were not ready to play major league baseball but could not be assigned to the minor leagues for training under existing rules because their bonus payments exceeded $4,000. Bonus spending had reached $700,000 in the club's first two years of operations.[42]

In September the board removed Ehlers as Richards's assistant, apparently because the powerless assistant general manager had been incapable of controlling his dynamic boss. In early November the power struggle reached its climax. Miles resigned. A new coalition leadership took charge. Real estate executive James Keelty took over as president while investment banker Joseph Iglehardt emerged as an active chairman of the board. Richards retained his dual position but publicly forswore further big gambles on expensive bonus players. He affirmed that the team had "reached the saturation point" and added a bit wistfully that he would spend no more on big bonuses "unless they were just too good to pass up."[43]

A seven-man coalition including Keelty, Iglehardt, and Zanvyl Krieger now controlled a voting majority of the club stock and made policy. However, these directors were often at odds, particularly over player development policy. McLaughlin described the board's infighting as "soft and silent," adding "you had to really be a party . . . to understand. Nobody came out in open confrontation." Some directors sided with either Richards or McLaughlin, fueling the simmering conflict between the two men. Keelty was McLaughlin's main source of support as well as Richards's financial watchdog. Iglehardt usually backed Richards. Krieger, perhaps the most civic-spirited of all the major stockholders, played the role of peacemaker within the board.[44]

While the new board wanted Richards to stay on in his dual role, it was determined to find a man who could maintain daily control over the club's finances. An intensive search for a skilled administrator to aid and restrain Richards began in the winter of 1955. A club representative met with Commissioner Frick over the rules violations and won Richards a "clean slate." Keelty confirmed the Orioles' commitment to continue to bid for the best talent. Richards promised that the days of "revolving door trades" were over. The club would build for the long haul. McLaughlin's careful methods had triumphed. The media-conscious Richards reaped most of the credit, to McLaughlin's disgust.[45]

McLaughlin did his work with little fanfare. Richards remained the club's dominant personality. He enjoyed a good rapport with the press. Richards's frankness and his endless supply of baseball recollections produced good stories for journalists. Moreover, the club had given him a massive initial publicity buildup as the savior of Baltimore baseball. The Orioles were committed to Richards's leadership and style for the long haul.

With player development in the hands of capable subordinates, Richards was free to apply his unquestionable talents in the area to which they were most adapted: molding a major league team. Richards was a great teacher for young players, a master at handling pitching, and an expert at getting the most out of journeymen. A few carefully thought out trades during the winter of 1955–56, together with Richards's good field managing, produced results: the Orioles won sixty-nine games in 1956, moving into sixth place. The following year, the team won half its games and finished in fifth place. Although the Orioles slipped back to sixth the next two years, they played better baseball. Richards's teams displayed characteristics that would mark later championship squads: good pitching and tight defense. However, a weak attack, particularly a lack of power hitters, made it impossible for the Orioles to move into contention. "Richards' DeLuxe Retreads," as one baseball publication dubbed the Orioles, always included a number of older players who faded after a good season or two. Attendance picked up in 1956 and 1957 before dropping back to 1955 levels in 1958. It rose again in 1959 as the first products of the farm system began to join the club.[46]

By the winter of 1957, Orioles officials were optimistic about the success of the minor league program. McLaughlin and Dalton adopted the motto "home grown by 1960" to indicate their confidence in the talent that Orioles farms were nurturing. A farm system of seven clubs and about 150 players had a number of outstanding young pitchers and two highly talented infielders, Brooks Robinson and Ron Hansen. Richards expressed satisfaction with the program, adding a strong dose of realism by telling reporters that "we've got to have five or six crops of young ball players for the effects to show." In 1959 the new Orioles began to make their appearance. Pitcher Jerry Walker was a standout in that year's All-Star Game. Robinson was building a reputation as an outstanding major league third baseman. By the end of the 1959 season, five young Orioles had established their major league credentials. Richards announced he would give other farm system products their chance in 1960. A new era was clearly beginning for the franchise.[47]

Back on the Farms

The Orioles success in player development took place while minor league baseball suffered through the worst years of its postwar crisis. A number of factors had undermined the minor leagues' market, but minor league executives continued to focus their complaints on television. By the mid-1950s, these long-standing fears were beginning to become real. Major league teams were creating regional television networks that threatened to capture the identification and loyalty of fans in minor league cities. Recognizing that the major leagues were of little help, the minors turned to Congress for assistance in preserving the remnants of their financial independence.

Congress was willing to listen; but as the decade wore on, minor league officials realized that legislative relief was unlikely. The forces arrayed against the minor leagues were too powerful. Foremost among them was the television industry. The networks repeatedly turned back the efforts of minor league supporters in Congress to enact legislation restricting broadcasting rights. Major league–minor league relations were tenuous. Minor league leaders made common cause with the majors before Congress but had little trust in the leadership of the big leagues. Major league determination to maximize television income regardless of the impact on the minors poisoned their relationship. When Commissioner Frick, one of the minors' self-appointed champions, suggested streamlining organized baseball's organization under a single individual, the minor leagues responded hostilely. They refused to surrender what remained of their independence to the major leagues without some form of financial compensation.[48]

The major leagues meanwhile were moving in an ad hoc manner toward a fundamental restructuring of the minors. They reduced the number of their own farm clubs and sold off most of their minor league subsidiaries to cut down on overhead. Through changes in the rules regarding bonuses and free agent acquisition, they virtually cut off access to talent for independent minor league teams, killing off nonaffiliated operators. By 1957 major league clubs owned the contracts of about 80 percent of the players in the minor leagues. The major leagues also began to subsidize their individual farm clubs in a more systematic manner in order to keep them financially solvent.[49]

The restructuring of the minor leagues was not a major league conspiracy. Each team moved independently to improve its operations and save money. By 1957 both major and minor league executives recognized the need to work out a modus vivendi. Over the next six years they slowly put together an agreement that finally brought a measure of stability to minor league baseball in exchange for the surrender of the minors' remaining independence.

The Orioles were one of the major league franchises that actively participated in minor league restructuring. Between 1953 and 1957 the club streamlined its minor league system and disposed of its sole wholly owned subsidiary. The Baltimore franchise inherited a thirteen-team minor league system from the Browns. At the end of the team's first season in Baltimore, McLaughlin laid out the condition of the farm system for a representative sent by new general manager Richards. The club simply had too little talent to justify a system that was the largest in the American League. Money used to maintain these players and teams could be better spent on scouting. McLaughlin and Richards agreed to cut back the farm system to eight teams and drop about a hundred players. At a 28 November 1954 press conference announcing these moves, McLaughlin explained: "Our one aim is to feed players to the parent club. The 100 players we released . . . had no chance ever to make the majors, so we got rid of them. Now, with our expanded scouting system we'll be acquiring new talent to test." The Orioles farm director added that working agreements were easily made with the bloated and economically strapped minor leagues: "We could snap our fingers in the . . . hotel lobby here and within an hour get twenty farm clubs that would be glad to form a working agreement with us."[50]

Even with a reduced minor league system, the Orioles ran a large-scale operation. An average of 250 players reported to the club's Thomasville, Georgia, camp for six weeks of "intensive scrutiny and instruction." The players, signed en masse over the previous year, were quickly weeded out. Those who remained joined the rosters of lower minor league clubs. After a season of play, some were promoted, the rest dropped. Between 1954 and 1959 the club signed 805 players and released 668. Earl Weaver, a young minor league manager, quickly learned that an Orioles employee had to restrain his desire to win with experienced career minor leaguers and concentrate on selecting and developing talent that might eventually play on the major league club.[51]

The size of Baltimore's minor league system fluctuated, but the trend was to a slight contraction from the eight teams of 1955 to six or seven teams between 1956 and 1960. Bonus spending slowed too. Between 1956 and 1958 the club spent only $200,000 on large bonuses. Few of the high-priced players signed in Richards's first years made the major leagues, a factor that diminished club enthusiasm for offering large sums to untried talent. Nevertheless, the club continued to spend heavily for talent, and the size of the average bonus rose relentlessly as sixteen major league clubs bid furiously against each other for premium amateur ballplayers. "The steady, continuous acquisition of the best potential talent is a costly, tedious process," a joint Keelty-Richards statement noted, "but the management of the Baltimore Orioles plans to spare no expense in acquiring and developing the best available youth." McLaughlin simultaneously increased the number of full- and part-time scouts. Overall spending on the minor league system rose relentlessly.[52]

By 1960 Baltimore's minor league system of about 150 players ranked in the middle of major league organizations in terms of its size. The total number of amateur signings declined from 204 in 1954 to 62 in 1959 as a result of increased competition, the rising costs of signings, and the limited number of minor league roster spots. In talent, however, Baltimore's was one of the premier organizations. Between 1954 and 1959 it sent more players to the majors than any other organization except that of the Cardinals. In 1959

Orioles farmhands dominated the selection for the Pacific Coast League's all-star team. Patient development of talented prospects and a superior scouting staff were about to pay off.[53]

While building a solid farm system, Baltimore management was simultaneously exploring changes in the rules governing major league–minor league relations. The club's initial interest was prompted by a desire to change the rules regulating the assignment of large bonus players to the major leagues and a need to find ways to cut down on the size of bonuses. The first objective was particularly troublesome for Baltimore. All major league teams were deeply concerned about the second. Richards also hoped to change the rules governing the minor league draft in order to exploit talent-laden systems like the New York Yankees farms. He found support among a number of other clubs.[54]

Reform of the rules governing both bonuses and the minor league draft was a piecemeal process. Too many vested interests were involved to permit sweeping changes. Veeck's 1952 proposal to expand the minor league player draft had laid the groundwork for his expulsion from baseball. Each team had too much money invested in its minor league players to permit an unrestricted draft. Richards, an ardent champion of rules changes that would expand the number of players eligible for a draft, began to change his mind as the Orioles farm system improved. Modification in the rules governing the player draft had to be tied to a plan limiting bonus payments to amateur free agents in order to build a majority for change among major league owners.[55]

In the mid-1950s the major leagues began experimenting with modest changes in the minor league draft rule and discussed a possible "free agent draft" of amateur talent. In 1957 they agreed that players with more than four years of minor league experience would be eligible for the draft. The majors also abandoned the old bonus rule, permitting major league teams to place players signed for sums larger than $4,000 in the minor leagues immediately. These rules changes assisted the Orioles player development program but, one Baltimore official noted, also reduced the already weak restraints on costly bidding for talented amateurs. In September 1958 the Orioles placed a representative on a special committee to study ways to restrain spending on bonuses through reform of the draft. In December 1958 the major leagues adopted a revised minor league draft rule designed to reduce bonus spending by further limiting the amount of time a minor league player could be protected from the annual draft.[56]

While the major leagues were restructuring the player acquisition process, minor league executives were organizing for a last-ditch battle against television. During the December 1955 winter meetings of baseball executives, the major leagues voted down a minor league plan that would have restricted broadcasting. Big league executives then endorsed Walter O'Malley's plan for a televised game of the week on Saturdays. The games would be beamed into minor league cities and blacked out in major league ones. To soften the impact, the National League proposed that half the expected income from the game of the week be turned over to the minors to compensate them for revenue losses. The American League vetoed this suggestion.[57]

Minor league baseball executives were convinced that a game of the week would cut deeply into their already limited revenues. The contraction of minor league baseball continued. Between 1953 and 1956 ninety-four minor league clubs folded. At the same time, the major leagues continued to sell their wholly owned subsidiaries. In 1951 the majors owned 207 minor league clubs; by the beginning of the 1957 season they owned 38. St. Louis Cardinals general manager Frank Lane explained the rationale for disposing of clubs to a meeting of civic leaders in Rochester, New York:

> We over invested in minor league properties. A fifteen club minor league system is far out of proportion to our needs. We are happy if we can realize a two player expectancy each year from the minors. We don't need fifteen clubs for this . . . and can not afford to operate two triple-A . . . clubs. Independent ownership can succeed because its primary interest is giving fans entertainment. Under St. Louis, Rochester was forced to operate with our player procurement program foremost in mind. As a consequence Rochester was saddled with special contract purchases, farming out of players, organization drafts, and heavy scouting expenses.[58]

In order to cut their losses, the major leagues encouraged the formation of "community baseball" through the sale of stock in minor league teams to local fans. The major leagues sold their minor league franchises and property, plus the contracts of older minor league ballplayers, to these newly created corporations. In the case of Rochester, the Cardinals sold their AAA franchise to local interests for $525,000 in January 1957. Eventually over 8,200 individuals bought stock in the club at ten dollars per share. Community baseball organizations helped to reanimate baseball in the higher minor leagues. By the early 1960s a majority of the AAA International League's teams were community owned. However, community ownership was economically unfeasible in small towns, and the D, C, and B leagues they hosted continued to fold.[59]

Baltimore adopted the community baseball strategy to unload its unprofitable wholly owned subsidiary, the San Antonio Missions. The Orioles inherited ownership of this money-losing AA team from the Browns. Baltimore needed a club in the high minors to train its prospects but had to decide if continued ownership of the team was the best financial strategy. The new owners expected the Missions to make a profit. In February 1954 Miles led a fact-finding mission to San Antonio to talk about the team's future with club officials and local civic leaders. Miles struck the right note with local leaders by stressing that the Orioles were "sincerely interested" in San Antonio, calling the Missions "our most prized possession" and promising to stock the team with the best available talent.[60]

Baltimore management made good on its promise to remold the team's personnel radically, and an improved Mission team rose to the top of the second division of the Texas League. Between 1954 and 1956 the Orioles continued to feed the best of their limited available talent to the team. San Antonio finished second in the 1955 Texas League but dropped into the second division in 1956. Local fans responded by staying at home. Missions attendance dropped from 100,000 in 1955 to 50,000 in 1956. The Orioles lost $125,000. In December 1956 Keelty led a second group to San Antonio to study the situation. The club considered selling the Missions but decided instead to bring in new management, led by promotion-minded Marvin Milkes. The Orioles purchased a top pitcher for the club, and Milkes promised improvements "on the field, in the office, [and in the] stadium." The fate of the San Antonio franchise lay in Milkes's ability to turn a profit, rapidly.[61]

After another money-losing season in 1957, Baltimore quietly searched for a buyer for its AA franchise. No one was willing to meet the Orioles' selling price of approximately $400,000 for the team and $750,000 for the stadium. At the beginning of December 1957, Baltimore management signed a working agreement with Louisville (AAA), and Richards announced, "We will not continue to operate the Missions." Richards's statement catalyzed the San Antonio business community. It formed a public corporation and negotiated a sale agreement. The Orioles turned over the franchise to San Antonio Community Baseball. The two clubs agreed to delay sale of the stadium until San Antonio Community Baseball could assume the additional debt. Three years later, the Orioles sold the stadium to the San Antonio club.[62]

Community baseball clubs were entering a very unstable market. During the same week that Baltimore announced its decision to dispose of the Missions, major league baseball agreed to offer the television networks a Sunday game of the week to complement the successful Saturday game. Baltimore was among the clubs that were negotiating independently with the Columbia Broadcasting System (CBS) for participation in the Sunday game.

Angry minor league officials mobilized to fight the Sunday game of the week. A committee representing the minor leagues "stormed" into a meeting of major league owners to demand they abandon the plan. The committee, which included the president of Rochester Community Baseball, Frank Horton, threatened legal action and an appeal to Congress. The majors were unmoved. A good deal of money was at stake. Commissioner Frick optimistically suggested that the minors' threatened action might even prompt Congress to grant baseball the right to regulate television, strengthening its monopoly position.[63]

Rebuffed by the major leagues, the minor leagues took their case to

Congress and to the Department of Justice. Horton got in touch with fellow Republican Kenneth Keating, Rochester's congressman. Keating helped arrange congressional hearings. Keating and Representative Emanuel Celler joined minor league officials in petitioning the Justice Department to look into the legality of the game of the week.[64]

The minor leagues, Horton admitted, were taking a leap into the dark by calling for further congressional investigation of organized baseball. House hearings in 1957 focused on franchise shifts had hurt the sport's image but had also demonstrated congressional reluctance to become involved in regulating professional sports. While many congressmen sympathized with the plight of minor league baseball, they were unlikely to take action that would limit their constituents' access to televised baseball. The Justice Department rejected the minor leagues' contention that baseball had to possess the power to establish blackout rules for broadcasting. The department held that organized baseball's arguments were of dubious legality and failed to serve the public interest.[65]

Ultimately, 1958 Senate hearings demonstrated the physical impossibility of creating a system of television blackouts that would protect minor league franchises while permitting major league telecasts to continue. The Senate declined to pass legislation introduced by Keating and supported by the major leagues, including the Orioles, that would have written baseball's antitrust exemption into the legal code.[66]

The 1957 House hearings and the 1958 Senate investigation did prompt joint action by the major and minor leagues to improve their relationship. The major leagues received a lot of unfavorable publicity from the hearings and wanted to avoid further public confrontation. More pragmatic minor league owners recognized that legislative or judicial relief was unlikely and decided to make the best of a bad situation. Over the next five years, pragmatists in the two wings of organized baseball designed a new system of financing, essentially on major league terms.[67]

Money was the minor leagues' Achilles' heel. As clubs continued to fold, the majors had increased the ad hoc subsidization of their affiliates. Independent minor league franchises also needed help, and in 1956 the National Association set up a minor league–financed emergency fund of $100,000 to aid troubled clubs. The major leagues then came to the rescue: each club contributed $31,500 to a minor league stabilization fund. By 1959 the major leagues had contributed $500,000 to assist the minors and firmly established the precedent of a common minor league aid program.[68]

Minor league officials accepted the money with bad grace, correctly fearing that the aid might portend the demise of their limited independence. Frank Horton recalled that at the time of the first major league grant-in-aid, he and Rochester general manager George Sisler wrote personal thank you notes to each of the major league clubs. They were startled to discover that the other minor league clubs took the money without thanking their benefactors. Another sign of minor league resentment was the rejection of a major league proposal for realigning the minor leagues.[69]

Some independent owners continued to fight against any concessions to the major leagues. Earl Mann of Atlanta tried to utilize television to market his product with some initial success. During the mid-1950s, however, the Atlanta franchise's attendance dropped drastically, and Mann joined the chorus of minor league owners blaming major league broadcasts for their problems. He attempted to build an alliance of minor league operators and to exploit 1959 congressional hearings in last-ditch efforts to "eliminate the farm system octopus with the attendant vicious Bonus evil . . . and . . . control the Television Monster." Commenting on Mann's specific proposals, National League president Warren Giles responded that "television and radio have created serious problems for many businesses." Noting the growing popularity of westerns and comedies like "I Love Lucy," Giles added that major league baseball broadcasts were only a marginal part of the minors' difficulty with television. He rejected Mann's suggestion that the major leagues stop signing amateur talent as impractical and bluntly concluded that the contraction of the minor leagues would continue "because Major League clubs do not have the need for working agreements and ownership clubs to develop their limited supply of players." Realistic minor league operators agreed with Giles's analysis. One commented that the Mann proposals were "fine in theory, but unfortunately . . . not practical."[70]

Ultimately, pragmatic minor league owners recognized the need for and the immediate advantages of a deal with the majors. With the number of major league affiliations dropping, prudent minor league owners were wary of confronting the big leagues. Moreover, the financially shaky higher minors faced an attempt at the unionization of their employees. In 1959 lawyer Gary Stevens formed an International League Players Association, enrolled about 160 players, and demanded that the IL set up a pension fund. The International League refused. Its leaders took this threat so seriously that they arranged a press conference to discuss the impact of unionization. The tactic worked. The press gave its support to the hard-pressed owners. The IL knew it could also count on major league support on this issue. The way toward cooperation was smoothed further when the majors established a $1 million "player development fund," a thinly disguised subsidy to assist the minors.[71]

By 1961 the majors and minors had reached agreement on the basic elements of a settlement. The major leagues were ready to provide continuing subsidization at set rates for minor league clubs in exchange for a fundamental restructuring that would reduce the number of franchises. Major league teams would provide the minors with prospects and coaching expertise. The minors would accept rules changes that favored major league player development objectives. Asked why the minors agreed to surrender their remaining independence, Horton replied that they simply could not continue to operate on their limited finances. They accepted a role in the major leagues' player development program in order to survive.[72]

The new arrangement removed many critical decisions from the hands of minor league executives, who increasingly focused their attention and energies on marketing activities. The drastic slimming down of the minor league system also had a significant impact on major league player recruitment. Scouts were no longer interested in signing marginal players since so few roster positions existed on minor league teams. The total number of minor league players declined drastically and, in the judgment of at least one veteran scout, so did the number of quality recruits. By the early 1960s minor league baseball had finally achieved a degree of stability by accepting full subordination to the major league player development program.[73] The Orioles benefited from the stabilization because it leveled off the costs of minor league operations and permitted the club to continue its aggressive player development program. The years of trial and error ended as professional management took over the direction of the Baltimore baseball club.

Putting the Pieces Together

On Labor Day weekend, 1960, in front of wildly cheering crowds that totaled over 114,000 for three games, the Baltimore Orioles proved definitively that they were a pennant contender. The New York Yankees, perennial American League champions, swept into Baltimore with a one-game lead over the young, upstart Orioles. On Friday, 2 September, rookie pitcher Milt Pappas beat the Yankees' best pitcher, the crafty Whitey Ford, 5–0, in a three-hit shutout. The following day, young Jack Fisher hurled a second shutout, 2–0. On Sunday, Chuck Estrada, another of the "Baby Birds," combined with the ageless relief pitcher Hoyt Wilhelm to defeat the Bronx Bombers, 6–2. The Orioles moved into first place with a two-game lead. Richards's "kids" were on the way to the franchise's first winning season.

Community Baseball— Major League Style

Looking back on the Orioles' first years, Jack Dunn wistfully commented: "An individual owner or one man at the top is probably better than trying to operate [by committee]."[1] On both the minor and major league levels community-owned baseball teams proved to be a short-term experiment. The trend in baseball ownership was to one-man control or purchase by a larger corporate entity that would use the team as a marketing tool or as a tax shelter. In the case of Baltimore, multiple ownership by members of the business community speedily evolved into a two-man combine and then gave way to control by a major brewery. The first stage in the passage from community baseball to private ownership was accompanied by major changes in the organizational structure of the club. The chaos and innovation that marked the Richards era gave way to the orderly administration of the classic baseball general manager, Lee MacPhail.

The Keelty-Iglehardt-Krieger leadership presided over the transition from one administrative style to another. These men and their fellow board members, motivated by community pride, plowed their profits back into the team in order to produce a winner for the city. They served without pay, bought tickets to the team's games, and paid their own way whenever they traveled with the Orioles.[2] Civic pride brought the franchise many benefits without providing coherent management. The Orioles' major stockholders were unable to give the club day-to-day supervision because they had to attend to the businesses that created their individual incomes. By late 1955 Orioles owners were actively seeking a proven administrator who could harness and discipline the talents of Richards and McLaughlin.

At the end of the 1956 season the board found a man they hoped would provide Richards with the administrative assistance he clearly needed while keeping a sharp eye on club spending. They chose William Walsingham, a forty-seven-year-old baseball executive with nearly thirty years experience in the Cardinals organization. The board simultaneously rewarded Richards with a three-year contract extension as both manager and general manager. By handing the two men overlapping grants of authority, the board set up a confrontation. Richards easily triumphed. He simply ignored Walsingham and continued to operate without any effective day-to-day restraints. Walsingham never established his authority over the club treasury or any aspect of the administration. Richards ran the major league club while McLaughlin managed his minor league operation with little interference.[3]

The maneuvering between the board and the club's front office never affected either player recruitment or the club's field performance. The Orioles continued their slow advance to respectability and made a profit in 1956, 1957, and 1958. Nevertheless, the owners concluded that Richards could not continue in his dual role and that the Walsingham experiment had not worked. News of their dissatisfaction leaked to the press. Team "sources" told reporters that Richards's one-man style of management was undercutting employee morale. Board members also complained that Richards's lack of interest in administration and his frequent absences hurt the team. The owners believed that the jump to contention required more effective management and that "Richards must be relieved of his front office duties." At the end of the 1958 season they fired the ineffective Walsingham and began interviewing candidates for the general manager's post. Richards, who recognized that he had to surrender one of his two posts, initially tried to hold on to the general manager's job. When the owners informed him of their determination to retain him only as manager, Richards shrewdly made the best of the situation by endorsing Lee MacPhail, the youthful head of the Yankees farm system, for the position of general manager. Joseph Iglehardt took Richards's advice.[4]

MacPhail took the Baltimore job only after he ascertained that he would have full authority over Richards and after a face-to-face meeting with the Orioles' often-difficult manager. MacPhail concluded that he could deal with Richards. In his first statement to the press on 10 November 1958, the prudent MacPhail warned Orioles fans that the club needed more time to build a contender and urged them to be patient. MacPhail's careful realism contrasted with the heady optimism of Richards's first months. It nicely mirrored the sobering experience of the club's first five years.[5]

MacPhail's hiring laid the groundwork for another change in the team's ownership. Between 1955 and 1959 control of a majority of the franchise's stock passed from the hands of the small group of seven stockholders into the hands of two men: Iglehardt and Krieger. Iglehardt had quietly acquired slightly over 30 percent of the club's stock. He joined with Krieger, holder of approximately 17 percent, to take operational control of the Orioles.

At the end of the 1959 season, Keelty, now a member of the board's minority, gracefully resigned, citing the need for a full-time administrator in the office of club president. Iglehardt and Krieger promoted MacPhail to president. Baseball operations were finally in the hands of a full-time professional administrator. MacPhail enjoyed the confidence of both owners and increasingly served as mediator between the two men.[6]

The Krieger-Iglehardt alliance temporarily blocked the ownership ambitions of the club's other major stockholder, brewer Jerold Hoffberger. Hoffberger had been using television successfully since 1947 to increase his market share of the regional brewing industry, and he was interested in purchasing a major league ball club to further improve the sales of his beer. In 1956 Hoffberger's National Brewery lost its television and radio contract rights with the Orioles to the Krieger family's Gunther Brewery. Hoffberger, who also owned a Detroit brewery, backed Bill Veeck's unsuccessful effort to acquire the Tigers the same year. When Theo Hamm's, an expanding Minneapolis brewery, acquired Gunther and the Orioles broadcast rights in January 1960, Hoffberger faced a powerful new rival in his home territory. Later that year he considered bidding for a franchise in Washington, another city where he used baseball to market his beer. Blocked from controlling his home town team by the Iglehardt-Krieger alliance, Hoffberger declined to join the Orioles board of directors but retained his interest in acquiring the franchise.[7]

Management by MacPhail

In the winter of 1957 *The Sporting News* commented that the Baltimore organization continually "raises eyebrows" in other major league front offices with its unorthodox management practices. In addition to Richards's having a dual function as manager and general manager, assistant general manager Jack Dunn performed the functions of both road secretary and director of public relations. Walsingham, who reported directly to club president Keelty, was supposed to assist Richards while providing oversight on his spending and his personnel moves. Overall, *The Sporting News* pronounced Baltimore's management style "unusual," implying it might also be ineffective.[8]

The Orioles' management style was innovative as well as chaotic. Moreover, it worked. The club's minor league system was producing a steady stream of young prospects, although they were still some years away from being major league players. "The possibilities are there," Richards commented in late 1957. The team pioneered an important area of marketing with its 1954 study of its fan base and its fans' preferences. The Orioles made effective use of television to promote attendance. The club's owners quietly made their weight felt in baseball's inner circles, gaining places on important committees and actively participating in management meetings. In a conversation with Branch Rickey about American League owners, Commissioner Frick expressed his admiration for Baltimore's "very able" Keelty, praising his sound and independent judgment.[9]

Lee MacPhail built upon the solid foundations laid by his predecessors, consolidating the club's gains and creating a more orderly organization. He arranged for Orioles participation in CBS's national game of the week, maintained a favorable stadium deal with the city, acquired a working agreement with Rochester, and took important steps toward ending Baltimore's anomalous position on racial issues. He also attempted to improve the club's public relations program and unsuccessfully tried to harness the contentious Richards and McLaughlin to his program.

The team's soft-spoken new general manager, a man of medium stature with a large oval face, was a cautious and patient operator. His geniality, politeness, and sobriety were in stark contrast to the qualities of his legendary father, Larry MacPhail, an aggressive, abrasive, and innovative baseball executive. Lee took a degree in economics at Swarthmore College and joined the Brooklyn Dodgers farm system in 1941. After wartime service, he went to work for the Yankees and rapidly advanced to director of the farm system under general manager George Weiss. MacPhail admired Weiss's organizational ability and arrived in Baltimore with plans to replicate his consolidation of the control of team operations in the general manager's office. He would use Weiss's management methods, MacPhail told reporters, because they were "the only ones I know." Weiss had built the most successful franchise in baseball's history, and that fact was certainly an important consideration in the Baltimore owners' decision to hire MacPhail as their general manager.[10]

MacPhail's reputation for fairness, attention to detail, and common sense served him well in his administration of the Baltimore franchise. "If you can't get along with Lee MacPhail, you can't get along with anybody," Dunn commented.[11] MacPhail quickly established an effective working relationship with the always-independent Richards while simultaneously assuming control of the personnel decisions that Richards formerly handled. He took command of the fragmented but talented Baltimore front office and won its loyalty by immediately ruling out major personnel changes. MacPhail's decision to retain the versatile and extremely popular Jack Dunn won praise and support from the press and within the organization. He showed a sure touch in dealing with important matters such as television, stadium facilities, race relations, and upgrading the Orioles' minor league system.[12]

Television was playing an ever-increasing role in the club's finances. Although the Orioles' market was geographically small, sales of television sets had skyrocketed in Maryland, and the state's population continued to grow. In 1950 there were approximately 70,000 television sets in the state of Maryland. By 1960 the number of sets reached 1 million. Maryland paralleled the rest of the United States in this trend. In 1950, 12.3 percent of all U.S. homes had sets. By 1955 that figure rose to 67 percent (34.9 million homes), and by 1960, to 87 percent (45.8 million out of a total of 52.5 million homes).[13]

The growth in the number of television sets and the consolidation of local stations into three major broadcasting networks opened new possibilities for major league baseball. During the early 1950s local television broadcasts proved that baseball was an efficient marketing tool for a number of products, foremost among them beer, followed by tobacco, oil, automobiles, and shaving equipment. In 1956 Gillette tripled its payment for five more years of World Series broadcasting rights. The following year, CBS and NBC paid a combined total of $1.3 million to individual clubs for the right to televise their games nationally on Saturdays. Local stations shelled out another $4.8 million for the right to telecast their home teams' games. Sponsors and stations placed limits on the rising costs of television sports by negotiating long-term contracts with fixed annual step increases. The teams benefited from these deals by having an assured income as they made longer-range plans.[14]

While increasingly lucrative, television remained a problem for organized baseball. Justice Department rulings forbade blacking out broadcast games in the home team's market or pooling major league broadcasting rights to make a single national contract with the major networks. Each club negotiated individually with the local stations and with the networks. The price a team could get for its broadcasting rights corresponded to the size of its market area and its won-lost record. Few baseball men were well versed in the requirements of the new entertainment medium or capable of fully utilizing its promotional potential. Baseball's clumsy efforts to win an exemption from the antitrust laws met defeat in Congress and aroused the broadcasting industry's ire.[15]

From the beginning, the Orioles' approach to television was more positive than that of many other clubs. The Orioles' strategy was to control television's more damaging side effects by a careful manipulation of its broadcast games. To further limit TV's depressing effect on attendance, Baltimore and Washington clubs agreed that neither team would televise into the other's broadcasting area during their respective home stands. In an effort to maximize its profits and exposure, the club initially split the rights to televise fifty-six games between two Baltimore stations. For a few years the Orioles also sold broadcast rights for select games to Washington television stations. With the aid of the Baltimore stations, the Orioles built a four-station network to carry baseball games into Pennsylvania and to Maryland's Eastern Shore. The team hired one of the best available sports broadcasters, Ernie Harwell, to handle both television and radio.[16]

Because the Orioles' market was constricted, its local television revenues were also compressed. Jack Dunn, who helped negotiate television and radio packages in the 1950s, recalled that little negotiation took place over the size of the rights payment. The Orioles had little bargaining leverage.[17]

By 1957 club officials believed that they had effectively harnessed local television to their marketing strategy. The Orioles accepted some loss in their paid attendance when broadcasting home games because they believed that television created new paying customers, stimulating interest in baseball among people who had never visited a ballpark. Club surveys showed that televised home games cut most heavily into attendance on nights with poor weather, and the Orioles generally avoided early- and late-season broadcasts. On the whole, the Orioles' experience reinforced the long-standing claim of television executives that attendance was pegged to field performance rather than television. In 1957, for example, the club played the best baseball of its brief life, and attendance rose to 1,029,581 even though the Orioles televised a record fifty-eight games, including twenty-one home contests. Nevertheless, the club's board decided to reduce the number of televised home games when the Orioles negotiated a new broadcasting agreement.[18]

In the second half of the 1950s television became more lucrative for all clubs. The prices that the television industry charged for advertising rose steadily, and baseball shared in the bonanza. Breweries in particular found televised baseball a useful marketing tool and were ready to pay higher rates for access to a heavily male audience. In Baltimore, the two leading breweries spent a combined total of more than $1 million for TV time in 1957, mostly on sports. The Orioles' broadcasting income rose by an estimated $150,000 under the terms of a 1957 agreement with Gunther Brewery.[19]

By 1958 television was so important to baseball in Baltimore that Iglehardt's initial choice for a general manager was CBS Sports executive William MacPhail. When Richards suggested brother Lee, he was promoting a baseball man with the right contacts in the broadcasting industry.[20]

Lee MacPhail broadened the club's television income sources while restructuring its broadcasting schedule. He negotiated a three-year television contract that, by industry sources estimates, provided the team with an annual broadcasting income rise from $400,000 in 1959 to $475,000 by 1961. Even so, the sum was only one-half the amount paid to the Yankees for their local rights. In addition, the New York club had a very lucrative contract with national television for Saturday and Sunday games of the week. The Yankees were plowing this income back into their player development program. In order to remain competitive, MacPhail resurrected the team's plan to join the national game of the week, selling the rising Orioles to the game's sponsors and increasing the team's overall income base. Convinced that home broadcasts were damaging in a restricted market like Baltimore, MacPhail wrote the 1959 pact with Gunther to permit the club to gradually cut back home game broadcasts while increasing the number of road telecasts. In 1958 Baltimore broadcast twenty-one home games, but by 1962 the number fell to four. Finally, MacPhail widened the team's broadcast sponsorship by selling part of its advertising time to tobacco companies.[21]

Even as television became baseball's primary marketing tool, league executives were becoming increasingly aware of the general weakness of the major league's promotional efforts and of the need to safeguard the sport's image from the assaults of congressional investigators and critics of its performance on racial issues. Public relations became more important because a growing number of teams were entering into long-term partnerships with city and state governments for the construction and maintenance of publicly owned stadiums.

By the mid-1950s, the commissioner's office was attempting to build an effective public relations program for organized baseball that would fill the stadiums with fans while building public support for baseball's less publicized agenda: creating political support on both the national and local levels for new publicly financed stadiums, greater team control over broadcasting, and a federal law solidifying baseball's antitrust exemption.[22]

Orioles public relations efforts mirrored those of the rest of the major league franchises. Commenting on the club's promotional efforts during the 1950s, MacPhail stated: "We didn't spend money on marketing, period . . . we didn't have any outside . . . professional help in marketing."[23] The Orioles had done little before he arrived. The club offered a variety of season ticket plans to attract fans. It held an occasional "night" honoring some individual or organization. In 1958, the Orioles sponsored the publication of an anecdotal "history" of Baltimore baseball. During the first years of MacPhail's

administration, the club made a few innovative efforts to improve its attendance. In 1960 it sold single tickets through an arrangement with the highly
popular S&H Green Stamps plan. The club set up the Orioles Advocates the
same year. The Advocates were members of the political and business elite
who promoted attendance at home games and helped the team's players to
find housing and off-season jobs. Borrowing an idea from the NFL Colts,
the Orioles set up so-called Birds' Nests, social clubs for fans. Other aspects
of the club's public relations effort were low-key. The Orioles loyally supported organized baseball's request for congressional enactment of a law
granting the sport antitrust immunity but declined to lobby actively in nearby
Washington, leaving this job to the commissioner and his lawyers.[24]

Improving its public stance on race relations was one of the areas where
organized baseball needed to act. The pace of integration of blacks into
baseball had been slow. By 1954, however, only a few teams remained segregated. Organized baseball congratulated itself on the success of its "great
experiment" and ignored the enormous problems its black employees still
faced in a largely segregated nation. Like the majority of Americans, baseball
executives felt that they had done enough. Organized baseball's reaction to
the national travail of integration was one of indifference to blacks and
incomprehension of their demands.[25] The Orioles' inability to deal effectively with Baltimore's black community was a case in point.

Black leaders recognized that both the Orioles and the American League
were dragging their feet on integration. Black criticism of the Orioles and
other American League clubs focused on the clubs' lack of colored major
league players. The American League had been slow to sign stars out of the
Negro leagues after Jackie Robinson finally broke the color barrier. It paid a
heavy price. The National League got most of the best available young talent
and a head start on recruiting blacks. When Bill Veeck took over the Browns
in 1951, he set out to rebuild quickly and cheaply by going after young black
athletes. However, Veeck's two years of intense recruiting produced few
major league players for the Orioles.

When the Orioles began searching for talent in late 1953, the Negro
leagues were in decline. The pool of remaining Negro league talent was filled
with aging players. Ehlers emphasized recruiting young players to build the
Orioles and declined to sign aging black stars. As a result, the Orioles' best
black prospects spent most of the 1950s slowly advancing through the team's
minor league system.[26]

Aware of blacks' mistrust, team officials made occasional efforts to address
their concerns. In 1955 Miles told a meeting of black civic leaders, "We'd be
the most stupid people in Baltimore if we didn't want a colored player." Few
black leaders were convinced. Columnist Sam Lacy of the *Afro-American*
repeatedly contrasted the Orioles' lack of black talent with the hiring practices of the Colts, "perhaps the most liberal organization in professional

sports."[27] In the early 1950s, Colt stars included black halfback Buddy Young and quarterback George Taliaferro. The criticism became even more pointed after the Colts won successive NFL championships in 1958 and 1959 with squads featuring black stars Lenny Moore, Jim Parker, and Gene "Big Daddy" Lipscomb.

In mid-1955 the Orioles attempted to meet black complaints and improve themselves by acquiring veteran outfielder Dave Pope from Cleveland. After the season, Jack Dunn told reporters that the Orioles were interested in acquiring Jackie Robinson. Lacy was skeptical, noting Robinson's age and high salary. Whatever credibility the Orioles built by picking up Pope, they dissipated during the following season by trading him a week before acquiring black pitcher Connie Johnson. The trades raised black suspicions that the Orioles maintained a racial quota.[28]

The veteran Johnson became the Orioles' first black "star," enjoying fine seasons in 1956 (9–10, 3.44 ERA) and 1957 (14–9, 3.20 ERA). The club attempted to exploit this success to improve its image among blacks by arranging a special ceremony honoring Johnson near the end of the 1956 season. Mayor D'Alesandro cooperated by proclaiming "Connie Johnson Day" and joined other civic leaders at a Memorial Stadium ceremony.[29]

Connie Johnson Day was a success, but black leaders continued to criticize club performance on racial issues and few blacks frequented Memorial Stadium. Paul Richards became a focal point for suspicion and criticism. Critics charged that the aloof Texan was insensitive to racial problems and unwilling to keep many blacks on his teams. The Orioles trained in racially segregated Arizona towns during most of the 1950s because of Richards's fondness for that area. The *Afro-American* noted that Richards never had more than four or five black players on his squads and rarely more than two. In the winter of 1957 the Orioles acquired an aging black star, Larry Doby. The club reported that advance ticket sales rose 15 percent that winter on the basis of a good showing in the 1957 season and the acquisition of Doby. Richards, however, traded Doby before the 1958 regular season began. Doby had reportedly complained about segregated conditions at the Orioles training camp. Lacy complained that Richards was consistently trying to find a replacement for .300-hitting black first baseman Bob Boyd. He also criticized Richards for naming only one black to the 1961 American League all-star team.[30]

Black concerns about racism in Orioles management were understandable although exaggerated. Like most major league clubs, the Orioles were insensitive to racial segregation in the cities that hosted their training facilities. However, no evidence exists that Richards's player moves were racially motivated. Doby, Johnson, and Pope were all aging athletes who essentially played themselves off the squad. Boyd was a weak fielder and a line drive hitter in a power hitter's position. Richards's interest in a better fielder was natural on a team that depended so heavily on good defense. However, it is easy to see why blacks were aroused by circumstantial evidence pointing to racism in hiring, especially in light of the American League's generally poor record on integration, which heightened their feeling that the Orioles practiced discrimination in employment.

Black spokesmen had stronger grounds for criticizing the Orioles' spending on bonus players. Bonus money went almost exclusively to talented whites. The practice was baseballwide. The Orioles were operating a business and were unwilling to lay out large sums of cash for players they could acquire cheaply. Black athletes got little bonus money because they were willing to play without the lure of extra cash. Nevertheless, the club created resentment by exploiting the eagerness of young black players to escape from the poverty created by generations of racial discrimination.[31]

The club's failure to support hotel desegregation in Baltimore fully merited harsh criticism. Baltimore's hotels remained closed to black players after all the other major league cities opened theirs. The situation was even more galling because, unlike most cities in the South, Baltimore had no city ordinances enforcing segregation. The city's hotels imposed it in deference to local racism and resisted Governor Theodore McKeldin's efforts to bring about change. The Orioles maintained a discreet silence during the controversy. Finally, in the spring of 1957 the Major League Baseball Players Association stepped in and negotiated a settlement that permitted black major leaguers to stay in the same hotels as their white teammates. Baltimore hotels maintained their segregation policy for all other blacks.[32]

MacPhail inherited a baseball club without a positive record on race relations in a period of growing racial tensions in Baltimore. In the winter of 1958–59 Baltimore faced an assault of "block busting," the practice of moving black families into previously white areas in order to undercut real estate prices and stimulate panic selling among whites. Unscrupulous realtors made large profits and inflamed racial tensions in the city and state. White flight to the suburbs accelerated, and more blacks flowed into the city. As black political power grew inside Baltimore, tensions increased within the white-dominated city Democratic Party.[33]

At the same time, racial issues again came to the fore inside organized baseball. A decade and a half after the major leagues put their first black into uniform, they continued to avoid taking action against segregation in the cities of the South and Southwest where teams trained. Baseball executives were reluctant to confront local authorities. However, the teams possessed unusual leverage since spring training was an important part of the lucrative tourist trade in both areas. Black activists and their white liberal allies recognized the potential power of organized baseball. They seized the opportunity to reach their larger social objective of open public accommodations for all while simultaneously advancing the interests of black athletes. Their struggle for desegregation received substantial assistance from the national press, which ran exposés of the living conditions and racial humiliations that black players endured during spring training.[34]

Between 1954 and 1961 the Orioles trained in segregated cities in Arizona and Florida. The club rarely had many blacks on its spring training roster and never made an effort to challenge local customs in the interest of its employees. In 1959 the Orioles moved their training facility to Miami, Florida. Marketing considerations motivated the move. The Orioles hoped to cut training costs and attract Baltimore fans to preseason games in Miami's 10,000-seat public stadium. In an innovative promotion, the club arranged package tours to bring paying customers to warm Miami from cold Baltimore. Because press coverage of segregation in Florida's "grapefruit league" was intense, the move to Miami placed the Orioles in the midst of the growing controversy over continued segregation at training facilities.[35]

Organized baseball's initial reaction to criticism of its "festering sore" was to hope the problem would go away. "Common sense will solve race problems," *The Sporting News* editorialized, suggesting that timely concessions by local authorities might save baseball from acting in the interest of its black employees.[36]

Gradually, under increasing pressure from black organizations, the Players Association, and the federal government, baseball reversed its position. A number of clubs forced their training hotels to end segregation by threatening to take their business to other cities. MacPhail, who recognized that baseball in general and the American League in particular had done little for its black personnel, decided to act. In February 1961 he secured an agreement from the Orioles' Miami training hotel to house the club's black players. Unfortunately, this action was little more than a gesture since the club had only one marginal black prospect, who chose to stay in segregated housing.[37]

MacPhail nevertheless won a measure of confidence for himself and the club from the city's black elite by taking a stand against hotel segregation. A frank appeal for support before a black civic group further improved his personal image and that of the Orioles. He convinced the influential and skeptical Lacy that racial considerations did not motivate the club's hiring or scouting practices. However, the team's improved relationship with the black community did not produce a box office bonanza. Blacks continued to stay away from Orioles games. To a long history of racial hostility and intimidation by white fans, the Orioles added a basic indifference to attracting black fans to Memorial Stadium. The club never marketed itself aggressively in the black community. Recalling those years, MacPhail commented that the Orioles had failed to do "as much probably as we should have done" to attract blacks.[38]

A second area of the club's public relations in which MacPhail made a strong mark was in the Orioles' critical relationship with local government. A good working relationship with city hall helped a team build a local identification, boosting attendance. Equally important, the municipal government was the Orioles' landlord.

MacPhail built on strong foundations of cooperation laid by Orioles management and Mayor D'Alesandro. Goodwill, however, was an inadequate substitute for money, and as Baltimore's urban problems mounted, the cost of Memorial Stadium's maintenance became a serious problem for both the club and the city.

The Orioles' relationship with the city of Baltimore began on a note that was very favorable to the franchise. D'Alesandro had given generous terms for the lease of Memorial Stadium to the NFL's Colts in 1951. He offered an even better deal to major league baseball. The Orioles would bring the city more revenue, after all, if only because they would use the park an average of seventy times a season, while the Colts had only six home contests annually.

The contract between Baltimore and the Orioles, signed on 12 November 1953, gave the club an option to use Memorial Stadium for twenty years at an annual rent of 7 percent of its admissions receipts after taxes. The city granted the club full control of all concessions for all events at the stadium in exchange for 5 percent of the after-tax revenues for the first five years of operations and 10 percent thereafter plus a further cut of 20 percent on nonbaseball concessions. In addition, the city granted the Orioles the right to operate the parking lots for all baseball games in exchange for 20 percent of the lots' after-tax revenues. Finally, Baltimore granted the club full income from the television rights for its home games for the first two years and requested only a minimal payment thereafter if its share of concessions income fell below $90,000. In return, the Orioles guaranteed the city a minimum compensation of $75,000 for the first two years of its operations and $90,000 thereafter and agreed to pay $250 for each night game to cover the lighting costs.[39]

The city had made sweeping concessions to bring in a baseball team. In addition to charging a minimal rent, Baltimore handed over the revenues from parking and food concessions, assumed all the costs for stadium maintenance, and provided the club with free office space. The city also promised to permit the sale of beer in the park's concession stands in spite of strong local protests, to invest $2.5 million in stadium improvements, and to install a new electronic scoreboard at a cost of $172,000.[40]

City leaders were pleased with the deal. They had a major league team. In 1954, Orioles games at Memorial Stadium netted Baltimore over $100,000, compared to the $9,000 that minor league baseball put into city coffers in 1953. Although a combination of operating expenses and debt service left Baltimore with an annual stadium deficit averaging over $200,000, income from major league baseball helped to cut city indebtedness in half and was five times greater than the income generated by professional football. Moreover, the city unloaded the cost of the electronic scoreboard: Gunther Brewery paid for the new scoreboard in exchange for exclusive rights to advertise on it.[41]

The club, too, was happy with the agreement. Walsingham pronounced the stadium a first-rate facility for playing and watching baseball. Located in a pleasant middle-class community in northern Baltimore, Memorial Stadium even aided the club's recruiting efforts. The Orioles frequently brought young amateur players and their parents to see the facility and neighborhood and then drove them to Washington's decaying Seventh Street area for a look at aging Griffith Stadium.[42]

In 1957 both the Colts and the Orioles actively began lobbying the D'Alesandro administration for improvements in the stadium. Walsingham, utilizing data developed in the club's fan survey, explained the Orioles' rationale for seeking improvements: "Public interest in baseball is a lot higher than it used to be. But there is a changing public demand. People today want better facilities. It used to be that baseball was almost strictly a male event. But now it has become a family affair. About 40 percent of our attendance is made up of women and children. Now, too, people come to the games in automobiles. So the demand is for better facilities in the stadium. You give the people these proper conditions and they'll turn out."[43]

From the Orioles' perspective, Memorial Stadium had three critical defects. First, it lacked adequate off-street parking. Approximately 5,000 parking spaces existed in the vicinity of Memorial Stadium, but only 2,800 were in stadium lots. In contrast, Milwaukee had 11,000 lot spaces. Parking space was critical because a majority of fans were coming to games in their cars. Limited parking in secure areas cut down on the appeal of baseball as a source of entertainment and also severely limited the value of the team's parking lot concessions.[44]

Second, too many of Memorial Stadium's seats were wooden bleachers, a form of accommodation that was unpopular with many patrons. Both the Colts and the Orioles wanted to replace the bleachers with individual chairs, a move that would reduce the stadium's total seating capacity but permit an increase in ticket prices that would more than compensate the clubs.[45]

A third and unresolvable problem was the construction of the upper deck. In an effort to save money, the city had built the second deck on large steel and concrete piers that created viewing obstructions from many seats on the terrace level. The decision to use piers instead of more costly cantilever construction severely restricted the number of higher-priced "choice" seats the club could sell.[46]

Talks between the two sports franchises and the city over stadium improvements began in earnest in the summer of 1957. D'Alesandro announced that the city would put $550,000 into a special stadium maintenance program to prepare for the 1958 All-Star Game. He came forward with a plan to spend another $4 million on stadium improvements but requested a one-third contribution from each of the two teams to cover the costs of new seats and of escalators to move fans swiftly to the second deck. Both clubs balked. Keelty stated that the Orioles had to channel their limited capital into player development and reward fan loyalty by "concentrating on the primary task" of building a championship team.[47]

Discussions on Memorial Stadium improvements took place as city governments throughout the United States were debating the relationship between professional sports and municipal development plans. Los Angeles and San Francisco were wooing two of New York's baseball teams, the National League Giants and Dodgers, with promises of new stadiums and attractive concessions arrangements. Commissioner Ford Frick stated that in the future municipalities would have to assume a larger share of the costs of major league baseball by providing the teams with publicly owned and maintained stadiums. A November 1957 article in *American City* entitled "Is Big League Baseball Good Municipal Business?" noted that all municipal stadiums were losing money and bluntly asked if the big cities with their declining tax bases and growing urban ills could afford to invest scarce public dollars in sports facilities.[48]

Mayor D'Alesandro believed they must. Professional sports were an integral part of his plans for long-term urban renewal. The Baltimore mayor affirmed that sports and other "cultural" activities brought needed revenue into the city and improved its tattered image. Baltimore would spend to improve the stadium and construct a downtown Civic Center "because we believe that the cities are fighting for existence and we intend to fight with every means at our command."[49]

D'Alesandro's view was widely shared in the city's business community. The Association of Commerce joined in the mayor's efforts to turn the 1958 All-Star Game at Memorial Stadium into a vehicle for a "distinctive and high caliber brand of advertising" for Baltimore. The subsequent December 1958 triumph of the Colts in professional football's championship game reinforced the political-business elite's sense that big league sports could play a useful role in urban renewal by building Baltimore's image. City leaders were willing to accept the costs of stadium improvements and grant the sports franchises various special concessions in an effort to improve Baltimore's image. The real issues were how much the city and state could afford to pay and whether the political elite could mobilize voter support for their plans.[50]

MacPhail inherited the city's general commitment to support Orioles baseball together with a much more problematical political situation. In May 1959 D'Alesandro lost a bruising Democratic primary to Harold Grady. The Baltimore Democratic Party was badly split between the reform elements that backed Grady and the city machine. The new mayor favored continued cooperation with the Orioles but lacked D'Alesandro's personal commitment and political clout. Moreover, the city paid off the last of its stadium debt service in late 1957. It could look forward to making a profit on Memorial Stadium, provided, the *Sun* noted, "that a need . . . has not arisen to make extensive improvements."[51]

MacPhail's immediate objectives were to improve seating and to sell beer in the stands. The Orioles president stressed the need for improved seating to attract fans and argued that most major league clubs, even those in publicly owned facilities, already offered vendor service to fans. Vending beer in the stands would increase concessions income for the club and the city.

MacPhail received a stinging lesson in the realities of local politics. Just before the opening of the 1960 season, the city's Park Board agreed to permit vendors to sell beer in the stands. The board action set off a confrontation between the club and the political elite. Temperance groups had long decried the close ties between baseball and the brewing industry, characterizing the game as "beerball." Baltimore temperance advocates denounced the Orioles' plan. Grady took note of the opposition among groups that had supported his election and decided to oppose the club's request. After the Baltimore solicitor backed the Park Board's decision, the city council approved legislation for a referendum to revoke the board's permission. MacPhail withdrew the club's request.[52]

Profiting from this first experience, the Orioles president did a better job of lining up support for improved stadium seating. Perhaps to repay the embarrassed Orioles for his desertion over stadium beer, Grady publicly committed his administration to increasing the number of choice seats in Memorial Stadium. The Greater Baltimore Committee gave its support, issuing a report endorsing the club's plan for adding 2,600 higher-priced seats. Both the political leadership and the business elite reaffirmed that professional sports were good business for Baltimore. In November 1962 city voters approved a $1.2 million recreation loan to upgrade the stadium to meet club needs. The city-club alliance continued to operate but strains grew in the 1960s as public funding became scarce.[53]

The Orioles continued to insist that the costs of minor league development ruled out a club contribution to the maintenance of Memorial Stadium even after the team's first winning season. MacPhail firmly maintained the policy of putting all available money into the minor leagues, telling reporters, "We intend to continue our aggressive policy in the competition for . . . talent."[54] Inheriting a superior system, MacPhail preserved it. He made only two significant changes in the Orioles' minor league operations during his first four years.

The first change was settling on a AAA affiliation. As the last step before the major leagues, AAA baseball was the most difficult and important step for minor league prospects. The choice of a AAA team was especially important for the Orioles, a club that had a bumper crop of prospects who could quickly turn it into a contender. During the early years of its player development program Baltimore signed "limited" working agreements with various AAA clubs because it did not have enough prospects to fill up a minor league roster. By 1959 the Orioles needed to acquire a full-time working agreement with a AAA club. The club ended its limited agreement with Vancouver of the Pacific Coast League after the 1959 season and signed a regular working agreement with Miami for 1960. Geographic and monetary considerations played a role in MacPhail's decision to drop Vancouver and pick up Miami, a member of the International League.[55]

Toward the end of 1960, Baltimore again shifted its working agreement. The Rochester Red Wings and the St. Louis Cardinals were breaking their thirty-three-year-old association as a result of the community baseball team's irritation with the National League club's player development policies. When the Cardinals had sold the AAA team to Rochester, they insisted that community baseball would have greater independence from the demands of the St. Louis player development program. The reality was quite different: "We said . . . Rochester had three teams: one on the way to the Cardinals, one on the way back, and one in Rochester," Horton recalled, explaining the constant instability of the Red Wings' roster and their consequent difficulties in fielding a winning team.[56]

In September 1960 St. Louis's operating style produced a revolt in Rochester. First, the Cardinals traded four Rochester players to rival Buffalo for one man who was immediately promoted to the major leagues. Rochester Community Baseball received nothing. Then, at the end of the season, the Cardinals announced that they wanted to fire the Red Wings' popular manager, Clyde King. President Horton immediately summoned the Rochester board of directors into session and secured their approval to end the club's affiliation with St. Louis. The board agreed with Horton that accepting St. Louis's decision would mean surrendering community baseball's "last vestige of independence."[57]

The "divorce" was amicable. At Horton's request, St. Louis general manager Bing Devine telephoned MacPhail to suggest a swap of AAA affiliates. MacPhail, who had sent a representative to scout the Red Wings in late September, jumped at the opportunity. Richards and McLaughlin were equally enthusiastic.[58]

The two community baseball clubs quickly reached an agreement on the terms of their association. The Orioles agreed to let the Red Wings retain control over the selection of a manager and, as far as possible, to refrain from recalling players from Rochester in mid-season. At an October 1960 joint press conference with Rochester officials, McLaughlin remarked that minor league teams were in the "entertainment business" and needed roster stability. MacPhail and Dalton stressed that the Orioles needed an "intelligent, aggressive," and independent Rochester operation.[59]

For Rochester, the deal with Baltimore was extremely attractive. In addition to obtaining pledges of cooperation that MacPhail and the Orioles honored, the Red Wings had linked up with one of the best minor league systems in baseball, assuring that Rochester consistently would be able to field a strong club and attract fans. For Baltimore, Rochester was a nearly "ideal place" to nurture its young talent. MacPhail proudly stated that the working agreement with Rochester was "one of the best deals" he ever made.[60] The Rochester-Baltimore arrangement has endured for nearly thirty years.

McLaughlin's appearance at Rochester was one of his last acts as the director of the Orioles' minor league system. A slowly simmering conflict between McLaughlin and MacPhail erupted shortly after the beginning of 1961, and MacPhail dismissed the team's highly independent farm director.

McLaughlin was unable to adjust to the new organizational arrangements. He believed that he had been unfairly passed over in the 1958 selection of a general manager. He continued to insist on maintaining the widest possible independence for his minor league operations at a time when MacPhail was trying to centralize control in the general manager's office. McLaughlin lost his most powerful supporter when Keelty left the team's management. MacPhail remarked that McLaughlin's power base within the organization was reduced to a loyal group of scouts.[61]

McLaughlin finally pushed himself out of the organization on the issue of bonus payments. Large bonuses remained a sore subject with the Orioles. MacPhail insisted that he had to clear all major bonus signings. McLaughlin decided to ignore this policy: "It all centered on one case, really . . . a last straw. . . . I ran the minor league operation independently. It was as though . . . we weren't in the same organization. . . . There was a left-handed pitcher named [Dave] McNally. . . . I didn't consult with Lee. . . . The bidding got pretty high on him and . . . Jim [Russo] said, 'I can get him if we go $80,000.' . . . I was in Appleton. . . . I . . . told him 'go ahead.' . . . I came back and they had a fit."[62]

McLaughlin recognized, as he put it, "I'd overstepped myself."[63] MacPhail replaced McLaughlin with his competent assistant, Harry Dalton. Under Dalton, the club would continue to produce a steady stream of top talent for another decade.

McLaughlin's departure broke the last physical link between the Orioles and the Browns. More importantly, it was a major step toward the centralization of authority in the general manager's office. MacPhail took firm control of the largest and most important part of the club's administrative structure.

Dalton was a capable administrator, content to operate within a well-struc-tured office hierarchy. Only Richards retained a reduced autonomy.

The Payoff

A few days before Christmas 1959, Bob Maisel of the Baltimore *Sun* took a look at the relative success of the city's two major sports franchises. Both teams, he noted, had started off with five-year plans. The Colts met their goal: winning National Football League championships in 1958 and 1959. They were the city's darlings. After six years, the Orioles were still in the second division although they had spent $928,000 on player development that year alone. The club lost nearly $54,000 in 1959 and seemed intent on spending itself into bankruptcy. Its stock fell in value, and, for the first time, the Orioles raised ticket prices, while increasing the number of night games by eleven to a total of fifty-nine, in order to cover losses.[64]

While the financial picture was bleak, Orioles officials were confident that their minor league system was filled with the talent needed to produce a major league contender.[65] From the lower minors to the club's AAA farm team, the system was stacked with young players who would soon make their mark in the major leagues: John Powell, Pete Ward, Dean Chance, Chuck Hinton, Steve Barber, Marv Breeding, Chuck Estrada, Ron Hansen, and many others.

The depth was great enough to permit the club to make some important trades during the December 1959 winter meetings. Baltimore picked up swift, talented, and eccentric center fielder Jackie Brandt from San Francisco in exchange for pitcher Billy O'Dell, its original big-bonus player. The club acquired a temperamental power-hitting prospect, Jim Gentile, from Los Angeles. Baltimore would go with youth in 1960, and to emphasize this decision it released, traded, or sent to the minor leagues thirteen members of its 1959 major league roster.

The Orioles opened their seventh season in Baltimore with a young and untried infield consisting of Jim Gentile (twenty-five) at first base, Marv Breeding (twenty-six) at second, Ron Hansen (twenty-one) at shortstop, and the "veteran" Brooks Robinson (twenty-two) at third. Twenty-five-year-old Jackie Brandt patrolled center field. Experience, and some power, were supplied by aging outfielder Gene Woodling and injury-prone catcher Gus Triandos. A youthful corps of starting pitchers—Jack Fisher, Steve Barber, Milt Pappas, Jerry Walker, and Chuck Estrada—backed by two tough veter-ans, Hal "Skinny" Brown and Hoyt Wilhelm, led the club into contention. The team played well from the early spring. One-third of the way through the season it held first place by two and a half games. Throughout a remarkable season, the Orioles won the close games. Gentile provided the home run power. The pitching and defense were excellent. The hard-throwing Barber proved the biggest surprise. Arriving from the lower minor leagues with a reputation for wildness, he won ten games. Estrada won eighteen, Pappas fifteen, and Brown and Wilhelm combined for twenty-three victories. Ron Hansen chipped in with power hitting and superb defense, becoming the American League all-star shortstop and rookie of the year. Nearly 1.2 million fans paid to get into Memorial Stadium to see the club play.

By late August, the American League pennant race was a two-team affair. The Orioles and Yankees alternately surged into first place and fell back. The veteran Yankees were a formidable opponent, featuring a powerful offense led by sluggers Mickey Mantle, Yogi Berra, and Roger Maris. Their pitching staff was anchored by Whitey Ford, one of the great left-handers of the modern era. New York played excellent defensive baseball and had the intangible factors of experience and the confidence born of a decade of championship baseball on its side.

In the end, the Orioles' bid for a pennant came up short. A four-game series at Yankee Stadium in late September decided the American League championship. The veteran Yankees simply outplayed the nervous young Orioles. Baltimore had to settle for second place.

It was, however, a most successful second-place finish. The club made a $315,000 profit after taxes in spite of spending over $1 million on player development that year. The value of Baltimore stock rose. The Orioles rewarded Richards for another excellent job of managing by extending his contract. Both fans and stockholders looked forward to an American League championship in 1961. The club encouraged their hopes with a new slogan: It Can Be Done in '61.[66]

Regrettably, the dream season of 1960 was just that. A number of veterans had exceptional years. All the young players had good years. The breaks went with the Orioles. In 1961 the Orioles proved they were indeed a first division team but also discovered that they were still short of having the talent needed to overtake the powerful Yankees. Six difficult years of franchise building were the prologue to six often-frustrating years of pursuing teams that were always slightly better.

Major League Frustrations

First baseman Jim Gentile was a weather vane of the Orioles' success in the early 1960s. Tall, handsome, graceful, "Diamond Jim" was a superior fielder and the club's top home run hitter. The Orioles plucked him out of minor league obscurity prior to the 1960 season. Gentile was twenty-five and had spent many frustrating years in the Dodgers farm system waiting for star first baseman Gil Hodges to grow old. By 1960 Hodges was still playing well and the Dodgers had a gigantic young prospect named Frank Howard ready to take his place. Gentile was an "old" minor leaguer with a reputation for brooding that affected his play. The Dodgers sent Gentile to a Baltimore club willing to gamble on his emotional state in order to get a power-hitting prospect.

In 1960 Gentile hit twenty-one home runs as he helped the Orioles to a second place finish. The following year, he hit a Herculean 46 homers and drove in 141 runs to carry the club to its best record yet. Unfortunately, the Yankee tandem of Mickey Mantle and Roger Maris combined for 115 home runs to lead their club to another pennant. The young Detroit Tigers repeated the Orioles' 1960 performance, battling the New Yorkers to the wire before stumbling in a critical September series at Yankee Stadium.

Babe Ruth once remarked that home run hitters drive Cadillacs. Essentially, baseball is a game of pitching and defense, briefly interrupted by scoring bursts. Fans pay to see these bursts and idolize the men who create them. The power hitter, the rare individual who regularly "puts 'em out of the park," is also the athlete who puts paying fans into seats. As a result, he is highly paid and under tremendous pressure from both fans and management to produce. After his 1961 success, Gentile was paid about $30,000, the highest salary on the team. Fans and management expected Gentile to repeat his remarkable 1961 achievements.

In 1962 Gentile stumbled. After an excellent start, he tailed off, hitting only .208 with thirteen home runs in the second half of the season. The Orioles plunged to seventh place. Gentile brooded and fought with his new manager. After a decent 1963 season (.248 and twenty-four home runs), the team traded him to Kansas City. Three years later, the thirty-two-year-old Gentile was out of professional baseball.

The saga of Jim Gentile goes to the heart of one of the central problems of baseball management. Only a few players ever achieve long-term consistency. Short playing careers are common at the major league level. The general manager's primary function is to keep a constant flow of talent moving to his club from the minor leagues, from trades, and, in recent years, from free agent signings. In the early 1960s, Baltimore had the nucleus of a contending club in pitchers Steve Barber and Milt Pappas and third baseman Brooks Robinson. Its major weakness remained a lack of power hitters. MacPhail traded repeatedly, hired new managers and coaches, and poured money and manpower into the minor leagues in an effort to find the players who could turn a contender into a champion. The Orioles kept coming up short. The Yankees simply had a larger nucleus of stars and could still acquire the right supporting players by trading off the surplus talent produced by their highly regarded minor league system. The Orioles' efforts to build to New York's level were further impeded when the American League expanded to ten teams and changes in the minor league draft tapped Baltimore's existing talent pool.

Expansion

Two months after the end of the 1960 season, the American League hastily added two new franchises and permitted the Washington Senators to move to Minnesota. The owners agreed to stock the new teams with players purchased from the major and minor league rosters of the eight existing clubs. The existing clubs would charge $75,000 for each player sold, and they strictly limited the number of players that they made available for this "expansion draft." Even so, the Orioles' well-stocked farm system was a prime target for the expansion franchises, and Richards went to extraordinary lengths to "hide" talented players he could not protect. In one case, he asked minor league manager Earl Weaver to have outfielder Chuck Hinton fake a serious injury. Weaver refused, but Richards set up an "accident" anyway.

The ruse failed and the Washington expansion club drafted Hinton. In addition to Hinton, the Orioles lost a number of other prospects, including future twenty-game winner Dean Chance and some important cogs from the 1960 campaign such as aging outfielder Gene Woodling and journeyman Gene Green. "We are not too happy to give up the men we lost," MacPhail commented as he surveyed the effects on his club's 1961 pennant chances.[1]

The desire to protect their farm systems and the wish to limit the competition for amateur talent were two factors that delayed the major leagues' decision to expand. Another factor was the Pacific Coast League's resistance to surrendering any of its territories. The large and wealthy cities of the Far West were the prizes that all three leagues coveted.[2]

In an October 1953 editorial welcoming Baltimore into the American League, *The Sporting News* noted that New York's Del Webb had extracted a pledge to expand from his fellow owners in exchange for supporting Baltimore's bid and announced that the "race for [West] Coast territory" was underway. Baseball's race west was cautious: conducted at a snail's pace and with a number of stops along the way. In the end, however, *The Sporting News* proved correct.[3]

The first stage in expansion was another round of relocation by existing major league franchises. At the end of the 1954 season, Webb and New York partner Topping arranged for the Mack family to sell the financially ailing Philadelphia Athletics to a business associate of the Yankees owners, banker and real estate magnate Arnold Johnson. The new owner immediately bought the rights to Kansas City from the Yankees and moved his team into the stadium that Webb's construction company had recently upgraded.[4]

The American League next set up an "expansion committee" to study possible sites for new franchises. The Orioles were one of the American League teams ready to support expansion. Commissioner Frick, however, requested that the clubs hold off. The American League shelved expansion plans with little complaint.[5]

The next move belonged to the rival National League. Walter O'Malley, the shrewd and ambitious owner of the Brooklyn franchise, decided that the time was ripe for his long-contemplated move to Los Angeles. O'Malley's Dodgers played to enthusiastic crowds in cramped Ebbets Field. The crosstown National League Giants were playing to a nearly empty stadium. O'Malley realized that if a West Coast move were to succeed, the Dodgers had to have a Pacific rival. Moving the two New York teams in tandem would carry an ancient rivalry west and make travel to the Pacific Coast economically feasible for the other National League clubs.[6]

Attorney O'Malley laid the groundwork for a move with his customary skill. He made a complex series of demands for a new stadium in Brooklyn that the city of New York would refuse to meet. O'Malley acquired the franchise rights to Los Angeles from fellow National League owner Phil

Wrigley. He negotiated a very favorable stadium and concessions deal with the city of Los Angeles and worked out a profitable contract with a California "pay television" company. All the while, O'Malley denied that he had made the final decision to move. Instead, Giants owner Horace Stoneham, pleading poverty, carried his case to the National League. The league approved Stoneham's request to move and granted O'Malley the same right if he chose to use it. At the end of the 1957 season, O'Malley announced he would be moving to Los Angeles.[7]

O'Malley's maneuvers generated considerable anger in New York and provoked a new congressional challenge to baseball's antitrust exemption. Brooklyn congressman Emanuel Celler subjected National League representatives to withering criticism during hearings in the summer of 1957. He warned the owners that by shifting franchises to enhance profits, organized baseball was acting like other businesses that had "no right to come in here and ask for an exemption from the antitrust laws." National League leaders pleaded ignorance of O'Malley's plans. In the end both the committee and the city of New York had to accept O'Malley's decision. He had the legal right to move his property. Los Angeles was a better market, columnist Red Smith noted, and "no matter how bitterly Brooklyn fans resent the departure of their team, nobody can fault O'Malley's decision on business grounds."[8]

While neither Congress nor the city of New York could halt the National League's move west, they could cooperate to challenge organized baseball's monopoly control over the sport. Mayor Robert Wagner set up an informal group to look into the possibility of attracting an existing National League franchise to New York. When the Cincinnati Reds and Pittsburgh Pirates turned down the city's overtures, Wagner asked politically well connected lawyer William Shea to organize a third major league.[9]

The idea of a third league startled organized baseball into action to protect its monopoly. Commissioner Frick had broached the idea before, primarily to pacify Congress without any apparent intention of taking action. After the Giants' and Dodgers' moves, Frick again talked about bringing more teams to New York, either through a third league or by expanding the two existing leagues. As an indication of organized baseball's "good will," the two leagues agreed to modify their franchising rules to permit a second team in any city with a population of more than 2 million. Frick, however, insisted that expansion or the creation of a third league must be an orderly process, following the secure settlement of existing teams in their new homes and a far-reaching reorganization of the minor leagues.[10]

Frick may have been sincere, or he may have been creating a smoke screen for inaction with his contradictory support for two mutually exclusive alternatives. In any case, his wavering between options only deepened Shea's mistrust of the baseball establishment. The New York lawyer pressed forward with plans for a third league. In the winter of 1958–59 he hired Branch

Rickey to put together the new league. The seventy-seven-year-old Rickey had lost little of his dynamism and none of his organizational ability. He soon made the Continental League, as the new circuit was dubbed, an unpleasant reality for the major league establishment. Rickey lined up experienced minor league operators to run most of the franchises together with wealthy business backers.[11]

In May 1959 the major league owners met at Columbus, Ohio, where they approved a resolution welcoming the formation of an eight-team third league and outlined their terms for formal recognition. The Columbus resolution was an invitation for Rickey's group to join in the existing monopoly. Shea cautiously welcomed the offer but coupled expressions of satisfaction with a warning that the Continental League's supporters in Congress were ready to enact legislation creating a third league if the major leagues stalled further.[12]

The Continental League had powerful political backers, particularly in states eager to have a major league team. Congressman Celler supported the idea, as did the chairman of the Senate Antitrust Subcommittee, Estes Kefauver. Kefauver held hearings on expansion in July 1959. Frick repeated baseball's formula: creation of a third league that operated within the framework of the existing monopoly. The commissioner and a number of minor league executives complained that a new league operating independently of the established leagues would damage their markets, indicating that negotiations over franchise rights would be complex and time-consuming. Shea countered that a new league would end the unpopular major league habit of franchise-shifting while providing employment for more athletes, increasing profits for local economies, and satisfying the civic pride of more communities.[13]

While Shea and Rickey pressed forward with plans for the third league, major league owners continued to employ delaying tactics that they hoped would kill the Continental League but permit them to avoid shouldering responsibility before Congress, the press, and the public. Although reluctant to authorize an expansion of the existing leagues, the owners were equally unwilling to let anyone else control the process. Major league tactics failed to fool Rickey or Shea, who appealed to Kefauver for support. Guided by Rickey, Kefauver's staff drafted a bill that would put an end to major league control of the minor leagues and, in short order, permit the third league to compete on an equal footing with the two older circuits in talent recruitment.[14]

In the midst of these maneuvers, Calvin Griffith, Clark's heir and successor as owner of the Washington Senators, became a new source of embarrassment for the major leagues. In late September 1959, shortly after the Continental League announced it would place a franchise in Minneapolis–St. Paul, Griffith announced that he would move his team to the Twin Cities for the 1960 season. Griffith had been maneuvering to take the Senators out of Washington at least since 1956. Once before, in 1958, he had a deal set to move to the Minneapolis area when the press found out. The news broke just as the U.S. Senate was holding hearings on baseball and set off an explosion in Congress. Kefauver hauled Griffith before his committee and extracted a pledge from the surprised and embarrassed Senators owner that he was through "exploring" options for a franchise move. The club's board of directors passed a resolution "discouraging" inquiries from other cities.[15]

Congress was not alone in its outrage over the proposed move. Frick called the idea "catastrophic." When Griffith revived the suggestion in 1959, in the midst of the Continental League crisis, the reaction of his fellow owners was apoplectic. Cincinnati's Gabe Paul called Rickey to assure him that the major leagues were not behind the Griffith move. Griffith, Paul explained, was a "nice boy who is baseball dumb and a terrible operator." Fearing congressional reaction, the owners met in mid-October and forced Griffith to abandon the move. Frustrated again, Griffith licked his wounds but held on to his plans.[16]

Griffith's action forced the American League's hand. League attendance had continued its decline from 9,142,361 in 1950 to 7,296,526 in 1958. Griffith was unable to make large profits in Washington and wanted to move. His fellow owners had already recognized both the right of owners to move and the mutual profitability of shifting franchises. As one baseball executive explained, "We've got to shift with our market. After all . . . we're merchandising baseball." A move from Washington, however, required putting a new team in the city to appease Congress. Thus, at the same October meeting during which they cuffed Griffith, the owners agreed to set up a committee to study expansion. The best available corrective to declining attendance was further franchise-shifting or expansion to build new sources of paying customers. Expansion would bring the existing clubs a tidy profit through the sale of franchise rights and players; it would also stimulate a rise in revenue from television rights, particularly if the new teams went into large markets.[17]

Rickey and Shea saw the American League's action as another proof of a major league conspiracy. They also faced growing opposition from minor league owners who they suspected had major league encouragement. Determined to force the issue, the Continental League turned to Congress. Kefauver held a new set of hearings in May 1960 at which Shea and Rickey flayed the major leagues for "extortionate demands" and "bad faith" while underlining their own desire to break with the sport's monopolistic practices and introduce innovations that would ensure better competition and fairer treatment of players.[18]

The Kefauver hearings were the springboard for new legislation aimed at ending major league control over the minors by strictly limiting the number of athletes major league teams could keep under contract. The major leagues mobilized their friends in Congress to defeat the legislation. In late June the baseball establishment won out over the Continental League when the Senate voted seventy-three to twelve to recommit the Kefauver bill, effectively killing it for that session. Realizing that it lacked the votes to do otherwise, the Continental League supported recommitment in order to avoid rejection in the full Senate. A Continental League strategy paper noted that the major leagues were able to mobilize the senators with baseball in their states into a nearly solid front to oppose the Kefauver bill. Both of Maryland's Republican senators supported the major league position. One of them, John M. Butler, underlined a serious weakness in the Continental League's position: "Basically . . . the Congress . . . should not attempt to govern the internal operations . . . of baseball. . . . Nor should Congress be put in the position of aiding private groups in a . . . business venture." Organized baseball skillfully played upon congressional reluctance to legislate rules for the sports business.[19]

In spite of their victory, major league owners realized that expansion could no longer be deferred. Rickey and Shea were threatening to set up a rival league outside their control. None of the owners thought this outside Rickey's ability or the new league's financial base. Frick recalled: "Whether or not Mr. Shea was bluffing, no one will ever know. Baseball was scared. The nightmare of the Federal League war was common knowledge. Pressure was being applied by the press and public opinion. The structure of baseball was under scrutiny by Congress. . . . A baseball war would be a calamity beyond comprehension. Compromise was in order, and it came quickly."[20]

On 18 July 1960 the National League voted to expand to ten teams and established a four-man committee, which included O'Malley, to meet with American League and Continental League representatives to map out a strategy. The American League responded by forming its own committee of four, including Baltimore's Iglehardt. A 2 August meeting of the three leagues led to a compromise solution: the two major leagues agreed to expand by four teams within two years and to add four other franchises thereafter. The major leagues promised the new franchises to Continental League syndicates.[21]

On 30 August 1960 the American League owners voted to add two teams by 1962 and set up a special committee of four to examine sites and recommend candidates. Iglehardt participated on this committee as well. Two months later, after reviewing the possibilities, the American League voted to move the Senators to Minnesota and to set up new franchises in Washington and Los Angeles. The league double-crossed the Continental League's backers and cut them out of the expansion. Rickey protested vigorously but to no avail.[22]

Del Webb apparently was the moving force behind the American League decisions. The Yankee owner had been pressing for Los Angeles as an expansion site since 1953. In August 1960 he won Commissioner Frick's public endorsement of the idea that Los Angeles, despite the Dodgers' presence, remained an "open city" for expansion where the American League could locate without paying compensation. Urged on by Webb and his partner Topping, American League owners decided to steal a march on the National League and plant a franchise in the West Coast's best market before the senior circuit returned to New York. The owners then granted Griffith's wish. Since the American League feared congressional antitrust action if the capital was without baseball, they moved the other new franchise back into the overcrowded East Coast market that Griffith had just vacated.[23]

The Sporting News judged American League actions "hasty and almost frantic." They were also ill-judged maneuvers because the American League totally underestimated the resolve of Walter O'Malley. National League baseball was returning to New York in response to the political power that Shea and his associates wielded. No parallel pressure existed for placing a second franchise in Los Angeles. O'Malley simply ignored Frick's "open city" statement. He invoked major league Rule 1 to claim exclusive territorial rights. Frick waffled, declining to enforce his August ruling that Los Angeles was an open city against O'Malley. The Dodgers owner forced a settlement on the American League that turned the Los Angeles Angels of that league into his paying tenants.[24]

The American League ended up with a single franchise on the West Coast, a money-maker in the Twin Cities, and a potential albatross in Washington. The league had put weak teams into highly competitive markets. The National League emerged with two very profitable markets in New York and Houston and continued to dominate the Far West with its perennial contenders in San Francisco and Los Angeles.

The Orioles owners had hardly distinguished themselves, following Webb's lead into the series of ill-advised franchise moves. Baltimore also backed the Yankees boss over the choice of new owners in Washington. In a decision tinged with delicious irony, Baltimore voted for the group led by General E. R. Quesada against a syndicate led by Edward Bennett Williams, the future Orioles owner, and supported by the Orioles' past owner Veeck and future owner Jerold Hoffberger.[25]

The Orioles' reward for supporting expansion was monetary. Operating in a restricted market and suffering from poor attendance, the club could use the money that came from an expansion draft. However, on balance, Baltimore needed talent more than money. Expansion was a one-time capital infusion. It simultaneously diluted both Baltimore's major league squad and its farm system, while it increased competition for amateur free agents. The three seasons that followed illustrated how difficult it is to maintain even a young club as a contender.[26]

Looking for Help

The 1961–65 Orioles bore the stamp of Lee MacPhail. Both Richards and McLaughlin had departed by the end of 1961, leaving the Orioles general manager with the major responsibility for improving 1960's second-place team.[27] During these years, MacPhail slowly reshaped the team that he had inherited, and after a series of experiments he eventually put together the right manager and the right players to win an American League championship. MacPhail's effort to build a pennant winner reveals a good deal about his character and about the nature of the general manager's job.

Improving the Orioles was a difficult task. The expansion draft had a major impact on the pool of available major league talent. By February 1961 *The Sporting News* reported a 45 percent turnover in American League personnel as the eight established teams attempted to replace men lost in the expansion through trading and by promoting minor league prospects. The Orioles lost five major league journeymen or aging frontline players, together with a number of minor league prospects, to the draft. In an effort to fill the holes in their roster, they traded another five men with major league experience as well as a number of prospects for bench strength.[28]

At the same time, Baltimore Baseball was paying the price of success in the form of rising salaries for its young stars. The team managed to offset major raises for Gentile, Pappas, Robinson, and other young players by unloading the salaries of highly paid veterans like Gene Woodling and selling off players in the draft. Nevertheless, a club payroll that reached $500,000 in 1960 continued to rise gradually. Attendance had to keep pace if the club was to cover its costs.[29]

The club was in a particularly tight bind because of heightened local expectations that the 1961 Orioles would capture the American League pennant. Orioles sales promotions built on the theme It Can Be Done in '61. Opening day 1961 festivities featured a parade with the Baltimore Symphony Orchestra playing on the floats. The Association of Commerce called the festivities "spectacular." The Orioles somewhat dampened local spirits by losing to the expansion Los Angeles Angels, 7–2.[30]

The team started slowly, playing poorly in the early spring. The Orioles temporarily lost a number of players, including shortstop Ron Hansen, to military call-ups that resulted from the tense U.S.-Soviet confrontation over Berlin. Hitting was generally weak and pitching ineffective. Highly touted rookie pitcher John Pappa was unable to adjust to major league competition and went back to the minors. Milt Pappas had arm troubles. Chuck Estrada performed erratically, while Jack Fisher was simply unlucky, pitching well but getting little offensive support. Fortunately, Brooks Robinson hit consistently and Jim Gentile put on an awesome display of power hitting with thirteen home runs by mid-May. Together, they kept the club afloat during a dismal spring.

By the time the Orioles finally began to play good baseball in June, the American League race was a two-team contest between New York and Detroit. The Orioles made a strong effort, going 31–17 between mid-June and August and winning 16 of 20 in one stretch, but could never pick up ground on the two leaders. Richards, who had predicted a Baltimore pennant the previous winter, admitted it was one of the most frustrating seasons he ever endured. The Orioles finished the season with their best won-lost record ever, 95–67, but managed only a third-place finish, thirteen and a half games behind the champion Yankees.

The team ended the season under a new manager. In August, Richards left the Orioles for the position of general manager of the National League's expansion franchise in Houston. Reports of a Houston offer to Richards surfaced in mid-July 1961 and followed the club through the remainder of the summer. By mid-August, Richards, with club approval, was talking to Houston's owners. The Houston financial offer was very large, and the new club was ready to give Richards the full authority he always craved. Nevertheless, the usually decisive Richards delayed making up his mind. Finally MacPhail, who felt that his manager's indecision was affecting the Orioles' performance, gave Richards a 1 September deadline to make a choice. On 30 August, Richards announced his resignation and immediately signed a contract as Houston general manager.[31]

With Richards gone, MacPhail faced two major, pressing problems: hiring a qualified replacement and preventing Richards from siphoning off management personnel and scouts from the Orioles. Initially, the team hoped that Luman Harris, Richards's highly regarded, longtime associate and third base coach, would take over as manager. Harris finished out the season as interim manager but then loyally followed Richards to Houston. Other departures from the scouting staff and front office were limited, and the Orioles avoided any serious disruption of operations.[32]

The selection of a manager was MacPhail's first endeavor in this tricky area where public relations was key. While the press normally celebrates the tactical acumen of a baseball manager, his real skills lie in accommodating the twenty-five individuals who make up a team: assessing available talent and getting the most out of it. The manager has to gain control over the players while allowing a great deal of latitude for their individuality. Earl Weaver, one of baseball's most successful managers, explained that he tolerated a large degree of individuality on his winning teams because "a ball club isn't a family, but it's together more than a family for seven months. You can't hold your feelings in that long."[33]

The manager is also the team's most visible representative, normally meeting with the press on a daily basis during the season. He controls team strategy during games. Thus, the manager quickly becomes the focal point for discontent with performance. Player talent is always in short supply, and when a season goes badly, the manager becomes the scapegoat.[34]

MacPhail's selection of a manager reflected his values. After interviewing a number of candidates, he chose Billy Hitchcock, a forty-four-year-old minor league manager in the Braves' system. In announcing his selection on 10 October 1961, MacPhail stressed Hitchcock's organizational loyalty. Teamwork and cooperation within the front office were the values that MacPhail hoped to instill in an organization still accustomed to Richards's individualism. Hitchcock was an easygoing man whom *The Sporting News* described as "kind, conscientious, understanding and patient." He was also skilled at dealing with the press. MacPhail hoped that the young and approachable Hitchcock would be able to get the most out of a team that relied so heavily on young players. Clearly Hitchcock was in personality the opposite of the austere and aloof Richards.[35]

Because Hitchcock had no major league managerial experience, he and MacPhail carefully selected their coaches from the Orioles' minor league system. The decision to rely on youth rather than experience was a calculated risk. MacPhail believed that hiring an ex-major league manager to assist Hitchcock might undercut the new field leader's authority with the players. He also preferred the enthusiasm of the younger men to the caution of the veteran ex-managers he interviewed. MacPhail was gambling with the Orioles' box office appeal by hiring the unknown Hitchcock instead of a veteran major league manager. The lack of a "name" manager could undercut fan interest, especially after the disappointment of the 1961 season.[36]

Recognizing that Hitchcock would need help to challenge the Yankees, MacPhail set about acquiring some new players and improving the club's public image. The Orioles' most obvious weakness was a lack of offense. The team needed another power hitter to take some of the load off Gentile. The outfield was strong defensively, but only Jackie Brandt hit well in 1961. Power-hitting outfielders, as usual, were in short supply, and MacPhail did not have the talent excess that would permit him to give up a regular to acquire a veteran. He told one reporter that he would deal away frontline players only if "it appeared that we were getting the better of it." Moreover, MacPhail believed that help could be found in the Orioles' farm system in the form of a hulking twenty-year-old prospect named John "Boog" Powell. The pressure to find someone increased when the Orioles' other home run threat, catcher Gus Triandos, demanded a trade. The team decided to bring Powell into the major leagues.[37]

The continuing tension over Berlin increased MacPhail's problems. During the winter of 1961–62, a number of the team's best players were called to active duty with their army reserve units. Hansen was recalled, as were pitcher Steve Barber and outfielder Barry Shetrone, a top minor league prospect. The status of Brooks Robinson and Chuck Estrada, two other reservists, was unclear.

Added to this were other concerns about the team's infield and pitching. The infield, the strength of the 1960 team, became a 1962 weakness. Marv Breeding hit a puny .209 in 1961. Young Jerry Adair, a good glove man, hit .264 with nine home runs that season, but with Hansen lost to the military, he would have to fill in as shortstop, leaving his second base position open. Anticipating this gap, MacPhail acquired veteran second baseman Johnny Temple. Jack Fisher finished the 1961 season with an 10–13 record. Mac-Phail picked up veteran pitcher Robin Roberts to augment his young staff. He was unable to make a deal for the discontented Triandos.

Recognizing that the 1961 publicity campaign had backfired, MacPhail appointed Bob Brown as the team's director of public relations and instructed him to come up with a new approach. Assistant general manager Jack Dunn wanted to try his hand at broadcasting, and the club hired him to do play-by-play of its games. Dunn tried to broaden the club's fan base by pitching his broadcasts toward children and women.[38]

MacPhail's increased interest in public relations was directly linked to financial considerations. Club attendance in 1961 dropped by 130,000 from its 1960 total, to 951,089. MacPhail estimated that the Orioles needed a minimum of 900,000 paying customers to break even and looked to a vigorous marketing campaign combined with improved play to reverse the attendance slump. The club trimmed the salaries of a number of athletes who had played poorly in 1961 in an effort to keep the books balanced and encourage better performances. Gentile and Barber got raises in recognition of their superior 1961 performances. Overall, the club's 1962 payroll probably rose slightly but remained near the $500,000 plateau.[39]

The 1962 season was a disaster. The team started as it had in 1961. The pitching was erratic and Gentile's hitting carried the offense. The big first baseman got help from Temple and Robinson. Barber, the club's best pitcher, was serving his army tour and only available for weekend duty. Adair, subbing for another unwilling warrior, Ron Hansen, got off to a slow start at the plate. Brandt slumped badly. Triandos was slowed by injuries. By May the Orioles desperately needed catching help and MacPhail swung a deal with the expansion New York Mets. The Orioles acquired Hobie Landrith in exchange for first baseman Marv Throneberry. A sports legend was born in New York. "Marvelous Marv" epitomized the hapless expansion Mets.

In mid-June the Orioles finally began playing with some consistency. MacPhail's acquisitions played a big role. Landrith had a fine year for Baltimore. Temple hit well and played good defense. Robin Roberts proved he was still a capable pitcher, winning ten games. Robinson emerged as a power hitter, with twenty-three home runs. Unfortunately, Gentile faded during the summer, and young Boog Powell had a hard time adjusting to major league pitching and the requirements of major league outfield play. The club slumped again in the early summer.

In late July the usually reticent MacPhail publicly blasted his club for listless play and threatened severe pay cuts if there was no improvement. Shortly thereafter, star pitcher Milt Pappas publicly criticized Hitchcock. Gentile, who had lived in fear of Richards, began to bait and defy his new manager. MacPhail admitted that the team lacked leadership and refused to guarantee that Hitchcock would return. Attendance took a nose dive as the Orioles floundered near the bottom of the American League standings. In an economy move, MacPhail sold Temple and his $30,000 salary to Houston.[40]

At the end of an unsatisfactory season, the Orioles were in seventh place, with a 77–85 record. Home attendance dropped another 160,000, to 790,254. The team drew better on the road than at home for the third time in four years. The club's minimal consolations were winning eleven of eighteen contests from the champion Yankees, including a five-game sweep in late August in Baltimore, and a small end-of-year profit produced by last-minute economies. MacPhail announced that a major personnel shake-up would follow the season and gave Hitchcock a new contract as a vote of confidence.[41]

The Orioles began their promised shake-up at the end of the 1962 season. MacPhail fired two of Hitchcock's coaches and announced that he would hire men with major league experience for the following season. The Orioles general manager found other positions within the organization for the two dismissed coaches, a tacit recognition that his decisions had been at fault.[42]

As the new coaches, MacPhail hired Hank Bauer—a gruff, crew-cut former Yankee star, ex-manager, and Marine veteran—and Luke Appling—a former star shortstop with a reputation as a "holler guy." Hitchcock pledged to cut down on "prima donna antics" by the players.[43]

Having fortified his manager with new assistants, MacPhail set about rebuilding his team and instilling it with a new sense of discipline. He placed a number of minor league players on the forty-man major league roster. Baltimore's farm system was a source of comfort. The Orioles' top two minor league teams had fifteen players who won all-star honors. They were available to bolster the Orioles directly or through trades.

Next, MacPhail cut the salaries of players who had performed poorly in 1962. The Orioles' profit margin was too narrow to permit the luxury of overlooking a bad year. Moreover, MacPhail, like most general managers, believed that money was the best incentive for good athletic performance. Key players like Barber, Hansen, Gentile, and Pappas got pay cuts. Adair, Robinson, and relief pitcher Dick Hall, who played well, were offered small salary increases. Player discontent was general. MacPhail was unmoved: "I am aware [that] there are a few unhappy athletes in this organization . . . and they are going to have to stay that way." He reminded the players that he had warned of pay cuts in July and that the club continued to play poorly. MacPhail insisted that the club could not afford another season of low attendance and pointedly reminded the players that their individual salaries were directly linked to the club's field success and profitability.[44]

In a move that surprised even the promanagement *Sporting News*, the gentlemanly, soft-spoken MacPhail publicly pressured Brooks Robinson to sign for only a modest increase. In January 1963 at Baltimore's annual Tops in Sports banquet, MacPhail produced a copy of Robinson's 1963 contract and invited the star third baseman and guest of honor to sign before a startled crowd. Robinson refused, telling the Orioles general manager that the raise was too small. He then enumerated his impressive 1962 accomplishments. *The Sporting News* remarked that not even Bill Veeck had employed such "outrageous" pressure tactics.[45] Ultimately, the Orioles settled on an increase closer to Robinson's demands. MacPhail's move testified to the club's financial problems and was symptomatic of baseball's labor relations.

MacPhail traded to bolster the Orioles. Gus Triandos took his large salary to Detroit in a deal for catcher Dick Brown. MacPhail sold the contracts of veteran pitcher Hal Brown and outfielder Dick Williams. Other trades followed. By February 1963 MacPhail had radically restructured the team, adding speed and power and improving its defense. He gave up Hansen for the American League's best shortstop, Luis Aparicio, and acquired four pitchers, two outfielders (both black), and another catcher. In exchange, MacPhail sent veterans Hoyt Wilhelm, Whitey Herzog, and Billy Hoeft, a number of top minor league prospects, and a few of the heroes of 1960 to other teams. In all, MacPhail unloaded twelve athletes and acquired nine as he searched for the proper player chemistry to return the Orioles to contention.[46]

The Orioles simultaneously pushed forward with a more active public relations program. The team introduced a season highlights film at the end of 1962. Professionally produced, the film stressed the team's strong minor league system in an effort to revive fan optimism for the 1963 season. Making the best of its dismal 1962 performance, the team launched its 1963 season ticket drive with newspaper advertising, illustrated with a battered bird, promising a comeback. A March 1963 article by MacPhail in *Baltimore* magazine stressed the hard-working attitude of the team. "There is no listlessness or lack of purpose on this squad," MacPhail claimed, and he added that "intangibles" like "enthusiasm" and "hustle" would spark a comeback. "For the first time the Orioles believe in themselves as a team." MacPhail promised a "new look" for the Orioles. The Baltimore Association of Commerce's Sports Committee picked up these themes and began a Boost the Birds campaign to build attendance.[47]

The 1963 Orioles were an improved team but no challenger to the Yankees. The revamped team got off to a good start, taking an early lead and winning thirty of their first forty-seven games. In late May, however, the team slumped badly, losing twenty of twenty-seven contests and dropping into sixth place. Hitchcock became the target of growing criticism from both fans and the press. MacPhail stood behind his manager but was unable to protect Hitchcock from the criticism that followed a series of unnecessary public relations gaffes. The team's always weak credibility with the black community received a setback when Hitchcock, suddenly and without adequate explanation, benched black outfielder Al Smith. Powell and Gentile struggled to provide the needed home run power for a team that was still short in this critical offensive department. Robinson slumped to a .251 average and eleven home runs. When the pressure cooker season ended, the Orioles were in fourth place with an improved record of 86–76.[48]

The improvement was insufficient to save Hitchcock's job. MacPhail realized that the easygoing manager was incapable of overcoming the team's personality problems. On 29 September 1963, the Orioles general manager tearfully announced that he had fired Hitchcock, "with great regret," and shouldered blame for the team's poor season. MacPhail explained: "It is not the intended policy of this club to make frequent managerial changes for insufficient causes or for publicity reasons. Under the present circumstances, it was decided a change for 1964 was necessary."[49]

MacPhail proceeded cautiously in his second effort to find an effective manager. Both management and the club's players agreed that the team needed a "tough guy" to knit together a contender. MacPhail also looked for a name manager who would assist the team at the box office. Finally, he settled on Hank Bauer. The new manager's wife prudently remained at the couple's Kansas home, commenting, "Baseball is so indefinite, you know."[50]

As the 1964 season approached, MacPhail again was active on the trade market, sending Gentile and Smith to American League rivals for outfielder Willie Kirkland and first baseman Norm Siebern in an effort to improve the club's offense, standings, and attendance.

The Orioles' lackluster play was an important reason for poor attendance, but it was not the only factor. The American League generally suffered declining attendance in the early 1960s. The long years of Yankees dominance were finally having their predictable effect. Shortly after the Orioles' August 1962 sweep of New York, *Sports Illustrated*, in an article entitled "That Old Yankee Soap Opera," noted that New York had blown a commanding lead but that this event created little optimism among the contending clubs. The Orioles' Jackie Brandt voiced the widespread defeatism among Yankee rivals: "If the Yankees had to they could win ten games in a row. They win when they have to. They're not going to blow anything."[51]

Jack Dunn, who returned to his post of Orioles assistant general manager late in 1962, commented during the following season: "I used to think that the League couldn't get along without the Yankees. I'm starting to think we'd be better off without them."[52] Even ex-Yankee MacPhail admitted that more than a decade of New York dominance was taking its toll. The lack of real pennant races was killing fan interest. Added to this was a drop-off in scoring that made games more boring to spectators. An enlarged strike zone, higher pitcher's mound, stadiums with larger and more regular playing dimensions, and the effects of expansion combined to reduce scoring. New stadiums and expansion briefly revived attendance, but it soon declined again and revived only some years after the Yankees' collapse, when a reduced strike zone, lower pitcher's mound, and the designated hitter rule revitalized the American League's offense.[53]

Continuing Yankees field dominance undermined the entire American League's financial base. The CBS Saturday and Sunday national broadcasts were virtually Yankees games of the week. The New York team played in most of these telecasts and took away the largest share of national television money, an estimated $500,000 a year to add to its $1.2 million in local TV rights. The league's other teams were hard-pressed to compete with the wealthy Yankees for amateur talent.[54]

In the case of the Orioles, continued dominance by the Yankees rapidly defused the fan enthusiasm that had exploded during the 1960 season. When the great expectations of 1961 collapsed, Baltimore baseball fans stopped coming. The poor play of the 1962 club simply accentuated the trend in Oriole home attendance that began after the 1954 season. The Baltimore club generally finished in the lower half of the American League in attendance. As a team playing in a smaller market, *The Sporting News* noted, the Orioles were on a treadmill. They had a limited fan base to draw on and clearly could not afford to match New York's large payroll. Yet in order to field a pennant winner they needed a larger financial base of support in the form of more paying customers.[55] Permanently breaking Yankees dominance meant introducing some fundamental changes in the rules of baseball.

Bonus Baby Blues

In 1959 Paul Richards addressed the problem of Yankees dominance in a *Look* magazine article entitled "The American League Is Dying." Richards argued that the Yankees' strength lay in the degree to which New York could corner young talent and protect the prospects developing in their farm system. As a corrective, Richards suggested a strict limit to the number of minor league prospects a team could protect, combined with an annual draft of minor league players to redistribute talent. The proposal had been made before, Richards noted, and a minority of major league teams with strong farm systems had been able to defeat it at the minor league level.[56]

In spite of the reforms introduced in the late 1950s, the existing minor league draft remained something of a farce. The rules governing the draft protected individual farm systems from raids. In 1959 some 3,000 players were eligible for the draft, but only a dozen were considered to have major league potential. The draft list usually was a compilation of "has-been" and "never-were" athletes. Moreover, the draft was costly. In 1961 the Orioles spent $62,000 to acquire three marginal players.[57]

By 1961 the steadily increasing cost of amateur signings had created a majority among the major league teams in support of a serious attempt to reform the minor league draft. Commissioner Frick set up a committee to study the minor league draft and appointed Lee MacPhail as chairman. The MacPhail group's recommendations, adopted at the 1961 major league winter meetings, limited the number of bonus players the major leagues could protect while on option to their minor league affiliates. It also increased the number of quality minor league players available for drafting while lowering the cost of each athlete.[58]

The rule passed over the opposition of a number of big-city franchises. Los Angeles owner Walter O'Malley denounced it as "socialistic." The Dodgers, Yankees, Mets, and Giants continued to spend heavily on amateur talent and defeated the rule's intent by filling their forty-man major league roster with these prospects. However, the other aspect of the new rule worked well. During the early 1960s, more minor league talent was available, and the possibility of equalizing team strength through the draft existed.[59]

The MacPhail rule hit heavily at the Orioles farm system. In the first draft of 1962, Baltimore lost eighteen prospects to its rivals, including a number of expensive bonus players. Orioles farm director Harry Dalton ruefully commented: "We aren't exactly overjoyed at the [draft] . . . we had to leave some pretty good boys unprotected."[60]

The Orioles also proved that a superior scouting staff could negate the harmful effects of the expanded minor league draft. By carefully scouting the minor league systems of other teams, Baltimore was able to draft a number of players who played important roles on future championship teams. Moreover, MacPhail informed the board of directors, the new rule induced the club to reduce its bonus spending by $250,000 in 1962. This savings enabled the Orioles to make a profit that year despite their seventh-place finish and resultant drop in attendance.[61] A superior scouting staff enabled Baltimore to continue rounding up top prospects at lower costs.

Because the new rule failed to curb costly bonus spending by richer clubs or to equalize talent quickly, it lost support among the major league teams. A majority rapidly coalesced around the idea of a free agent draft of amateur talent. An amateur draft offered a cheap solution to both of baseball's basic economic problems. It would eliminate costly bidding wars between competing clubs for individual players; it would also reduce the money advantage traditionally enjoyed by the big-city franchises with their larger fan bases, thus creating more competitiveness on the major league level. As a result, the Yankees and Dodgers, the two wealthiest teams in the two best markets, spearheaded the opposition to an amateur draft.[62]

Opponents briefly derailed the amateur draft idea at an August 1964 owners' meeting. Their victory was short lived. Frick strongly favored the draft, and, because he was nearing retirement, took an unusually strong stand with the majority of the owners. He appointed MacPhail to chair a second committee that studied and endorsed an amateur draft. MacPhail felt that the 1961 minor league draft was only a partial success because the rival clubs failed to "follow sound business sense." Their fierce competition for "scarce" amateur talent led to intense bidding wars. Since the revised minor league draft had failed to discourage competitive bidding, MacPhail began contacting other general managers to build support for an amateur draft.[63] He discovered that a consensus already existed: "The general feeling was that we should do whatever we could to . . . spread the talent and give all the clubs . . . an equal opportunity to develop talent that would be based on the ability of [each] organization."[64]

On 2 December 1964 the major leagues enacted a draft of amateur talent similar to that existing in professional football over the objections of the Yankees, Mets, Dodgers, Angels, Twins, Senators, and Cardinals. Under the new draft rule each team selected exclusive negotiating rights to individual players. The clubs made their selections in reverse order of the standings at the end of the previous season. Each team then had a limited time to sign its selections. Athletes who declined a team's offer would be placed in a pool and would be eligible for a supplemental draft later in the year. Amateur players who were not drafted could negotiate with any club. The draft was designed to assist the teams with the worst records in their efforts to build a contender. Ultimately, however, the ability to improve rested with the competence of the management of individual teams.[65]

The amateur draft was an unusually daring move for a business as conservative as baseball. In an era when the major leagues remained concerned about retaining their cherished antitrust exemption, they installed a recruitment mechanism that their own lawyers warned was of dubious legality.[66] The cost of amateur talent had simply become too great, forcing baseball into a bold revision of its rules that flaunted antitrust law.

Organized baseball held its first amateur draft at New York's Hotel Commodore on 8 June 1965. Following the rules adopted in December 1964, the teams drafted in order of their previous season standings during the first three rounds, with the worst club selecting first. Thereafter, the order of selection was determined by lots. The draft continued until all teams had finished making their selections. The Kansas City Athletics chose first, selecting future major league outfielder Rick Monday. On average, clubs selected twenty to thirty players. The Orioles made seventy selections. Dalton explained that the club wanted to be assured that it could continue to sign as many players as under the old system of competitive bidding. The Orioles came to the meeting with a list of 350 players their scouts considered potential major leaguers. The club was committed to continuing its policy of aggressively pursuing all available talent.[67]

Overall, the amateur draft succeeded in both its objectives of equalizing talent and holding down the costs of player acquisition. Dalton felt that Baltimore could make the system work to its advantage, and during the subsequent decade the Orioles continued to select a steady stream of top-quality players.[68]

The amateur draft contributed significantly to equalizing competition in major league baseball. Even before its enactment, however, the Orioles general manager had succeeded in building his team into a serious contender. The Orioles' field fortunes improved in 1964 and 1965 just as its management structure took the final steps from community to corporate baseball.

Changing the Guard

The deal was simple and breathtaking in its effects. For six years the Orioles had sought an "impact" player—a man who would provide the leadership and consistent offensive and defensive play that would turn a contender into a pennant winner. Players of this caliber are rare. Sporting dynasties are built around them. Early in December 1965 outgoing club president Lee MacPhail passed a slip of paper to Harry Dalton, the club's new vice president for player personnel. On it, MacPhail had summarized the terms of a deal that would send three Orioles players, including pitcher Milt Pappas, to Cincinnati for outfielder Frank Robinson. The deal, MacPhail added, was Dalton's to decide. Dalton never hesitated. Baltimore wrapped up its first pennant on that December day.

A New Era

In 1964 the Orioles surged back into contention. The team got off to a good start and by mid-July was in first place. Throughout the summer Baltimore and Chicago battled for first place while New York hung on grimly a few games off the pace. Boog Powell put together a fine year. Nineteen-year-old rookie pitcher Wally Bunker won nineteen games. Another rookie, outfielder Sam Bowens, hit twenty-two home runs with seventy-one RBIs. Aparicio and Brooks Robinson won golden glove awards for their defensive play. Brooks Robinson (.317 average, 28 home runs, and 118 RBIs) also captured the American League's most valuable player award. The Orioles were in first place until 16 September when the Yankees mounted a come-from-behind charge, winning eleven straight games and taking the American League pennant. The Orioles finished third with a 97–65 record, two games behind the champions.

Baltimore fans responded to the improved Orioles. Attendance jumped by almost 350,000, to 1,116,215, and the club reported a profit of $304,400. For the first time in its history, Baltimore Baseball, Inc., declared a dividend for its stockholders. Optimism reigned again among both management and fans. The Orioles farm system was stocked with top prospects who appeared to be ready for the major leagues. MacPhail confidently told *Sun* columnist Bob Maisel that the addition of one defensively solid, power-hitting outfielder could mean a pennant in 1965.[1]

The Orioles returned to contention in a period of major change for both the American League and professional baseball. The minor leagues moved closer to economic stabilization and complete subordination to the major leagues. The New York Yankees changed owners and collapsed. Jerold Hoffberger took control of the Orioles, ending the era of community baseball in Baltimore and bringing a new management style to the club.

Probably no event in sports history was more surprising or dramatic than the sudden and generally unanticipated collapse of the New York Yankees. The major long-term objective of the draft rule adopted in December 1964 was to equalize talent and end the Yankees' domination of the American League. The owners wanted other teams to catch up with the Yankees, not to destroy the club that was baseball's most powerful box office and television attraction. The Yankees escaped the leveling effects of the amateur draft by collapsing on their own in 1965. Their decline almost certainly began when owners Topping and Webb fired their aging general manager, George Weiss, and manager, Casey Stengel, after the 1960 season. Weiss had built the Yankees dynasty of the 1950s, and the players he collected carried the team forward for four seasons after his dismissal. However, the Yankees player development program was never the same. The team's best scouts retired. The first signs of the impending collapse of the greatest of baseball dynasties appeared in 1963. The New York minor league system, the base of the team's dominance, posted an overall losing record. The Yankees' top four minor league clubs finished last or next to last in their leagues.[2]

A few astute baseball men recognized the danger signals in the early 1960s. Gabe Paul first suggested that other American League clubs were catching up in the battle for talent in 1962. A few months later, Lee MacPhail predicted that the Yankees soon would lose a number of key players to age and that the team would be unable to find suitable replacements. The collapse of New York's minor league system occurred at precisely the time when age finally caught up with the superb athletes who had carried the

Yankees into thirteen World Series in fifteen years. Yogi Berra retired after the 1963 season. Mickey Mantle had reached his mid-thirties plagued with injuries. Roger Maris burned out trying to cope with the expectations of the New York press and fans after his epic 1961 season. The reserves simply did not match up. In a clear talent mismatch, Los Angeles swept the 1963 World Series from New York in four games. The Yankees owners recognized that their team was in trouble. In a major shake-up, Topping and Webb ousted general manager Roy Hamey and replaced him with manager Ralph Houk. The popular Berra took over as field leader.[3]

The following year, the proud Yankees rallied once more to narrowly win the American League championship. Topping and Webb meanwhile agreed to dissolve their long-standing partnership. In August 1964 they sold majority control of the team to CBS. The Yankees lost the World Series to the St. Louis Cardinals. The club fired Berra, replacing him with Cardinals manager Johnny Keane, a move that infuriated both the press and fans. At the start of the next season the Yankees fell into the American League's second division and, to the surprise of most fans and journalists, resolutely remained there for the rest of the season. The era of Yankees dominance was over. No team would again dominate baseball as New York did between 1949 and 1964.

The first and most evident effect of the Yankees' demise was to accelerate the decline in American League attendance. In 1961, the first year of expansion, the ten-team American League drew 10,163,016 customers. Attendance then fell steadily until it reached a low point of 8,860,764 in 1965. The Minnesota Twins ran away with the 1965 American League pennant in the manner of the old Yankees, further depressing fan interest. Orioles farm system director Harry Dalton reflected the general feeling that New York's sudden fall was bad for baseball when he wistfully expressed the hope that the Yankees' minor league prospects were "the kind you pay your way in to see."[4] For decades, other American League teams had relied on the Yankees to draw big crowds and had failed to develop effective marketing programs. Now, the king was dead. The American League would have to solve its attendance problems without the drawing power of a star-studded Yankees team.

Corporate Baseball

In an editorial comment on CBS's 1964 purchase of the Yankees, *The Sporting News* labeled the trend toward corporate ownership of baseball clubs "disturbing." Baseball's Bible, as *The Sporting News* was known, argued that the game would inevitably suffer if its management passed from men with a primary interest in sports to corporations who viewed teams as subsidiaries and utilized them as part of a broader marketing strategy. The Yankees deal was particularly troubling because CBS was in the entertainment business. Critics, including baseball men like Bill Veeck, charged that CBS would remold and warp the game in order to make it more marketable on television. *Sport* magazine agreed, adding that baseball faced the danger of coming under total network dominance. Clearly, the Yankees' already powerful influence grew when the American League's most important media market passed under the control of the network that produced both Saturday and Sunday national baseball broadcasts. A number of team owners shared these concerns over the impact of CBS's ownership. When the Yankees announced the CBS deal in August, American League president Joe Cronin conducted a swift telephone poll of the owners and then announced that the league approved the move. Kansas City's Charles Finley and Chicago's Arthur Allyn immediately protested, forcing Cronin to call an owners' meeting for a formal vote on the CBS sale. In accord with Section 8 of the American League's constitution, a three-quarters majority of the owners again approved the sale at a 9 September 1964 meeting in Clearwater, Florida.[5]

Baltimore's vote swung the American League behind CBS by giving supporters of the sale the three-quarters majority needed. Veeck charged that Orioles board chairman Joseph Iglehardt, holder of a large portfolio of CBS stock and chairman of the TV corporation's financial committee, was responsible for the decision. Press inquiries revealed that a number of league owners had financial ties with the giant television network. The CBS-Yankees deal raised the specter that organized baseball would soon be a tool of the television industry. Once again antitrust issues came to the fore and Congress prepared to investigate the sport.[6]

Iglehardt, in fact, did not determine the club's policy on the CBS purchase. The Orioles board was deeply divided on the issue. MacPhail, the brother of a CBS executive and Iglehardt's confidant, favored the sale. Krieger opposed it. With the team's principal owners deadlocked over such a major issue, the final decision rested with the minority stockholders. On 4 September 1964, the board appointed a three-man committee of Krieger, MacPhail, and Jack Dunn to attend the owners' meeting and empowered them to decide how to vote. The setup of the committee clearly left the decision to minority stockholder Dunn.[7]

Dunn was the perfect symbolic choice to make the last major decision taken by Baltimore community baseball. No man outdid the pleasant Dunn in civic devotion. He had willingly sacrificed his sole ownership in the minor league Orioles when the opportunity arose to bring in a major league team. Throughout the next decade, Dunn handled a variety of administrative jobs for the team with professionalism and skill. The board selected Dunn because of its confidence that he would act in the club's best interests. Dunn recalled:

It cost me a lot of sleepless nights [be]cause I could anticipate the situation. . . . The votes were lined up so . . . that Baltimore would determine whether or not the Yankees could be sold to CBS. I agonized over that, I really agonized. . . . I voted [for CBS] because I felt that there was no reason they shouldn't own the club. I was reasonably certain there would be endless litigation if we turned them down because we had no "legitimate reason." . . . There was no moral turpitude. There was no reason to arbitrarily turn them down.[8]

Dunn's vote was weighted with significance for the future control of the Orioles. The issue of the CBS purchase of the Yankees accentuated the widening split between Iglehardt and Krieger. The causes of the split are obscure but certainly included Iglehardt's growing desire for sole control over the franchise. "Iglehardt wanted all or nothing. . . . He wanted to own the club," Dunn explained.[9] Krieger had lost his influence over the Colts and was determined to retain a major say in the future of Baltimore baseball. Moreover, he continued to favor multiple ownership of civic institutions like professional sports.[10]

The CBS purchase put the Orioles chairman of the board in a difficult personal position. Major league rules prohibited participation in the ownership of more than one baseball club. Iglehardt, as a CBS shareholder, was in technical violation of the rule. He resigned from the CBS board of directors immediately after the American League approved the Yankees sale. The league would still have to determine if possession of CBS stock constituted a conflict of interest.

With a congressional investigation pending, league president Cronin wanted to avoid any appearance of conflict of interest. In November 1964 he ordered Iglehardt to sell either his CBS or Orioles stock. Iglehardt balked, saying that his "heart" lay with the Orioles, while making clear that his major financial interests lay in holding onto the highly profitable CBS stock. Cronin declined to challenge Iglehardt, in part because a league survey revealed three other owners who held stock in CBS.[11]

Fortunately for organized baseball, the Senate's February 1965 hearings favored its interests. The new chairman of the Antitrust Subcommittee, Senator Philip Hart (D.-Mich.), wanted to assist professional sports to regularize their anomalous antitrust position. Moreover, he took a positive position regarding CBS's acquisition of the Yankees. At the beginning of the hearings Hart stated that he could find no antitrust problems with television ownership of a baseball team. He then introduced a bill designed to give limited antitrust protection to all sports. CBS and organized baseball supported the legislation. Aided by the sympathetic Hart, CBS attempted to reassure the public that its ownership of the Yankees would never endanger the sport of baseball. The CBS presentation stressed that the company had retained experienced baseball men Topping and Houk to run the Yankees as an independent subsidiary.[12]

Shortly after the hearings, the American League office announced that Iglehardt could retain his CBS stock by placing it in a blind trust while he remained associated with the Orioles. The Baltimore board chairman agreed immediately, adding "I intend to remain a member of the Orioles directors indefinitely."[13] Indefinitely turned out to be less than two months. In the spring of 1965 a two-year power struggle between Iglehardt and Hoffberger climaxed with the victory of the city's brewery king.

Hoffberger waged his initial campaign for control of the club in the fall of 1963 as disagreements between Iglehardt and Krieger intensified. Hoffberger announced his decision to seek control at a moment when the franchise's financial position was weak. Season attendance for 1963 dropped to 774,343, forcing the Orioles into a series of stringent economies. After looking over the attendance figures and the club's financial report, the *Sun*'s Bob Maisel suggested that Orioles treasurer Joseph Hamper deserved a medal for squeezing out a $99,262 profit. Concern over the club's financial picture apparently was one of the factors that led Krieger, the corporation's treasurer, to accompany the team's baseball men to the 1963 winter meetings.[14]

Talking about his decision to acquire control of the Orioles after the 1966 season, Hoffberger stated, "I knew a financial risk was involved" but added that he believed he could turn the team into a money-maker. He then explained the reasons behind his move: "I wanted to gain control, first of all, because I am a sports enthusiast. Secondly, I thought I could do something with the franchise. And, thirdly, I had no idea where the control might go if Iglehardt decided to sell. It might have gone out of town, and I think it's important that Baltimore own the club—not necessarily me."[15]

Two other factors appear to have weighed heavily on the timing of Hoffberger's decision: marketing considerations and the deterioration of the Krieger-Iglehardt relationship. National Brewery had reacquired rights to broadcast Orioles games in 1963. Hoffberger wanted a contending team to increase the impact of his advertising campaign. The Krieger family was out of the brewing business, smoothing the way for an entente between two men who additionally shared a number of civic and charitable interests.[16]

Initially, Hoffberger tried to buy out Krieger. He was frustrated by an existing "buy-sell" contract between Iglehardt and Krieger. Under the terms of this agreement, which ran through the end of 1969, each man had to offer his stock to the other first if he decided to sell out. Krieger rebuffed an offer from Iglehardt to purchase his stock. The three men were deadlocked. Hoffberger announced that his plans were "temporarily deferred."[17]

Defeated on this front, Hoffberger continued to acquire more club stock. By November 1964, Hoffberger's National Brewery owned 29 percent of the stock in the Baltimore Orioles, Inc., the club's holding company. Krieger held 17 percent and Iglehardt owned 32 percent. None of the three men had enough stock to control the club, but Iglehardt's links to Krieger were badly frayed, while Hoffberger was busily courting his former family business rival.[18]

The deadlock continued throughout the 1964 season. Eventually, Iglehardt became frustrated: "I for some time had been unhappy with my associates in the ownership of the Baltimore Orioles. I had been attempting for some time to acquire the stock of one of the other two large stockholders, whose stock, together with the stock I already owned, would have given me control of the club."[19]

"Being unsuccessful," in his bid to take over control of the club, Iglehardt decided to offer his own stock for sale to Krieger. Krieger transferred his option to Hoffberger, who bought out Iglehardt for an estimated $1.5 million. Krieger picked up a small amount of club stock at the same time, increasing his holdings to 18 percent. Three other transactions took place as part of the deal. Minority stockholders Robert Gill (2,000 shares), Phil Iglehardt (1,001 shares), and the estate of Hugh Baker (450 shares) sold out to the Hoffberger-Krieger interests. National Brewery emerged with 65 percent of the voting stock in Baltimore Orioles, Inc.[20]

The club announced the sale on 26 May 1965. The pending realignment of control threatened MacPhail's position. The Orioles president was closely tied to Iglehardt, while Hoffberger was a close friend and former backer of Bill Veeck who was anxious to return to baseball. MacPhail offered his resignation. Hoffberger immediately rejected it, stressing his confidence in the team's president. On 11 June the board of directors dutifully elected Hoffberger chairman. He immediately formed a three-man executive committee with Krieger and MacPhail to run the club. Noting his lack of experience in sports management, Hoffberger reaffirmed his confidence in Mac-Phail, adding "I now begin my education in baseball."[21]

While following MacPhail's lead in baseball matters, Hoffberger speedily established his control over the franchise. The new owner had two main business objectives: to keep the team profitable and to improve its marketing potential. "Not many owners make much money out of baseball . . . but that doesn't mean they shouldn't," an optimistic Hoffberger told an interviewer. He added that the club was well run "on the baseball side" but that "there appeared to be fan promotion aspects that were missing."[22]

Krieger's influence over the club rapidly evaporated. "Poor Zan," Mac-Phail commented: "He was always in the forefront of bringing teams there [Baltimore] and he always somehow ended up getting squeezed out of the main ownership position. He thought he had an agreement with Hoffberger that regardless of what the stock [situation] was, he would have a lot to do with the operations. Just as much as he ever did."[23]

The Rochester Story

In the minor leagues, too, the short era of community baseball was ending. Even with major league subsidization, the number of minor league franchises continued to decline. AAA baseball, which should have been the most financially secure, was particularly hard-pressed. A number of publicly owned teams failed. Rochester proved capable of maintaining a community ownership scheme but only when the team's directors effectively handed over control of the club to a few dedicated men. Ultimately, wealthy, civic-minded businessman Morris Silver put Rochester Community Baseball on firm footing.

Rochester's working agreement with Baltimore was critical to the minor league team's survival. Red Wings baseball's executives and management were delighted with the talent the Orioles supplied, as well as with the cooperative attitude of MacPhail and farm system director Dalton. Baltimore was willing to leave local baseball men with a wide degree of latitude in administering their franchise and to provide direct and indirect assistance that enabled the AAA club to break even financially.[24]

The talent that Baltimore supplied enabled the Red Wings to make the International League playoffs repeatedly and stave off serious financial problems. The Orioles usually refrained from recalling the best of Rochester's athletes until the team finished its playoff competition. Red Wings general manager George Sisler, son of the Browns' Hall of Fame first baseman, estimated that the team's improved play in 1961, particularly an exciting late season playoff drive, was worth an extra $45,000 in a year when Rochester Community Baseball lost $33,127.[25]

At the season's end, the Baltimore club presented Rochester with an even bigger gift, covering its deficit to the enormous pleasure and relief of team president Frank Horton and general manager Sisler. Red Wings officials signed a renewal of their working agreement with Baltimore and listened as MacPhail extolled the franchise to the press as "the best."[26] Attempting to build a long-term relationship, MacPhail invited Sisler to the Orioles' winter instruction league so that the Rochester general manager would become familiar with the best talent in the Baltimore minor league system.[27]

In spite of the Orioles' support, community baseball faced serious problems in Rochester. The team operated under an extremely strict budget limitation. A few rained out games could be the difference between breaking even or losing money. The team had very limited broadcasting income and at times was unable to sell out all its radio advertising time. Sisler was so concerned about team finances that he worried about lost baseballs.[28]

Rochester's problems were typical of minor league baseball. At the end of the 1961 season, the Yankees announced they were dropping out of one A team affiliation after its losses mounted from $10,000 to $100,000 annually.

Even minor league officials gasped at the size of the financial bath New York had taken.[29]

Weak finances made the International League, and indeed all three AAA leagues, very unstable. The International League had a hard time finding cities that were large enough and wealthy enough to host its teams. Its Havana franchise moved when the Cuban Revolution created a climate that was distinctly unfavorable to capitalism. Montreal's team folded, and the IL awarded the franchise to Syracuse. Jersey City moved. The league set up a team in San Juan, Puerto Rico, only to have it fail in its first season. When looking for a suitable city in which to relocate the San Juan team, the IL found itself debating sites in Charleston, West Virginia, and Montreal—both cities that had recently dropped out of the league.[30]

In order to solve these problems, International League owners implemented economy measures. At the end of the 1961 season they cut their rosters from twenty-one to twenty players and reduced the number of playing days (although not the number of games) by eliminating the players' off-days. Syracuse worked out a highly unusual arrangement with two of the major league expansion teams, Washington and New York, fielding a squad comprised of the limited number of AAA prospects both teams possessed. Rochester kept its overhead low by maintaining an extremely small front office. Red Wings general manager Sisler also acted as business manager, park supervisor, public relations specialist, concessions manager, and stadium director.[31]

Recognizing that they needed to cooperate to assure their mutual survival, the teams of the International League set up a watchdog financial committee in July 1962 to oversee league and individual club expenses. They approved new rules for the division of ticket receipts, designed to encourage each club to improve its promotions. Further impetus for careful management came at the end of the 1962 season when the American Association, one of the three AAA leagues, folded.[32]

Major league affiliation had become essential to the survival of any minor league team. The major league–minor league player development program of May 1962 was a boon to the International League. The agreement had two aspects: a minor league stabilization program and a financial subsidization plan. The stabilization program reorganized the minor leagues, further reducing their number. The two AAA leagues remained. The class AA and A leagues merged into a new class AA, while the Class B, C, and D leagues were consolidated into A leagues. A few major league teams also purchased individual Class D clubs for the purpose of providing basic training to players just entering professional baseball. These clubs were the basis of so-called rookie leagues that played abbreviated schedules. Baltimore purchased the team in Bluefield, West Virginia, as its rookie league entry. Overall, the major leagues guaranteed financial support to one hundred minor league teams. An agreement between the minor and major leagues determined the level of subsidization the big leagues provided to their farm clubs. Each major league club agreed to cover the salaries of its farm system players above a certain minimum level. The major league club also covered the costs of spring training for its affiliates and paid the salaries of minor league managers. All of the major league clubs except the four new expansion franchises committed themselves to support a minimum of five minor league teams.[33]

The "player development contract" replaced the centralized player development fund at the end of the 1962 season. Thereafter, the minor leagues lobbied to increase the size of major league subsidization by having the big leagues lower the level at which automatic support payments took effect. The process was slow but relentless. Eventually, a three-way division of the costs of minor league baseball emerged. The major leagues covered most salaries for players and coaches together with the costs of spring training. The host cities generally assumed most of the costs of stadium maintenance and set modest rental fees. The owners of the minor league franchises paid for uniforms, the players' base salaries, transportation, and equipment and hoped to make enough of a profit to continue their association with organized baseball. Sisler estimated that the player development contract provided the Red Wings with an additional $30,000 in annual income.[34]

Meanwhile, baseball's talent pool continued to contract as a result of competition from other sports for athletic talent and as a result of the bonus system. Young men were increasingly unwilling to sign baseball contracts without receiving a cash bonus. Consequently, minor league clubs had to rely on the major leagues to recruit talent.[35]

George Sisler remarked in 1962 that the price of major league subsidization was a further surrender of Rochester's already limited autonomy. The Red Wings retained a good deal of latitude in matters relating to marketing but surrendered control over both player acquisition and the selection of a manager and coaches. In November 1961 the Orioles traded away the Red Wings' best catcher to acquire a major league player. Rochester had to wait annually until Baltimore had set its major league roster at the end of spring training before putting together its squad. Still, the wait was worthwhile since the Orioles farms were brimming with talent. Better players enabled the Red Wings to post a second good season in 1962 and to end the year in the best financial situation since Rochester Community Baseball came into being in 1957.[36]

On the issue of selection of managers and coaches, the Red Wings surrendered to Orioles desires after making a brave last show of independence. At the end of the 1962 season, manager Clyde King resigned. Sisler announced that the Red Wings would have the final say on their next manager, even if this meant that the club had to pay his salary. He virtually ruled out hiring the new manager from Baltimore's minor league system. Two weeks later, the

Red Wings and Orioles jointly announced that Rochester's new manager would be Darrell Johnson, a MacPhail protégé and Baltimore's most highly regarded minor league manager. Sisler endorsed the "Orioles' choice."[37]

The trend toward Orioles control of personnel matters continued throughout the 1960s. The nature of the squads Rochester fielded changed. The team used fewer veteran players and just prior to the 1965 season released the last former major league player it had directly under contract. Increasingly, the veterans playing for Rochester were slumping or ailing Orioles whom the team sent to the minor leagues to work themselves back into physical or mental shape. This policy angered many Rochester fans, who felt, with reason, that it hurt their team's pennant chances.[38]

In spite of the continuing loss of independence that a major league association brought, Rochester's management remained pleased with its pact with the Orioles. In October 1962 Rochester president Morris Silver outlined the reasons for the Red Wings' pleasure. First, the Orioles were ready to cover Rochester's financial losses. Second, in spite of a poor year, the Baltimore club continued to limit its raids on the Red Wings' roster during the season. "There's no disagreement anywhere," Silver affirmed, adding, "The Orioles have been 100 percent honorable with us. They have lived up to the letter and spirit of our agreement."[39]

The player pipeline continued to function satisfactorily for both organizations. In 1963, Rochester fielded a contending team that included five top prospects. The following year, three of the Orioles' six minor league teams took first place. Rochester could look forward to receiving further quality reinforcements. The Red Wings won the International League playoffs for the first time since 1956 with the players Baltimore provided. Victory in the playoffs meant a larger financial gain for the hard-pressed Red Wings.[40]

Rochester's success owed much to its leadership. From 1958 to 1962, the triumvirate of Morris Silver, Frank Horton, and George Sisler kept community baseball afloat in the face of extremely difficult conditions. The club's costs continued to rise. The citizens and corporations of Rochester could not cover continuing major financial losses. Horton, and later Silver, served without pay. Silver and Horton had played leading roles in creating the Rochester Community Baseball operation. Silver retired after serving briefly as club president. Horton, who succeeded him and served as club president from 1957 to 1962, was a lawyer and local politician with larger ambitions. He proved to be a quick study in baseball matters and played a useful role in the talks that finally produced a major league–minor league player development agreement. Sisler provided Rochester with skilled management. He acquired the players, negotiated the working agreements with the Cardinals and later the Orioles, hired the club's few other management personnel, and dealt with the myriad details needed to keep minor league baseball operating on a daily basis. Sisler spent most of his free time meeting with local groups in the Rochester area in an effort to boost attendance. The club's marketing efforts continued throughout the calendar year, with Sisler carrying an enormous share of the burden.[41]

In 1962 Horton resigned to seek election, successfully, to Congress. The club's board of directors asked Morris Silver to take over as president. Silver, a successful salesman with a great sense of civic pride, was Rochester Community Baseball's largest individual stockholder. Horton had regularly consulted with Silver during his term as president and credited him with a major if unofficial role in the club's decision making. Silver returned to the helm only at the board's insistence and with the intention of serving out the remnant of Horton's term.[42]

The board's decision to recall Silver in 1962 testified to the severity of the crisis that the International League faced. Following the collapse of the American Association, the IL assumed two of its franchises, becoming a ten-team circuit. The extra expenses involved in managing a ten-team league, particularly large transportation costs, were a severe strain; and in December 1963 the International League formally requested an extra subvention from the major leagues to cover its enlarged travel expenses. When the major leagues declined to provide the money, the International League, at Silver's insistence, returned to an eight-team format. The two excluded franchises then joined the Pacific Coast League to create a costly geographic monstrosity: a twelve-team minor league that stretched from Little Rock, Arkansas, to Honolulu, Hawaii.[43]

The IL's decision to return to an eight-team format angered major league owners. With expansion, the major leagues required a minimum of twenty AAA teams to service their twenty franchises. They had insisted on the 1962 expansion of both the PCL and IL to ten-team circuits so as to meet this need. However, the major leagues were unwilling to pay the extra costs of the expanded minor leagues. The International League's president, Tommy Richardson, was incapable of leading a strong opposition to the major leagues and their spokesman, Commissioner Frick. The IL owners recognized that the league needed a strong spokesman and elected Silver league vice president. Silver met with Frick to present the IL case. The talks, which Silver characterized as "unpleasant to say the very least," led nowhere. Frick accused the International League of "blocking progress" by reverting to eight teams. Silver responded that the IL could not have completed the 1964 season with ten teams and refused to reinstate the two dropped franchises. In the end, the major leagues accepted the International League stand but retaliated by offering the twelve-team PCL the extra financial assistance they had previously declined to provide the IL.[44]

By the winter of 1965 both Rochester and the International League again needed Silver's leadership. The player development contracts had helped to stabilize the size of the minor leagues, but the individual clubs, particularly in the more costly higher minors, continued to operate in extremely strained financial circumstances. Attendance at minor league games remained very low. From a postwar high of 42 million in 1949, minor league attendance fell to 9.9 million in 1963. Minor league owners continued to feel that the major leagues simultaneously ignored and exploited them. The higher minors actively sought more financial assistance. IL president Richardson summed up their frustrations. On the eve of December 1964 major league discussions of the minors' woes, he complained: "If an outfit owned fifty-nine gas stations and lost only five of them, something would be done in a hurry. But these people—they've lost baseball in 320 cities, so suddenly now they're going to talk about it."[45]

By December 1965 the higher minors were again on the verge of collapse. A number of community baseball operations had folded. The leagues either sold the franchises to local limited partnerships or to owners who moved the teams. Fan interest remained tepid. The AAA teams appeared to be little more than development grounds for major league clubs that regularly recalled the best minor league players in the midst of pennant races. As a result, the AAA leagues lost much of their local identification. *The Sporting News* urged expanding major league assistance to offset these problems.[46]

International League owners decided that they had to present a more united front to the major leagues. They pushed the ineffective Richardson out of his job and elected George Sisler to replace him. Rochester, in turn, needed an experienced executive to run its baseball operation and recalled Silver from his second brief retirement, investing him with "full authority" to run the Red Wings. Acting as both president and general manager, Silver quickly put his personal stamp on the Red Wings. He secured the Orioles' consent to oust incumbent manager Darrell Johnson and hire the best available manager in the Orioles' minor league system, thirty-six-year-old Earl Weaver. Weaver was enormously successful as manager, leading the Red Wings to championships in 1966 and 1967. The club's finances improved greatly as attendance rose and Silver kept a tight lid on administrative costs. In 1966 the champion Red Wings made a profit of $161,472. "I'm astounded," New York Mets general manager Bing Devine told reporters after hearing about Rochester's profit.[47]

A heart attack in December 1965 briefly sidelined Silver and forced him to place a greater administrative burden on a series of young general managers. Nevertheless, he firmly controlled the club's operations for the next eight years. Silver devoted the rest of his life to the Red Wings, providing Rochester with one of the most successful eras of minor league baseball it has ever enjoyed. "He was almost like a general manager-owner. He had a hand in everything," Horton recalled, adding, "That was his life."[48]

At the same time, Sisler was quietly and effectively dealing with the financial issues that made major league–minor league relations so tenuous, gradually securing increased support payments from the big leagues for AAA baseball. The long-hoped-for stabilization of the minor leagues began to take effect in the late 1960s. Individuals or limited partnerships took over owner- ship of minor league clubs. The era of community baseball was a brief and only partially successful experiment, but Rochester's experience indicated that with aid from the major leagues, competent men could make minor league community baseball work.

Mr. Hoffberger's Team

Management issues also dominated the first months of the Hoffberger re- gime, as corporate ownership replaced community baseball on the major league level. Jerold Hoffberger took control of an Orioles organization that was once again facing financial difficulties. The 1964 club turned in a profit of $301,092 after its exciting battle to the wire for the American League championship. The 1965 Orioles slumped badly at the gate as Minnesota ran off with the American League championship and the Yankees collapsed. Nevertheless the club retained a number of important assets. MacPhail's building efforts continued to yield significant benefits on the playing field. The team had a good stadium contract, profitable concessions and television contracts, and the lowest seating prices in the American League. Its farm system was laden with talent. The price of team stock continued to rise.[49]

Hoffberger attempted to capitalize on these assets with innovative man- agement techniques. The new owner was forty-five years old. An active civic leader and ardent supporter of Israel, he was highly protective of his personal and business privacy, living quietly in the Baltimore suburb of Riderwood and generally avoiding publicity and interviewers. A liberal on social issues, Hoffberger was also a hard-headed businessman who had taken over the family business, National Brewery, in 1946 and turned it into Baltimore's dominant regional brewery. In 1946 National was a strictly local operation, selling 230,000 barrels a year and rated as the 150th largest brewery in the nation. By 1965 National was the eighteenth largest brewery in the United States with annual sales of nearly 2 million barrels of beer. The company had plants in Baltimore, Detroit, and Miami and employed 900 people. Hoff- berger tried to run his businesses as semiautonomous and mutually support- ing profit-makers. He was determined to turn the Orioles into a consistently profitable venture.

As a manager, Hoffberger preferred to delegate authority to men he trusted. Harry Dalton characterized his style as "hands-off" management, explaining:

When Jerry gave me the job . . . he said "I've only got one piece of advice for you: as long as you make more right decisions than wrong ones, you'll never have any trouble." He was a hands-off operator. I mean he'd be interested. I'd do something . . . and he might say to me a week or month later, "I don't understand why you made that move." But that was just a personal comment by Jerry who knew that you understood that and you weren't supposed to get panicked . . . because the boss didn't agree. Jerry . . . gave you support. When you did something he didn't like, he'd tell you. Then it was over and you went on from there.[50]

While Hoffberger had no previous experience with baseball management, he had a close friend with considerable knowledge and a great desire to impart it: Bill Veeck. Throughout the early 1960s Veeck lived on Maryland's Eastern Shore while recovering from a series of operations that seriously impaired his health. During this period he and Hoffberger had frequent conversations, which appear to have influenced the new owner's views considerably.[51]

Veeck was a constant critic of baseball's public relations and marketing efforts. He attacked organized baseball's indifference to racial issues and unwillingness to experiment with changes in the game's structure. In a 1964 *Esquire* article on the "Baseball Establishment," Veeck surveyed the Orioles management with a jaundiced eye. Veeck felt that MacPhail was a competent general manager and Bauer a good major league manager, but he labeled board chairman Iglehardt a nonentity. Overall, he appraised the Baltimore operation as "dullsville."[52] Veeck had consistently stressed the need for combining good baseball with superior marketing in order to turn a club into a profit-maker. In his 1962 autobiography, Veeck laid out a philosophy that was very much in accord with Hoffberger's outlook: "A baseball team is a commercial venture operating for a profit. The idea that you don't have to package your product as attractively as General Motors packages its product, and hustle your product the way General Motors hustles its product, is baseball's most pernicious enemy."[53] Some years later, Veeck told an interviewer: "I've never suggested that promotions do much if you are not winning. . . . What I do say is promotions plus a winning team will break attendance [records]."[54]

Hoffberger clearly listened to Veeck's views on marketing. He admitted his debt both verbally and by his actions. The Orioles were a team with a winning record and low attendance. Hoffberger moved to take advantage of the winning record to increase the club's income and not incidentally to help boost National's beer sales. In October 1965, after consultations with Mac-Phail, he announced that J. Frank Cashen, his longtime assistant at National Brewery, would join the Orioles as executive vice president to run the team's marketing activities. Hoffberger explained that while MacPhail was a solid baseball executive, he needed experience in public relations. Cashen understood marketing. Hoffberger also hoped that Cashen would learn about baseball management from MacPhail and Dalton.[55] Dalton defined Cashen as "Jerry's man," a trusted aide whom Hoffberger would tap whenever he needed assistance. As Dalton explained Hoffberger's motives: "Now he's going to buy this major league ball club, so he said, 'I want my man in there just seeing everything and knowing what's going on.' So he sent him out to head up the administration."[56]

Cashen was a former sports reporter who had also managed a racetrack for Hoffberger. He was accustomed to the Hoffberger style: "Jerry's phone worked twenty-four hours a day. There'd be meetings Saturday morning at 7:30 and Sunday nights and sometimes holidays. When Jerry wanted something done because he wasn't happy, he'd just have a meeting. Many times early mornings at his place. Frank fit that style."[57]

At the same time that Hoffberger moved Cashen over to the Orioles, he promoted Jack Dunn, the club's administrative jack-of-all-trades, as a reward for his loyal and solid service. The Orioles' new management team was beginning to take shape. The competent MacPhail would concentrate on building a winner. Cashen would build fan support and also give Hoffberger a trusted man within a group of managers with whom the owner had only limited experience.[58] Hoffberger had the men he wanted, but he had achieved this at the price of somewhat reducing MacPhail's authority. MacPhail accepted the new owner's decision with his customary grace, but the changes in ownership and management encouraged his departure. As a result, Hoffberger's initial reorganization was a prelude to a far-reaching restructuring of the Orioles two months later.

Meanwhile, the Orioles had completed the 1965 season with an excellent overall record of 94–68 but a disappointing third-place finish, eight games behind the champion Minnesota Twins. The team had enjoyed good pitching but weak hitting. Boog Powell, in particular, had an off year, while 1964 phenomenon Sam Bowens slumped badly. Regulars John Orsino, Norm Siebern, and Jackie Brandt had subpar seasons. Manager Bauer benched all three. Once again the lack of consistent power hitting undercut the Orioles' pennant chances. Attendance dropped drastically to 781,649, a loss of nearly 350,000 paid admissions and the second worst figures in the club's history. MacPhail again looked to trades to improve the club's offense. This time, however, the Baltimore president and general manager was ready to deal one or more of his best players to acquire a home run–hitting star. The precipitate drop in attendance meant that the Orioles could no longer wait on their own farm system to produce the catalyst needed to turn a good team into a pennant winner.

A New Lineup

Recalling the events of the fall of 1965, Lee MacPhail explained his decision to leave Baltimore: "Jerry asked me not to leave [but] I sort of got myself involved. . . . I . . . got myself in a position where it was pretty hard to say no. The second thing was that I've always felt that when someone buys something they ought to have complete ability . . . of putting their own people in . . . and . . . in as much as I had someplace to go, it was only fair that he had a right to put his own people in."[59]

MacPhail had become "involved" and had "someplace to go" because the owners made a major blunder in choosing a replacement for retiring commissioner Ford Frick. Baseball's problems called for a strong man with wide powers of intervention. Both leagues were facing politically embarrassing demands from unhappy owners in Milwaukee and Kansas City who wanted to move their franchises because of declining attendance. Other outstanding problems included the continuing general decline in major league attendance, the noncompetitive nature of the expansion teams, and numerous irritants in major league–minor league relations.

A year before his retirement, Frick bluntly told the owners that his successor needed expanded powers to deal with baseball's complex problems. The owners disregarded Frick's advice. Buzzy Bavasi, the Dodgers' general manager, suggested that organized baseball simply drop the commissioner's post. While few owners agreed with such a drastic idea, their search committee clearly ruled out strong personalities. *Sports Illustrated* complained that the owners were consciously searching "for someone of stature whom they can boss."[60]

Under the circumstances, few competent individuals wanted the job. As the list of candidates dwindled, MacPhail's name emerged in the speculation. The Orioles president, who understood what the job entailed, politely but firmly discouraged interest in his candidacy. His active and public opposition to further franchise shifts ruled out support from owners like Kansas City's Charles Finley. In any case, the owners were fixated on hiring a nonbaseball man. Hoffberger believed that the sport badly needed to bring in an expert who could improve its image and deal with complex issues like a national television contract and franchise shifts.[61]

Recognizing that a commissioner hired from outside organized baseball would need assistance from experienced executives, the owners approved a plan to provide him with special aides. They then elected a man who surely would require a lot of assistance. Retired air force general William D. Eckert was a pleasant nonentity who lacked the ability to handle the position the owners thrust upon him together with a seven-year contract and a $65,000 a year salary. The press quickly dubbed the bumbling Eckert baseball's "Unknown Soldier." He became a growing embarrassment to the owners who hired him.[62]

The owners' search committee maneuvered MacPhail into the unhappy job of trying to assist Eckert. In November, MacPhail announced he was resigning as Orioles president.[63] MacPhail's departure threw Hoffberger's reorganization into chaos. The new owner, with less than six months of experience, had to select a veteran baseball executive to run his team. The choice was made more difficult by the fact that two highly qualified candidates already existed within the Baltimore organization: farm system director Dalton and the reliable, versatile Dunn. In addition, Hoffberger's ties to Veeck raised speculation that the former Browns owner might return to baseball with the Orioles. A long delay in making a choice might build factions and ill will within the organization, but too quick a decision by the inexperienced Hoffberger could create serious problems for the franchise.[64]

Hoffberger moved slowly, talking with both Dunn and Dalton while insisting that MacPhail remain in charge of the team until the conclusion of baseball's winter meetings in December. After the meetings, Hoffberger announced his decision: a general reorganization. He left the president's job open, retained Cashen as his executive vice president and "decision maker," and promoted Dalton and Dunn to vice president for player personnel and vice president for administration respectively. Hoffberger abolished the position of general manager. The advantage of the reorganization, the *Sun*'s Bob Maisel commented, was that it kept everyone happy. The question was whether a baseball franchise could operate with this sort of delegation of authority. The specter of administrative confusion characteristic of the Richards era again loomed in Baltimore. This time, however, two nonbaseball men, Hoffberger and Cashen, would be in charge instead of the combative but experienced Richards and McLaughlin.[65]

In the late afternoon of 14 December 1965, the Orioles front office personnel uncorked champagne bottles to toast their outgoing president. Dalton led the toasting. He was honoring more than the end of one man's career with the Orioles. MacPhail's departure snapped one of the last ties to the community baseball era in Baltimore. It also opened the club's championship years. Just before leaving, MacPhail presented the club with the impact player it needed to capture four pennants over the next six years. In a complex series of player trades that began on 2 December, MacPhail unloaded a number of players who had failed to contribute and picked up the surplus of athletes needed to acquire the power-hitting outfielder the club had long craved. On 9 December the Orioles announced that they had acquired Frank Robinson in exchange for Milt Pappas and two other players. Ten months later, Robinson was the American League MVP, winner of baseball's triple crown, and undisputed leader of baseball's champion Orioles.

2 The Hoffberger Years

Up and Down
the Greasy Poll

I find it a distasteful piece of irony that I must make this plea in light of the fact that without Frank Robinson, a person who would be excluded by such businesses, we would probably have no World Series.
—Mayor Theodore McKeldin, urging tavern owners to serve blacks, October 1966

We were astonished at Weaver's attitude. . . . We're not used to managers who just show up . . . take what's available and go to work.
—Frank Lane, October 1968

Benjamin Disraeli, nineteenth-century prime minister of Britain, once defined achieving success in politics as climbing to the top of a greasy poll. The analogy is pertinent for professional sports in general and baseball in particular. Winning a World Series is difficult enough, but maintaining that level of play is even more taxing. Harry Dalton, who built champions in Baltimore and Milwaukee, recalled:

> Success . . . especially in baseball is almost self-defeating because you get to the World Series . . . and especially if you win it, for the next four months you're larger than life. . . . You take normal young American men who are competitive and combative and reasonably intelligent and you pluck them out of an almost normal sports environment . . . and they think they're gods. By the time they come to spring training in March, they really think they are larger than life. Winning . . . doesn't seem quite as important and isn't much of an incentive. . . . It's just not the same.[1]

The 1966 Orioles climbed to baseball's heights. The 1967 Orioles, essentially the same team, fell quickly into the second division. Rebuilding a contender required changes in both personnel and management, the recovery of individual and team motivation, and the return of a number of key players from serious injury.

Limping Away with It

The 1966–71 Orioles were Harry Dalton's teams. Tall and slender, the youthful, personable, and easily accessible Dalton was very popular with the sports press. An affable man, who by his own admission disliked salary negotiations with his players, he was, nevertheless, a tough labor negotiator. His career paralleled that of his amiable predecessor, Lee MacPhail. Neither man had been a professional baseball player. Both headed up successful player development programs before taking control of the Orioles. Each replaced a successful field manager with a man more in line with his outlook and style. MacPhail needed two tries to find the right man. Dalton, profiting from a decade-long familiarity with the management personnel in the Orioles' minor league system, was able to select the right man on the first try. Finally, first MacPhail and then Dalton made critical player trades that carried Baltimore to a pennant. MacPhail acquired the star outfielder needed to bring a first pennant to Baltimore. Dalton's efforts to build a pennant winner centered around finding pitching.

The trade that brought Frank Robinson to Baltimore left a gaping hole in the Orioles pitching staff. Milt Pappas, who had been the mainstay of the rotation for six years, went to Cincinnati for Robinson, as did reliever Jack Baldschun. A number of young pitchers would get a shot at their slots, but Orioles management was taking no chances. It drafted veteran relief pitcher Moe Drabowski during the off-season. In June, the Orioles traded for another veteran reliever, Eddie Fisher. The team would rely on power hitting and a good bullpen to bolster its youthful and often erratic or injured starting pitching.

Sports Illustrated, in an April preview of the 1966 season, pronounced the revamped Orioles the favorite in the American League pennant race in spite of questionable pitching and a rookie starting catcher. Manager Hank Bauer happily noted that the team had unloaded six players who had slumped during the 1965 season. Harry Dalton admitted that the team had a lot of "question marks" but added that it had "cannons at the four corners," in first baseman Powell, third baseman Brooks Robinson, right fielder Frank Robinson, and left fielder Curt Blefary. If some of the talented younger players contributed, Baltimore would be a serious contender.[2]

A bigger issue than where the 1966 Orioles would finish, *Sports Illustrated* contended, was whether Baltimore was a major league town. Local support had rarely been vigorous. Hoffberger's management team had embarked on a major marketing campaign to stimulate attendance. The 1966 Orioles would be contenders; their local support was another matter.[3]

The local press responded defensively to charges that Baltimore was giving the team insufficient support. Even the city's defenders admitted, however, that Baltimore, with its shrinking population, would be hard-pressed to increase its support beyond certain levels. The Orioles would have to attract a larger part of their attendance from suburban Maryland. In the general reorganization of the team front office that followed Dalton's promotion, Cashen had created a fan relations department, designed to respond speedily to complaints, suggestions, and requests for information. The team increased the number of promotional nights at the stadium.[4]

In 1966, these efforts bore fruit, with the considerable assistance of a superb baseball club. The pennant race was over quickly. Orioles' power hitting ignited the team's early surge into first place. Brooks and Frank Robinson pounded opposing pitching as Baltimore won twelve of its first thirteen games. A number of the younger players also contributed—in particular, catcher Andy Etchebarren, pitchers Jim Palmer and Wally Bunker, and second baseman Davey Johnson, who took over for the veteran Jerry Adair, providing solid defense and key hits.

At mid-season the Orioles were leading the American League in just about every offensive category. Four of six players in the league hitting above .300 were Orioles. The league's three RBI leaders played for Baltimore. Three Orioles led in runs scored, and three of the four leaders in total hits played for Baltimore. While the young starters were often erratic, a strong bullpen was winning games for the Orioles. Finally, team defense, especially infield play, was remarkable.

The 1966 Orioles had built such a lead by mid-August that none of their rivals could catch them even though they hit a slump in the second half of the season and played only .500 baseball. Injuries, especially to the young pitchers, slowed the club. A number of hot hitters cooled off. In late August, Dalton commented that his team was "limping away with it," with the timely aid of players recalled from the minor leagues.[5]

In late September the Orioles limped into the American League championship, nine games ahead of Detroit and solid underdogs to the still-undecided National League winner in the World Series. The series, *Sports Illustrated* opined, would pit the "inconsistent Orioles" against the "snarling survivor" of a hard-fought National League pennant race.[6] Pessimism over the Orioles' chances only increased when the defending champion Los Angeles Dodgers won the National League race. The Dodgers pitching staff was anchored by two of baseball's best, Sandy Koufax and Don Drysdale. The speedy Dodgers were expected to run wild on the bases against the Baltimore pitching staff. *New York Times* sportswriter Arthur Daley expressed a widely held view when he predicted that Los Angeles would sweep the Orioles in four games.[7]

Orioles players and management were pleased to be getting a chance to play Los Angeles, one of baseball's major markets, since that would mean the series would be the most profitable possible. In an effort to build fan loyalty, the club endeavored to see that season ticket holders got as many seats as they wanted. It also made an unusually large block of reserved seats available on a single-seat basis to attract more individual fans.[8]

The series was over in four games. But, "against all odds and all expectations," the Orioles had swept the Dodgers.[9] The turning point in the series came early in the first game. Home runs by the two Robinsons gave the Orioles a three-run lead after the first inning. The score was 4–1 in the third when Dave McNally walked the bases full of Dodgers. Moe Drabowski came out of the Baltimore bullpen to snuff out the Dodgers' rally. Drabowski gave up another run in the next inning, but he escaped further damage and shut out Los Angeles for the rest of the game. Jim Palmer, watching from the sidelines, decided that he could beat the Dodgers with a steady diet of fastballs.[10]

The next day Palmer threw a four-hit shutout against Los Angeles, beating the great Koufax with the aid of some terrible Dodgers fielding. The series then moved to Baltimore, where Wally Bunker matched Palmer's performance with a six-hit shutout. McNally compensated for his bad outing in the initial game by pitching still another shutout, a four-hitter, in the fourth contest. Appropriately, the only Orioles run came on a fourth-inning Frank Robinson home run. Brooks Robinson snuffed out a Dodgers rally in the fifth with a great defensive play, and approximately an hour later the 1966 World Series ended.

Victory was worth $11,683 for each Orioles player. Bauer had already received his reward, a two-year contract renewal that Hoffberger apparently decided upon in the enthusiasm of the Orioles' first American League pennant and announced at a "hastily arranged" press conference on 30 September.[11] He also rewarded the club's financial mastermind, comptroller Joe Hamper, with promotion to vice president. The baseball press showered Baltimore players and executives with awards. MacPhail appropriately won *The Sporting News*'s major league executive of the year award. Bauer was manager of the year. Frank Robinson was the series and American League MVP. Dreams of a baseball dynasty on the shores of the Chesapeake Bay filled the minds of Baltimore fans and management alike. They were a welcome relief from some of the harsher realities of life in Maryland in the mid-1960s.

A "Grade A" Negro

As his players celebrated clinching Baltimore's first American League pennant, a champagne-soaked and exhilarated Jerry Hoffberger called Cincinnati's Bill De Witt from the clubhouse party to thank him for trading Frank Robinson. Robinson's arrival had boosted the Baltimore franchise months before he stepped onto the playing field. Ticket sales rose as soon as the team announced the trade. WJZ, the station that held the Orioles' television rights, suddenly found that selling advertising time was easy. As *The Sporting News* inelegantly noted, Robinson was the first "grade A Negro" to play for the Orioles, a man who could attract both black and white fans, simultaneously improving the club's play and its record on racial matters, which had remained clouded in spite of MacPhail's efforts.[12]

The Orioles' racial problems were an accurate reflection of baseball's situation. By the mid-1960s organized baseball was habituated to congratulating itself on past achievements while ignoring continuing problems of discrimination. *The Sporting News*, reflecting management's views, complimented Ford Frick for "superb" congressional testimony in support of civil rights legislation and claimed that professional sports had shown the nation how to carry off integration.[13] The reality was more complex. Baseball was integrated on the playing field and at its spring training sites. Even here, however, disturbing patterns of discrimination remained. Moreover, blacks made only the most limited progress into the ranks of baseball management and professional umpiring and faced persistent discrimination in the areas of housing and public accommodations.

Discrimination in both subtle and blatant forms remained an integral part of baseball in the 1960s. At the entry level, a vast majority of bonus money went to white amateur players. Blacks continued to face strong and open racism in the minor leagues, leading one study of the minors to comment: "Listen to the stories the Gibsons, the Robinsons, the Stargells relate and you can't help wondering if baseball organizations were insensitive to the problems of blacks . . . or actually determined to make life as difficult for them as possible."[14] Racial incidents were largely ignored by minor league management, and black players recognized that their continued advancement depended on accepting these slights in silence.[15]

Blacks escaped from the most overt forms of racism if they won promotion to the major leagues. However, they continued to face a number of discriminatory barriers both inside and outside their working environment. Black athletes were frequent victims of racial stereotyping by the press. By the mid-1960s two other subtle patterns of discrimination had appeared. "Stacking" was the practice of employing blacks only at certain positions, particularly in the outfield and at first base. Stacking reduced the total number of blacks playing in the major leagues. A 1967 study concluded that blacks had to outperform white players consistently in order to win spots on major league teams. The blacks who played in the major leagues tended to be star players. Whites generally monopolized utility roles on baseball teams.[16]

Another area of continued discrimination against blacks was housing. Black baseball players earned higher salaries than many other members of their race, but they faced the same problems in trying to find decent housing in a nation where residential segregation remained widespread.

Racial barriers placed strict limits on the length of black careers in professional sports. White players who wanted to remain in baseball after their retirement had the option of signing on as scouts, coaches, or minor league managers or of joining front office operations. After twenty years of baseball's "great experiment," these options effectively remained closed to blacks. In 1962 the Chicago Cubs signed baseball's first black coach. Chicago's action failed to set off a stampede by other clubs. In 1966 the American League hired the first black umpire, Emmett Ashford. That same year CBS television hired the first black sports announcer for its football games. The proportion of blacks broadcasting football has since risen, but few blacks are employed in this or any other nonplaying capacity by major league baseball teams. As late as 1982, a survey of twenty-four baseball clubs reported that blacks filled only 32 of 913 available white-collar management jobs. Only 15 blacks were included among baseball's 568 full-time major league scouts.[17]

During the mid-1960s, baseball's reluctance to hire a black field manager became the focus of public criticism. The issue was highly charged because it involved placing white athletes under the control of a black man and inviting a black into baseball's decision-making process. By 1970 even the conservative *Sporting News* was critical of the major leagues' failure to hire a qualified black manager.[18]

Orioles management rarely took advanced positions on racial matters prior to Frank Robinson's arrival. As late as 1973, Baltimore was among the least integrated teams in the major leagues. MacPhail recognized that the American League had to develop its own black stars in order to remain competitive on the playing field and at the box office. He made serious efforts to recruit top black athletes, but the process was slow. The National League had an inside track on signing the best black talent.[19]

MacPhail's honesty and his occasional forays into the black community helped to defuse some criticism aimed at his club. However, by the mid-1960s black patience with the club was wearing thin. The Orioles had few black employees on the field and none in management. In 1965 the club had 16 black players in its approximately 150-man minor league system. In the same year it hired a lone black scout. Critics charged that the lack of quality black players decreased the Orioles' chances of winning a pennant and limited their ability to build a strong fan base.[20]

Frank Robinson was aware of the racial problems in Baltimore but was very anxious to play for a team that was a contender and that wanted his skills. His relationship with Cincinnati Reds owner De Witt had become increasingly antagonistic, and Robinson suspected that the owner's hostility included a racial animus.[21]

The Orioles' new outfielder was at that time no civil rights militant. Asked by the NAACP to join its efforts, Robinson replied that he would join only on the condition that he would not have to make public appearances or take any other action in support of "their cause" as long as "I was in baseball."[22]

Although not actively involved in the civil rights movement, Robinson became a prime symbol of the demands of black athletes during his career in Baltimore. His search for suitable housing for his family during the 1966 and 1967 seasons and a postseason controversy over the desegregation of city taverns underlined the continuing existence of discrimination in Maryland's largest city. In the later part of the 1960s, Robinson emerged as one of the prime contenders to become baseball's first black manager.

At his first meeting with the Baltimore press in January 1966, Robinson announced that he would bring his family to the city during the 1966 season. The Orioles found housing, but, as Robinson recounted, "When my wife saw it she was appalled. It was dirty and rundown and she felt it was unfit for the kids." Robinson moved to a hotel until he could find a satisfactory house in a black neighborhood in Baltimore.[23]

Robinson's housing problems gave Jerold Hoffberger and his new management team an opportunity to assist the cause of racial equality. They hardly distinguished themselves. In fairness, Hoffberger had shown sensitivity to racial issues. In 1963 he hired former Colt star and front office executive Buddy Young as National Brewery's contact with black athletes. Hoffberger got along well with his black players, including Robinson, who found his new boss's friendly and unassuming ways a refreshing change from the behavior of De Witt.[24] Moreover, the team's ability to change patterns of racial discrimination was strictly limited in the area of open housing. Segregated housing was at the center of the battle for equality in Maryland in the mid-1960s.

Change loomed for the city of Baltimore in the spring of 1966. After nearly a decade of slow progress in desegregation, the city's black community was demanding faster progress. The civil rights movement was flush with a string of successes in the South and anxious to break down barriers of discrimination in the cities of the North. In the spring of 1966 the Congress of Racial Equality (CORE) announced that Baltimore would be one of its "target cities."[25]

The moderate white establishment that had patiently guided Maryland's slow-paced desegregation during the 1950s and early 1960s was rapidly losing control of the state's politics. In 1963 moderates had steered an antidiscrimination bill through the state General Assembly designed to open public accommodations to blacks. The bill was loaded with exemptions, including provisions that it would not apply to twelve counties, primarily on the conservative Eastern Shore, and exempting taverns. Violence against black civil rights workers on the Eastern Shore that summer gave the impetus to passage of a more comprehensive bill the following year.

The 1964 bill consolidated white resistance. A referendum to overturn the new antidiscrimination law barely failed to win passage in the fall elections. Alabama's segregationist governor, George Wallace, campaigned actively in Maryland's summer presidential primary, stirring racial tensions. White moderates leading the state, headed by Governor J. Millard Tawes and Baltimore mayor Theodore McKeldin, were in a race against time, trying to speed up the pace of change while avoiding a violent white backlash.

Baltimore was one of the centers of growing black anger and white resistance. City urban renewal programs were eliminating housing for blacks. The rate of demolition of substandard housing rose from 600 households per year in the late 1950s to 800 per year in the early 1960s before accelerating to 2,600 per year by the late 1960s. Nine out of ten of the evictees were black. Black activists charged that the city redevelopment program was "Negro removal" rather than urban renewal. The program stimulated the flight of many essential services: stores, banks, and doctors and other professionals. One study done some years later painted a frightening picture of Baltimore that applied in the 1960s as well: "The core of Baltimore is shared by greater than average proportions of abandoned wives, unwed mothers, the unemployed and the underemployed, the scarred and maimed, high school dropouts, alcoholics, [and] old people."[26]

Urban renewal cut into the city's tax base, reducing the availability of essential services such as public transportation, while the migration of paying jobs to suburban sites continued to increase. The urban black poor could neither travel to where the jobs were nor hope to follow them to the suburbs. Baltimore County maintained its barriers to black migration into the suburbs, cutting off a potential safety valve for urban tensions. The more rural parts of the state resembled the Deep South in their segregation and overt racism.[27]

Blacks made up approximately 40 percent of Baltimore's population but remained seriously underrepresented in city government and city services. Redevelopment of the central business district was the chief priority of the white political elite and a major drain on the city budget. The city's ethnic groups retained a disproportionate share of political power and defended their geographic enclaves and share of city services from penetration by blacks. White-dominated unions enforced seniority rules that effectively denied employment in blue-collar jobs to blacks. A 1966 survey by the International Association of Police Chiefs condemned the city police department as blatantly racist. Governor Tawes forced the resignation of the city's police commissioner and his lieutenants. Tawes then took control of the police force, appointing successive commissioners and establishing mechanisms for improving relations with city blacks. A potential exploding point was removed, and the purged city police did yeoman service during the tense summer of 1966.[28]

While the Orioles soared toward their first championship, the streets of

Baltimore were the scene of a summer of CORE's strategy of "creative tensions." Responding to black demands, Mayor McKeldin suspended the construction of high-rise public housing and commissioned a survey of the city's services. The report illustrated the legitimacy of black leaders' complaints. Baltimore offered its largest minority substandard housing, understaffed welfare services, and inadequate public health programs, and tolerated an appallingly high infant mortality rate.[29]

CORE took to the streets to protest. So did racist groups like the Ku Klux Klan. Moderate black leaders warned Mayor McKeldin that they would be unable to restrain black counterviolence if the Klan continued to incite white anger. The Klan and other racist freebooters urged whites to "buy guns." In August racists ignited a riot by a mob of about 1,200 angry whites. The police managed to control the outburst after a one-hour rampage, arresting eight whites.[30]

At the heart of city tensions was housing. The Maryland General Assembly was debating an open housing law that would finally knock down the legal barriers that had contained Baltimore's large black population within the city. The state real estate industry, a segment of the moderate establishment, and a large portion of the suburban population lined up in opposition to the bill. Frank Robinson's efforts to find decent housing fell afoul of this resistance.[31]

Robinson also unwittingly became involved in another aspect of the racial struggle in the city of Baltimore. During the first days of CORE's spring offensive, Mayor McKeldin had secured the voluntary desegregation of many of the businesses in Baltimore's infamous "Block." City taverns, however, remained segregated. In October as the city prepared to host its first World Series, McKeldin attempted to expand the availability of public accommodations by convincing tavern owners to open their doors to blacks. The mayor pointedly reminded sports fans and saloon keepers that "without Frank Robinson . . . we would probably have no World Series."[32] Tavern owners were unmoved, claiming that their bars were neighborhood institutions that would not accept strangers easily, especially blacks. McKeldin gave up. A disgusted Sam Lacy summed up black feeling: a black man had brought the city its championship but Baltimore was still segregated. Its baseball team reflected this pattern of discrimination. The Orioles employed the fewest blacks in the major leagues.[33]

Robinson was faced with another example of the realities of racial segregation in the winter after the Orioles' triumph. He found that a black athlete's efforts to capitalize on his series heroics and triple crown through personal appearances and endorsements were likely to be far less lucrative than those of a star white player. Robinson was a capable public performer. One admiring report described him as "poised, completely at ease, and reflecting . . . polish."[34] Robinson set his sights low—a conservative $20,000 to $30,000 in extra money—but was able to earn less than $10,000. "Not one endorsement came my way. I did make ... personal appearances, but the majority were for expenses only."[35]

The following spring, Robinson again ran into difficulties when he tried to secure housing. Racial tensions remained high in both the city and state. CORE leaders informed city officials that they intended to continue their efforts to desegregate the city. White conservatives reacted angrily. Open housing remained the flash point of racial conflict. Robinson's real estate agent spent the winter in an unsuccessful effort to find the Robinson family a suitable house. Finally the frustrated star called on Orioles management to help resolve his problems. Before Hoffberger could live up to a pledge to help, Robinson's real estate agent secured housing by informing neighbors of the identity of the prospective black renter. Robinson was happy to get a good house but added realistically: "If I was Frank Robinson, just plain Negro, I'd probably still be looking."[36]

Robinson was the only Orioles player who successfully broke the racial barrier in housing during the late 1960s. Stars such as Paul Blair, Mike Cuellar, and Don Buford had to settle for segregated housing. Race relations in Maryland got worse during the last years of the 1960s. McKeldin, possibly the state's most progressive leader in race relations, retired after a single frustrating term as Baltimore mayor. The Democrats retook the city government in a campaign marked by charges that the party machine retained a strong antiblack bias. The moderate Tawes left the statehouse. Clarence Miles participated in a bruising Democratic gubernatorial primary, dominated by the issue of housing, that concluded with the triumph of a segregationist candidate, George Mahoney. Mahoney's campaign slogan, Your Home Is Your Castle, was an undisguised appeal to white fears and racism. His victory drove moderate Democrats into support of the Republican candidate, Spiro T. "Ted" Agnew, who campaigned as a racial moderate. The Maryland General Assembly passed an open housing law in 1967, but a state referendum overturned the law.[37]

In April 1968, in the wake of the assassination of Martin Luther King, Jr., Agnew displayed his "moderation" by inflaming racial tensions. At the height of the rioting sparked by King's murder, the governor convened a meeting of the state's leading civil rights activists. A majority came to the meeting directly from the streets, where they were trying to end the violence. Agnew accused the civil rights leadership of secretly encouraging and abetting the rioters. About eighty of the one hundred black leaders walked out. White backlash appeared to be in control of the state government. Baltimore's new mayor, Thomas D'Alesandro III, struggled unsuccessfully to bridge the gulf that separated the racial factions in an increasingly impoverished city. Frustrated in his efforts to improve city services and moderate racial conflict, D'Alesandro quit politics after a single term as mayor.[38]

Ultimately, the power of the federal government restored social peace in

Maryland. In 1968 Congress passed a national fair housing bill. Three years later, the Maryland General Assembly followed suit. The barriers to black migration into the suburbs fell, relieving but not ending inner city tensions. Federal legislation, including the Johnson administration's creation of programs in the war on poverty and the Nixon administration's enactment of revenue sharing, placed money in the hands of local government and permitted astute city leaders to deal with some of the underlying causes of racial conflict in the cities.

Robinson meanwhile openly challenged racial barriers inside baseball. This time his actions had the aid of the Orioles. In June 1967 Robinson publicly criticized continuing racism in baseball, citing California Angels pitcher Jim Coates as an example of a white pitcher who regularly threw at black batters and got away with it. Orioles management supported Robinson. The following year, Robinson announced his interest in becoming a major league manager when his playing days were over. The team backed Robinson's successful application for the job of manager of a Puerto Rican winter league team. The move indicated that the Orioles were ready to open coaching positions to blacks. More important, it put Robinson in a position to claim a major league manager's job when he retired. The black star improved his resumé with several successful seasons as a winter league manager.[39]

A Faceless Fungo Hitting Coach with a Politician's Mind

As Maryland racial problems grew more perplexing, the state's major league baseball team slid back down the greasy poll. The champions of 1966 became the also-rans of 1967. The team's management was aware of the need to prevent a postsuccess letdown but proved unable to reverse the slide without major changes. As Frank Cashen commented in late 1966, it was hard to concentrate on the future while still reveling in a World Series triumph. He admitted that this feeling infected management as well as the team.[40]

Dalton had decided to stand pat over the winter of 1966–67, counting upon the Orioles' well-stocked farm system to meet any personnel problems that might arise during the 1967 season. The decision reflected Dalton's confidence in his player development program. In line with that approach, the team was active in the free agent draft, making twenty-seven selections. The Orioles continued intensive scouting of other clubs' minor league systems since Baltimore had acquired four valuable members of the 1966 team via the minor league draft.[41]

Rising salaries were a significant factor influencing the Orioles' decision not to make any major trades. A World Series triumph meant a $500,000 profit for the club and hefty pay raises for a number of players. Frank Robinson became the team's first $100,000 a year player. Brooks Robinson won a large raise. The payroll rose to an estimated $850,000. The addition of more major league veterans would increase the financial drain on a club that was hard-pressed to attract 1 million paying customers and was supporting a large and costly minor league development program. The Orioles increased their ticket prices to meet these rising costs.[42]

In 1966 the club had gambled with its pitching and won. In 1967 it again gambled and was badly embarrassed. Two starters showed up at spring training nursing sore arms. Shortly thereafter, Jim Palmer came down with arm trouble that would effectively disable him for two seasons. Dalton, however, remained optimistic about the ability of his young pitchers to re-bound from their injuries and reluctant to trade away any of his firstline players or top minor league talent for pitching assistance. He was playing with the club's financial health. The Orioles' off-season ticket sales rose after the World Series triumph but were far short of the club's objective. Dunn believed that a good preseason performance by the team would be critical to the profitability of the 1967 Orioles.[43]

By opening day, Dalton was forced to reevaluate his decision. Barber, Palmer, and Bunker were on the sidelines, and Frank Robinson was suffering from the first of a series of injuries that would impair his performance during the 1967 season. The club's top minor league prospect, first baseman Mike Epstein, boldly refused to accept another year at AAA-level baseball. Cor-rectly believing he was ready to play in the major leagues, Epstein walked off the team, returned home, and demanded a trade.[44]

Dalton initially took a firm stand. Epstein was bound by the reserve clause. If he refused to play in the Baltimore system, he would never play again. Discussing his top prospect in October 1966, Dalton had stated that his "potential was too great to consider letting him to go to another organiza-tion." The club had already rejected offers from three other clubs for a trade. Dalton recognized that Epstein's prospects of promotion were limited as long as Boog Powell played for Baltimore but took the classic management stand: "There is no set formula on the advancement of an outstanding prospect. Their advance varies according to a club's needs and to the individual play-er's ability."[45] During 1967 spring training, the Orioles tried to convert Epstein into an outfielder, but the young power hitter simply could not adjust to the position's defensive requirements.

At the end of spring training, the Orioles decided to send Epstein back to Rochester. Epstein, however, refused to comply with management's fiats. Aided by the rash of injuries affecting the pitching staff, he forced the Orioles to trade him by refusing to play. In late May the Orioles sent Epstein to the Washington Senators in exchange for pitcher Pete Richert.

Richert performed well for the Orioles over the next five seasons but could hardly stem the disaster that overwhelmed the 1967 team. Dave McNally joined the list of pitchers with arm problems. Opposing hitters repeatedly clobbered Stu Miller, one of the stars of the 1966 bullpen. The club traded player representative Steve Barber after a series of clashes with management. In June, Frank Robinson was involved in a violent collision with Chicago second baseman Al Weiss that took him out of the lineup for six weeks. Robinson returned but was bothered by double vision for the rest of the season. Brooks Robinson had a poor first half, while Powell slumped throughout the year. Epstein, Barber, and utility man Woody Held, another player traded during the season, helped their new clubs repeatedly beat the Orioles.

Dalton tried without success to resuscitate the team, acquiring pitching help through trades and calling up minor leaguers. The director of player personnel was heavily criticized in the press for his slow response to the club's woes.[46] The Orioles limped into a tie for sixth place, with a 76–85 record, fifteen games behind the American League champion Boston Red Sox. Home attendance plunged by about 350,000, to 860,390. The Orioles lost $57,412 in 1967. In spite of a bad season, the team payroll remained stationary. Dalton cut a few athletes' paychecks but found himself involved in acrimonious salary disputes with players who insisted on large raises based on good individual performances.[47]

Dalton wasted little time in shaking up the team. Shortly before the end of the season he assigned special scout Jim Russo to follow the Orioles and report on the causes of their poor performance. After hearing Russo's report, Dalton concluded that the team was affected by complacency and that Bauer and his coaches had failed to motivate the players. When the season ended, the club released coaches Gene Woodling, Harry Brecheen, and Sherm Lollar; to take their places, Dalton called up three members of the Orioles' minor league coaching staff, Earl Weaver, George Bamberger, and Van Hoscheit. Dalton dismissed the three coaches for different reasons. Brecheen was the scapegoat for the siege of arm miseries that hit his pitching staff. Woodling had clashed with both management and players during the season. Lollar's major sin appears to have been his closeness to manager Bauer. Dalton's relationship with the manager was strained. While he and Hoffberger agreed that Bauer deserved another opportunity to lead the team, Dalton, like MacPhail before him, was determined to surround a "players manager" with tough, hard-working coaches. Dalton counted on the new men to instill motivation and workmanlike habits in a team that management believed had lost its self-discipline.[48]

The key figure in the coaching shake-up was the short, raspy-voiced former manager of the Rochester Red Wings, Earl Weaver. Weaver incarnated the values and work habits of the Baltimore minor league system. A career minor league player, the thirty-seven-year-old Weaver had managed in the Orioles system for eleven years, working his way up from a Class D team to the top. Along the way, he consistently produced winning teams.

Commenting on his player development philosophy in 1966, Dalton stated that, unlike many other minor league system directors, he was never satisfied with simply training athletes. "I want our players to develop the habit of winning."[49] No manager did a better job of inculcating a will to win than the fiery Weaver. Dalton, who hired Weaver in 1956, watched his progress with increasing interest. In 1961, when Dalton and Paul Richards decided that the Orioles' minor league system needed a single instruction book, they assigned Weaver to write it. When Dalton created an opening on the Orioles coaching staff, he wanted Weaver to fill it.

"As soon as he was made coach, I think we all knew that Earl would be made manager eventually," Brooks Robinson recalled. "He was Harry Dalton's boy."[50] By placing Weaver on the 1968 coaching staff, Dalton gave him an opportunity to evaluate the Orioles' talent objectively. If Bauer faltered, Weaver would be ready to take charge. The difficulty with this plan was that both Bauer and his players were fully aware of Dalton's thinking. The manager's authority had been undercut, and Bauer was naturally very resentful.[51]

Recognizing that the Orioles could not enter another season without reinforcing their pitching, Dalton dealt off a number of veterans to acquire young pitching and a capable utility infielder/outfielder, Don Buford. He relied on the minor league system to provide a replacement for Luis Aparicio and to bolster the pitching staff. The Orioles system lived up to Dalton's continued confidence, as Mark Belanger moved into Aparicio's shortstop role while pitcher Jim Hardin became a mainstay of the 1968 staff.

With his job on the line, Bauer vowed to be "tougher" with his players. Management instituted a winter conditioning program for the team. It enrolled some players in health clubs and set reporting weights for others. Spring training for 1968 was a strenuous experience for the players. Weaver, Bamberger, and Hoscheit did most of the organizing for a manager who kept his distance from his assistants, particularly his potential successor. Bauer's attitude harmed his already shaky standing. Dalton had made clear that management expected organizational loyalty to smooth over any personality conflicts between the manager and his new coaches. Bauer, however, could not overcome his resentment and suspected that the team was trying to force his resignation.[52]

The Orioles left spring training in April 1968 with the look of a contender. Palmer was lost for another season, but McNally had recovered from his arm problems. The club opened the season with a healthy pitching staff. Unfortunately, the offense failed to ignite. Centerfielder Paul Blair had broken an ankle playing winter baseball and was healing slowly. Frank Robinson again was dogged by illness and injury. At the beginning of July, Blair was hitting .199, Curt Blefary a weak .208, and Frank Robinson .229. The Orioles trailed the league-leading Detroit Tigers by ten games. Attendance was as poor as it had been in 1967. Bauer stuck loyally with his slumping veterans rather than inserting Dalton's winter acquisitions or other players on his bench.

Dalton decided to replace Bauer in June. He won Hoffberger's agreement just before the All-Star Game, arguing that Bauer was not utilizing the talent he had and that continued poor play would be disastrous for the club's attendance. During the three-day break surrounding the All-Star Game, Dalton flew to see Bauer at his Kansas City home and inform him of the club's decision and then returned to Baltimore to introduce the new manager to the press.[53]

Weaver signed a contract to finish out the season. He failed to close the gap with Detroit significantly, but under Weaver the Orioles began to play an enthusiastic and exciting brand of baseball. By the end of the season, the press, players, umpires, fans, and Baltimore management were aware that Weaver was a unique personality. The "faceless fungo hitting coach" of spring training emerged as a master strategist and motivator.[54] Umpires discovered a man whom they could instantly dislike. After an early confrontation with the volcanic Weaver, infuriated umpire Larry Napp told a reporter, "That man shouldn't be managing in the minor leagues let alone the majors."[55]

Orioles management discovered that Dalton's man was indeed the antidote to the complacency that infected the 1967 squad. Utilizing the potential of his full twenty-five-man squad, Weaver drove the Orioles into a second-place finish, far behind the Tigers, but with a 91–71 record that indicated the team could be a contender in 1969.

That Terrible Machine

Weaver's success was of critical importance to a team that was drawing poorly at the box office and depending heavily on its television revenues for a limited profit. In February 1966 *The Sporting News* noted that increased television income enabled Baltimore to offset rising costs, the loss of special tax benefits, and poor attendance.[56] Still, local television income was limited. If the club was going to remain profitable, it needed a larger and more consistent amount of revenue from national network television. Washington, Kansas City, Cleveland, and Chicago were other American League teams in the same position. In the middle of the decade organized baseball took a number of important steps toward stabilizing its relationship with the television networks and increasing its income.

Organized baseball recognized the importance of the networks for its long-term profitability. In 1961, when local television revenues provided an overwhelming part of each team's broadcasting income, Commissioner Ford

Frick appeared before the House Antitrust Subcommittee to support legislation aimed at permitting the two professional football leagues to pool individual team television rights and sell them to the networks as a package. Frick
stressed that baseball should enjoy "a similar permissive right to deal with its
television problems on the same basis."[57]

In September 1961 Congress passed and President Kennedy signed an act
that amended antitrust laws to authorize professional sports leagues to enter
into television contracts on behalf of their members with the networks and
also granted professional and amateur athletic teams the right to black out
television coverage in areas immediately contiguous to the site of a televised
game.[58]

Organized baseball's foresight in supporting this legislation brought a
quick reward. Local rights payments began to level off around 1963. In the
case of the Orioles, the payment situation was complicated by the club's
television and radio arrangement with National Brewery. Under terms of the
National-Orioles contract, National purchased rights to the entire advertising package and then resold most of the advertising time to other sponsors.
The 1962 contract granted the Orioles a sizable increase. In 1963 National
began to experience difficulties selling advertising on Orioles broadcasts. As
a result, National leveled off the annual rate at which payments increased
during 1963 negotiations for a three-year contract. The contract base payment rose from $617,000 for 1964 to $650,000 for 1966.[59]

In the face of a general leveling off of their local television and radio
revenues, hard-pressed American League owners placed the question of a
national contract on the agenda for the 1963 winter meetings. They hoped to
put together a plan for pooling both rights and revenues. Under this scheme
the leagues would offer a package of games for competitive bidding by the
three networks, and each team would receive an equal share of the profits
from the sale of combined rights.[60]

The Sporting News warmly supported the revenue sharing idea. The Yankees, Dodgers, and Giants, baseball's biggest money-makers, were naturally
unenthusiastic since a pooled national contract would substantially reduce
the profits they made under the existing game of the week scheme.[61]

News of the 1963 agreements between CBS and NBC and the two professional football leagues ended whatever chance the game's traditional powers
had of defeating a pooled national contract. Professional football's growing
popularity plus the existence of two competing leagues drove payments "sky
high," *Television Age* commented.[62] CBS concluded a two-year deal with the
National Football League for $28.2 million, while NBC bought five years of
games from the upstart American Football League (AFL) for $36 million.
The deal enabled the AFL to compete on a level of parity with the NFL in
talent acquisition and gave the new league psychological reinforcement by
validating its claim to equality with the older circuit.

The size of the two football leagues' TV deals astonished baseball men. Their total profit from the game of the week scheme was $1.7 million. The $3.5 million that organized baseball took from the sale of World Series and All-Star Game rights was earmarked for the pension plan. Reacting quickly, the owners formed a committee under Detroit's John Fetzer to work out a package sale proposal.[63]

Baseball's choice of Fetzer was shrewd. A longtime television station owner, he knew the broadcasting industry well. As an American League owner, Fetzer had an immediate financial interest in broadening his income. He speedily came forward with a plan for putting baseball on prime-time television: a Monday night game of the week. Under the major league proposal, baseball would basically vacate its Monday night schedule to showcase a single game on national television. The major leagues would gain an enormous advantage: rights payments for prime-time television were much greater than those for Saturday or Sunday afternoons.[64]

The networks were unenthusiastic about the Monday night proposal. In the first place, baseball was not prime-time material. With a 162-game schedule, individual games rarely stirred great fan excitement. Moreover, fans were primarily interested in their local teams. They were unlikely to be enthusiastic about a game matching two teams from other cities or the other league. The networks were not interested in paying the major leagues $10 million for a prime-time game when they believed that television was already oversaturated with baseball. In April 1964 the president of American Broadcasting Company (ABC) cut the number of major league games his network would broadcast under its game of the week arrangement, telling organized baseball "to make itself scarce."[65]

After the collapse of this first approach, opponents of the idea of pooling rights and sharing income raised new objections. They briefly delayed major league approval of a new set of Fetzer proposals. The sale of the Yankees to CBS and congressional pressure in favor of revenue sharing facilitated the triumph of organized baseball's first experiment in profit sharing.[66]

Fetzer's second effort to sell the networks on a Monday night game of the week also failed. All three networks turned thumbs down. Fetzer then offered an alternate proposal that achieved his basic objectives of both pooling rights and sharing revenues. On 15 December 1964 eighteen of the twenty major league teams signed a $5.7 million game of the week agreement with ABC. Under the terms of the contract, ABC had the exclusive right to select for national broadcast games that the eighteen participating teams played on Saturdays. Each team would receive a $300,000 payment for its participation. ABC had an option to renew the pact for a second year, and the size of the payment would increase if all twenty major league teams signed up. The Yankees remained outside the pact because of contractual obligations to CBS. The Phillies indicated they would probably join later. Fetzer hoped to

entice New York into the arrangement with the promise of eventually sur-
passing the rights payments that its corporate parent would offer.[67]

Fetzer had mastered "that terrible machine," television, *The Sporting News*
editorialized proudly. The pact appeared to satisfy everyone. CBS continued
to broadcast baseball's most attractive team, the Yankees. ABC had eighteen
other teams to match up. NBC retained the World Series and the All-Star
Game, the crown jewels of baseball broadcasting. Each of the participating
teams had substantially increased its television revenues. In the case of
Baltimore, the $300,000 in extra rights payments represented a 50 percent
increase in its broadcasting income, a significant shot in the arm for a team
with serious attendance problems.[68]

The dream arrangement collapsed within a year. ABC lost money on its
game of the week package and dropped its option for 1966. Organized
baseball responded by putting the World Series and All-Star Game into the
same package with the Saturday game of the week and the Monday night
prime-time plan and then inviting bids. NBC picked up the package for three
years at $11.8 million a year.[69]

The biggest element in the package was a 65 percent increase in network
payments for the World Series and the All-Star Game. The nineteen participating clubs, now including the Phillies, received the same $300,000 pay-
ment as in 1965. The experiment in televising baseball in prime time was a
ratings failure, closing off an avenue to a major rise in television profits for
organized baseball.[70]

Nevertheless, the package deal with NBC worked out well for both the
network and baseball. Saturday game of the week ratings picked up, enabling
the network to sell its advertising time. Improved ratings, in turn, enabled
Fetzer and his committee to increase the size of the payments baseball would
receive when the agreement was renegotiated in 1968. "Baseball and the
tube have formed an alliance that should prove durable," *The Sporting News*
commented.[71]

For the Orioles, television money remained the rock upon which the
franchise built financial stability. The 1965 deal with ABC proved to be the
difference between a profitable and a losing season. When attendance fell in
1967 and 1968, national and local broadcasting provided the club with over
$1 million, about 25 percent of its total income. Unlike income from ticket
sales, concessions, and player sales, which fluctuated, broadcasting income
consistently if gradually increased. Veteran baseball man Frank Lane, Dalton's executive aide, predicted that the future of the attendance-poor Orioles
and the sport in general rested with TV: "Within ten years the baseball parks
of America will be mere studios for pay television."[72]

The Orioles attempted to capitalize on their 1966 World Series triumph in
order to build a stronger and larger broadcasting network. The club signed a
two-year pact with WJZ television that included both an increase in its basic

rights and an agreement that all telecast games would be in color. Simultaneously, the club concluded a new deal with WBAL radio that included plans for an expanded network of sixty stations stretching from Delaware to Florida to Louisiana.[73]

The players too were ready to capitalize on the television bonanza. By 1969 the long-dormant Major League Baseball Players Association had assumed a significant role in the sport and was eager to assert its right to an increased share of World Series TV profits. Baseball's profitable national television contract became the catalyst for labor-management confrontation.

7 Championship Years

Brooks Robinson was the Orioles' first "home-grown" star: the initial success of what became a prolific farm system. A personable, courteous, and straightforward man who was readily accessible to both fans and the press, he was the team's most popular player for most of his twenty-year major league career. A consistent, durable athlete, he revolutionized the way third basemen played their position and won election to baseball's Hall of Fame in 1983. Robinson reached the peak of his playing career in 1969–71 as one of the leaders of the best team ever to play in Baltimore. In 1969, he hit twenty-three home runs and drove in eighty-four runs despite a .234 batting average. The next year, Robinson hit .276 with eighteen home runs and ninety-four RBIs. He topped off this fine performance by dominating the 1970 World Series in a way few players ever have. In five games against Cincinnati, Robinson hit .429 with two home runs and six RBIs. His defensive play at third base choked off a number of rallies by the Reds' powerful hitters. "He's the whole series," said Cincinnati's Pete Rose. "Brooks Robinson belongs in a higher league."[1]

During these years Robinson took an equally important step off the field. In the winter of 1968 he inherited the job of Orioles player representative. Robinson accepted the assignment because of a sense of responsibility to his fellow players, and he carried it out with the same determination that marked his play. Believing that change in baseball's labor relations was long overdue, Robinson led the Orioles players through a revolution in player-management dealings. In the years when the Orioles reached the heights of success, organized baseball began the long and difficult process of adjusting to the realities of modern labor-management relations.[2]

Palace Revolt

Throughout the 1960s, publications like *The Sporting News* repeatedly bemoaned major league baseball's loss of the "sportsman owner" and his replacement by the corporate businessman. Jerold Hoffberger represented the new type of owner who regarded baseball as an interlocking part of a larger corporate empire. The prelude to management's confrontation with the players was an effort by Hoffberger and other baseball businessmen to modernize the structure of the game and increase profits.

In 1967 Hoffberger had optimistically predicted to stockholders that the Orioles would overtake the Colts as Baltimore's major sports attraction. By the end of 1968 he was uncomfortably aware that major league baseball faced severe problems.[3] Social and political tensions mounted inside American society. The nation was at war in Vietnam. The black struggle for civil rights had entered a increasingly violent phase. Younger Americans appeared obsessed with political causes to the virtual exclusion of essentially "frivolous" pursuits like attending professional sports contests. Fans and sportswriters complained that the game was slow, low-scoring, and generally boring. In spite of box office gains during the exciting pennant races of 1967 and 1968, American League attendance remained low and unevenly divided, with a few franchises showing large gains while the others struggled with poor attendance. Orioles attendance dropped drastically after the 1966 championship team failed to repeat. The long-standing racial tensions that exploded after the assassination of Martin Luther King, Jr., reinforced the tendency of white fans to stay away from the city. The Baltimore Bays soccer team, a wholly owned subsidiary acquired by the club in 1967, was an unprofitable venture, losing $400,000 the first season and $500,000 in 1968. The club made its 1968 profit of $551,305 from the sale of player contracts to two new expansion teams. Without this one-time-only infusion of cash, the Orioles would have taken a $200,000 loss.[4]

Faced with widespread attendance problems, the Orioles and all of major league baseball put greater stress on marketing efforts. Hoffberger turned the Orioles publicity campaign over to W. Donner Co., the same advertising company that handled the National Brewery account. The commissioner's office set up a wholly owned subsidiary to market organized baseball's "official" products: sports clothing and recreational equipment bearing major league team logos. Baseball executives hoped that in addition to providing another source of revenue, sales of these materials would deepen fan identification with the sport and boost lagging attendance.[5]

In another move designed to increase attendance, the major leagues decided on a divisional realignment for the 1969 season. Each major league would divide into two geographic divisions. The champions of each division would then have a playoff series with the league winners advancing to the World Series. The divisional realignment and playoff series were pressed on a reluctant National League by the American League. As was the case with its promotional company, major league baseball was here borrowing an idea that the National Football League had utilized with success to increase its profitability. Realignment permitted the leagues to shuffle their schedules, cut back on travel costs, and build fan interest by increasing the number of contending teams. A playoff series prior to the World Series also increased baseball's television revenues.[6]

The American League resorted to another method of building attendance when it agreed to expand to twelve teams. The League acted with considerable reluctance, deciding on expansion only after it had maneuvered itself into a politically embarrassing position and then made a poor choice of one of the expansion sites.

The 1961–62 major league expansion was not a major long-term financial success. Neither of the new American League teams drew well its first year, although both did better in their second seasons. Thereafter, the novelty wore off and fewer fans were willing to pay money to see noncompetitive expansion teams. Major league expansion also created serious problems for AAA baseball, forcing it out of some of its best markets. Expansion aroused discontent among major league players, who demanded higher wages when they saw the payments the new teams made for journeymen and borderline minor league prospects. By the end of the 1962 season, baseball owners were clearly wary of the effects of another round of expansion.[7]

Within a few years, however, the major leagues were fending off political pressures for further expansion created by the actions of restless owners in Kansas City and Milwaukee. In 1961 the colorful, ambitious, and independent Charles O. Finley, a Chicago insurance executive, purchased the Kansas City franchise. Finley inherited a bad baseball club in a small market. He decided to move the club. After a bit of scouting, Finley concluded that Oakland, California, was the ideal site for a franchise transfer. The eager city establishment offered a modern 50,000-seat facility at attractive terms and a five-year broadcasting contract worth $1.1 million per annum.[8]

Finley approached his fellow owners for permission to move in 1963. The American League was badly embarrassed and initially tried to keep the matter away from the press. Less than a decade earlier the American League had approved shifting the Philadelphia franchise west to Kansas City. Allowing the team to move again would be an admission of past bad judgment. Moreover, Finley was already highly unpopular with his fellow owners, who were unwilling to do favors for the maverick. The Kansas and Missouri congressional delegations, aroused by news of the proposed transfer, threatened legislative action. Baseball remained concerned about its antitrust exemption. The city's leaders offered to meet Finley's specific demands for stadium improvements and organized efforts to increase attendance at A's games. The league blocked Finley's initial effort to move the team.[9]

Kansas City's reprieve was short lived. The syndicate that owned the Milwaukee Braves was anxious to move and had a very attractive bid from Atlanta. Milwaukee was a small market with a poor team and declining attendance. The Braves faced severe competition from two Chicago teams less than a hundred miles to the south. Milwaukee's local television income was very restricted. Atlanta, on the other hand, had a new stadium, enjoyed no major league competition, boasted a larger population base, and, most important, was a major television market.[10]

Unlike their American League counterparts, National League owners were ready to back the Braves' move. A confrontation with Congress ensued, and baseball won. The Wisconsin delegation, led by Senator William Proxmire, was unable to round up the support needed either to strip organized baseball of its antitrust protection or to force it into revenue sharing arrangements that would equalize income between teams, negating the attraction of larger markets like Atlanta.[11]

Finley renewed his bid to move to Oakland. In October 1967 the American League granted Finley's wish. Simultaneously, the league voted to expand, putting new teams in two cities in 1969. The owners awarded one of the expansion teams to Kansas City in response to strong pressure from the Kansas and Missouri congressional delegations. In December they awarded the other expansion team to Seattle, a city both leagues coveted as a market. The move to two Pacific Coast cities was a direct challenge to long-standing National League supremacy in the Far West. The senior circuit responded by voting to expand by two teams in 1971.[12]

The Orioles were the only team to vote against the Finley move. The team's owners harbored a strong mistrust of Finley. Iglehardt had campaigned unsuccessfully against accepting the insurance man's 1961 bid for a franchise. Dalton argued that Kansas City had supported its team and suggested that rather than forcing the city's loyal fans to endure the long building process that characterized an expansion franchise Finley should sell his club and the league should then award him an expansion franchise in Oakland. Cashen was openly critical of the Finley move. Moving existing franchises, he warned, "doesn't create the kind of image we want in baseball." It was a "bad precedent. . . . Once you start it, where do you stop?" Stability, Cashen opined, was the key to successful marketing of major league baseball. "I'm just afraid we're opening the door toward turning baseball into a series of one night stands."[13]

Expansion and the Kansas City transfer provoked a flurry of press criticism. The owners prepared to cash in on expansion by charging the new teams $175,000 for each player contract they purchased. However, they recognized that baseball could not afford a repeat of what happened in the first expansion. It needed a more equitable drafting system that would permit the new teams to be more competitive from the start than the 1961 expansion franchises had been. The owners appointed a special committee to set up new rules for the draft.[14]

Harry Dalton represented the Orioles on the four-man expansion committee that came up with revised draft rules in January 1968. The committee's plan allowed each of the existing teams to protect only fifteen of the forty men on its major league roster in the first round of the draft and an additional three men in each subsequent round. The two new clubs would each draft thirty players off the rosters of the ten existing teams.[15]

The Orioles front office was extremely concerned about the draft's impact on Baltimore's status as a contender. Weaver and Dalton drew up a list of players they felt were key to a successful championship bid. The team ran a number of mock drafts, attempting to predict what players it could leave unprotected but still retain. The club chose to leave a number of journeyman major league players unprotected in order to hold on to top minor league prospects. Even so, a number of attractive minor league prospects remained unprotected. Holding its breath, the team left the injured Jim Palmer off its protected list. The planning worked. Baltimore lost a number of good players from its minor league system but held on to its outstanding prospects. Dalton remarked that he was "unhappy" with the losses, "but under the circumstances not too unhappy."[16]

Surveying the problems created by expansion, television, the growing militancy of the Players Association, drooping attendance, and the need for a coordinated industry response on these issues, Hoffberger took an active role in organizing the ouster of Commissioner Eckert, with the aim of replacing him with a dynamic younger man who understood the television industry and labor relations.

Eckert, while well-meaning, simply was not up to the demands of the job. Commenting that "we can't go floundering around . . . without leadership," Hoffberger joined younger men like New York's Mike Burke, Cincinnati's Francis Dale, and St. Louis's Richard Meyer who convinced a majority of league owners to buy out the remaining five years of Eckert's contract during the December 1968 winter meetings. The "young Turks" won passage of a resolution creating a special committee to propose a wide-ranging reorgani-

zation of baseball's management structure. Hoffberger chaired the committee that was to report its recommendations at the December 1969 winter
meetings.[17]

Having granted the younger men a series of concessions, the game's
traditional forces, led by Walter O'Malley, then closed ranks and blocked
Burke's candidacy for the commissioner's job. After a two-month deadlock
with the reform forces, the old guard secured a compromise that replaced
Eckert with an interim commissioner, lawyer Bowie Kuhn. Kuhn appeared to
be an admirable compromise choice since he was a younger man with expertise in television and labor relations matters. In May the owners offered
Kuhn the job on a permanent basis.[18]

Players' Revolt

Kuhn's appointment came not a moment too soon, as organized baseball's
management faced its most difficult labor crisis of the postwar era. Baseball's
labor-management relations changed dramatically and speedily. As late as
1958, Robin Roberts, the National League player representative, professed
total confidence in management, telling a congressional committee, "I feel
definitely that what is good for the owners is good enough for us players."[19]
Less than a decade later, baseball's labor-management relations moved from
peace to confrontation.

The pension plan remained a source of friction because of Commissioner
Chandler's 1949 decision to make baseball's national television income the
source of pension funds. Twenty years later, the size of the major league
pension had increased to five times the original payment, but major league
television and radio revenues were forty-five times larger. The owners rejected repeated efforts by the Players Association's lawyer, J. Norman Lewis,
to increase the players' share. When Lewis asked for a 25 percent cut of
television revenues for the players, an Orioles official responded that the
request was "ridiculous," adding, "If they want to share in the profits, they
should be willing to share in the losses."[20] The owners rejected this demand
without making any counteroffer. An indignant Tom Yawkey of Boston told
reporters that he might sell out as a result of the players' insulting demands.[21]

Apparently seeking to mollify angry owners, the player representatives
dismissed Lewis in early 1959. Later that year, they affirmed full confidence
in Commissioner Frick's handling of television issues and hired a new legal
adviser, Judge Robert Cannon.[22] Cannon, who had ambitions to succeed
Frick, managed the players' affairs in the interest of labor peace and the
owners' pocketbooks. He supported the reserve clause, praised the pension
as the "finest in existence," and insisted that relations between labor and

management were "magnificent." In 1964, Cannon told Congress that the "thinking of the average major league ballplayer" was "we have it so good we don't know what to ask for next."[23]

Judge Cannon's idyllic view of labor-management relations overlooked signs of player unhappiness. Labor-management tensions were building because of players' discontent over issues like minimal salary levels, inadequate pensions, continued racial discrimination, large bonus payments to untried amateur players, and restrictions that management imposed on their lives.[24]

Player resentment over the low minimum salary was long-standing. The owners repeatedly rejected player requests for an increase and refused to negotiate the issue. Increases came when management decided to give them. The owners were equally unsympathetic with player efforts to have a say in matters such as scheduling and playing rules. Typical of the restrictions that management imposed on players were the efforts of first the Cincinnati Reds and then the Chicago White Sox to force pitcher Jim Brosnan to give up his lucrative second career as a writer. In 1964 the White Sox fired Brosnan when he refused to stop writing about baseball.[25]

In 1934 sportswriter John Lardner noted that baseball labor peace was rooted in the lack of player unity. Playing careers were short and most athletes were satisfied if they could increase their individual salaries. Thirty years later, Orioles player representative Steve Barber echoed this view, telling a reporter that a union offered players nothing. The individual athlete, Barber stated, had to earn a better salary by his on-the-field performance and with his own negotiating skills. In 1934, however, Lardner added a prophetic warning: "Yet there is reason to suspect that the players would be stronger under a united front than either they or the [baseball] magnates imagine."[26] In 1966 the players took the first steps toward creating a united front.

In January 1966 the player representatives, with the owners' full approval, offered Cannon the post of "administrator" of their affairs with an annual salary of $50,000. The owners were so pleased with the choice that they voted to set aside 35 percent of the profits from the All-Star Game to pay for the expenses of a New York office for Cannon.[27]

To the surprise of both players and management, Cannon declined the offer, citing pressing business concerns. The players then formed a search committee to seek another qualified adviser. In March the search committee announced its choice: a forty-eight-year-old professional in labor relations, Marvin Miller of the United Steel Workers.[28]

Miller toured baseball's spring training sites in March and early April 1966, outlining his plans for revitalizing the long-moribund Players Association, identifying issues the players wanted him to pursue in talks with management, and requesting a vote of approval from the players. Miller won the players' endorsement, 489 to 136.[29]

The owners reacted to Miller as if he carried an infectious disease. His labor background aroused deep-seated hostility. Moreover, Miller labeled baseball's minimum salary "unreasonably low," laying the groundwork for a confrontation with management.[30] The owners expressed their displeasure with the choice of Miller by refusing to allocate the $150,000 in All-Star Game proceeds they had previously pledged for a Players Association central office. They also appear to have blacklisted at least one member of the committee that selected Miller. Veteran pitcher Robin Roberts never found further employment in organized baseball.[31]

Management and labor met for their first serious negotiating session on 6 June 1966. The owners refused to carry through on their pledge to fund Miller's office, claiming such action would violate the Taft-Hartley Act. Miller would not back off. The first meeting ended in a deadlock in which "neither side scored, but Miller looked strong."[32] Eventually, the owners found a way out of the corner into which they had painted themselves. They raised the size of their contribution to the pension fund and eliminated the requirement for a player's regular contribution. The players were told that they were free to contribute the money they formerly put into the pension fund to cover the costs of Miller's office.[33]

The owners made an expensive mistake when they assumed responsibility for funding the entire pension program to escape contributing to the upkeep of the Players Association office. Miller, on the other hand, had held his ground in his first confrontation and succeeded in improving the players' pension. Miller's success as leader of the Players Association was based on his ability to protect and advance the interests of the majority: the average players. Miller concentrated on improving minimum salaries, pension benefits, spring training money, and scheduling. In so doing, he quickly won the trust and support of the players. Explaining Miller's ability to win player confidence, Brooks Robinson stated, "He was able to do it because he was honest and everything he said was the actual truth."[34] The owners' unconcealed hostility solidified Miller's position; as he himself said, "The owners did it for me. . . . They have been my biggest allies."[35] The owners' handling of labor relations over the next fifteen years was a textbook case of bad industrial management.

In December 1966 Miller announced that he would seek to negotiate a contract with management covering all the basic issues involved in the players-owners relationship, except salaries. Negotiations began in February 1967. The talks continued as management tried to wear down and break up the Players Association. To the surprise of the owners, the players stood solidly behind Miller. The owners then took over control of the talks from the ineffective Commissioner Eckert, hired John Gaherin, a veteran negotiator, to represent them, and established a Player Relations Committee (PRC) to supervise labor-management discussions and set policy. They elected Hoffberger to the committee.[36]

Calling for the establishment of a "dignified and mutually respectful relationship," Miller laid out a union agenda for major changes in its relations with organized baseball's management. The Players Association wanted a new minimum wage, an enlarged pension fund, guaranteed contracts, independent arbitration of contract disputes, a larger voice in defining its working conditions, and significant modifications in the reserve clause. Miller coolly added that "fundamental changes" in baseball's labor relations were a "matter-of-fact forecast."[37]

The drawn-out negotiations reached a flash point in December 1967 when the owners refused to meet with Miller and the player representatives during baseball's winter meetings. Tempers flared, with Miller threatening "action" and Paul Richards, who was now Atlanta's general manager, labeling Miller a liar. The angry Richards added that, if necessary, management would be ready to "get down into the gutter with him" in order to defeat Miller. Management then agreed to meet with Miller in mid-December.[38]

In January 1968 Miller finally secured a series of major concessions from management by threatening to call in federal mediators. Baseball's first "Basic Agreement," a two-year contract, improved working conditions, set the size of the owners' contribution to the pension fund, and raised the minimum salary from $7,000 to $10,000. It also established an arbitration procedure under the commissioner. Miller found this last compromise unsatisfactory but had established a precedent for the eventual use of an independent arbitrator.[39]

The Players Association's requests, presented in a "restrained and reasonable tone" by the low-key Miller, touched on the owners' most cherished prerogatives. As Brooks Robinson recalled: "They were adamant that nothing was going to change because it had been that way for a hundred years."[40] The owners' relationship with Miller and the Players Association became more antagonistic. Chicago White Sox owner Arthur Allyn urged his athletes to quit the association, arousing Miller's ire. *The Sporting News* complained that Miller was turning the Players Association into "a hard-nose labor union." Even columnist Red Smith, an early union supporter, admitted a bit of nostalgia for the "feudal and paternalistic" Cannon years.[41]

Miller, meanwhile, was involved in yet another marathon negotiation with management over the renewal of the pension plan. The association's objectives were twofold: to increase the size of the owners' payment and to link the pension plan firmly to baseball's national television income by establishing the principle that management would pay a set percentage of its TV rights into the pension fund. Annoyed by management's continual use of stall tactics, Miller threatened a player boycott of spring training if the pension issue remained unresolved.[42]

The players rallied to Miller. Among the major stars expressing public support was the Orioles' new player representative, Brooks Robinson. The pleasant, easygoing Robinson was impatient for change. His list of grievances included management attitudes, the reserve clause, and the owners' negotiating techniques. "The owners," he recalled, "never understood that nothing is forever."[43] Robinson's growing union activism was a warning sign that the players were serious about their demands.

The Orioles' player relations were like those of other major league teams. Hoffberger had favored raising the minimum salary and encouraged his athlete employees to get "organized help to plan their lives."[44] He advised Baltimore players to seek tax and investment help, to pursue higher education, and to exploit any off-season job opportunities that their association with baseball provided. Brooks Robinson was one of the players who followed this approach, turning his affairs over to a professional management organization. Frank Robinson testified to the "good atmosphere and close feeling" that the Orioles front office created.[45]

Management's cooperative attitude ended when the players began to assert their rights. Paternalism, heavily laced with self-interest, was a trademark of baseball management, and Orioles management was no exception. The fate of Orioles player representatives was a clear sign that Baltimore management would brook no interference with its prerogatives. Between 1960 and 1968 the club had nine player representatives in nine seasons. It traded them, released them, or left them available for restocking drafts. In the most notorious case, the club quickly unloaded veteran pitcher and player representative Steve Barber after he announced that the players would charge set fees for interviews with reporters. The club immediately appealed to Marvin Miller, who told the players that the proposed action violated their contract. The whole incident was over in five hours, but even Miller's intervention could not save Barber from the club's wrath. Cashen told reporters that the club was "hurt and disappointed" by the players' action and particularly irritated with Barber, who had failed to clear his moves beforehand with management.[46]

Barber had violated another elementary rule by damaging the club's rapport with the press. When relief pitcher Eddie Fisher was charged with assault during the same season, the club declined to comment on the incident and quietly traded him as soon as possible. The Orioles were particularly sensitive to negative press coverage in a year when the team played poorly.[47]

Another sensitive area in player-management relations was salary negotiations. The Orioles and the other major league teams insisted that the players negotiate directly with the club without professional help. Even star players had their problems. Brooks Robinson, a veteran of many contract squabbles, had an extended duel with Dalton over a $500 salary increase. Frank Robinson's first year in Baltimore began with a salary dispute. While Frank Robinson's unique skills enabled him to command a hefty salary, the average player's ability to negotiate was severely restricted by the reserve clause. The player either accepted management's final offer and played, or he gave up his career. "You couldn't go anywhere else," Brooks Robinson recalled; "if you didn't like it, tough."[48]

Harry Dalton explained that he determined a player's salary based on management's evaluation of what "his performance warranted, what I felt he should earn next season, and a figure which I felt he might be willing to sign for." Dalton described negotiations as "no easy task" and "not a part of my job which I relish. . . . It is a job that has to be done . . . and I try to exercise the responsibility with fairness to both players and management."[49] Dalton and other general managers doubtless acted responsibly but operated within a system governed by the reserve clause and other baseball laws that heavily stacked the deck in management's favor.

Brooks Robinson was one of a growing number of players who were beginning to object to the ground rules of labor-management relations in baseball. Even before his selection as player representative, Robinson had been critical of major league scheduling and a number of rules changes, decisions the owners regarded as their preserve. He was also aware of the club's habit of quickly disposing of player representatives but concluded that his status as the game's best third baseman and his enormous popularity with Baltimore fans would provide protection against club retaliation.[50]

Robinson assumed his new role at a tense moment in baseball's labor relations. Management continued to drag out talks, convinced that it could break Miller's hold on the union with a tough stance. Paul Richards, who nurtured a violent hatred for Miller, became a spokesman for the management hardliners. He told reporters, "Miller speaks mainly for a few rabble rousers and greedy ballplayers."[51] The hardliners proved their determination to resist when American League president Joe Cronin fired Al Salerno and Bill Valentine for seeking to organize their fellow umpires into a union. In December 1968 the owners underlined their stance by enacting a new rule that permitted teams to refuse to pay the contracts of players injured in nonbaseball-related activities. Marvin Miller denounced the rule as a "vicious anti-player action." Dalton endorsed the new rule, noting that baseball was seasonal employment and arguing that the players had a responsibility to keep the club's needs in mind during the months when they were engaged in other activities.[52]

On 17 December 1968 the owners made a new pension plan offer of $5.1 million. Miller immediately rejected the offer as "inadequate" and "fraudulent." The Players Association's chief complained that the proposed increase of $1 million would only cover the hundred new players that would join the major leagues as a result of the projected four-team expansion. Further, the increase was not linked to the major leagues' growing television revenues. The owners responded that the Players Association's claim to a fixed percentage of the major leagues' television income was "a property right

[that] they do not now have, nor ever had."[53] On 2 January 1969 the union called on its members to refuse to sign their contracts. The threat of a baseball strike loomed.

Brooks Robinson set an example for Orioles players by announcing that he would refuse to sign a new contract until the pension issue was satisfactorily settled. Other stars like Boog Powell and Dave McNally joined Robinson. Robinson urged management to enter into serious negotiations. In early February he led an Orioles delegation to New York for a players' meeting that unanimously endorsed a boycott of spring training camps unless the pension issue was resolved.[54]

The owners unanimously reconfirmed their position on 3 January. They offered to continue the talks. The Players Association then asked management to come up with a new compromise offer and repeated its suggestion that the two sides submit to arbitration. Miller indicated that his union was willing to accept a deal on the television issue under which the clubs would increase the size of their contribution to the pension fund rather than agree to set aside a percentage of their TV rights. On 17 February, the eve of the scheduled opening of most spring training camps, the owners rejected the union's suggestion of arbitration but increased their cash offer by $200,000.[55]

The owners' strategy continued to be predicated on the belief that time worked for them. Clubs usually lost money during spring training and thus would save by delaying the opening of the camps. The owners expected that their unpaid employees would soon abandon Miller and report to training. The union was gambling that it could turn the militant stances of the off-season into player solidarity and force the owners to compromise or risk losing the regular season and its profits. On 20 February the Players Association rejected management's latest offer.[56]

Management soon discovered that its calculations were flawed. The television networks were appalled by the prospect that a players' strike might extend into the regular season and began to exert pressure on the owners to settle. Noting the possibility that the owners might have to field teams composed of unknown youngsters and career minor leaguers, an NBC executive warned that his network would refuse to pay "major league prices for minor league games."[57] The Orioles, who were heavily dependent on television income, faced the prospect of serious income loss. In addition, the club's effort to enlarge its regional network was imperiled by the threat of a strike.[58]

Management found player unity equally discouraging. The White Sox opened their camp early, and almost all the team's major league veterans stayed away. A week later, 391 of the 402 players who had voted to strike were missing from camps. Most players continued to work at their off-season employment.[59]

Management mixed tough talk with pleas designed to entice as many players as possible into camp. The Orioles' Frank Lane warned the holdouts to report or an aroused management would "kick their pants off."[60] Frank Cashen claimed that the owners had agreed to "virtually 100 percent of the players' requests" and urged "the players on our club to give serious consideration to accepting this proposal." Cashen stood firm on the issue of television money: "The players have no special right to such revenue. . . . Ownership's position [is] that the benefit plan shall be funded from general assets of the corporation." Brooks Robinson responded that he was ready to "sit it out."[61]

With a potential contender, Orioles management was particularly eager to get its players into camp and avoid creating unnecessary bitterness. Hoffberger assured a meeting of club stockholders that "there has never been an iota of rancor in these negotiations and I do not expect any to carry over once the players get to camp."[62]

The club was encouraged by the decision of a number of its players to report to training camps. On 18 February pitchers Jim Palmer and Pete Richert signed new contracts. Center fielder Paul Blair also announced he would report. Former player representative Dick Hall, a free agent, signed. On 19 February nineteen of thirty-one invited pitchers, catchers, and infielders reported to the Orioles' Miami training camp. Dalton expressed his pleasure at the size of the turnout. Brooks Robinson assured the players in Miami that he and the union held "no animosity" toward them, and gently added that he "wished they wouldn't [report]."[63]

Robinson could afford to remain calm. The numbers were impressive, but the Orioles camp was populated by fringe players. Both Palmer and Blair were rebounding from injuries and fighting for a job. The thirty-eight-year-old Hall was a walk-on with an uncertain future. Richert came to camp because he lacked the savings to join the holdout. The core of the team was sitting out. In addition to Robinson, Powell, and star second baseman Davey Johnson, the team's three top pitchers refused to report. One, pitcher Jim Hardin, came to Miami for contract talks and then walked out, complaining Dalton was unwilling to deal with him in good faith.[64]

The trend was baseballwide. The skilled veterans and stars refused to report. Recognizing that the union had maintained sufficient unity, management decided to compromise quickly. On 22 February, the PRC rejected the latest union compromise offer and suspended the next session of talks. The next day, under pressure from the new commissioner, management changed its mind and asked for a meeting on 24 February. Twenty-four hours later, the two sides reached an agreement. The owners increased their pension fund contribution to $5.45 million, lowered the age at which a former player could begin drawing income, increased the scale of retirement benefits, and lowered the playing time needed for eligibility. The union came down from its original demand of a $6.5 million owners' contribution and agreed to leave unsettled its claim to a percentage of television money.[65]

Each side had achieved an important victory. The players had displayed an unexpected unity of purpose and increased the size of the pension fund without sacrificing their claim to a share of baseball's television income. The owners had achieved their objective of avoiding linking the pension fund to their television income. However, they had also created lasting mistrust between themselves and the union. Miller resented management's use of stalling tactics as a crude effort to destroy the union. *The Sporting News* prophetically warned that the next confrontation between labor and management would likely be "more severe" as a result of the "wounds" the pension battle had opened. Jerold Hoffberger, who, as a member of the Player Relations Committee, was intimately involved in the negotiations, agreed that "it might even be more difficult next time," adding, "I'm positive we'll have this thing every three years. You can bet your bottom dollar on that."[66]

City of Champions

Once the pension issue was settled, management, the players, and the fans settled down for three years of play in which the Orioles were baseball's dominant franchise. The Orioles teams of 1969–71 had all the qualities of a dynasty: power hitting, superb pitching, defense, speed, a blend of age and youth. The team won 318 games on its way to three American League pennants and one World Series championship.

The Orioles' success was paralleled by that of the Colts, who won an NFL championship in 1968 and two years later, following the merger of the AFL and NFL, won the championship of the professional football world. The Baltimore Bullets of the National Basketball Association were also highly successful in these years.

The triumph of its sports teams came at a psychologically critical moment for the city and for its political-business elite. After more than a decade of efforts at urban renewal, the riots of 1968 put into doubt their master plan for reviving Baltimore. The triumphs of Baltimore's sports franchises were proof that the city still retained vitality. On 10 April 1968, a week after the murder of Martin Luther King, Jr., and less than two days after a modicum of order was restored to the areas where rioting occurred in the wake of the assassination, over 22,000 fans braved the passage through a still-smoldering city to gather at Memorial Stadium for opening day. Mayor Thomas D'Alesandro III was present to throw out the first ball and to show the city's determination to continue about its normal business.[67]

Selling Baltimore as the "City of Champions" was a central marketing tool for the political and business leadership in the late 1960s and early 1970s. In 1971 Mayor D'Alesandro explained what championship sports teams had provided his city: "It's realistic to say that everyone benefits—merchants, fans, government, and, through the psychological uplift of being number one, the city as a whole."[68] William Boucher, executive director of the Greater Baltimore Committee, agreed, stressing that the success of the sports franchises created a sense of "unity . . . a city searches for desperately these days."[69] To their traditional belief in the value of professional sports in attracting new business investment, city leaders added a new faith in the efficacy of Baltimore's champions for promoting social and racial harmony, building the local tax base, and directly creating economic prosperity. Football and baseball championship games, in particular, were big money-makers. D'Alesandro estimated that every World Series game brought $250,000 into the city economy.[70]

Realistically, the major value of sports to the city was still indirect. The economic impact of championship games was too small to have a significant effect. Championship games did not create new jobs or significant long-term cash inflows for the city economy. However, the success of its professional teams helped build Baltimore's image and assisted the city in showcasing the progress of its urban renewal. By the late 1960s Baltimore had an impressive record in urban renewal and was on the verge of a major new initiative that would build on these earlier projects to provide the city with a new urban center.

In the late 1950s the Greater Baltimore Committee and the city administration, with support from the state of Maryland and the federal government, had launched a three-pronged assault on the city's ills. The political and business elite believed that improved transportation systems, a new city center, and the redevelopment of the harbor were the keys to a prosperous Baltimore. In 1956 the state established a Baltimore Port Authority with instructions to rebuild the city's decaying harbor areas and attract new private investment. The Port Authority began by revamping the outer harbor's cargo facilities. By the mid-1960s it launched a "Decade of Progress" investment program, committing $90 million to provide Maryland with a technologically modern facility at the Dundalk Marine Terminal for handling containerized cargo. Federal assistance paid for costly dredging of harbor channels that would permit the Dundalk facility to accommodate the largest merchant vessels in use.[71]

The Greater Baltimore Committee was moving forward at the same time with its plans to rebuild the central business district. In 1958 the committee unveiled its plans for Charles Center, a complex of nine new commercial office buildings, retail outlets, a federal office building, a hotel, and two residential apartment complexes, all linked by walkways and underground passages, designed by architect Mies van der Rohe, and financed with public money. By the mid-1960s Charles Center was winning the acclaim of architects and city planners.[72]

If the rebuilt port facilities and central business district were to succeed, Baltimore had to improve its transportation system. In 1957 the Baltimore harbor tunnel opened, offering a direct, economical route for shipments between Washington and points south and the major cities of the Northeast Seaboard. The city and state, using large federal highway construction funding grants, built expressways to link the central business district and port facilities with major interstate freeways and the harbor tunnel. By the end of the decade Baltimore had plans for a rail mass transit system that would link the redeveloped city center with the suburbs.[73]

In the mid-1960s the political-business elite determined to cap their earlier projects with a bold new idea: the redevelopment of Baltimore's commercially valueless Inner Harbor into a showplace of shops, offices, residences, and places of entertainment.[74]

Baltimore's leaders believed that they had to act boldly in order to adjust to economic competition and avoid the collapse of the city. The redevelopment of the inner city carried heavy economic and social consequences. Urban renewal, particularly the building of new freeways, destroyed many inner city neighborhoods. In pouring tax dollars into Charles Center, Baltimore business leaders proposed to alter the city's traditional reliance on heavy industry for income and employment and compete with the suburbs for nonpolluting, high-paying service industries like real estate, insurance, and banking. Diversification would create a healthier city economy. However, the social costs of economic diversification were serious. Diversification required a new type of work force, one that was more mobile and highly educated. Blacks and many of the ethnic groups that relied upon declining traditional industries for employment lacked the job skills to move into the developing sectors of the city economy. Many lower-paying service jobs went to women, changing the relationships within traditional urban families. Concentration on creating service industry employment promised new wealth but also threatened to widen the gap between haves and have-nots in Baltimore and to build a larger class of unemployables.[75]

The role of professional sports in this effort was to build the sinews of city unity, to give Baltimore's residents a sense of shared local pride. In 1971, for example, city businessmen took a leading role in preparing for the Pittsburgh-Baltimore World Series. The business leaders were particularly concerned to build popular enthusiasm by creating events that would encourage public involvement. Many local businesses contributed services to the public celebration, while the city budgeted $10,000 to cover the cost of events.[76]

Baltimore was acutely sensitive to any media criticism that might cast it in an unfavorable light. When ABC newsman Howard K. Smith poked fun at "Bawlmerese," the local style of English pronunciation, during the 1971

World Series, acting mayor William Donald Schaefer immediately unleashed a counterattack against a national media that, he claimed, belittled Baltimore constantly. "They are all so envious of our world champion Orioles and Colts," Schaefer explained in a Greater Baltimore Committee press release, adding that visitors would find that Baltimore was a big league city worthy of its championship sports teams.[77]

Sports, of course, could not single-handedly create a sense of civic identification. City leaders relied upon other means as well to build identification with and support for the new Baltimore. The political and business leadership invited the city's ethnic groups to participate in the revitalization of the Inner Harbor. In 1970, the city inaugurated the first of its annual city fairs at the site of the Inner Harbor development. In the years that followed, Baltimore created individual Inner Harbor fairs to honor each of its major ethnic and racial groups.[78]

No minority group was fully satisfied with the city's redevelopment programs. None was more at odds with the political-business leadership than Baltimore's largest and fastest growing minority, its black population. The riots of 1968 were a response to the failure of the city's leadership elite to meet basic black needs for housing and employment. In the 1971 mayoral election, black demands moved to the center of Baltimore's political agenda. City council president William Donald Schaefer, with the backing of the city's traditional elite and ethnic voters, defeated a black candidate in a divided and tense city.[79]

The new mayor, a pragmatic reformer, had fully supported the Inner Harbor development strategy and was firmly convinced of the utility of professional sports in building civic pride and a positive image of the new Baltimore. Schaefer soon discovered that the city's two major sports teams were developing a political agenda of their own, one that would require massive investment of tax funds. In the 1960s the Baltimore Colts began campaigning for a new publicly financed stadium located in the rebuilt city center. The stadium issue became a major political problem in the succeeding decade. Retaining Baltimore's champions would be a very expensive proposition for a mayor and a city already burdened with the costs of creating a new economic base.

And on the Field

The Orioles certainly did their part in creating the image of a city of champions. Dalton proved capable both of building and of maintaining a championship squad. Assisted by two shrewd judges of talent, Weaver and a recently rehired Jim McLaughlin, he established a baseball dynasty in Baltimore.

In the wake of the 1968 expansion draft, the Orioles had reshuffled their forty-man roster. Pitching remained a major concern in spite of good performances from McNally, Hardin, and Tom Phoebus. The club lost four pitchers in the expansion draft, including veteran reliever Moe Drabowski and young prospect Roger Nelson. Dalton picked up free agent Dick Hall, a former Oriole, to replace Drabowski. The club still needed another starting pitcher. In December 1968 Dalton got left-hander Mike Cuellar from Houston in exchange for power-hitting Curt Blefary. By the time spring training began, Dalton had assembled six candidates for Weaver's four-man rotation and a number of good utility players for his bench.

The Orioles opened the season with a loss, but they took over first place on 16 April. They never surrendered their lead, clinching the American League Eastern Division title on 13 September. Frank Robinson hit .308 with thirty-two home runs and one hundred RBIs. Boog Powell hit .304. McNally won twenty games and Cuellar twenty-three, while Jim Palmer rebounded from two injury-plagued years to post a 16–4 record. The club concluded with a 109–53 record and swept Minnesota in the first American League championship series.

The club's major problem that season was attracting paying customers. Although attendance rebounded by almost 200,000, to 1,062,094, the Orioles averaged only 14,000 fans per game to watch one of the finest teams ever to play professional baseball. One critic remarked, "This is the only town in America that will have to have 'bat day' [promotions] to get 20,000 people in here for the playoffs."[80] Baseball writer Roger Angell took a kindlier view, commenting that "Baltimoreans do care about the Orioles, but their curious affair is mostly conducted at long distance, by radio and television." He also noted that a deep pessimism hung over Baltimore sports fans in the wake of losses to New York teams by the Colts and Bullets in championship games earlier that year, "and the Orioles' success fills their townsmen's hearts with despair."[81]

The pessimism proved well grounded. For the third time in 1969 a superior Baltimore team lost a championship to a New York squad. The Mets outpitched and outhit the Orioles, made great defensive plays, and silenced the vaunted Baltimore attack to win the World Series in five games. Amazin'.

In the aftermath of a crushing defeat, Dalton tried without success to improve baseball's best team by acquiring another top pitcher. Failing in this effort, he relied on the team's well-stocked minor league system to bolster the squad and on Earl Weaver to provide the motivation for a return to the World Series. Dalton believed that Weaver's efforts received a welcome boost from a crowd of 5,000 that turned out to welcome the dispirited Orioles back from the disaster in New York. "People say rah-rah only goes so far these days," Dalton recalled a year later, "but I know after the players saw how the fans reacted that they became more determined than ever to win it all."[82]

The 1970 team, which *Sports Illustrated* labeled the "superlative Orioles," lived up to expectations.[83] The Orioles cruised into first place on 26 April, clinched their second straight American League Eastern Division title on 16 September, and ended the season with a record of 108–54. The pitching was formidable. The starting pitchers completed sixty games. Cuellar and Mc-Nally won twenty-four games apiece, and Palmer had twenty victories. Powell was the American League's most valuable player, hitting 35 home runs and driving in 115 runs. Overall, the team hit 179 home runs, as it finished fifteen games ahead of the second-place Yankees.

Minnesota once more provided the opposition in the American League championship series, and the Orioles again swept the Twins. The National League champion Cincinnati Reds put up only slightly greater resistance, as the Orioles redeemed their 1969 setback by winning the 1970 World Series in five games.

After the 1969 World Series defeat, Dalton had declared, "We don't want to stand pat just because we won our division by nineteen games."[84] In the wake of victory, Dalton continued to search for a top pitcher to team with McNally, Palmer, and Cuellar. He finally got his man by swapping two pitchers to San Diego for right-hander Pat Dobson. Further improvement, Dalton said, would come from the Orioles' highly productive farm system.[85]

Dobson fit nicely into manager Weaver's 1971 pitching rotation. After a slower start, the Orioles claimed first place for good on 5 June, took their third straight division title on 24 September, and finished the season with a 101–57 record. All four starters won twenty games. Outfielder Merv Rettenmund, a product of the Baltimore farm system, led the team in batting. Thirty-six-year-old Frank Robinson contributed twenty-eight home runs and ninety-nine RBIs. Brooks Robinson hit .272 with twenty home runs, while driving in ninety-two runs.

The Oakland A's provided the opposition in the 1971 American League championship series, which the Orioles won in yet another sweep. The World Series pitted heavily favored Baltimore against Pittsburgh. A hard-fought struggle that went to the full seven games ended with a Pittsburgh triumph. Superb Pittsburgh pitching throttled the Baltimore offense, while the Pirates offense proved a bit better than Orioles pitching. Following the loss, a confident Weaver predicted his team would win a hundred games again in 1972 and avenge its setback in the World Series.[86]

Weaver proved wrong. Eight years passed before he led a Baltimore team into another World Series. The fall of 1971 marked the end of another era in Baltimore baseball. In October, Harry Dalton, feeling that he had nothing left to conquer in Baltimore and eager for a new challenge, accepted an offer from the California Angels to take charge of their faltering franchise and build it into a winner.[87] Two months later, the Orioles traded the aging Frank Robinson to the Los Angeles Dodgers. Both men would be sorely missed. Without Robinson's leadership and hitting, the 1972 Orioles lacked offensive power. Harry Dalton had created a baseball dynasty in Baltimore with shrewd trades and attention to minor league operations. Due to low attendance, the club's financial viability was increasingly tied to its participation in postseason play. In 1972, following the departure of Dalton and Robinson, the Orioles fell from the heights. Baltimore baseball entered a period of prolonged financial crisis.

A new franchise gets off to a shaky start in September 1953. A worried Mayor
Thomas D'Alesandro, Jr., attempts to peer into the room where major league owners
were debating the proposed shift of the St. Louis Browns to Baltimore. (copyright
Washington Post; reprinted by permission of the D.C. Public Library)

Bill Veeck at the time of his purchase
of the St. Louis Browns (copyright
Washington Post; reprinted by permission of the D.C. Public Library)

Clarence Miles (copyright *Washington
Post*; reprinted by permission of the
D.C. Public Library)

Jack Dunn, *left*, and Paul Richards, *right*, display the field uniform of the new Orioles manager/general manager in 1954 (courtesy Babe Ruth Birthplace/Baltimore Orioles Museum)

Mayor D'Alesandro meets with the Orioles' reorganized management team in April 1956 as part of efforts to promote the team's upcoming season. *Left to right*: team president James Keelty, assistant general manager Jack Dunn, Mayor D'Alesandro, public relations director E. Paul Walsh, and manager/general manager Paul Richards (courtesy Babe Ruth Birthplace/Baltimore Orioles Museum)

Lee MacPhail (courtesy Baltimore Orioles)

Hank Bauer
(courtesy Baltimore Orioles)

Zanvyl Krieger
(courtesy Baltimore Orioles)

Jerold Hoffberger
(courtesy Baltimore Orioles)

As part of the effort to build a new Baltimore, Mayor D'Alesandro, *right*, meets with representatives of the Greater Baltimore Committee, including Orioles board member and builder Thomas Mullan, *center*, to endorse their plans for a $25 million bond issue to finance Charles Center, the beginning of the reconstruction of the central business district (courtesy Baltimore City Archives)

The new Baltimore, as seen in a 1976 photograph showing the completed Charles Center, *upper center*, and the initial stages of the Inner Harbor redevelopment project. The arrow points to the future site of Harbor Place, the crown jewel of the Inner Harbor development. (copyright *Washington Post*; reprinted by permission of the D.C. Public Library)

Another side of Baltimore appears in this scene of a CORE worker attempting to form a tenants' association in one of the city's black areas during the tense summer of 1966 (copyright *Washington Post*; reprinted by permission of the D.C. Public Library)

Mayor Theodore McKeldin (copyright *Washington Post*; reprinted by permission of the D.C. Public Library)

Harry Dalton
(courtesy Baltimore Orioles)

Earl Weaver
(courtesy Baltimore Orioles)

Series MVP Brooks Robinson hugs winning pitcher Mike Cuellar as shortstop Mark Belanger and a Memorial Stadium crowd celebrate the Orioles' triumph in the 1970 World Series (copyright *Washington Post*; reprinted by permission of the D.C. Public Library)

Dave McNally heads toward first base after hitting the first grand slam home run by a pitcher in World Series competition, 13 October 1970. Outfielder Don Buford looks on. Six years later, McNally and fellow pitcher Andy Messersmith mounted the challenge that ended baseball's perpetual reserve system. (copyright *Washington Post*; reprinted by permission of the D.C. Public Library)

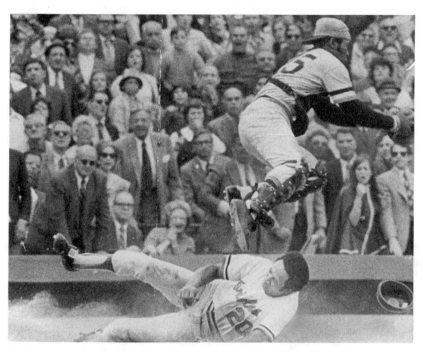

Frank Robinson slides home to score the winning run in the tenth inning of the sixth game of the 1971 World Series. Robinson's intelligent, aggressive play made him the natural leader of the 1966–71 Orioles teams. (copyright *Washington Post*; reprinted by permission of the D.C. Public Library)

Jim Palmer, the mainstay of the Orioles pitching staff in the 1970s and early 1980s, hurls a strike during the 1971 World Series (copyright *Washington Post*; reprinted by permission of the D.C. Public Library)

Memorial Stadium, the bait that initially attracted a major league team to Baltimore, soon became the central issue in a twenty-year debate over public funding of privately owned sports franchises in Maryland (courtesy Baltimore Orioles)

Frank Cashen
(courtesy New York Mets)

Henry J. Peters
(courtesy Baltimore Orioles)

Eddie Murray homers during the 1979 World Series. A remarkably consistent offensive and defensive player, the quiet Murray was a clubhouse leader and the offensive heart of Baltimore's superb 1979–83 teams. (copyright *Washington Post*; reprinted by permission of the D.C. Public Library)

Edward Bennett Williams
(courtesy Baltimore Orioles)

During the strike of 1981 an empty clubhouse and piled up mail give mute testimony
to a summer without major league baseball (copyright *Washington Post*; reprinted by
permission of the D.C. Public Library)

Union leader Marvin Miller leaves a federal mediation session during the 1981 players' strike (copyright *Washington Post*; reprinted by permission of the D.C. Public Library)

Joe Altobelli (courtesy Baltimore Orioles)

Edward Bennett Williams, *left*, President Ronald Reagan, *center*, and Commissioner Peter Ueberroth, *right*, watch the first game of the 1986 season from the Orioles dugout. One of Williams's many marketing triumphs was capturing the presidential opener for his club. (courtesy Ronald Reagan Presidential Library, National Archives and Records Administration)

Roland Hemond
(courtesy Baltimore Orioles)

Cal Ripken, Jr., the young star around whom the Orioles' rebuilding effort would begin (courtesy Ronald Reagan Presidential Library, National Archives and Records Administration)

A new era begins for Baltimore baseball, as Governor William Donald Schaefer, *right*, introduces and gives his blessing to Eli Jacobs, the new owner of the Orioles, at a December 1988 press conference (courtesy Governor's Office, State of Maryland)

A World Turned Upside Down

The world of athletics has burst its fiscal seams in every direction and is now big, big business.
—Arthur Daley, *New York Times,* February 1972

Robert Short, the last owner of the Washington Senators, was a bad parody of Bill Veeck. The round, short-tempered, and very persuasive Short was a wealthy Minneapolis businessman and a power to be reckoned with in the state and national Democratic Party. In 1968 he purchased the lackluster and money-losing Senators from local businessmen. Like Veeck's, Short's financing was limited. He reportedly bought the club with a cash outlay of $1,000, using his other businesses as collateral for a $9.4 million loan. Like Veeck, Short relied on promotions to build his fan base. Unlike Veeck, he knew nothing about running a baseball club.

Short's first move was a public relations stroke of genius. The Senators' new owner hired the legendary Ted Williams to manage his club. In 1969 Williams led a group of journeymen to what constituted dizzying heights for Washington baseball: a fourth-place finish with a winning record (86–76). Attendance jumped by nearly 350,000. The following year, the Senators played at their true level of competence, and the club dropped back to last place with a 70–92 season record. Attendance fell by nearly 100,000. No help was in sight. Short had inherited a weak farm system and did little to improve it. Looking for a name player to bring in fans, he traded away the left side of his infield, one of the club's few strengths, together with the team's best pitcher, Joe Coleman, for Detroit's troubled former Cy Young award-winner, pitcher Denny McLain. Short increased his promotions, setting a major league record for giving away pantyhose in an effort to attract female fans. McLain proceeded to lose twenty-two games for the inept 1971 Senators as attendance dropped another 170,000. Short criticized the fans for nonattendance, proclaimed that the stadium was unsafe, demanded major concessions in the terms of his lease from the municipally operated Robert F. Kennedy Stadium operations board, and raised ticket prices until they were the highest in the major leagues. At the end of three years, Short had alienated the Washington fans, press, and political establishment.[1]

Fortunately for Short, the city of Arlington, Texas, a community located between Dallas and Ft. Worth, was willing to provide a $7 million loan and a rent-free stadium if he would move his team. Two decades earlier, in parallel circumstances, the American League's owners had driven Veeck to the edge of bankruptcy and forced him to sell to local ownership before approving a franchise shift. When Short, having displayed his managerial incompetence, demanded the right to move, his fellow owners acted with alacrity. Short successfully hamstrung local efforts in Washington to purchase the team. He easily convinced fellow owners to approve a shift by reminding them that each had the right to move his property whenever profit called. The owners overrode the objections of Commissioner Kuhn, Jerold Hoffberger, and Chicago's Arthur Allyn and voted 10–2 to approve Short's request to move the franchise on 21 September 1971.[2] In an editorial sarcastically entitled "How to Succeed in Baseball," *The Sporting News* took the owners to task for their handling of Short's move: "One of the most objectionable aspects of the Washington franchise loss was the premium it put on failure. . . . Short has been miraculously rewarded. His American League lodge brothers have handed him the key to the bank vault."[3]

The Senators' relocation to Texas was the first of a series of off-the-field developments that convulsed baseball between 1971 and 1973. A players' strike and a major court test of the reserve clause followed, as the battle between labor and management entered a new phase. For players, for owners, and especially for fans, the baseball world was truly turned upside down. The fans' anger focused on the players who had upset the stable world of professional baseball and were launching the sport into a decade of unprecedented chaos. The Orioles found themselves embroiled in these industry-wide problems while simultaneously facing a major management reorganization, the loss of profitability, a growing stadium controversy, and the difficulties of rebuilding their major league club.

A Strange Way to Do Business

Hoffberger's opposition to the Senators' move was an act of principle. More than any owner except Short, he would gain from the relocation of baseball to

Texas. Moving the Senators opened up a vast new territory to the south for a team with one of the smallest geographic markets in baseball. Nevertheless, Hoffberger assisted Commissioner Kuhn's efforts to find a local buyer for the Senators and twice voted against the relocation. The team had consistently opposed franchise shifts in the 1960s. Cashen told reporters: "We've always maintained there should be a team in Washington. It's a matter of principle." He added that the Orioles had informed the other owners that, despite talk of their sometimes playing in Washington if the Senators moved away, the team would continue to play all its home games in Baltimore: "We made that infinitely clear at the meeting. We feel [that] we are the Baltimore Orioles and will remain so."[4]

Once the move was made, Hoffberger was determined to defend his new territory from intrusion by either league. The club's continued profitability was at stake. In the fall of 1970 Frank Cashen noted the first symptoms of financial trouble for Baltimore Baseball. Attendance during the 1969, 1970, and 1971 championship seasons averaged 150,000 less than during the 1966 World Series year. The Orioles drew better on the road than at home. The club declared a $1.40 dividend in 1970, but Cashen warned stockholders, "It is troublesome but true that the club would have done no better than break even on [its] regular season income. It was the extra income generated by the Championship series and World Series which provided the corporation's profit."[5] Between 1968 and 1974 the team's net income from games fluctuated between a low of $2,340,757 (1968) and a high of $2,624,212 (1970). Broadcasting income rose steadily until the 1972 season. It dropped by almost $200,000 when the team failed to make the playoffs. Concessions sales grew robustly between 1968 ($358,661) and 1974 ($575,327) but constituted the smallest increment of the club's major income sources. Overall, while club income rose by approximately $750,000 in the seven-year period 1968–74, operating expenses rose by $850,000. Player salaries, spring training expenses, player development costs, and the rental fee on Memorial Stadium all increased.[6]

Orioles management recognized that the team could not count on continuous participation in highly lucrative postseason play. By the end of the 1972 season, Hoffberger and Cashen were convinced that they must expand their market. Building a new stadium, combined with the cautious pursuit of former Washington fans, appeared the best way to solidify the club's financial base. The Orioles hired a Washington public relations firm to begin a low-key marketing campaign designed to attract an extra 75,000 paying customers a year to Orioles games.[7]

The flight of the second Senators franchise spurred the creation of a coalition of Washington businessmen and congressmen who began to apply pressure on the major leagues to put another team in the nation's capital. Joseph Danzansky, the wealthy and civic-spirited owner of Giant Foods, the largest grocery chain in the area, put together a syndicate to purchase a team. Members of Congress, led by Representatives B. F. Sisk and Frank Horton, lobbied the major leagues, warning of possible antitrust legislation. Their efforts had the sympathetic support of Commissioner Kuhn, a Washington native, who sought to bring a team back to the nation's capital while dissuading the congressmen from taking legal action to end baseball's antitrust exemption. For the next seven years, Hoffberger avoided a direct clash with these powerful forces while tenaciously holding on to his new territory. The Orioles' ability to attract Washington fans was severely constricted by the ongoing efforts of these groups to find a team for Washington.[8]

Hoffberger's determination to protect his new territories was a logical response to the chaotic way in which the baseball cartel operated. The Washington franchise relocation was another example of the weakness of baseball's central management. Kuhn had been powerless to stop the move. Hoffberger, in company with other baseball men, urged that the sport reorganize and put more power in a single authority. In 1969 the committee on structural reform that Hoffberger chaired recommended a considerable increase in the authority of the commissioner over playing rules, umpiring, marketing, broadcasting, legal matters, and public relations and urged the diminution of the role and power of the leagues and their officials.[9]

The Hoffberger committee's proposals were quietly buried by oldline owners like Los Angeles's Walter O'Malley. Bowie Kuhn's initial success as commissioner seemed to weaken the argument that the office needed wider powers to do its job. Kuhn, who worked closely with the Hoffberger committee, was keenly aware that baseball had to improve its marketing, its public image, and its relationship with the major television networks. He restructured the commissioner's office to achieve these goals.[10] Kuhn, however, lacked authority over critical issues such as labor relations and interleague cooperation. Hoffberger had to act independently to secure his club's interests.

In late 1971 the Orioles' problems were pressing but local. The club's margin of profit was evaporating, and Hoffberger faced a major job rebuilding an old ball club without the assistance of his top baseball man.

The 1971 Orioles were an aging collection of extremely talented athletes. Frank Robinson was thirty-six, and Brooks Robinson was thirty-four, as was leadoff man Don Buford. Powell, although only thirty, had trouble staying in top physical condition, and his play suffered as a result. Pitching ace Mike Cuellar was thirty-five. The Orioles farm system had not produced a top pitcher since the mid-1960s and was without a good prospect, although it was loaded with highly regarded infielders and outfielders. Two young outfielders, Merv Rettenmund and Don Baylor, had played their way onto the major league roster.

Harry Dalton's October 1971 departure was a major blow to Hoffberger.

The Orioles owner resented what he believed was the Angels' "tampering" with his employee. He handed complete control of club operations to his trusted aide, Frank Cashen, on a "temporary" basis. The *Sun*'s Bob Maisel observed shrewdly that this temporary appointment could last a long time. Hoffberger tended to promote from within the organization, and years could pass before another man of Dalton's quality emerged.[11]

Before leaving, Dalton agreed to refrain from raiding the Orioles scouting staff for a year. This enabled Cashen to take control of a stable organization, evaluate its personnel, and utilize the advice of experienced baseball men. Weaver's influence over club policy increased since he was an extremely good judge of talent.[12]

Cashen soon revealed that he had both the boldness and skills to play the role of a baseball general manager. The plainspoken, stocky Cashen moved quickly to restructure the team and keep it competitive over the long term. On 2 December 1971 Cashen traded Frank Robinson and pitcher Pete Richert to Los Angeles for four young prospects, among them pitcher Doyle Alexander. The Robinson trade was logical. Robinson himself had suggested that with the development of Baylor and Rettenmund "the club has to do something" to clear up an overcrowded outfield situation.[13] Nevertheless, the Orioles were taking a big chance. Robinson was the team's leader and, although thirty-six, was still one of the best hitters in the game. Weaver, who had an important role in working out the deal, was convinced that although the task would be difficult, the Orioles could win a fourth consecutive pennant without Robinson. He labeled the trade "a 1974–1975 type deal for us,"[14] admitting that "there is no way we can look good . . . for a couple of years."[15] Most Orioles players expressed concern and puzzlement over the trade. Detroit's manager, Billy Martin, was more succinct: "They're dead without Robinson."[16]

Strike!

Before the American League could test Martin's prophecy, baseball endured the first regular-season strike in its modern history. At immediate issue were the size and source of the owners' contribution to the player pension fund. Behind this important issue, however, lay the hidden agendas of the two sides. The reserve clause was under serious attack. A powerful minority of owners wanted to break the union before it undermined their control over the players. The Players Association and its leader, Marvin Miller, were equally determined to modify the reserve clause, increasing the bargaining leverage of players in contract talks. The hardline minority of owners played into Miller's hands.

On 8 October 1969 the St. Louis Cardinals and Philadelphia Phillies announced a major player swap. The Cardinals sent their talented center fielder, Curt Flood, to Philadelphia for Richie Allen, a temperamental power hitter. Allen offered no objections. The proud Flood balked and refused to report. While Flood was delighted to leave the Cardinals, he had business interests in the St. Louis area and regarded Philadelphia as a hotbed of racism. Flood sought advice from the Players Association. Miller was ready to support a court test of the reserve clause but warned Flood that it would be time-consuming and would probably end his career. The legal precedents involved in Flood's suit ensured that the U.S. Supreme Court would ultimately decide the case. Flood convinced the labor chief of his determination to fight for the right to play for whatever team he wanted. Miller arranged for former Supreme Court justice Arthur Goldberg to take the case.[17]

On 24 December 1969 Flood sent a letter to the commissioner reiterating his refusal to play for Philadelphia and asking Kuhn to inform the other clubs of his availability. Kuhn rejected this request on 30 December, stating that the reserve clause gave Philadelphia the exclusive right to Flood's services in perpetuity. Three weeks later, Flood filed suit against major league baseball in federal court in New York City, charging that the clubs, by invoking the reserve clause, were denying his right to gainful employment, thus engaging in a conspiracy that violated interstate commerce and antitrust provisions of the law. Flood also sought an immediate injunction that would permit him to play in the 1970 season.[18]

Responding to Flood's suit, organized baseball accused the outfielder of failure to maintain his contractual obligations, charged the Players Association with acting in bad faith by providing support to Flood, and warned that the overthrow of the reserve clause would destroy the game. In an apocalyptic description of the sport without a reserve clause, the major leagues claimed that all the talented players would gravitate to a few larger-city franchises for higher salaries, causing smaller franchises and the minor leagues to collapse.[19]

Management and players were on a "collision course," *The Sporting News* warned, urging the owners to avoid a confrontation by offering modifications to the existing system.[20] Brooks Robinson took essentially the same line. Noting his personal desire to remain in Baltimore, the Orioles player representative stressed the players' interest in modifications of the reserve rule that would permit them to try out the market at some point in their careers rather than overthrow the entire system.[21]

A majority of the owners rejected concessions. The old way of doing things was under attack, and the owners as a group were psychologically unable to accept compromise. As their legal position eroded, resistance to change increased. In December 1969 the National Labor Relations Board (NLRB) had intervened in another baseball dispute to order union elections for umpires. The NLRB's action effectively placed all professional sports under the jurisdiction of U.S. labor law and opened the way for the introduction of arbitration procedures in labor-management relations.[22]

This setback produced a hardening of the owners' position in the talks for renewal of the Basic Agreement. While the negotiators carefully avoided the issues raised by the Flood suit, it hovered over the talks. The owners put forward a take-it-or-leave-it offer that the players rejected on 27 January 1970. The talks continued throughout the spring of 1970. Ultimately the owners made significant concessions to secure labor peace. The new Basic Agreement increased both the minimum salary and playoff money that players received, provided termination pay for players released during spring training, and set formal limits to the amount by which a team could cut player salaries. Most important, the new agreement established the principal of independent arbitration on all issues that did not involve the "integrity of the game." In return for these concessions, the players temporarily abandoned their demand for a reduction of the 162-game schedule.[23]

The second Basic Agreement was a major victory for Miller. He solidified his support among the majority of players by winning an increased minimum salary and termination rights. At the same time he laid the groundwork for the introduction of arbitration into salary disputes, which would significantly increase the individual player's bargaining ability. The big loser under the second Basic Agreement was Commissioner Kuhn, whose claim to impartiality was repudiated by the owners when they agreed to independent arbitration of a majority of issues. Miller had insisted that the commissioner was the owners' employee and therefore ineligible to participate in labor-management discussions as an impartial arbitrator. The owners tacitly accepted Miller's viewpoint.[24]

Meanwhile, the Flood suit moved into the courts. In testimony before Federal District Judge Irving Cooper, organized baseball tried to establish its case that the abolition of the reserve clause would destroy the game's balance. Management also claimed that the players enjoyed "equal" bargaining strength with the owners under the existing reserve system. On 12 August 1970, Judge Cooper ruled in favor of organized baseball, noting that a district court could not "lightly" overrule a decision of the Supreme Court.[25]

The judge's ruling, combined with an almost simultaneous court victory in the suit of two former umpires fired in 1968 for union organization activities, seemed to reestablish management's position. In fact, the owners' victories were built on sand. *New York Times* columnist Leonard Koppett observed that the end of the reserve clause under the impact of a players' strike or other maneuvers was "only a question of time" and urged the owners to compromise with the players. *The Sporting News* also renewed its plea for compromise, noting that Judge Cooper had urged it, that Commissioner Kuhn endorsed it, and that the Players Association was ready for a deal. A majority of the owners were unwilling to accept this advice.[26]

The owners got a foretaste of the effects of a policy of confrontation with their employees in October 1970 when the umpires struck at the opening of the major league playoff games. Capable replacements were available from the minors, but the major leagues hastily settled after one day and granted umpires a four-year contract that increased both their cut of championship game income and their health benefits. The owners could not afford the appearance of questionable officiating on televised championship games, so they capitulated. The sport's credibility and their television incomes were at stake.[27]

During 1971 baseball enjoyed a brief respite of relative labor peace. The Flood case was working its way up to the U.S. Supreme Court on appeal. An appeals court upheld Judge Cooper, again stressing that only the high court could reverse its 1922 Federal League decision. The Supreme Court agreed in October 1971 to hear the Flood case during its 1972 spring term.[28]

The calm preceded a new storm. Negotiations for a renewal of the pension agreement were underway. Management and labor were at loggerheads over the issue of the clubs' television income. The pension plan traditionally was funded from 60 percent of the national television payments from the World Series and 95 percent of All-Star Game TV money. After signing its lucrative new national TV pact in 1965, organized baseball took the position that it would pay a lump sum out of its revenues into the pension plan and refused to divulge information on its television income to the union. Eventually, under pressure from the union and the press, the owners yielded and turned over the information in late 1971. Armed with this information, the Players Association demanded a major increase in payments into the pension fund.[29]

The labor-management confrontation of the spring of 1972 was a classic mismatch. In spite of appearances, the Players Association was much stronger than management. Marvin Miller had created a cohesive union by following a strategy that increased the basic benefits of all players. He was consistently flexible in tactics, winning concessions incrementally over a period of years. As a result, the players were better informed about the issues, wealthier, and deeply grateful to Miller.[30]

Management hid its fundamental disunity behind an apparently unyielding hardline stance. The owners disliked the union but were unable to agree on how to deal with it. Without exception, they had a difficult time adjusting to the end of paternalism and the introduction of a pattern of labor-management relations prevailing in other industries. Most owners had bought clubs for reasons that had more to do with psychological reinforcement than achieving a high rate of return on their investment. Still, none enjoyed losing money. The owners relished the prestige that went with possession of a club and also reveled in the opportunity to have special access to the youthful heroes who played the national sport. They became deeply resentful when these young men began to demand higher wages and increased benefits. Harry Dalton recalled: "I think all the clubs had a feeling . . . that they treated their players well. When they saw that the players were standing up and saying: 'well you're not doing right by me and I need professional help and union help,' a lot of owners . . . resented it and some . . . were hurt by it. I know Hoffberger was."[31]

A few owners, including Hoffberger, realized that management would have to make substantial concessions. Others, like St. Louis's August Busch, believed that they could destroy the Players Association by forcing a strike and then return to the halcyon, pre–Marvin Miller days of owner paternalism.[32]

In the spring of 1972 the owners began preparing for a confrontation with the union. They cut back on spring training to save money and simultaneously proposed to increase their pension contribution by $372,000 over three years. Miller claimed that the owners' offer failed to offset inflation and in effect asked the players to accept a 17 percent erosion of the value of their pension. He warned that the Players Association would strike rather than accept the offer.[33]

The union wanted a $700,000 increase in the owners' payment into the fund. On 10 March 1972 Chicago White Sox players voted 31–0 to authorize a strike. Orioles players followed suit a few days later.[34]

The owners met on 22 March and voted to stand pat on their pension offer. Hoffberger, a member of the Player Relations Committee, publicly endorsed management's position, telling reporters, "I am certain—as certain as one can be in this life—that there is no more money available."[35] Both Hoffberger and Cashen were anxious to avoid further provoking the union and disavowed Busch's open challenge to Miller to call a strike.

A strike would put the Orioles in a difficult position. Cashen noted that lagging attendance was a major problem in Baltimore and, indeed, throughout baseball. He reiterated that without the extra income provided by three successive World Series appearances, the club would have lost money. A large pension hike combined with the club's rising salary scale would make the Orioles unprofitable. Cashen cautioned the players that a strike would probably lead to cancellation of the entire 1972 season. In the event of a cancellation, the club would take moderate but acceptable financial losses. The long-term effects worried the Orioles: "Your fans [may] discover while you're out that they don't really need baseball that much." The potential loss of paid-in-advance season ticket holders would be particularly damaging for the financially strapped Orioles.[36]

Hoping to maintain some influence with the players and avoid an extended walkout, Hoffberger requested a meeting with his team prior to a 26 March spring training game with Texas. He presented management's case, outlined the current state of the negotiations, and warned that in the event of a strike he would have to shut down team operations.[37]

Neither Hoffberger's explanations nor other owners' threats dissuaded the players. On 31 March the player representatives voted 47–0 with one abstention that unless the negotiators reached an agreement or the owners agreed to submit the pension issue to binding arbitration, they would strike the following day.[38]

The Orioles and the twenty-three other major league teams suspended operations on 1 April. While the official line was that management meant business, Orioles officials were already looking toward a quick resolution of the impasse and avoided any criticism of individual players. As one official noted: "Our team's success has been based on getting along with each other. We could destroy that."[39] Prior to the players' departure, Hoffberger again met with them for four and a half hours. In a meeting that Brooks Robinson characterized as "frank," Hoffberger labeled "Marvin Miller's position" on pension funds "ridiculous," and urged the players to "take the leadership, change their votes and accept the [owners'] proposal."[40]

After an impassioned presentation, Hoffberger withdrew and the players debated the issues. The players confirmed the strike vote. Brooks Robinson explained that he respected Hoffberger, but the issue was "a matter of principle." Second baseman Davey Johnson, the team's alternate player representative, remarked that the owners had "decided to test us" and that the players had to stand united behind Marvin Miller.[41]

Although rebuffed, Hoffberger continued to take a conciliatory, if somewhat demeaning, approach: "I am not angry with my players, I am disappointed in them. I am not angry because I do not think they knew what they were voting for." Cashen echoed this thinly veiled attack on Marvin Miller, warning that the players were in for a "rude awakening" when neither management nor the fans came on "hands and knees" to beg them to play.[42]

Management continued to believe that, as *Sun* columnist Bob Maisel put it, Marvin Miller was an "Edgar Bergen with 600 Charlie McCarthies." The owners cherished this illusion, to their own detriment, for more than a decade. The players rallied around Miller because of his skill at winning concessions and because he addressed issues that they recognized as central to their long-term well-being. The owners' belief that they could return to a paternalistic relationship with their employees if Miller left the scene encouraged them in their efforts to break the union.[43]

The owners' tendency to take a hard line and expect their employees to surrender was reinforced by their own lack of solidarity and by fan and player reaction to the strike. The owners were rarely able to agree upon a flexible negotiating strategy. Public opinion polls showed consistent fan support for management's positions. Finally, the players were genuinely reluctant to strike. The *Sun* noted that the Orioles players' reaction to the strike was "a mixture of bewilderment, disappointment, and regret." Brooks Robinson probably expressed their views succinctly when he commented that if they had to strike, he wanted to get it over with as soon as possible. The owners counted upon public pressure to drive the reluctant players into accepting their offer. However, the players proved to be remarkably immune from public pressure and as the possessors of unique skills, they were irreplaceable. Moreover, the players were united by substantive grievances rather than simply by a charismatic leader. Management repeatedly had to swallow compromises it disliked.[44]

The 1972 strike set the pattern for future labor-management confrontations. The union offered a series of compromise proposals that management initially rejected. Once owner unity was badly frayed, management accepted the substance of one of the union's offers. In 1972, the union initially proposed that an existing surplus in the pension fund be applied to make up the difference between the players' demands and management's offer. After the owners rejected this, Miller offered to reduce the size of the Players Association's demands in exchange for greater control over the administration of the pension fund. Next, the players suggested that they would play while the issue was submitted to binding arbitration. Finally, after a ten-day strike, the owners' unity broke down, and amid a chorus of attacks on Marvin Miller, management presented a financial proposal that met the players' demands.[45]

The strike was a trying experience for Hoffberger and his baseball staff. Manager Earl Weaver got the club into an unnecessary clash with the union when he told reporters that sixteen of his players had been willing to play the canceled 1 April game and that he would shortly poll his team to see how many were ready to play. Weaver estimated that fully 50 percent of all major leaguers were ready to play, adding, "I just want the fans to know that it is not entirely the Baltimore players' fault, because a majority . . . wanted to play." Frank Cashen suggested that only four or five "diehards" were preventing the team from playing.[46]

Brooks Robinson politely corrected Weaver's account of the players' meeting. An angry Marvin Miller accused Hoffberger of coordinating an effort to break the strike, labeling the Orioles owner a "hardline reactionary." Miller added that Hoffberger had tried to coerce his players into repudiating the union by giving them false information on the Players Association's views. He flew to Baltimore on 5 April to meet with eighteen players at Robinson's house.[47]

The meeting produced a display of union solidarity. Miller threatened Hoffberger and Weaver with legal action under the Taft-Hartley Act if they continued to interfere in union activities. Cashen poured fuel on a smoldering personal dispute by suggesting that Miller and a few radical associates were coercing the players to strike while he and Hoffberger had the athletes' "best interests" at heart.[48]

Brooks Robinson attempted to maintain a level of civil discourse between management and labor. As the leader of the Baltimore players and a member of the union's four-man pension board, Robinson was well informed about the state of negotiations. He recognized that Hoffberger favored a compromise, but warned that the PRC was dominated by a group of owners determined "to bring us to our knees and break us." While encouraging the players to work out in expectation of an eventual settlement, Robinson attempted to defuse public discontent at an 8 April press conference. The union, Robinson told reporters, was anxious for a compromise but wanted a fair one. He criticized local newspapers for taking a generally promanagement stance in their coverage of the issues. Robinson recalled: "It was a very unpopular movement. . . . No one expected people to understand, but it was our fight and we were going to do what we had to do."[49]

Hoffberger faced a difficult task in attempting to win over a majority within the PRC for compromise. By his own admission, Hoffberger had little influence in owners' councils. He was usually in the minority on key issues. In April 1972 Hoffberger was part of a three-man minority trying to convince five other owners that the PRC should offer a new proposal to the union. Eventually, aided by the two league presidents, the minority won its point. Management made an offer the union could accept. Final settlement was delayed for four days while the owners and players squabbled over whether to make up the games canceled by the strike. Finally, on 13 April 1972, the hardliners yielded to the moderates and settled.[50]

The terms of the new pension agreement constituted another success for the union. The owners increased their payment by $500,000 over their original offer, to $5.9 million. They insisted, however, that they would not replay the lost games and would dock the players' pay. Miller agreed since he favored reducing the number of games. Some owners then took out their ire by trading or sending to the minor leagues a number of player representatives.[51]

And So They Played Baseball

The 1972 season opened ten days late to small crowds. For the first time since William Howard Taft occupied the White House, the sport had no presidential opener. The heavily favored Orioles began the defense of their American League championship on 16 April, after rain washed out their scheduled opening game. Baltimore's new mayor, William Donald Schaefer, threw out the first ball and, together with a sparse crowd, watched as the Orioles defeated New York in a rain-shortened contest, 3–1.

The 1972 season was a financial and athletic disaster for the Orioles. The team played poor defense, failed to hit, and, as a result, wasted many well-pitched games. Observers compared the 1972 Orioles to the 1967 team, the last to post a losing record, complaining that it lacked confidence and hustle. Boog Powell slumped badly. Brooks Robinson, who management hoped would fill the role of the departed Frank Robinson, played superb defense but hit only .250, while his home run and RBI totals dropped from twenty and ninety-two in 1971 to eight and sixty-four respectively in 1972. Shortstop Belanger and catchers Etchebarren and Elrod Hendricks were all hitting under .200 at mid-season. At the All-Star break, the team batting average was a puny .217.

Through it all, the Orioles hung close to the division leaders. Weaver shuffled his lineups to squeeze out whatever offense was available. The pitchers—McNally, Cuellar, and Palmer—kept the games close. Rookie infielder Bobby Grich and outfielder Don Baylor played with distinction. Veteran outfielder Tommy Davis, a late-season addition, added some needed offensive production. In late September three teams—the Orioles, Yankees, and Tigers—staggered toward the division title. The Orioles, however, simply could not overcome their anemic batting and continued defensive miscues. The team finished third with an 80–74 record.

The Orioles took a big beating at the box office. Resentment over the player strike was nationwide but particularly strong in Baltimore. The Orioles enjoyed the additional dubious distinction of leading the league in rained-out ball games. The games had to be played as part of doubleheaders, and the team lost the revenues. Attendance dropped by 130,000, and the club balance sheet plunged into the red, with a loss of $214,582.[52]

By late June, Weaver had concluded that the team needed a major overhaul. At postseason meetings, Orioles management decided that the team's primary need was for a power-hitting catcher. Cashen began negotiations with the Yankees for Thurman Munson and with Atlanta for another young hitter, Earl Williams. Grich's superb performance made veteran second baseman Davey Johnson expendable. "Get me Williams," Weaver told Cashen, "and we'll win the pennant."[53] In December, at the winter meetings, the Orioles landed Williams together with a minor league prospect in exchange for Johnson, catcher Johnny Oates, pitcher Pat Dobson, and a minor leaguer. The house cleaning continued during the winter as the team sold the contracts of outfielders Don Buford and Roger Repoz to Japanese clubs.

Here We Go Again

The owners arrived at the 1972 winter meetings with major problems but with renewed confidence. In June 1972 the Supreme Court upheld baseball's antitrust exemption by ruling 5–3 against Curt Flood's suit. The decision was hardly a ringing endorsement of the owners' legal position. Chief Justice Warren Burger, in the majority opinion, noted his grave doubts about the constitutionality of the exemption. However, the Court was unwilling to overturn a previous decision. It again urged Congress to take action to clear up the legal tangle the Court's previous decisions had created.[54]

The Supreme Court decision strengthened the resolve of hardline owners to resist further concessions and increased militancy among many ball-players. Kuhn and moderate owners like Hoffberger favored negotiating the revisions of the reserve clause. They scored a victory when the owners increased Kuhn's authority in the player relations area and elected a moderate majority to a streamlined PRC. Talks between the union and PRC on revisions to the reserve clause began in early September 1972.[55] However, the hardliners, including St. Louis's outspoken Busch, were unwilling to bargain away their prerogatives. Harry Dalton commented:

> They should have anticipated the problem on the reserve clause and tried to work out something in advance: try and work out some sort of alternative solution before it all came crashing down. . . . There were some in the ranks that wanted to see that happen. . . . [The clubs] were separate entities. . . . That was the weak point in management's position with the players. . . . While there were some that were liberal owner-ships and some that were paternalistic and . . . ran very caring, solid organizations, . . . some . . . didn't. The ones that didn't were the ones that created this situation. . . . It did get confrontational.[56]

When the Supreme Court announced its decision, Curt Flood's immediate response was: "Baby, I gave them one hell of a fight."[57] The fight, as both sides knew, would simply move to other venues. A legal setback to their challenge to the reserve clause hardened the players' determination to force concessions either through direct talks with the PRC or in the bargaining on a new Basic Agreement. Since neither the courts nor Congress was ready to help them, the *New York Times'* Arthur Daley warned, "The ball players now know they will have to use their own muscle if they are to pry concessions from the owners."[58]

Talks on both the reserve clause and the Basic Agreement continued throughout the Fall of 1972 without success. Finally, on 29 November, Commissioner Kuhn publicly presented the owners' "final" position. The proposal offered free agency at the end of five years to any veteran making less than $30,000 or to any player with eight years' experience making less than $40,000. Men with ten years' playing time on one club would enjoy the right to veto prospective trades. The owners also offered to cut reserve lists from forty to thirty-eight names, to contribute $6 million to the pension fund over three years, and to raise the minimum salary to $15,000 by 1975 and the guaranteed minimum payment to players in the World Series to $20,000.[59]

The union rejected the Kuhn plan out of hand. Its provisions for free agency would apply only to journeyman players. The proposal to reduce the number of players on the reserve list was an unsubtle way of cutting rosters, a direct threat to player livelihood that would further cheapen the value of free agency. Similarly, so few players stayed with a single club for ten years that that part of the owners' offer was virtually worthless. The union wanted a minimum of salary of $15,500 in 1973, rising to $17,500 by the 1975 season. Union leaders were particularly incensed by Kuhn's decision to make the offer public. They saw this move as a blatant public relations ploy by the owners. Noting that only 5 of 960 current players on major league rosters would be eligible for free agency under Kuhn's plan, Marvin Miller labeled the owners' proposal "mischievous and destructive."[60]

From the union's perspective, Kuhn's offer was an effort to avoid addressing the key issues: the players' demands for a major modification of the reserve clause and arbitration. The Players Association insisted that all players must have the right to free agency at the end of a specified period of time. Further, the players wanted to institute a system of binding arbitration for salary disputes. Kuhn responded that organized baseball could accept neither free agents nor arbitration as part of a loosened reserve clause system.[61]

The winter meetings ended with the two sides deadlocked. Its major achievement was a significant change in the rules of play. Convinced that more offense would reverse sagging attendance, American League owners voted to substitute a "designated hitter" (DH) to bat for the pitcher when his team was at the plate. The DH rule infuriated baseball traditionalists, who spent the winter—and indeed the succeeding decade and a half—denouncing the change, while American League owners watched their attendance grow. The brouhaha over the DH rule helped distract fans' attention from the showdown between labor and management. As the winter of renewed labor-management confrontation continued, the owners prepared for a lockout. The *Sun*'s Bob Maisel warned his readers: "Fasten your seatbelts. Here we go again."[62]

Mr. Hoffberger
Takes Stock

The 1973 baseball season started on time. Moderates on both sides prevailed, and the negotiations ended with a compromise settlement. For a while, however, another confrontation between management and labor appeared imminent. The players were anxious for a compromise, but Brooks Robinson warned that if they went on strike, the issue would be the reserve system, not pensions or salaries. "We . . . think a man sometime in his life should have a chance to decide his destiny," Robinson explained. However, Robinson admitted that he was weary of conflict, calling the 1972 strike the "worst thing that ever happened to me." As a result of that experience, Robinson and his fellow players were willing to settle for signs rather than immediate proof of owner willingness to resolve the reserve issue.[1]

On 5 January the players made a new proposal designed to break the deadlock and avoid a strike. They offered to drop their demand for a shorter season and to delay talks on the reserve system for one year to allow for further study by the two sides. After a month's delay, management offered its counterproposal on 8 February as all but two clubs simultaneously instructed their players not to report to their spring training sites for the normal pre-March workouts. Commissioner Kuhn labeled this action a "routine matter," noting that these workouts were "voluntary." In reality, management was signaling the players that they faced a lockout if the two sides failed to agree on a new Basic Agreement.[2]

The Orioles were one of two clubs that declined

to join the lockout threat. Cashen had so few athletes under contract at that point that, as he explained at the time, "It doesn't make a whole lot of difference." "Anyhow," he added, "I'm optimistic that negotiations will be settled in a few days."[3]

Brooks Robinson, speaking after a union meeting, also expressed confidence that the two sides could reach accord. "I'd hate to see [a strike]. The players have not made a strike threat, have not taken a strike vote, and don't intend to. We've expressed our willingness to continue bargaining, if necessary, without disruption of spring training or the regular season."[4]

The new management offer was full of terms that the union would find unacceptable. It proposed granting the right to salary arbitration to players with three years' experience, but never in consecutive years. The owners wanted a three-year moratorium on changes in the reserve system. Marvin Miller rejected the arbitration proposal as a sham and warned management that a lockout while negotiations were in progress violated U.S. labor law.[5]

Miller's firmness provoked a display of toughness by management. Cashen declared: "I am not in favor of opening spring training under the conditions outlined by Marvin Miller." He informed Orioles players that the scheduled 23 February opening of training camp was highly problematical.[6]

On 17 February, with the scheduled opening of camps less than two weeks off, the two sides renewed talks. After a week and a half of intense negotiations, they reached a compromise. The owners agreed that an athlete could request binding salary arbitration in any year after the termination of his contract. Salary arbitration would begin before the 1974 season. The owners increased the minimum salary from $13,000 to $15,000 in 1974 with further incremental steps that would increase it to $16,500 by 1976. Management increased its contribution to the pension fund and raised spring training benefits. In return the union agreed to a study of the reserve system prior to negotiations on its future.[7]

Impartial, binding salary arbitration was one of Marvin Miller's greatest successes. The psychological impact of the arbitration system was immense. Under the system a three-man panel made up of representatives of labor and management and an independent labor relations expert heard each case. The independent arbitrator inevitably decided each case. Since the arbitrator had to choose between a club's offer, which usually represented at least some increase in the athlete's salary, and the player's inevitably higher claim, the player had every incentive to request arbitration. Conversely, the club had little reason to use the procedure. Just the threat of arbitration repeatedly led clubs to increase their salary offers to players out of fear of paying more in the event of a loss. The arbitrators' decisions were based on an analysis of very complex variables and often appeared totally capricious. A 1978 study of the first four years of baseball salary arbitration concluded that the arbitrators' main guideline was not the difficult-to-judge merits of the individual cases but a desire to have each side win about half the disputes. Under these conditions, arbitration had an immediate inflationary effect on the entire salary scale of baseball. It sparked a general and continuous rise in the median income of all ballplayers.[8] For Jerold Hoffberger's talent-rich but attendance- and income-poor Orioles, the implications of arbitration were very serious.

A Tale of Two Earls

Once baseball settled its labor problems, the Orioles eagerly opened camp. The personnel of the 1973 team differed considerably from that of the 1971 American League championship squad. Only twelve of the twenty-five members of that team remained. The 1973 team was brimming with fast, talented, young players. It had few power hitters, and for the first time in years, entered the season with only three established starting pitchers and an untried relief corps. The key to success in 1973 appeared to rest in the ability of manager Earl Weaver to motivate the Orioles' newly acquired, talented catcher, the power-hitting Earl Williams.

Weaver entered the season under pressure. After a disappointing 1972 season, Weaver had to take a young team, turn it into a contender, and guide it into postseason play. Neither Weaver nor his club got off to a good start. The inexperienced Orioles needed time to find themselves as a team and played erratically during the first weeks of the season. Weaver was arrested for drunk driving on 16 April. Because of weak attendance, the club was acutely sensitive to its public image. With his team floundering, Weaver appeared to have placed his job on the line.[9]

Adding to Weaver's woes was Earl Williams's performance on and off the field. Williams enjoyed hitting but disliked catching. His lackadaisical attitude and frequent tardiness enraged teammates and fans. By mid-season, Williams was without doubt the most unpopular player ever to appear in an Orioles uniform, the subject of fan taunts and racial epithets. Weaver stuck with him, using him in 132 games. The Orioles needed his bat. Williams produced twenty-two home runs and eighty-three RBIs for a power-starved offense. The Orioles also benefited from the introduction of the designated hitter. Tommy Davis, a defensive liability with a good bat, was the team's primary DH. He drove in eighty-nine runs. These two consistent hitters had plenty of opportunities to drive in runners. Lacking power, Weaver relied on speed, provided by outfielders Baylor, Blair, Al Bumbry, and Rich Coggins and infielders Grich and Belanger. The Orioles led the American League with 146 stolen bases. Solid pitching from Palmer, McNally, Cuellar, and rookie Doyle Alexander, together with good defense, kept the team in contention throughout the summer. In August the Orioles began an impressive stretch run, reeling off thirteen straight wins, to take a commanding lead in the American League East.[10]

Unfortunately for Baltimore, the American League championship pitted them against the best team in baseball. The Oakland A's took the championship, three games to two, and went on to win the World Series. Nevertheless, 1973 was a successful season for the franchise and for Weaver. Faced with a must-win situation and handicapped by a lack of power hitters and by the Earl Williams problem, the Orioles' manager had platooned players, adopted a new strategy, and won. The team turned a profit as a result of its championship series appearance.

Success in 1973 created no complacency in the Orioles front office. The team was too delicately balanced and needed help in two critical areas: pitching and offense. Team management was worried about the continued effectiveness of Cuellar and the thirty-two-year-old McNally. High-salaried Boog Powell's best days were clearly behind him as he suffered through a third straight subpar season. During the off-season Cashen sought to acquire a pitcher and unload Powell.[11]

The winter of 1973–74 produced a number of shocks. The nation suffered through a serious oil shortage. The Orioles and major league baseball in general appeared likely victims of a continuing shortage of fuel. The club, whose modest attendance goal was set out in the slogan A Million or More in '74, began laying plans for a return to energy-saving day baseball. Cashen noted morosely that such a strategy would be a disaster for the Orioles. The club had enough trouble attracting paying customers without playing its games when most fans were working. The unfavorable effects of continued gasoline rationing on attendance was a subject that sent baseball officials into depression.[12]

Fortunately, the energy crisis was abating by the time the Orioles opened spring training in late February 1974. Led by Commissioner Kuhn, organized baseball introduced a number of energy-saving ideas—cutting light use by 20 percent, taking batting practice in daylight, avoiding charter flights, and changing game starting times to avoid energy peak use periods—that permitted the sport to continue playing at night while winning the praise of the federal government.[13]

Cashen succeeded in acquiring another starting pitcher in Ross Grimsley, but his efforts to trade for a badly needed power hitter failed. The Orioles discovered that they could not unload Powell and his contract. After failing to deal off his aging, high-paid star at the winter meetings, Cashen ruefully remarked: "I suppose you could say Boog's off the market because there is no market for him."[14] Weaver would have to win in 1974 by relying on essentially the same cast that had won in 1973, including the temperamental Earl Williams.

The club was also burdened by labor unrest. Arbitration began in February

1974. The owners had already clashed with the Players Association over Marvin Miller's request for salary data. The owners refused to release the information. Only an NLRB order led them to surrender the data. Fifty major league players filed for arbitration. Three were Orioles: Grich, McNally, and Blair. In order to avoid other cases, the club had to increase the salaries of a number of stars. Pitcher Jim Palmer signed for an estimated $135,000. The team's aging hero, Brooks Robinson, won a $5,000 "token raise" to $115,000 despite an average 1973 season. Eight other players who were ineligible for arbitration initially refused to report to spring training, demanding salary increases.[15]

Faced with an explosion of salary demands, the Orioles decided to contest the three arbitration cases. The club won two. However, it paid all three players substantially more than they had received the previous season. Overall, arbitration cost the Orioles an extra $28,000 in salaries. It also embittered relations between management and individual players. McNally, who won his case, was particularly outspoken, calling arbitration "a hell of an experience to go through" and charging that Cashen had violated confidences during the appeal.[16] Baseballwide, arbitration helped to raise the number of players with salaries of $100,000 or more to thirty-three.

Cashen took a firm line with the holdouts. By early March four of eight had signed contracts. He invoked the option clause on the contracts of the remaining four, meaning that they would be required to play either at their previous salary or at a reduced wage set by management. Jerry Kapstein, the agent for one of the four, pitcher Doyle Alexander, instructed his client to refuse to sign a contract and indicated he would challenge the validity of baseball's perpetual option clause in court.[17] Ultimately, Alexander signed a new contract with a sizable raise, nullifying the possibility of a court challenge.

Meanwhile, Earl Weaver was leading this company of discontent players in pursuit of another American League East championship. It wasn't easy. The Orioles played under .500 until August. Jim Palmer was injured for most of the season, and Doyle Alexander was ineffective. Powell went into a near-season-long batting drought. Earl Williams was as incorrigible as in 1973 but this time failed to hit as consistently, dropping to fourteen home runs and fifty-two RBIs. "We stank until late August," McNally admitted.[18]

As luck would have it, none of the Orioles' rivals played much better. In late August the team suddenly came alive. Powell briefly regained his batting eye and hit a torrid .351 with four home runs. Palmer returned from injury to pitch well. Davis, Grich, Blair, Robinson, and Baylor all contributed to the attack, as did rookie Enos Cabell. The club won ten in a row in late August and continued to run up victories during the rest of the season. After a tense pennant race, the Orioles won the American League East on the next to last game of the season.

Once again the Orioles were unable to overcome the A's, losing the championship series, 3–1, despite four well-pitched games. Postseason play again proved to be the difference between profitability and a money-losing season. However, total attendance of 962,572 after one of the most exciting seasons in the club's history "left Orioles officials in a morose state."[19] Even Baltimore booster Bob Maisel leveled a blast at local fans. The team failed to sell out its playoff games. Brooks Robinson expressed the frustration that both players and management felt when he told reporters that Baltimore fans could not expect the Orioles to remain if they gave the team such pitiful support.[20]

The 1975 Orioles would be a vastly different team. Frank Cashen spent the fall of 1974 acquiring badly needed power hitters. By the end of the 1974 winter meetings he had acquired the players he wanted: Houston's Lee May and Montreal's Ken Singleton, together with pitcher Mike Torrez, in exchange for a number of top prospects and the discontented Dave McNally. Boog Powell and Earl Williams had become "extra baggage."[21] Management once again had improved a contender. However, superior Orioles clubs had repeatedly failed to attract solid support. Cashen reminded stockholders that "financially speaking, in the past eight years the Baltimore Orioles have been in a win or else lose money situation."[22] Continued poor attendance increasingly focused the attention of both the club and the public on the suitability of Memorial Stadium as a major league park and forced Baltimore's business and political leadership to evaluate carefully the costs and benefits of professional sports in the context of their development strategy.

The Schaefer Era

By the mid-1970s Baltimore was in the midst of an "urban renaissance" that won national attention. Mayor William Donald Schaefer presided over the emergence of a new Baltimore, dominating city politics for sixteen years (1971–87). He carefully balanced the demands of the business community for redevelopment with those of the city's racially and ethnically diverse masses for improved services.

Schaefer's large, droopy jowls and sad eyes gave the Baltimore-born German-American a placid and sympathetic appearance. Looks were deceiving. Schaefer possessed a fierce temper that prompted the *Sun* to refer to his administrative style as government by "tantrum" and seemingly limitless energy.[23] A bachelor who lived in an unpretentious West Baltimore row house, Schaefer devoted himself to city politics. He rose to prominence as a ward politician, performing mundane but necessary jobs for his constituents. In 1955 Schaefer won election to the city council and by careful attention to the needs of his constituents and fellow council members advanced to the post of council president during the administration of Thomas D'Alesandro III. In 1971, Schaefer succeeded D'Alesandro.

The new mayor was a problem solver with little interest in ideology or party affiliation. He improved basic city services such as road repair, sanitation, and public transportation with hands-on management. Schaefer literally worked day and night, touring city areas in his automobile to check on the progress of municipal services, noting problem areas, and insisting on quick action from his bureaucracy. Schaefer's ability to provide efficient responses to constituent needs built wide support among both city ethnic groups and blacks.[24]

The mayor was equally skilled at meeting the basic requirements of the city's business community. He had strongly supported the redevelopment of the central business district, and, as mayor, Schaefer carried to completion the initial phase of the Inner Harbor project. By the end of Schaefer's tenure as mayor, the city center teemed with gleaming office complexes, exclusive shops, new restaurants, and hordes of tourists and shoppers who put cash into Baltimore's economy.[25]

Schaefer carried forward the redevelopment of the city center while holding together a broad and shifting coalition of often-conflicting interest groups. During the 1970s Baltimore's population dropped by approximately 120,000 people, primarily whites. The economic, racial, and political make-up of the city altered. Its tax base shrank further, endangering the quality of city services. By 1980 blacks comprised 55 percent of Baltimore's total population. The whites who remained in the city tended to be more affluent and included a larger share of liberals, who frequently supported black demands. A number of well-financed young white professionals became "urban homesteaders," buying abandoned row houses and refurbishing them. Urban homesteading and an influx of real estate speculators from Washington in the late 1970s drove up the price of city housing while contributing to a growing shortage of rental units for the poor. Schaefer shifted with the times. The mayor of 1971 who protected the interests of ethnic neighborhoods became the politician who during the next decade and a half handed blacks a larger role in the administration of city government and promoted the return of affluent whites.[26]

One of the keys to Schaefer's success was his ability to funnel state and federal money into Baltimore. Theodore McKeldin had pioneered in this area, taking advantage of his friendship with President Lyndon Johnson to win large grants from the programs of the war on poverty in the mid-1960s. Schaefer took Republican McKeldin's technique a step further. An apolitical politician, he eagerly courted each president from Nixon to Reagan. The mayor could point to an impressive record of success in utilizing federal funds. By 1981 Schaefer had brought an estimated $295 million in federal aid into Baltimore. He had less success with Ronald Reagan, the amiable ideologue whose economic policies deprived the urban poor of basic assistance, enriched the well-to-do, and turned the United States into the world's biggest debtor nation.[27]

On the state level, Schaefer found a partner and kindred soul in Governor Marvin Mandel. Mandel, a product of Baltimore's machine politics, succeeded Spiro Agnew in 1969. The new governor was a political operator and deal maker who, like Schaefer, saw himself as a pragmatic problem solver. These two political professionals formed a successful partnership until the governor was convicted on political corruption charges. Mandel understood the need for wealthy Maryland suburbs to support Baltimore's redevelopment and ensured that the state's largest city got its share of state budget outlays.[28]

Schaefer helped Baltimore rediscover a sense of urban identity. Appraising the Schaefer years in 1987, the *Sun* stated: "Schaefer took stewardship of a city stopped by the 1968 riot . . . plagued by crime and bypassed by tourists. . . . In a city losing self-confidence, he installed pride and boosterism. Whatever 'Baltimore is best' may mean, people believe it."[29]

Professional sports played an important role in Schaefer's plans for building an urban identity. He was proud of the city's reputation for sports champions and, like his predecessors, worked to exploit this reputation to attract corporate investment. The mayor took evident delight in assisting Orioles promotional efforts by appearing at opening day ceremonies and honoring the team's successes. He formed a committee of local businessmen and civic leaders to promote attendance at professional sports events. The rediscovered sense of identity helped Baltimore live with many of the ills that it could not cure. Crime, drug abuse, and an alarming rise in teenage pregnancies afflicted Baltimore, which was further troubled by declining traditional industries, a weakening tax base, and a growing gap between haves and have-nots.

Schaefer's administration of the city found support among a majority of blacks but left many of their leaders dissatisfied. The mayor's relationship with the black community was a case study in the success and limitations of his governing style. The mayor realized that the city's white political and business leadership had to reach an accommodation with Baltimore's emerging majority. In the wake of the April 1968 riots, Schaefer joined in Mayor D'Alesandro's efforts to eliminate the causes of urban violence. The Schaefer-led city council passed legislation to end block busting and ensure equality in housing opportunity. City leaders convinced the Federal Highway Administration to reroute major freeway projects away from black neighborhoods. The city fairs launched under D'Alesandro and continued by Schaefer became a means of defusing urban tensions.[30]

Schaefer continued his predecessor's effort to bring area residents into the planning for low-income housing projects. By 1975, the city had built 15,000 new low-income units. Baltimore's Gay Street was the epicenter of the April 1968 riots. Between 1968 and 1978 the city, with federal assistance and community input, built 748 low-income residential units in the riot-scarred corridor. The new housing units, however, were islands of stability in a neighborhood beset by continuing problems of poverty, crime, drug abuse, and segregation.[31]

The mixed legacy of the Schaefer administration created division among black leaders. Civil rights leader Clarence Mitchell supported Schaefer's 1983 reelection bid, while his brother, Congressman Parren Mitchell, opposed the mayor. In 1981 Parren Mitchell defined Baltimore as "a city with a split personality." Critics stressed that the black majority of the city was not receiving its fair share of the budget. Too much money was going to Harbor Place, capstone of the Inner Harbor development, and other central city business projects. Blacks owned only 15 percent of these businesses. Their unemployment rate was at least twice that of whites. The black majority was badly underrepresented in the city council and, despite Schaefer's efforts, in the higher levels of city administration.[32]

Given enough resources, Schaefer probably would have met black demands more fully. Baltimore's major weakness was a limited control over its economy. The city's prosperity was linked to the decisions of larger economic units: the state, large corporations, and the fluctuations of the world economy. The port of Baltimore, the nation's fourth largest, was heavily dependent on foreign automobile imports. The vulnerability of the city to world economic trends was graphically demonstrated when the 1973 oil crisis set off a recession. In 1975 only two Baltimore-based corporations were among the so-called Fortune 500. Both the growing service industries and the declining smokestack industries of Baltimore were overwhelmingly branch plant operations. Their corporate headquarters were located elsewhere—and in times of recession, major corporations tend to cut employment and production at these branch units.[33]

The city's economic weaknesses were very evident as Schaefer sought to retain local ownership of the Orioles and struggled with the question of Memorial Stadium's future.

The Dowager of 33rd Street

In April 1973 *The Sporting News* reported that "a showdown [is] coming in Baltimore" over the issue of Memorial Stadium. The city, baseball's Bible warned, faced the stark choice of building a new facility or losing its professional football and baseball franchises.[34]

The twenty-three-year-old facility was the center of a tug-of-war between local and state government and the city's two major sports franchises. Both clubs claimed that their future profitability was directly linked to providing better facilities for their fans. However, Hoffberger and successive Colts owners disagreed over the type of facility they wanted. The city was incapable of bearing the costs of a new stadium, while the state legislature was divided over whether to bail out Baltimore.

The growing debate over Memorial Stadium was the product of its initial design, a boom in stadium construction, powerful egos, and the Orioles' straitened financial circumstances. The stadium, which journalist Thomas Boswell described as "the brick and wood dowager of 33rd Street," was fundamentally unsuitable for the type of profit making both football and baseball owners wanted.[35]

The decision to construct Memorial Stadium as inexpensively as possible meant that many of the seats in the lower deck offered only an obstructed view and had to be sold at a cheaper price. Its horseshoe configuration was well suited for playing baseball, but not football. One end zone was crammed into the closer end of the facility, and the layout of the field created poor lines of vision for many spectators.[36]

The boom in stadium construction that began in the early 1960s increased pressure for a new ballpark. Between 1960 and 1966 seven new multipurpose stadiums went into operation in major league cities. Other new facilities followed in the later part of the decade and the early 1970s in Oakland, Pittsburgh, Philadelphia, San Diego, and Arlington, Texas. Changes in the federal tax code that exempted interest on municipal bonds encouraged this construction boom. By the early 1970s almost every National League team had a new home, while the California Angels, Kansas City Royals, Oakland A's, and Texas Rangers of the American League had modern parks. Other American League owners could only cast envious glances at the largesse of National League cities and soon began to employ threats of franchise moves to extract new facilities.[37]

The American League owners achieved their objectives at a much slower pace than their National League rivals. The 1970s were a period of economic instability. The inflationary effects of the Vietnam War and the rising price of energy cut heavily into both state and local government budgets. In the case of Baltimore, local political and business leaders remained favorably inclined toward the needs of professional sports but were unable to fund a new stadium. Ultimately, they dumped the question into the lap of the governor and General Assembly of Maryland, where it remained, unresolved, for over a decade.

Schaefer inherited a simmering conflict over Memorial Stadium that pitted the city against one of its sports franchises. Baltimore had kept its initial commitment to maintain a suitable facility for its professional sports tenants. In 1960 the city began a $2 million, six-year improvement program for Memorial Stadium. In 1963, at the request of the Orioles, the city installed

4,264 chairback seats and contracted to install escalators to the upper deck at an additional cost of $130,000. The 1965–70 Baltimore capital improvement plan committed another $1 million to stadium upkeep. The city permitted the Orioles to make a number of capital improvements in the park, including the construction of a restaurant, in order to improve club profitability. Baltimore absorbed large losses from stadium operations.[38]

These improvements failed to satisfy the Colts' blunt, aggressive, millionaire owner, Carroll Rosenbloom. In September 1965 Rosenbloom announced that he was putting together financing to build a domed stadium at an unspecified location and that Hoffberger was ready to join the initiative. He denounced conditions at Memorial Stadium and warned city leaders to build a new stadium or risk losing major league sports in Baltimore.[39]

City leaders politely ignored Rosenbloom's threats and his demand for a new facility. The Colts owner was a persistent man, and two years later Rosenbloom repeated his demand for a new facility, again claiming Hoffberger's support. Rosenbloom stressed that he could "easily" raise financing for a private stadium, and reiterated that without city action to build a new park, professional sports might flee Baltimore.[40]

This time the city responded. Douglas Tawney, the director of the city's Department of Parks and Recreation, bluntly replied that the city could not afford a new stadium when it was hard-pressed to maintain Memorial Stadium. The city would continue its efforts to modernize the existing facility, recognizing that "to fail to keep the present structure in an up-to-date well-maintained condition is the best method to have the . . . major league franchises locate elsewhere. . . . The city of Baltimore would certainly be left with an $8 million white elephant."[41]

Mayor Thomas D'Alesandro III attempted to pacify Rosenbloom by ordering a special study of Memorial Stadium improvements. Tawney met with Colts and Orioles officials and then drew up a list of improvements that he claimed the city could make in the existing stadium. Tawney's final report recommended a major overhaul: enclosing the park, putting a dome over it, increasing the number of seats by approximately 5,000; providing a total of 15,000 parking spaces; improving lighting, concession stands, and toilet facilities; building offices for both clubs; and installing luxury boxes. Tawney estimated the total cost of these extensive renovations would be $10 million.[42]

Rosenbloom, who had already angrily rejected Tawney's preliminary report, continued his campaign for a new stadium. Hoffberger took a more moderate stance, expressing his willingness to discuss the proposed improvements with city comptroller Hyman Pressman.[43] Hoffberger's comments were significant since they indicated that a considerable gap existed between his position and that of the Colts owner.

The city moved forward with its study of major stadium renovations. In the winter of 1969 Mayor D'Alesandro commissioned a New York consulting firm to draw up plans for improving Memorial Stadium. The consultant's report of July 1969 offered the city three alternative plans ranging in price from a minimum of $5 million to a maximum of $19.3 million. None of the proposals included the cost of placing a dome on the facility. D'Alesandro immediately ruled out the two more expensive plans and announced that the city would attempt to meet the goals of the $5 million renovation project on a piecemeal basis. He indicated that Baltimore would seek contributions from its professional sports franchises to support the work.[44]

The debate over Memorial Stadium became more complex during 1970–71. Rosenbloom continued to insist that a new facility was the price of retaining the Colts in Baltimore. He quarreled with Hoffberger and took the city and Orioles to court over his rights to use the stadium for a Monday night football game.[45]

Rosenbloom's pique with Hoffberger had multiple roots: the natural rivalry between the two franchises, anger that the Orioles had a better stadium contract, and a belief that the baseball club enjoyed a privileged relationship with city government. The city sided with the Orioles when the baseball team claimed that a Monday night football game would do serious damage to the stadium playing field. Rosenbloom was angry about the Orioles' control of stadium concessions. At a November 1970 press luncheon he complained that his club was a "second-class citizen" in Memorial Stadium utilization and planning.[46]

In February 1971 Rosenbloom announced that he would pull out of Memorial Stadium when the Colts' lease expired in 1972 and move his team into a new stadium outside the city limits.[47] Initial reaction to Rosenbloom's announcement was polite indifference. Neighboring counties showed no enthusiasm for having the Colts as tenants. However, Rosenbloom's threat suddenly awakened state leaders' interest in the stadium issue.[48]

On 3 April 1971, Governor Marvin Mandel summoned representatives of the city, Colts, and Orioles to Annapolis. Mandel pledged state action to assure the modernization of Memorial Stadium.[49] Mandel's subsequent actions and comments showed that the governor believed that the impasse between city and sports teams had to be broken by outside action. Mandel faulted D'Alesandro for unnecessarily antagonizing the proud Rosenbloom. The governor became convinced that the only way to retain both sports franchises in Baltimore was by building a new stadium.[50]

State involvement in the Baltimore stadium issue complicated an already difficult issue. It raised fundamental questions about the use of public funds to assist a select few businessmen in making a profit. It also made settlement of the issue more difficult since the whole population of Maryland, through their elected representatives, became involved in the special concerns of Baltimore.

On 28 March 1972 the Mandel administration introduced bills in both houses of the legislature that would establish a Maryland Sports Complex Authority. The General Assembly approved the bill on 8 April and Mandel signed the legislation on 5 May. The bill authorized the Authority "to provide for a sports complex and related facilities in the greater Baltimore region" and to find means of financing the project without the use of state funds.[51]

The Authority began its work in June 1972. Its membership of five was weighted toward the city's progrowth political and business establishment. It included William Boucher III, the executive director of the Greater Baltimore Committee, who had already publicly supported building a new facility, and William Sondheimer, Jr., who was chairman of the board of the corporation redeveloping the city's business center and Inner Harbor. Sondheimer, like Boucher, was receptive to arguments favoring the construction of a stadium as part of the city center renewal.[52]

The Authority's efforts were aided by the July 1972 departure from Baltimore of Carroll Rosenbloom. The Colts' contentious and embittered owner swapped his NFL franchise for one in Los Angeles. Rosenbloom wreaked a probably unintended revenge on the city when he turned the Colts over to Robert Irsay, a pugnacious, devious, and emotional Chicago-area businessman. Irsay speedily ruined one of professional football's model franchises. However, the initial effect of Rosenbloom's departure was to open the way for renewed cooperation between the Colts and Orioles.

In early August the Authority arranged an Irsay-Hoffberger meeting that resulted in an apparent accord on the requirements for a new stadium. Meanwhile, the members of the Authority toured new stadiums in other cities and discussed problems related to their construction and maintenance with local officials. They also met with the officials of the Colts and Orioles and with the representatives of the city Department of Parks and Recreation. They reviewed the previous consultant's study on rehabilitation of Memorial Stadium and discussed acquiring the Camden Yards (old railroad yards) in downtown Baltimore as a new stadium site. The Authority hired a new consulting firm to draw up plans for both a total upgrading of Memorial Stadium and a new stadium in the Camden Yards.[53]

In January 1973 the Authority issued its preliminary report. It began with a review of the history of the construction and installation of improvements at Memorial Stadium. The Authority concluded: "Comprehensive planning for Memorial Stadium was non-existent at the time of initial construction as well as during several modifications. Although the present stadium is approximately only 20 years old it is beset with adverse conditions."[54]

Among the defects the report cited a lack of parking; 3,000 obstructed-view seats; wooden seats; poor leg room; no handicapped seating; problems of converting the stadium for use by baseball and football teams; inadequate concession stands, restrooms, and press and administrative facilities; and the difficulties of maintaining a natural turf playing surface on nearly a year-round basis. The study pointed out that the Memorial Stadium neighborhood had become poorer, racially mixed, and older. Finally, the report assessed city revenues from the stadium, noting that while city income derived from football was steadily increasing, baseball rental payments were erratic. The Authority concluded that baseball was not a growth sport in Baltimore.[55]

The Authority's final report, issued 21 February 1973, endorsed the construction of a new stadium in the Camden Yards. It estimated that the cost of a 70,000 seat domed facility with underground parking for 4,500 cars would be $114.1 million. The report concluded that a complete renovation of Memorial Stadium would cost $91.7 million but stressed the difficulties in acquiring financing for this project and estimated that a new stadium would produce twice as much revenue for the city.[56]

Irsay had already endorsed a new park. The Orioles stated they could live with either project. The critical question, the *Sun* editorialized, was "who will pay?" The Sports Authority act prohibited the state from shouldering the cost, and opposition to the use of state revenues remained strong inside the General Assembly. The city of Baltimore was so hard-pressed for revenues that its initial 1974–79 development plan did not include major improvements to Memorial Stadium.[57]

Both Colts and Orioles officials attempted to build support for a new stadium by discreetly hinting that, although they wanted to stay in Baltimore, failure to provide improved facilities would force them to look for new homes. As a practical demonstration of their determination, both teams refused to renew expiring long-term agreements for the use of Memorial Stadium.[58] In December 1973 the Orioles and Colts provided the Sports Authority with written assurances that they would sign long-term agreements to play in a new stadium. Significantly, Cashen reversed the Orioles' previous position, telling reporters that Memorial Stadium "is incapable of being remodeled in such a way as to make it attractive for fans over the long term."[59]

Governor Mandel and the Sports Authority launched a publicity campaign designed to rally popular support behind the Authority's plan to sell bonds to finance construction. The campaign collapsed when both the Colts and the Orioles refused to sign a thirty-year lease until stadium construction began. The Authority declined to request the General Assembly's permission to sell bonds without signed leases. Plans for a new stadium had reached an impasse. The city rushed forward with an improved lease for Memorial Stadium that provided the Orioles with low rental and a city commitment to continue improvements on the park through 1979. The team had the option of withdrawing from the agreement at any time.[60]

In early March 1974 Jerold Hoffberger assessed the future of baseball in Baltimore. He was "disappointed but not discouraged" by the Stadium

Authority's refusal to forward a bond authorization request in 1974. He stressed that a team's financial situation was conditioned by the type of facility in which it played. The Orioles continued to be hampered by poor attendance that Hoffberger felt was at least partially attributable to the stadium. The club was saddled with the largest payroll in its history and remained dependent on participation in postseason play for its profit. Toronto, Seattle, and New Orleans were actively seeking a major league franchise. Hoffberger stressed that he had no plans to sell the club but as a prudent businessman faced with the possibility of serious losses, he would have to listen to any offers. "If I see the losses are great, I'm going to have to do something. . . . I'm not giving up any of my options." If attendance stayed low and the team remained without a satisfactory stadium: "I will bow to the will of the people. I think then the people of Baltimore will have told us what they want to tell us. First, they don't want a new park and, second, they don't want a club."[61]

Nine months later Baltimore voters approved a referendum barring the use of public funds to build a new stadium.

Baseball on the Block

One of the most most obvious explanations for the willingness of rich businessmen to own apparently money-losing professional sports teams is that they derive major tax benefits from them while basking in public approval. Another appealing factor for the businessman-owner is that sports franchises almost invariably bring major profits when sold. In a classic example of the law of supply and demand, the scarcity of major league franchises and the surplus of rich men ready to buy them have generally kept purchase prices high. One Orioles vice president observed in the early 1970s that the combination of a five-year tax depreciation benefit and the lure of large profits from the sale of teams created a fast turnover in ownership because the two factors encouraged quick sales to maximize profits.[62] He might also have added that the frustrations of maintaining a profit on a year-to-year basis provide another incentive for selling out.

While these factors have had a major impact on baseball, alone they are inadequate to explain industry trends. The economics of baseball is difficult to fathom because each team is a separate economic entity. Many are profitable enterprises. A few are tax shelters for larger corporations. Others are subsidiaries whose profitability is less important to their owners than their "fit" into a larger (usually broadcasting) market strategy. In the case of the Orioles, the major tax benefit of ownership, amortization of contracts, had long since expired. Another obvious benefit of ownership that was specifically applicable to Hoffberger, utilization of the team to sell his major product, beer, was of limited value. In fact, during the decade of public identification of the Orioles with National Brewery, the brewery, the centerpiece of Hoffberger's business empire, lost its primacy in the regional market. In the 1960s a few large breweries consolidated control over a major share of production and distribution. Hoffberger's far-flung regional operations were unable to compete. In January 1975 National made small cuts in its Baltimore work force and began to consider shutting down its Miami brewery. The company was able to recoup a major share of the dominance it once enjoyed in the local market with the introduction of Colt 45 malt liquor. However, National's production costs were rising, and the need to improve its competitive position led Hoffberger into a merger with Canadian giant Carling before the end of the year. As part of the merger agreement, Carling took over Orioles broadcast rights. Hoffberger transferred his family's Orioles stock into the O-W Fund, Inc., a holding company.[63]

The Orioles were an independent corporation again. Hoffberger needed higher attendance to offset rising player salaries or he would face major losses. He wanted a new stadium to stimulate higher attendance. Adding to the Orioles' difficulties, the team's radio network was collapsing. WBAL, the team's 50,000-watt flagship station, reported that it had lost $300,000 over the previous three years because of lack of sponsorship.[64] WBAL declined to renew a long-term contract with the Orioles, insisting upon yearly pacts that would permit the station to reduce its rights payments if sponsorship remained weak. The team's network fell from its 1960s' high of eighty-five stations to twenty-four in 1974. Washington station WEAM dropped the Orioles in the middle of the 1974 season due to lack of sponsor interest. Faced with persistently low attendance, falling broadcasting revenues, and a deadlock over stadium financing, Hoffberger acted like a prudent businessman. In January 1975, Cashen reported to stockholders: "For the Baltimore Orioles, 1974 was very similar to many previous years. The club was successful on the field and less than successful at the box office." Although participation in postseason play again permitted the Orioles to show a profit of $82,700, Hoffberger had decided to throw in the towel: "The club is for sale. Discussions are taking place with interested parties."[65]

The financial problems of both the brewery and the baseball club were the proximate cause of Hoffberger's decision to sell. Cashen commented that Hoffberger decided to quit "when we kept playing brinkmanship with the budget."[66] However, money apparently was only one motivation for Hoffberger's decision. He was clearly disillusioned with the players after five years of labor unrest. He was also tired of dealing with Commissioner Kuhn, whose efforts to put a new team in Washington were sabotaging the Orioles' best hope for increasing attendance and profits. Hoffberger had major charitable and personal interests that demanded greater attention, among them an increasingly active participation in Jewish community affairs.[67]

The absence of baseball from the capital of the United States was a particularly grating issue for Orioles management. Washington's business and political elite was determined to secure a new team and its gaze repeatedly settled on the Orioles. In September 1972 two congressmen approached Hoffberger to sound him out about the possibility of arranging a sale of the team and its transfer to Washington. Hoffberger, a man of immense civic pride, showed them the door. Commissioner Kuhn continued to encourage the efforts of Washington's leaders to acquire an existing franchise. After Walter O'Malley blocked a Washington group's bid to buy and move the San Diego Padres in 1973, Baltimore became the major target.[68]

In 1974, with Kuhn's blessing, the American League tried to nudge the Orioles toward Washington. The league suggested that the Orioles play a number of games in Kennedy Stadium. Hoffberger initially refused. On reconsideration, however, the Orioles high command decided to agree in principle to the league request. As Cashen explained: "It was just a question of keeping our options open."[69] The league office came up with a plan for playing fifteen games in the capital but never put it into operation. By agreeing to the league's Washington plan, Hoffberger succeeded in reducing league pressure on himself while building a small fire under Baltimore city officials. A clause that the team negotiated in its 1974 lease agreement permitted the Orioles to schedule twelve of eighty-two home games outside Memorial Stadium. While Cashen and Hoffberger vehemently denied using pressure tactics, they scheduled three exhibition games for New Orleans during the 1975 spring training season. New Orleans was on the verge of completing a massive new indoor stadium, so large it was to be called the Superdome. The chairman of the new facility contacted Hoffberger about the terms for purchasing the Orioles.[70]

The Orioles' willingness to play baseball in Washington and New Orleans produced desirable results for the franchise. Washington leaders were indifferent to the suggestion, effectively killing the American League plan. The Orioles gladly let the project die. When the plan initially surfaced, Cashen had reacted negatively: "I really can not foresee . . . any great windfall over there. In the past, playing here, we always outdrew the Senators."[71] The threat of an Orioles move, reinforced by Hoffberger's announcement that he would sell the club, finally galvanized Baltimore's leaders into action to save their major league franchise.

In October 1974 Hoffberger set $12 million as the "starting point" for bidding on the Orioles and reiterated that he would accept "any reasonable offer." At the same time, Hoffberger repeated his desire to keep the team in Baltimore and urged city interests to step forward.[72]

The outlook for local purchase of the franchise was poor. One city businessman told the *Sun*'s Bob Maisel that there was "absolutely no way you could pay $12 million for the Orioles and come close to breaking even in

Baltimore." Money markets were tight, the team's salary structure was inflated and its operating expenses were rising, and Baltimore appeared unable to provide the attendance and television rights income needed to offset these factors.[73]

While Krieger and Hoffberger maintained that a new stadium would mean a major increase in attendance, other observers were uncertain. One Orioles official, overlooking the club's record of indifference on racial issues, suggested the city's changing racial composition would be lethal for baseball: "White people are moving to the suburbs. And the Blacks don't support baseball." Blue-collar workers, an important part of baseball's traditional base of support, were hard-pressed to maintain their standard of living and as a result had little money to spend on entertainment.[74]

By mid-October 1974 Baltimore political and business leaders were discussing three options to save the team: forming a private syndicate to buy out Hoffberger, city purchase of the franchise, or finding funding to build a new stadium. Mayor Schaefer favored building a new stadium and was trying to encourage the formation of a business syndicate to purchase the team. City comptroller Hyman Pressman wanted the city to buy the team and rehabilitate Memorial Stadium, arguing this approach was cheaper and would ensure the permanence of the franchise.[75] All three plans faced the same difficulty: financing. The city needed authorization from the General Assembly in order to build or rehabilitate a stadium or to float a bond issue to finance a municipal purchase of the Orioles.

Mayor Schaefer believed that private participation in the effort to save the Orioles for Baltimore was the best way to avoid a franchise shift. On 16 October 1974 the mayor appointed a group called the Committee to Save the Orioles, under the chairmanship of former Johns Hopkins University president Milton Eisenhower. The committee included many of the city's business leaders. Schaefer instructed it to meet with Hoffberger to discuss ways to arrange a sale of the club to local interests. The Orioles owner announced that he would hold off discussing the sale of the club to outside interests until the Baltimore group had a chance to put together a syndicate with adequate financing.[76]

By the end of October at least three Maryland groups were trying to put together financing to bid on the Orioles. The most serious was backed by Baltimore businessman F. Barton Harvey, a stalwart of the Greater Baltimore Committee and co-chairman and spokesman for Eisenhower's committee. Harvey wanted to meet Hoffberger's purchase price with a combination of public and private funds: private capital providing $5 million and the city assembling another $5 million through a bond issue. While the Harvey plan was $2 million under his asking price, Hoffberger agreed to give the local group thirty days to come up with its half of the financing package. If it reached this goal, he would be ready to wait until the city could arrange its part of the package. American League president Lee MacPhail, who wanted to save Baltimore baseball, found the plan "feasible."[77]

The victory of the 5 November 1974 referendum barring public financing of a new stadium indicated that little public support existed for spending tax dollars to retain professional sports in Maryland. Nevertheless, the effort to retain the Orioles in Baltimore appeared to be picking up ground. In mid-November, Harvey announced that developer Ralph De Chiaro had put together a syndicate with $6 million financing. While many legal questions about financing the city's share remained unsolved, both sides appeared confident of finding a way to swing the deal. The mayor and the Baltimore Chamber of Commerce began a campaign with the goal of selling a record 15,000 season tickets for 1975, ensuring the club of a profitable season while the sale moved forward.[78]

The Orioles' future was a prime topic of the 1974 baseball winter meetings, appropriately held in New Orleans. Commissioner Kuhn assured Baltimore leaders that organized baseball was committed to retaining a franchise in their city through the 1975 season. The owners discussed a number of proposals designed to provide the Orioles and the equally impoverished Oakland A's with assistance, but they failed to act on them.[79]

On 13 December 1974, shortly after the winter meetings, De Chiaro broke off talks with Hoffberger upon learning that the Orioles owner was discussing the sale of the franchise with another group led by Bill Veeck. The sudden reappearance of Veeck on the baseball scene added color and drama to the bidding for the Orioles. Veeck, as usual, was working with shoestring financing. He was convinced that his marketing skills would permit the Orioles to make a profit even in an old stadium. In addition to his being Hoffberger's friend, Veeck's strengths were his past record as a successful owner in Chicago and Cleveland and his stated desire to keep the franchise in Baltimore while building a fan base in Washington. Veeck could count on a careful hearing and influential support for his bid.[80]

Veeck's appearance as a bidder sparked concern and new action from city groups. In late January the mayor's committee launched a publicity campaign to build support for a bond issue to finance a local buyout of the Orioles. The chamber of commerce sponsored a fourteen-hour phone-a-thon that sold $29,918 in Orioles tickets. Baltimore's General Assembly delegation placed the issue of the Orioles' prospective sale before the legislature in a bid to rally statewide support to retain the franchise. Hoffberger indicated that if the other stockholders approved, he might offer his 68 percent of the club at an $8.2 million price tag that city interests could meet.[81]

De Chiaro officially withdrew his bid for the Orioles at the end of January 1975, ending the likelihood of a Baltimore group buying the club. At the same time, a Washington syndicate, led by developer Theodore Lerner, announced it would bid on the Orioles. Governor Mandel decided to throw his support behind the Veeck bid. In an effort to discourage the Washington group, Schaefer announced he would take legal action to prevent a franchise shift. The chamber of commerce unveiled plans for a second phone-a-thon to reach the elusive goal of 15,000 season ticket sales.[82]

Baltimore's retention of the Orioles appeared more problematical when former General Motors president Edward Cole entered the bidding for the club. Cole's syndicate enjoyed the support of Commissioner Kuhn, who had decided that the best solution to the lack of baseball in Washington was to turn the Orioles into a regional franchise playing a split schedule.[83]

Hoffberger denied that political pressure from Annapolis or his own community loyalties would influence his decision on a bidder: "Terms pick the buyer . . . the thing that influences me . . . is the price he is paying and the way he is going to pay it."[84] Nevertheless, he spurned the Cole group's bid as "an insult to my intelligence." Bob Maisel commented that Kuhn's backing was probably the kiss of death for the Cole bid. Hoffberger had developed a strong dislike for Kuhn as a result of the commissioner's efforts to bring baseball back to Washington.[85]

New Orleans backed out of the bidding at about the same time. Construction delays pushed back the opening of the Superdome to late August 1975. Moreover, the stadium's configuration was less than ideal for baseball. By late February, Veeck appeared to be the next owner of the Orioles. The Veeck bid, however, remained nebulous. Veeck wanted full control of the club, since owning anything less than 80 percent of the stock meant the loss of tax depreciation benefits. He lacked the $12 million in financing Hoffberger wanted. Further, while committed to playing the 1975 season in Baltimore, Veeck repeatedly warned that the team would move to Washington, which he regarded as a "gold mine," unless it got solid attendance.[86]

Hoffberger was having second thoughts about selling. On 1 March, he met with the players in Miami and informed them that a sale appeared unlikely and that he wanted buyers who would stay in Baltimore and retain the team's existing management.[87]

Mandel, nevertheless, pushed forward with his plans, apparently convinced that Veeck was the best bet, in the long run, for retaining the team in Baltimore. In March the governor asked the General Assembly to provide $4 million for a loan that would permit Veeck to buy the club while binding him under terms of the loan agreement to remain in Baltimore.[88]

The Veeck loan passed the lower house of the Maryland legislature but ran into a stone wall in the state Senate. A meeting between Veeck, Mandel, and Senate opponents of the bill was fruitless. The upper house rejected the proposed legislation on 6 April 1975.[89]

In spite of this setback, Veeck pressed his bid and began negotiations with the city over terms of a Memorial Stadium lease. The two sides appeared on the verge of a deal when Commissioner Kuhn intervened. Committed to a regional franchise, he sought to derail a Veeck purchase by reintroducing his handpicked candidate, Edward Cole. In early May, Cole suddenly offered $12.6 million for the Orioles. Red Smith sarcastically labeled the commissioner, "Promisin' Bowie, the Franchise Peddler." An outraged Hoffberger told Smith: "The Commissioner and I can get along fine as long as he sticks to being commissioner and doesn't take over as peddler of my ball club."[90]

A few days later Hoffberger told a luncheon of the Advertising Club of Baltimore that "most but not all" of the details of a deal with Veeck were completed and that the sale would probably be finalized after the end of the 1975 season.[91]

Less than three weeks later Cashen stunned Veeck and the city by breaking off the negotiations. Hoffberger subsequently refused to explain the reasons for his decision to terminate the talks. A temporary improvement in National Brewery's profitability may have had some influence. Reporters close to club management have speculated that Hoffberger was concerned about Veeck's readiness to move the club. Another factor may have been that the Orioles' financial picture improved as a result of favorable stadium terms and increased ticket sales. Whatever the reasons, Hoffberger's decision had major personal consequences, ending a long friendship with Veeck, who commented: "This means the loss of a friend, a ball club, and a lot of dollars and—for me at the age of sixty-one—a loss of innocence."[92]

Within a few months Hoffberger had cause to regret the decision to remain in baseball. In 1975 the sport entered into a new period of intense labor-management confrontation and spiraling costs. Simultaneously, the Orioles lost their dominating position in the American League East and, with it, their only assurance of making a profit.

10 Free Agency

The Orioles' 1975 baseball season mirrored the team's off-the-field trials. Spring training was marked by continued player unrest, as athletes raised their salary demands and many refused to report. Orioles general manager Cashen was openly exasperated with the players and their agents. Preseason brought major change as the team traded Boog Powell to Cleveland and finally succeeded in sending Earl Williams, together with some of its limited cash, to Atlanta. The Orioles stumbled badly in the season's first two months. Ineffective relief pitching and a lack of hitting dropped the team into last place in early May. In late May, shortly before Hoffberger finally took the club off the block, the Orioles began to revive. Between June and September the team compiled the best record in the American League, 74–43. Don Baylor blossomed as a power hitter while Singleton and May provided major contributions to the offense. Jim Palmer led the starters with a 23–11 record that won him a Cy Young award, newly acquired Mike Torrez won twenty games, and journeyman Dyar Miller contributed an outstanding season of relief pitching. In spite of these efforts, the Orioles spent 1975 in a desperate and ultimately futile chase of the Boston Red Sox. Rookie outfielders Fred Lynn and Jim Rice paced a devastating Boston attack and a veteran pitching staff put together an excellent year to catapult the Red Sox into the World Series.

Nevertheless, the 1975 season provided many reasons for optimism. The addition of Singleton and May had improved the Orioles attack. The starting pitching was solid. Moreover, the club's anemic gate improved slightly as the Orioles attracted just over 1 million fans in a rain-shortened home season. Improved attendance, however slight, combined with lowered Memorial Stadium rental, player sales, and interest income allowed the Orioles to end the 1975 fiscal year with a loss of only $3,192.[1]

The Messersmith Case

In the winter of 1975–76 professional baseball faced the most severe labor relations crisis in its 106-year history. Sweeping change in the nature of labor-management relations occurred just as the Orioles began restructuring the team's front office. On 15 December 1975 veteran baseball executive Henry J. Peters replaced Cashen as club general manager. Eight days later, 23 December 1975, independent arbitrator Peter Seitz handed down a decision that overturned the perpetual reserve system and forced baseball executives to negotiate a new relationship with the players.

Hoffberger's decision to replace Cashen was a necessary consequence of his decision to sell National Brewery to Carling. Under terms of the agreement announced on 31 October 1975, Hoffberger became chairman and chief executive officer of Carling's U.S. operation, Carling National Breweries. Hoffberger wanted his top assistant at the brewery, and on 3 November the club announced that Peters would replace Cashen after the winter meetings.[2]

The appointment of Peters was part of a gradual process in which Hoffberger reduced his involvement with professional baseball. After the setbacks of the late 1960s Hoffberger became less active in owners' politics. Thereafter, the Orioles owner usually avoided attending major meetings of the owners. In July 1975 Hoffberger briefly resumed an active role, joining Oakland's Charles Finley in a quixotic effort to oust their common nemesis, Commissioner Kuhn.[3]

Walter O'Malley rallied the National League owners in support of Kuhn, while the American League's new president, Lee MacPhail, brought wavering club owners back into line to defeat the Hoffberger-Finley alliance. This latest in a long series of defeats at the hands of his fellow owners appears to have confirmed Hoffberger's decision to distance himself from the game.[4]

The choice of Peters fit this pattern. The new general manager had extremely wide minor league experience as well as a successful tenure as general manager of the Oakland club and a term as president of the National Association. Calm and cautious by temperament, the self-confident, dignified Peters could operate independently without undercutting or embarrassing the owner. Cashen gradually withdrew from management of the financial end of the operation while assisting Peters's transition.[5]

Meanwhile, the era of free agent players arrived. Ironically, Charles Finley, Oakland's abrasive, innovative, and tightfisted owner, played a key role in triggering a revolution in owner-player relations. No owner ran a more economical organization than Finley, who during the later stages of his baseball career virtually abolished his front office staff and consistently had one of the smallest payrolls in professional sports.

Salary disputes were a regular feature of Finley's operation. So were confrontations between the owner and his players. In the middle of the 1968 season Finley had a personal disagreement with one of his outfielders, Ken Harrelson. The angry A's owner placed Harrelson on waivers. By releasing a player in the prime of his career, Finley set off a bidding war for Harrelson's services that the pennant-contending Boston Red Sox won. Six years later, Finley refused to live up to a contractual arrangement with star pitcher Jim "Catfish" Hunter. Hunter took Finley to arbitration and won his case. On 15 December 1974 arbitrator Peter Seitz declared that Finley had breached Hunter's contract and that the star pitcher was, as a result, free to offer his services to any club. The owners initially tried to form a united front to force Hunter to sign with Oakland. The cash-poor, pitching-rich, Orioles announced that they would decline to enter a bidding war for the star pitcher.[6]

The owners' front collapsed within two weeks. Hunter was one of the best pitchers of his era. George Steinbrenner, the wealthy owner of the rebuilding New York Yankees, offered the pitcher a five-year, $3.75 million contract. Other owners and general managers gasped in amazement at the size of the offer that more than tripled what had previously been the sport's highest salary. Hunter signed and helped turn the Yankees back into a contender after nearly a decade of futility. "Baseball's establishment will live to regret the Catfish Hunter case," *The Sporting News* correctly predicted, "and baseball's players will live to profit by it."[7]

More bad news was on the way for the owners. A few days after Hunter signed, former Cincinnati star outfielder Bobby Tolan and the Players Association announced that they would utilize the arbitration procedure to challenge the validity of the reserve clause. Tolan would play the 1975 season without signing a new contract. He claimed that the reserve clause in his previous contract applied only for one year and after the season he could negotiate to play for any other team.[8]

The *New York Times'* Murray Chass characterized the owners' reaction to Tolan's challenge in a single word: "hysteria."[9] They heaped abuse on arbitrator Seitz, who would hear the case, and loudly warned of the imminent collapse of the sport.

Marvin Miller suggested that the reserve clause issue could be settled better through negotiations. The owners balked. Meanwhile, Tolan, who was coming to the end of a distinguished career, opted for job security and signed a new contract with the San Diego Padres. The confrontation was postponed.[10]

In March 1975, the fate of the reserve clause passed into arbitrator Seitz's hands. Montreal's newly acquired pitcher, Dave McNally, refused to sign a contract, as did Los Angeles pitching star Andy Messersmith. The Expos and Dodgers invoked the reserve clause to force the two pitchers to report. Both men did report but announced their intention of playing without contracts for 1975.[11]

Miller had his case. Messersmith was a player in his prime, who, like Hunter, could expect to make a fortune on the free agent market. McNally, while in his mid-thirties, remained one of the game's stars, and, in addition, was a tough-minded individualist. Both men resisted the subtle and direct pressures and blandishments that management mounted to induce them to sign new contracts. The union gained extra leverage in its efforts to secure a negotiated settlement of the reserve issue as part of a 1976 renewal of the Basic Agreement.

Although Miller had offered to compromise on the reserve clause, the union leader was determined to modify the rules under which players negotiated their salaries. Baseball clubs were raking in huge profits from their lucrative television contract revenues and a general rise in attendance. Attendance stood at 11.4 million in 1972 and surged to 13.4 million the following year. After remaining level for two years, it jumped to 14.6 million in 1976. The following year, after expansion and the first free agent draft, baseball attendance reached 19,639,551. Television income followed suit. From $41 million in 1972, the total for local and national payments to baseball steadily climbed to $52.1 million in 1977. Miller insisted that the players' salaries adequately reflect these profits. Ending the perpetual reserve system would make this objective a reality.[12]

Miller's plans met with fierce owner resistance. Baseball management already felt that it was making too many wage concessions as a result of the arbitration procedure. Cashen condemned arbitration, claiming that it was producing an atmosphere of "crisis bargaining" and as a result was "not working."[13] In fact, the system was working very well for the players whose individual incomes rose steadily and dramatically. The players were attacking the sole dike holding back further salary inflation, the reserve clause. The owners believed that they had to stand fast to preserve the reserve clause or lose their remaining control over baseball's salary structure. Shortly after the season ended, management filed suit in federal court to prevent an arbitrator from hearing the challenge to the reserve clause.[14]

Union efforts to achieve a compromise met with unyielding owner opposition. In June 1975 the Players Association presented a package of proposals designed to modify but not abolish the reserve clause. The union proposed that players with a combination of five years' service in the major and minor leagues have the right to play out their options and offer themselves as free agents to any club willing to bid for their services. The plan was hedged with a series of restrictions designed to preserve competitiveness among the teams.[15]

The owners delayed making a final answer to the union offer until 23 October 1975, when they suddenly informed the Players Association that management would terminate both the Basic Agreement and the pension plan at their expiration in 1976. Organized baseball's chief negotiator, John Gaherin, assured reporters that the move was simply a technicality. The union claimed that the clubs were positioning themselves, first to create an impasse with the union through their negotiating tactics, and then to dictate the terms of a new agreement to athletes without the protection of a Basic Agreement.[16]

Since management had closed off the avenues to a compromise, the Players Association proceeded with its direct challenge to the reserve clause. McNally's part of the case was moot because arm problems forced the veteran to quit baseball in mid-season. In mid-November a federal judge threw out baseball's suit challenging Messersmith's right to seek arbitration. On 21 November 1975 Players Association counsel Richard Moss presented the Messersmith case to a three-man panel chaired by independent arbitrator Seitz.[17]

Prior to rendering his decision, Seitz urged both sides to attempt to negotiate a settlement to their problems. The owners refused. Baseball's attorneys and Commissioner Kuhn were convinced that they could successfully appeal a negative arbitrator's decision in the court. Moreover, the owners' hostility to Seitz was intense as a result of the Hunter decision. They were looking for an excuse to dismiss him.[18]

On 23 December 1975 Seitz ruled that Messersmith was a free agent since the reserve clause bound a player to his team for only one year after the expiration of his contract. The decision also meant that every baseball player with a one-year contract (the vast majority) could become a free agent simply by refusing to sign and playing out the 1976 season. Players' agents carefully studied their options. Management gloomily faced the probability of skyrocketing salary scales. The exasperated owners responded by firing Seitz and announcing they would challenge his decision in court. Lee MacPhail warned, "This decision could have a disastrous effect on baseball."[19] Seitz's decision changed the fundamental nature of player-management relations, as Henry Peters and his Orioles players soon discovered.

Lockout

Initially both players and management took cautious public positions on the effects of the Messersmith decision. Orioles player representative Brooks Robinson downplayed fears of mass player holdouts for higher salaries, suggesting that the arbitrator's decision would usher in a new era of job security as the owners offered players multiyear contracts to stabilize their budgets and squads. Multiyear pacts would be "good for the players," and the sport would survive free agency: "I don't see it as that big a deal. It's not going to shake the foundation of any game. The owners said the same thing when salary arbitration came into being. I don't think any of the players are jumping up and down over the decision."[20] Center fielder Al Bumbry agreed with Robinson's initial analysis, adding that "in all probability I'll sign my contract."[21]

The outlook was less comforting for newly installed Orioles general manager Peters: "On the surface you could say that all 900 players would not sign their contracts. But I don't know what the situation will be. I do think that salary negotiations will be very, very slow and that everyone will be confused. If a player should ask about free agent status, all I can tell him is what happened and that is not final."[22] Hoffberger tried to sound optimistic, recalling that "in adversity there are always opportunities," but clearly was dismayed by the latest players' success.[23]

To further increase management disarray and depression, the appeal of the Messersmith decision was on thin ice. Baseball's attorneys had convinced the sport's lawyer-commissioner, and through him the owners, that they had a strong appeal. However, U.S. courts have regularly upheld arbitrators' decisions. On 8 January 1976 federal judge John W. Oliver opened the hearing on management's appeal and suggested that baseball attempt an out-of-court settlement with the unions. The judge warned the owners against collusion to deny free agent Messersmith employment. Management refused to take the hint. A month later Oliver upheld Seitz's ruling, praising the arbitrator's efforts.[24] *The Sporting News* urged owners to bargain with the union. Management, however, decided to appeal the case while threatening a lockout of spring training camps to force the union to offer concessions. Management, with some justice, complained that it was in a no-win position. Peters explained: "Right now the players have the best of two worlds. They have the benefit of collective bargaining and that's gotten them the best pension plan in the world, and wonderful insurance and health plans. But they can also enter into private negotiations on their personal contracts."[25]

The Players Association offered concessions on free agency but insisted that management negotiate a new Basic Agreement that would include a modified reserve rule. The union took the position that it would not surrender in negotiations the rights it had won in arbitration and the courts. A revised reserve system had to permit a player the option of selecting among salary offers from various clubs at some point during his career. The union reiterated that it sought changes in the reserve structure rather than its total abolition. Direct negotiations rather than court confrontations, it said, were the best means of settling baseball's problems.[26]

As long as they had a chance, however slim, of overturning the Messersmith decision, a majority of the owners were unwilling to bargain. By keeping the camps closed, the owners increased the pressure on individual players to sign a contract and start earning a salary. Hoffberger, usually a leading moderate, supported a lockout, indicating both the appeal of this strategy and the Orioles owner's personal weariness with player demands. Peters and Weaver dutifully claimed that a delay in training would have little effect on their veteran squad. In any case, Peters had only eight players under contract by mid-February and foresaw long, tedious talks before he could sign many more.[27]

On 23 February 1976 the Player Relations Committee officially postponed the opening of spring training "indefinitely." The Orioles immediately announced they would support the PRC decision. Marvin Miller warned that the owners were once again "misjudging [the] players."[28]

The PRC was also misjudging the unity of the owners. Bill Veeck was back in baseball as owner of the Chicago White Sox. As usual, he was underfinanced and could scarcely afford a prolonged lockout that might easily continue into the regular season. Veeck denounced the PRC decision as a violation of his rights. Three days later, Veeck announced he would open spring training for all nonroster players.[29]

By late February the intermittent discussions on the Basic Agreement were again in session. Marvin Miller reiterated the players' desire for a compromise, tabling another proposal that would modify but retain the reserve system. The owners held fast. Both sides waited for a court decision on the owners' appeal of the Messersmith case. Meanwhile, few veterans were signing contracts, frustrating part of management's strategy. Miller kept up the pressure. He called on Kuhn to intervene for the good of the game and open the camps. He suggested that the players might form their own leagues, and, simultaneously, offered to arrange a meeting of player representatives and the PRC to settle the issue.[30]

On 9 March a federal appeals court upheld Seitz's ruling. Within twenty-four hours, the Orioles broke a decade-long policy by offering pitching star Jim Palmer a multiyear contract. On 11 March fifty player representatives met with the PRC to discuss a deal. The two sides were unable to reach an accord. The owners maintained the lockout.[31]

"Time is growing short," *The Sporting News* nervously warned the owners, as the scheduled opening of the baseball season loomed only three weeks distant. Faced with an imminent loss of profits, a united union, and a defeat in the courts, and apparently again under pressure from moderates within the ranks, the owners finally took a step back from confrontation with the players. On 15 March, over the objections of the Orioles, the PRC offered a new proposal that accepted the Messersmith decision and suggested a formula for modifying the reserve clause. The players rejected this "final offer" because it placed too many restrictions on the freedom they had won under Seitz's ruling. Nevertheless, the two sides were again negotiating seriously.[32]

Two days later, Commissioner Kuhn intervened to push the talks toward conclusion and ensure that the baseball season would open on time. He ordered the teams to open their spring training camps immediately. Kuhn felt that the owners had overreacted in closing the camps. He recognized that the Players Association was ready to bargain. His intervention was well timed to avoid another embarrassing public break between moderate and hardline owners. The commissioner won the accolades of the press.[33]

The commissioner's order also won him public condemnation from Orioles officials. Frank Cashen, who remained on the PRC, expressed his "shock" at Kuhn's "unilateral" action. The commissioner, however, achieved his basic objective of pushing forward the negotiations. The union announced that the owners' proposal could serve as the basis for an agreement.[34]

Negotiations for a Basic Agreement continued into the summer of 1976. Both sides showed a willingness to compromise but the talks were slow moving because of the complexity of the issues and because the major leagues were involved simultaneously in expansion. In July 1976 the two sides agreed to a modified reserve clause. Under the new Basic Agreement, all major league players were eligible to opt for free agency in 1976. All future players became eligible for free agency after playing six full seasons in the major leagues. The clubs would participate in a postseason draft of free agents. Each free agent could negotiate with a maximum of twelve teams. To further restrict the ability of the richer clubs to corner talent, the agreement set limits on the number of players each team could acquire. Teams that lost free agent players would be compensated with choices in the amateur player draft. All players with two to six years of major league experience could request salary arbitration. At the insistence of the union, Commissioner Kuhn pledged nonintervention in the operation of the draft. Finally, the owners increased their contribution to the players' pension fund by nearly $2 million.[35]

The 1976 Basic Agreement moved the players a step further toward a dominant position in labor-management relations. As the owners had foreseen, the combination of arbitration and a free agent draft had an explosive impact, driving salary scales upward for a decade. Multiyear contracts that provided greater security for players became normal. The size of the pension increase was remarkable. Three years earlier the owners had risked a strike over the union's demand for a much smaller sum. Owner efforts to reverse this trend by limiting the rights of free agents met with firm union resistance, setting up future confrontations. Rising salaries also forced a number of clubs, including the Orioles, into a major restructuring.

Reggie

In obedience to the commissioner's decree, the Orioles opened spring training on 19 March 1976. Twelve players appeared. Peters expressed his disappointment at the small turnout of athletes. However, he could hardly have been surprised. The Orioles had been unable to sign many of their top stars. Most were holding out on the advice of their agents, who emerged as major powerbrokers in the mid-1970s.[36]

The growing influence of agents was a development that troubled both management and labor leaders. Marvin Miller voiced his concern over the way some agents were exploiting their clients. Frank Cashen repeatedly expressed his anger at agents and their tactics. Looking back a decade later, Harry Dalton explained the change in labor-management relations in the 1970s: "There used to be reasonably close dialogue between general manager and player . . . and you got to know the player better. . . . Then if the player had any problems . . . [he] came to the general manager and the club, because that was his big brother. . . . When the [Players] Association came in . . . and then beyond that . . . the agent . . . [they] gave the player two sources of comfort and put the club in third place. . . . I miss the old way."[37]

One of the most resourceful agents was Jerry Kapstein, a New York lawyer who quickly established a reputation as a tough bargainer. Kapstein utilized every technique at his disposal to force salary concessions for his clients. These tactics, particularly the refusal of his clients to report for training, infuriated Cashen. Kapstein, however, got results and more clients. By 1976 these clients included six Reds, five A's, four Phillies, four Padres, and seven Orioles. The calm, careful Peters faced a major challenge in his efforts to get these players and five others to sign contracts.[38]

Throughout the winter and spring crisis ignited by the Messersmith decision, Peters had been a voice for compromise and moderation. He was keenly aware that the Orioles were operating within very restricted financial parameters and that a failure to achieve some reasonable compromise on the reserve clause would destroy the club's ability to compete. In early March 1976, he estimated that 60 percent of the team could be free agents within two years.[39]

Peters's initial objective was to sign the veteran nucleus of the club. He offered a multiyear deal to Palmer, the best of Baltimore's pitchers, but released designated hitter Tommy Davis, an aging, one-dimensional athlete with a reputation as a "clubhouse lawyer." Peters confidently expected to sign older players like Brooks Robinson and Paul Blair, who had subpar 1975 seasons, at reasonable salaries. Other players presented difficult choices. They included outfielder Don Baylor, infielders Bobby Grich and Doug DeCinces, and pitchers Mike Torrez, Doyle Alexander, and Wayne Garland. Kapstein was advising six of his clients, including Baylor, DeCinces, and Grich, to hold out pending the conclusion of bidding for the services of free agent Messersmith.[40]

Peters was unwilling to further increase his offers to players like Baylor, and he believed that the club's pennant chances would improve with the addition of one of the game's best players, Oakland's Reggie Jackson. On 2 April 1976 the Orioles announced that they had swapped Torrez, Baylor, pitcher Paul Mitchell, and a minor league player for Jackson, pitcher Ken Holtzman, and another minor leaguer.

The trade sparked pennant fever in Baltimore and confusion on the team. Both the Orioles and A's were dealing off discontented athletes in the expectation that they would quickly come to terms with their new club. Jackson, in fact, had privately assured Orioles scouts that he was eager to play for Baltimore. It was a management strategy that had worked in the past and would work again, but it failed in the chaotic labor situation of 1976. Both Baylor and Jackson were shocked and hurt by the last-minute deal. Each refused to sign a new contract. Baylor recalled that initially he was devastated. Then he realized that baseball was a business. Baylor decided to sign only if the salary offered met his personal evaluation of his worth as a ballplayer. Jackson, who had put up with six years of Charles Finley's quixotic rule, had no illusions about management. Nevertheless, he too was disoriented and resented being forced to leave his teammates. Jackson was determined to make the Orioles pay highly for his services. While Baylor reported to the A's, the Orioles' new slugger holed up in Arizona, demanding a long-term contract and a hefty salary increase.[41]

Jackson's demands placed Peters in a difficult position. The club needed Jackson to contend in 1976. At the same time, granting Jackson's demands would have a serious effect on the entire team salary structure. While Peters was trying to entice his new outfielder into signing for a large raise, the club announced that it would cut the salaries of eleven other holdouts by the maximum 20 percent. Kapstein, who was the agent for six of the eleven, justifiably labeled the Orioles' position inconsistent. He demanded that the club rescind the 20 percent cut and negotiate long-term deals with his clients.[42]

On 6 April, with the season opener just three days off, Peters flew to Arizona for a meeting with Jackson and his agent. The slugger demanded a three-year pact for $675,000. Peters rejected the demand, as he would subsequent ones. He explained:

The one thing we had to recognize, and, I think we did immediately—maybe some other clubs didn't— . . . was the precedent setting contract. . . . Now in the spring of 1976 we signed Jim Palmer to a multiyear contract—three years—and it was at terms that recognized his superb performance . . . and we viewed it as a huge risk . . . on our part in giving him . . . a big, big chunk of money. . . . Then when we got into negotiations with Reggie Jackson and the others and we found out that their demands far, far exceeded what we had given to Jim Palmer, we felt we would not . . . want to go back and renegotiate with Jim Palmer and yet we felt we would have to do that.[43]

Although Peters held the line on the salary issue, he made three trips to Arizona for negotiations with Jackson's agent and never indicated he would cut Jackson's pay. Management's apparent willingness to bend its rules in order to accommodate one holdout created deep dissension on the club. Jim Palmer publicly criticized Jackson, calling his attitude "depressing." The club got off to a poor start, losing eight of its first twelve games. On 27 April Orioles management further damaged morale by carrying out its threat to cut the pay of ten players who remained unsigned by 20 percent. Jackson was not among the players disciplined. Peters, aided by Hoffberger, was attempting to talk the holdout into uniform, blaming his agent for the difficulty and threatening legal action against Jackson for breach of contract.[44]

On 30 April 1976 Jackson ended his holdout and reported to the club, still unsigned. He had negotiated an arrangement under which he would receive a reported $200,000 for playing in 1976 while negotiations for a new contract continued. If Jackson remained unsatisfied with the Orioles' offer, he would become a free agent at the end of the 1976 season.[45]

News of the Jackson deal set off an explosion in the Orioles clubhouse. Newly acquired pitcher Ken Holtzman, one of the unsigned players, demanded the restoration of his 20 percent salary cut and set his own deadline for signing a new contract. Later, Holtzman declared he would refuse any offer in order to become a free agent. Bobby Grich, another unsigned athlete, blasted the club for its double standard in player treatment and warned he might leave the team. Kapstein again demanded "consistent treatment" for his clients.[46]

Peters refused to rescind the cuts but also indicated that the money would be restored to any athlete who signed with the Orioles. Simultaneously, the Orioles general manager was seeking a trade that would relieve him of some of the unsigned and dissatisfied players.[47]

By early June, Peters had decided that he must act. The Orioles continued to play poorly. Peters attributed the club's inability to win to the continued clubhouse turmoil created by some of the ten unsigned players. He labeled Holtzman "a cancer on our club." Trading disgruntled, unsigned players was difficult. Few teams were interested in acquiring players who would become free agents at season's end. Peters contacted the division-leading Yankees, one of baseball's richest teams, and offered them Holtzman and the equally difficult and talented Doyle Alexander, together with a steady reliever, Grant Jackson, and aging catcher Elrod Hendricks for veteran pitcher Rudy May and four young, promising players. The trade would clearly help the Yankees in their bid for a 1976 pennant. Peters was gambling that by ridding himself of two major malcontents and acquiring some young players he could end the team dissension and put his club into the pennant race at the same time. The Orioles would make a serious effort to sign the remaining holdouts.[48]

For a moment, it looked as if Peters's strategy would backfire. Charles Finley of Oakland recognized that the onset of free agency would destroy his club's already limited profit margin. He decided to rid himself of many of the skilled and still-young athletes who had made the A's one of baseball's great teams. The trade of Jackson was a prelude to a major reorganization of his club. In June, Finley arranged to sell pitching star Vida Blue to the Yankees and relief ace Rollie Fingers as well as outfielder Joe Rudi to Boston. The clubs announced the sales on the same day that the Orioles and Yankees completed their major player swap. Commissioner Kuhn, who claimed that the sales would destroy the competitiveness of the American League, first suspended and then voided both of Finley's arrangements.[49]

Kuhn's actions aroused an enormous public debate. Many observers suspected that Kuhn was acting to put the brakes on baseball's escalating salary structure. Finley, of course, was outraged by actions that took away both his autonomy and his profit. He filed a $10 million restraint of trade suit against Kuhn and initially refused to permit the athletes involved in the sales to play for Oakland. Jerry Kapstein saw a sinister precedent for free agency in the commissioner's action. Marvin Miller agreed and insisted that Kuhn forswear any intent to interfere with player contracts as part of the deal for a new Basic Agreement. Jerold Hoffberger defended Finley's "right" to trade his "assets," then laughed and added: "We're not in a pennant race. What we are in . . . is a lawyers' full-employment program."[50]

Hoffberger could laugh. The Orioles were major beneficiaries of Kuhn's decision. The commissioner had prevented the Orioles' two principle rivals from stocking up on quality players who could turn the 1976 season into a two-team battle. Peters's June trades, combined with renewed efforts to negotiate with the remaining unsigned players, took the edge off team dissension, although it failed to quell it entirely. After a slow start, Jackson provided a major offensive boost and, together with pitchers Palmer, Garland, and the newly acquired Tippy Martinez, carried a major part of the load as the Orioles pursued the Yankees.[51] In the end, however, the team was unable to overcome its poor early season and finished in second place, ten and a half games behind the champion New York squad.

The Great Auction

In the middle of the 1976 season *Sports Illustrated* ran a long piece on Jim Palmer, the articulate, outspoken ace of the Orioles pitching staff. The article noted the sad condition of what was "only recently the finest franchise in baseball": the organization was "threadbare," with a fifth of the unhappy team playing out their options while other malcontents were traded for what the magazine labeled the "odds and ends" of Yankee farm clubs. Not to be outdone in pessimism, Palmer took up the owners' persistent theme that free agency would divide baseball into have and have-not franchises and stated that the Orioles were doomed to be among the second division clubs.[52]

In truth, the Orioles' situation did look perilous. The potential for personnel problems was created not only by the free agent draft but also by the fact that baseball was expanding by two teams for the 1977 season. The Orioles had only a slight chance of holding on to players like Jackson, and they would be drained of talent to stock the new teams. By August a number of teams were greedily casting their eyes on potential Orioles free agents and publicly discussing how these athletes might fit into their 1977 plans. Jackson remarked, "I'll soon be an overpaid athlete." Peters appealed to Commissioner Kuhn, charging tampering with his ball club. Pitcher Wayne Garland, on his way to winning twenty games, added to the picture of a club in dissolution by stating that he would only agree to play for Baltimore if the club replaced manager Earl Weaver.[53]

The Orioles still retained some strengths, however. Peters doggedly continued his efforts to sign a number of younger players and accelerated efforts to get key veterans under multiyear pacts. In June third baseman Doug DeCinces, a bright prospect, came to terms with the club. In September pitcher Ross Grimsley agreed to a contract. By the end of the season, only five of the original ten players entered the free agent pool. In addition, the Orioles' Rochester farm had one of the finest crops of prospects in its history. Finally, club attendance rose slightly and remained over 1 million for the second straight year.[54]

Rochester's 1976 team was so good that the Orioles placed seven Red Wings on the protected list of fifteen players excluded from consideration in the expansion draft. The team added eight of its major league players while leaving a number of aging veterans like Brooks Robinson, together with the five unsigned players, unprotected. The club held its breath. Veteran scout Jim Russo labeled the consecutive expansion and free agent drafts "a traumatic experience." The club was "waiting to be stripped" of many of its best players.[55]

The first major league free agent draft took place on 5 November 1976 in New York. The Orioles secured the right to negotiate with ten free agents, in addition to its five unsigned players. Peters initially believed that he could sign a few of the players on his list. He was quickly disabused of this notion. "At the end of the '76 season . . . we went through the first free agent draft. A pitcher named Bill Campbell . . . was drafted by the Red Sox . . . and about twenty-four hours later they announced he had signed a five-year $1 million contract, which was almost unheard of. . . . That contract knocked us all for a loop because it set a precedent . . . not only for other free agent players."[56]

By mid-November most of the top free agents had signed elsewhere. Jackson's agent, Garry Walker, explained Baltimore's dilemma in a demeaning fashion: "Baltimore is not going to get anyone. There's nothing wrong with the Orioles' management, or the players, or anything like that. It's just not a city where ballplayers want to play. It has no charisma. Why play in St. Louis or Baltimore when there are other cities to choose."[57] A dispirited and physically ill Peters commented: "I'm afraid its turning out exactly as a lot of us thought it might. The so-called glamour cities, and the big money, are certainly off to good starts in signing free agents. . . . It isn't easy to be optimistic."[58]

By late November the Orioles faced a complete defeat. They had lost all of their free agents and were priced out of the competition for the other available talent. The loss of Jackson, who signed a multiyear, multimillion dollar deal with the Yankees, was particularly painful. The Orioles had given up Baylor to get him, and the club had little spare talent with which to swing another big trade aimed at improving its weakened offense.[59]

The club got a boost from the expansion draft. The strategy of protecting young players worked, and the Orioles escaped without serious loss of talent. Ironically, the 1977 expansion also brought an unexpected but ultimately highly beneficial bonus for the Orioles. The American League owners rejected Commissioner Kuhn's demand that they award one expansion franchise to Washington. The defeat finished Washington as a site for American League expansion. Hoffberger had won a major battle, and the club finally had the opportunity to boost its perennially weak attendance by building support in baseball-starved Washington.[60]

By the time the December 1976 winter meetings ended, the winners of the 1977 season appeared clear. "The free for all is over," *Sports Illustrated* announced, and the likely pennant winners were the big spenders in the first free agent bidding war, the Yankees and the California Angels. Their wealthy owners, George Steinbrenner and Gene Autry, had set off a salary skyrocket by paying unheard-of sums for five top players. Autry signed his three, including former Orioles Bobby Grich and Don Baylor, to long-term contracts worth $5 million. The Yankees acquired pitcher Don Gullett and Reggie Jackson. The big losers were Oakland and Baltimore, each stripped of many of their best players. Peters was bitter, telling reporters: "We've seen . . . a handful of clubs that have been unsuccessful at building teams go out and use checkbooks to achieve things they couldn't accomplish through organizational efforts. And it's very clear that to some players loyalty means nothing."[61]

Nevertheless, Orioles management was more optimistic than either the sporting press or its own players about the club's 1977 chances. Peters explained: "We still think we have a decent ball club left but naturally we don't have as much excess talent as we once had."[62] He would try to acquire a few utility players and rely on the club's minor league system to fill in the gaps.

The other major item on Peters's agenda was convincing the club's veteran nucleus to sign long-term contracts with a franchise that appeared doomed to the second division. The difficulty he faced was daunting. In addition to Palmer, veteran outfielder Ken Singleton indicated that he was uninterested in playing with a team doomed to the second division. Peters stressed the need for team "harmony" and broke with previous policy by inviting his unsigned players to the team's 1977 spring training camp. "This year I want to concentrate on baseball while we're in Miami."[63]

The prognosis for Baltimore baseball was guarded as the team assembled for spring training. Six players remained unsigned. More ominously, the club had taken a $102,531 loss in 1976. This loss was offset by the one-time-only $875,000 the franchise made by selling players in the expansion draft. The Orioles raised ticket prices for 1977 in an effort to compensate partially for rising costs, particularly escalating major league salaries. While season ticket sales ran ahead of those for 1976, the team's drawing power was clearly linked to remaining in contention for the American League East title against the powerful Yankees. "I'm optimistic about the club," Peters commented wistfully; "I wish the financial picture wasn't quite so pessimistic."[64]

Without question, the club had to improve its attendance to survive in Baltimore. Team officials were pessimistic. Peters estimated the Orioles had to draw 1.2 million fans to break even in 1977 but noted that they had reached that figure only in the 1966 championship year. Even with big-name stars, Peters believed there was "simply no way" the Orioles could reach the 1.5 to 1.8 million attendance level that would assure a comfortable profit.[65]

On the eve of the 1977 season Jerold Hoffberger took a look at his team's financial prospects and issued what the *Sun* called an "ominous warning":

> We're going to be able to keep hacking it I guess. But frankly hacking it is not good enough. Individuals and businesses say to me: "Oh, come on, Hoffberger, keep the bloody club in Baltimore. You owe it to the city." Well, maybe I do owe things to the city, but I think my family and I have given a lot back to the city. I think right now it's up to the fans. They've got to understand, if they don't come out, we can't stay. Nobody can stay. . . . We can't continue to have the player payroll and the costs we have and not draw.[66]

Looking back from the perspective of the 1980s, Bowie Kuhn remarked that the Messersmith decision and the free agent bidding wars that followed "doomed" a number of owners. Among the victims of the inflation of salaries accelerated by free agency were a number of "traditional" owners and the commissioner's two most relentless critics. Within four years of the Messersmith decision both Finley and Hoffberger sold their franchises.[67]

11 Miracle on 33rd Street

I do not think this team is being supported the way it should be. I don't think the season ticket sale is as good as it ought to be, and I don't think the attendance is good.
—Jerold Hoffberger, March 1977

Our trading surplus has evaporated. Our ability to put together a deal is knocked way down.
—Henry Peters, April 1977

During the winter of 1976–77 the prospects of Baltimore Baseball and of baseball in Baltimore appeared bleak. The team had lost three top players to free agency. General Manager Hank Peters's efforts to trade for skilled replacements were unsuccessful. Brooks Robinson was clearly reaching the end of his great career. He would retire in mid-season 1977. The club's sole free agent signing, utility infielder Billy Smith, came to terms only after the other twenty-five teams declined to make an offer. Jim Palmer, Baltimore's outspoken pitching ace, was blunt: "This club stinks. They're lucky if they finish fourth."[1]

At the same time, Commissioner Bowie Kuhn was again maneuvering to bring baseball to Washington. Jerold Hoffberger reacted forcefully, telling reporters the commissioner's plan to move the Oakland A's to Washington "has as much chance of happening as I have of flying the Graf Zeppelin."[2] Introduction of a club into the nation's capital would destroy the Orioles' extremely shaky financial position by undercutting the club's radio and television market and reducing its attendance. At a 22–24 March owners' meeting in Tampa, Hoffberger headed off efforts to move a team from either league into Washington. When Kuhn's allies proposed reorganizing the majors into two thirteen-team leagues, Hoffberger responded: "Baltimore continues to oppose the introduction of an American League team in[to] Washington and will continue to oppose the transfer of an American League team into the National League for the purpose of putting a team in Washington."[3]

If the owners simply wanted to create two thirteen-team leagues, Hoffberger continued, he would willingly move the Orioles into the National League. Hoffberger and Peters extolled the benefits of offering Baltimore fans new "natural rivalries" and interleague play. Interleague play was anathema to the National League. American League teams refused to surrender the Orioles, a consistently good draw on the road. Kuhn's ploy collapsed.[4]

Hoffberger's victory was the first in a series of triumphs for the Orioles both off and on the playing field. Defying the predictions of the experts and continued losses to the free agent draft, the Orioles fielded a contender. In 1977 an Orioles team that mixed a small nucleus of veterans with a strong injection of first- and second-year players gave the powerful New York Yankees and Boston Red Sox a race to the wire for the American League East championship. The Orioles tied Boston for second place, posting 97 wins, 7 more than the 1976 team that had included the departed stars Jackson, Grich, and Garland. Injuries crippled the 1978 team, but it finished fourth with a respectable 90–71 record. In 1979, the Orioles raced into first place in early May, playing at a torrid 51–16 pace between 19 April and 1 July. The Orioles ended the season with a 102–57 record and quickly eliminated California for the American League title before losing a seven-game World Series to the hard-hitting Pittsburgh Pirates.

The 1977 and 1978 Orioles played to small home crowds. Hoffberger reopened his search for a buyer. The city's political and business elite unsuccessfully tried to put together a syndicate capable of meeting Hoffberger's price. The state once more declined to bail out Baltimore. Then in 1979 attendance boomed and Hoffberger's search for a buyer ended. Pledging to remain in Baltimore, Washington attorney Edward Bennett Williams completed a deal to purchase the club in August 1979, ushering in an era of championship baseball, rising attendance, and growing profits.

Mr. Hoffberger Bows Out

In spite of the Orioles' continuing success on the field, the 1977–78 seasons were among the most difficult Jerold Hoffberger weathered in his long stewardship of Baltimore Baseball. The club faced enormous, uncontrollable financial pressures created by the rising salary demands of players and a continued inability to increase fan support. Overall baseball attendance surged by over six million between 1976 and 1977. The Orioles were one of the few franchises that failed to follow this trend. Although the 1977 Orioles registered an increase of almost 140,000 fans, the team's home attendance of 1,195,769 was paltry in comparison to the more than 2 million fans drawn that season by each of its major rivals, New York and Boston. When the

Orioles failed to contend the following year, attendance dropped by approximately 140,000.[5]

Peters had to find a way to pay his successful club in an era of free agency. In March 1977 he won Singleton's agreement to a five-year contract with a substantial increase in salary. The following month Peters renegotiated Palmer's contract, granting another hefty raise and offering additional cash performance incentives to baseball's premier pitcher. Overall, the Orioles payroll rose by $500,000 in 1977 despite the loss of three quality players to free agency.[6] Looking over the club's future in April 1977, Peters was less than optimistic. He projected the "absolute top" Orioles attendance as "1.2 million," adding that "more realistically" the club's average was around 1 million. "You project your future attendance, then apply it to a budget and a payroll. If you put the financial jigsaw together and the pieces don't fit, you have to take a look at what you're doing."[7] Given his club's payroll and attendance figures, Peters came to the reasonable conclusion that signing a few expensive free agent stars in hopes of attracting higher attendance was a very bad gamble.

The Orioles continued efforts to retain their own free agent players and to sign others with moderate talent and correspondingly modest salaries. At the end of the 1977 season the club lost the services of pitchers Ross Grimsley and Dick Drago and outfielder Elliot Maddox. Peters pursued a number of other players, promising to make "damn fine offers" for their services.[8] He admitted, however, that the Orioles' ability to compete for free agents hinged on the financial restraint of other clubs. In the free agent market of the 1970s, owner restraint was rare. The Yankees' success in utilizing free agents like Reggie Jackson and Catfish Hunter to win pennants served as a prod to other owners. Bidding wars ensued. The Orioles failed to sign any of their selections. Peters condemned the "limited number of clubs [that] continued to pass out extravagant contracts to free agent players." In a January 1978 report to club stockholders, he warned that "the exercise of financial restraint is absolutely essential to the long-term future of not only our franchise but of major league baseball as a whole."[9]

Caught in a squeeze created by rising costs and limited attendance, the club created additional revenue by the only means available to it: raising ticket prices in 1977 and again in 1978. Peters reminded fans that Orioles ticket prices remained among the lowest in baseball. The club was gambling that the price hikes would not trigger a serious attendance slump. The sale of player contracts to two expansion franchises had enabled the Orioles to make a profit in 1977. In 1978 the club would depend on traditional and essentially fixed income sources: broadcasting revenues, concessions, and a weak attendance.[10]

Frustrated in his efforts to sign free agents and once again bled of a number of important players, Peters attempted to reinforce his club through trades. In December 1977, over the objections of manager Weaver, he sent veteran pitcher Rudy May and two minor league players to Montreal for reliever Don Stanhouse and two promising minor league prospects. He acquired outfielder Carlos Lopez from Seattle in an effort to bolster the team's attack.

The club discovered unexpected and potentially important information about its attendance as a result of a 1977 survey by marketing students from Baltimore's Loyola College. The survey produced some startling information: approximately 10 percent of the club's total attendance was coming from the Washington, D.C., area. Orioles business manager Al Harazin commented: "I would say that's a very high percentage when you stop to think we haven't put a major marketing effort into the area. It's a surprise to me it's that high. I think there's something substantial there. I don't know whether all these people are Orioles fans, but that's immaterial. They're baseball fans."[11]

Peters agreed with this assessment, adding that the team would be in a better position to exploit the Washington area if organized baseball finally determined its policy regarding expansion to the nation's capital. At the 1977 winter meetings, the owners again avoided making a commitment to Washington. Bolstered by this decision, the Orioles acted to expand their D.C. attendance base, negotiating a contract with Washington's WTOP radio to broadcast all the club's 1978 games. Peters recalled:

> Actually, it was out of concern that despite the good ball club we were putting on the field here that our attendance seemed to have been stonewalled. . . . We were very much concerned, particularly as we recognized what was happening economically. . . because of the free agents system . . . and the spiraling payrolls. In 1976 . . . the advice was don't fool with Washington. They are still bitter about losing the Senators. . . . After a couple of years . . . we decided we just had to do something down in Washington. The first thing we did . . . was to buy our way onto WTOP, because we felt we had to have a strong radio voice in Washington. . . . That was the beginning of our marketing efforts. We didn't have the dollars to spend on launching a massive sales effort. . . . We were just trying to feel our way along.[12]

The 1978 season was a financial disaster for the Orioles. The club lost $234,141 and was forced to raise its ticket prices for the third straight year. Neither a strong marketing effort nor head-to-head competition with traditional rivals like the Yankees and Red Sox drew fans. Sometime during the season Hoffberger decided to actively seek a buyer for the club.[13]

Hoffberger's decision was motivated primarily by the Orioles' failing financial condition. Other factors affecting the timing of the move were rumored family pressures and the end of his relationship with Carling Breweries. Between 1976 and 1977 National's share of the Maryland market dropped from 18 percent to 11 percent as well-financed national breweries such as Anheuser-Busch and Miller increased their sales in the state. In May 1978 with Carling National sales figures dropping, the Canadian brewery removed Hoffberger as a chief executive officer. At the same time, Hoffberger's family was apparently pushing him to divest himself of the time-consuming baseball business and, with it, a great deal of unwanted publicity. Talking with the *Sun*'s Bob Maisel in September, Hoffberger publicly confirmed that the club was on the market: "If somebody comes along with a pile of money and wants to meet certain terms, I'll listen and go to my board of directors with the proposal. The right guy just might buy himself a ball club."[14]

Bidding for a Ball Club

Hoffberger's hints quickly flushed out a number of potential bidders for the Orioles. Frank Cashen, ousted by Carling along with his longtime boss, began to sound out financial backers in an effort to return to baseball. Commissioner Kuhn, still trying to bring baseball back to Washington and eager to rid himself of an old adversary, caught wind of Hoffberger's interest in selling in May 1978. He urged former treasury secretary William Simon to enter the bidding. Simon, an outgoing, aggressive, and impatient business-man, was intrigued. Kuhn suggested to Simon that wealthy Washington attorney Edward Bennett Williams, the president of the NFL's Redskins, would be an excellent partner. Williams, a crafty, eloquent, and politically well connected member of the Washington establishment, knew Hoffberger. Simon held talks with Frank Cashen about the general manager's job.[15]

By early December 1978 Simon and Hoffberger had held a series of talks that Simon judged "positive." Hoffberger's assessment was more guarded: "I told him that we've gone through this before and if he liked [baseball] so much to send me a contract. I read where the club's 90 percent sold. . . . It's not 3 percent sold." Encouraged by Kuhn and, reportedly, by some members of the owner's family, Simon met with Hoffberger on 27 December, present-ing the Orioles owner with a contract offer designed to nail down a deal. Once again, Hoffberger refused to be pushed into finalizing an agreement: "We had a nice talk, and we drank a lot of coffee and ate cookies. It was very nice," he told reporters, adding that "nothing happened."[16]

The prospective new owner sought to assure Baltimore's fans that he intended to keep the club in the city. Nevertheless, the Simon bid stimulated a strong if uncoordinated reaction within the Baltimore business and political elite. In spite of his pledges to create a regional franchise anchored in Baltimore, Simon's ties to Washington, and his suggestions that the team play thirteen games in the capital, aroused Baltimore city leaders. They believed that Simon would be unable to withstand the allure of the nation's capital and would quickly move the franchise.

Losing the Orioles to Washington would be a severe blow to Baltimore's rediscovered sense of urban identity. By the late 1970s Baltimore was basking in favorable national attention. Under Mayor Schaefer's leadership the city was financially solvent, with a small surplus in its treasury. By limiting its annual bond sales, reducing the number of city employees, and relying on the state to cover most of the costs of large, expensive programs like mass transit, school construction, and welfare, Schaefer was able to continue providing adequate services to his constituents. The partnership of the city government, community associations, and the business elite produced solutions to some of the city's problems and gave Baltimore a national reputation as a "model of urban rehabilitation."[17] The first phase of the Inner Harbor redevelopment was nearing completion. Baltimore led the nation in public housing construction and by 1979 had more than twice as many urban homesteading starts as any other U.S. city. The city had taken over and renovated 2,800 row houses for low-income families.[18]

James Rouse, the developer of the planned community of Columbia, Maryland, and other successful suburban projects, was one of the driving forces behind Baltimore's urban renewal. Rouse, one of the founders of the Greater Baltimore Committee, believed that the United States had to rescue its central cities through an innovative partnership of local and federal government with business and community groups. Baltimore became a showplace for Rouse's concepts. With the support of Schaefer, he provided the leadership for the Inner Harbor redevelopment, mediating between preservationists and growth advocates by producing projects that combined their objectives.[19]

Professional sports had played a role in reshaping the city's image of itself and the image it projected throughout the nation. The Orioles and Colts champions of the 1960s and 1970s had helped Baltimore create a positive civic identity. City business and political leaders remained sensitive to any criticisms that might imply that Baltimore was less than a "major league city." In 1976 Peters demanded an apology from ABC television after one of its sports broadcasters made comments disparaging Baltimore. Two years later city comptroller Hyman Pressman attempted to present another ABC broadcaster, Howard Cosell, with a "Doghouse Award" for slighting Baltimore on a Monday night baseball telecast.[20]

No city more challenged Baltimore's pride and new urban identity than Washington. The nation's capital, with its ongoing urban development programs, monumental buildings, spacious parks, and abundant wealth, as well as its new role as a major cultural center, was simply in another class. Now, the arrogant Washingtonians appeared poised to steal a part of Baltimore's special identity. In early January 1979 Baltimore developer Herbert Siegel announced he would bid for the team. Another Baltimore group stated its interest on 10 January. Three days later, Siegel met Hoffberger for lengthy discussion about the terms of the Orioles' sale. Hoffberger assured both Siegel and the press that the team was available for sale to local interests. Hoffberger promised Mayor Schaefer that he would give first preference to local bidders but warned that he wanted a concrete offer by 1 February and urged Baltimore interests to coordinate their efforts and to act quickly and quietly, avoiding contact with the press.[21]

Mayor Schaefer reacted immediately to Hoffberger's suggestion, uniting various interested businessmen into the Mayor's Committee to Save the Orioles for Baltimore. The committee included such civic stalwarts as F. Barton Harvey, W. Wallace Lanahan, Harvey Meyerhoff, and Bernard Manekin. Seeking to solidify the committee's financing, the Achilles' heel of the 1974–75 failure, Schaefer arranged to bring wealthy Detroit businessmen Max M. Fisher, a Hoffberger friend, and Alfred Taubman into the group. The group set about raising $12 million to meet Hoffberger's selling price under intense local press scrutiny.[22]

Hoffberger, accompanied by Fisher, left for Israel on 23 January for a meeting of the board of governors of the Jewish Agency of Israel. Prior to his departure, the Baltimore group presented a plan to pool its funding with that of Fisher and Taubman to reach the $12 million selling price. However, the committee still lacked the financing to meet this goal. The group expanded from six to nine and eventually to thirty-two members but still failed to put together a solid financial package. One Baltimore banker commented that the team was clearly worth $12 million but its weak attendance history made the Orioles a very bad investment. As a result, prudent investors would commit only limited sums, while financial institutions would be reluctant to offer loans, particularly since tax advantages of franchise ownership were available only to purchasers of teams that made a profit.[23]

Lacking solid funding, the committee turned to the city and the state for financial support, suggesting that government provide $6 million of the purchase price. Mayor Schaefer was ready to contribute, but city funds were limited. Maryland's new governor, Harry Hughes, initially expressed cautious support, then began to back off, citing legal difficulties in providing such a large amount of state aid for a private business.[24]

When Hoffberger returned to Baltimore at the end of January, he faced a situation reminiscent of his unsuccessful 1975 effort to sell the club. Local interests had plans but lacked financing. An outside bidder backed by Bowie Kuhn had the money but might move the franchise. Hoffberger urged local bidders to continue their efforts and once again stressed the need to avoid publicity. He steered clear of finalizing a deal with Simon.[25]

On 5 February Simon's patience snapped. Talking with a Baltimore *Sun* reporter, an angry Simon announced that he was withdrawing his bid and denounced Hoffberger in strong terms: "I've never seen such duplicity in a deal in my life. It's like dealing with the scarlet pimpernel. . . . Mr. Hoffberger wants to play both ends against the middle. Well, he can forget this end . . . . The game is over."[26]

Hoffberger responded mildly that he regretted Simon's decision, commenting that the former treasury secretary was "a gentleman. He would have been an asset to baseball as would his partner."[27] The Orioles owner strongly hinted that Simon's departure hardly mattered, announcing that he had had six to eight other bids on the club. Hoffberger's revelation increased pressure on Baltimore's business community and on the state's politicians to put together a solid offer.

The following day, the committee unveiled its latest plan to the press. F. Barton Harvey, acting as spokesman for the group, announced that Hoffberger had offered the prospective buyers a five-year, $4 million loan at 6 percent interest. Harvey explained that the committee members would provide $6 million and that they would "use the $2 million in the Orioles treasury to make up the balance." The new owners would issue an "intrastate" stock offering "to replace the treasury" and provide working capital. While the new plan avoided making major demands on the state treasury, Harvey warned, "We will also need some help from the city and state if we run into operating losses."[28]

The newest committee plan was a financial house of cards. In spite of the Orioles' recent history of losing money, the prospective owners proposed to start operating by emptying the club's cash reserves. Further, they wanted a commitment from the city and state to provide $250,000 each for a five-year period to assure the club working capital. Finally, an intrastate bond issue might fail to attract the capital needed to run the franchise, much less repay the Orioles' depleted cash reserves. Team season ticket sales were running well behind their usual slow pace, causing both Peters and Hoffberger to complain publicly about the lack of fan support. American League president Lee MacPhail, a friend of Baltimore baseball, reacted tepidly to the committee's proposal. Governor Hughes was even more skeptical.[29]

Hughes had run for office as a careful administrator and reformer who would avoid the excessive and flamboyant management style of his scandal-ridden and disgraced predecessor. Marvin Mandel was indicted for corruption in November 1975, eventually forced to hand over his office, and finally convicted in the summer of 1977. (The conviction was overturned in 1987.) The Mandel trial was a great embarrassment to the state political establishment and to the citizens of Maryland. They turned to a man who offered a different style of government. Hughes preferred to leave major political initiatives to the state legislature. He referred the committee's "unusual" proposal to an aide with instructions to test its legality, commenting: "I'm not sure the state should become involved in protecting the losses of a private venture."[30] While the governor waited for a legal opinion, important state legislators poured cold water on the plan. Baltimore's Senator Harry Mc-Guirk, chairman of the upper house's Economic Affairs Committee, expressed strong reservations about providing state money to make the Orioles profitable. Senator Laurence Levitan of Montgomery County, a Washington suburb, flatly predicted that the legislature would reject the proposal.[31]

Complaining that "we're trying to get a lousy $250,000 [from the state] and everybody's trying to figure out why it can't be done," an angry Mayor Schaefer vowed to find funding for a local purchase of the Orioles.[32] To demonstrate their ability to manage a club and build attendance, the committee, with the mayor's backing, launched a ticket sales drive. At a 10 February meeting of the prospective buyers with the media and officials of the Greater Baltimore Committee, Schaefer set an attendance goal of an unprecedented 1.5 million fans for the 1979 season. Harvey explained, "We want to show such strength in advanced sales that we'll overwhelm the American League executives when we ask them for approval" of the prospective sale.[33]

Schaefer's efforts got a temporary lift when Governor Hughes announced that state assistance to the purchasers would be legal. On 16 February two Baltimore legislators introduced a bill that would authorize the state to provide a $2.5 million grant to assist Baltimore interests in financing the purchase of the Orioles. The bill, amended to make the state assistance a loan rather than a grant, passed the lower house on 28 March 1979.[34]

By that time the local effort to acquire the Orioles had grounded to a halt. Fisher and Taubman quietly withdrew their offer of assistance by mid-February. Two weeks later, Baltimore investors rejected an offer from a wealthy Pennsylvania businessman who demanded controlling interest in the club. Without outside financing, Baltimore investors were $2 million short of the money needed to cover their part of the purchase plan. The final blow to local hopes came in April. The Maryland Senate killed the bill authorizing state aid for the purchase of the Orioles. Two weeks afterward, Hoffberger indicated that he would move forward with the sale of the team to any buyer who could meet his price and conditions.[35]

Turnaround

The possible sale of the Orioles faded from the newspapers and public attention until mid-season. Oriole fans focused attention on their club's torrid run for the American League East title. The 1979 club was an attractive blend of homegrown young talent, role players acquired by trade, and a few moderately priced free agent players, together with the leaven of veterans from earlier Baltimore championship teams. In the winter of 1978 Peters had acquired the contract of a left-handed hitting outfielder, John Lowenstein, for $20,000. He signed free agent right-handed pitcher Steve Stone. A minor league trade brought hard-hitting, but defensively limited, outfielder Benny Ayala to strengthen the Orioles bench and provide a right-handed designated hitter. The development of rookie outfielder Gary Roenicke and relief pitcher Tim Stoddard improved the club's hitting, pitching, and defense.

The division-leading Orioles played before the largest crowds in club history. A sudden surge of local concern about the sale and loss of the team, combined with prodding by Mayor Schaefer and the Committee to Save the Orioles, built attendance. The Orioles' play attracted even more cash customers. By late May the club was performing before large, enthusiastic crowds. At the end of the season, the Orioles had attracted 1,681,009 paying customers despite weather problems that limited the club to seventy-two home dates. In September, stunned but happy club officials realized that they would make the largest profit in team history. The always understated Peters commented: "We certainly have broken into some uncharted territory." Peters credited intense off-season media coverage of the potential sale of the team with building great interest in the Orioles. The team capitalized on this coverage. The Orioles had signed radio and television contracts with two new stations after the 1978 season. Both stations, but particularly youth-oriented WFBR radio, were able to attract new fans. More promotional events also helped. The Orioles' on-the-field performance, particularly a June surge that saw the club win repeatedly in dramatic fashion, cemented fan interest. "By the time the All Star break arrived, the town was turned on." Still, Peters remained cautious. The team would have to wait some years to be confident that the attendance surge was no "fluke": "Next year is going to be highly interesting. . . . And five years from now if we're averaging 1.6, 1.7 million, then we'll know it's for real. I hope the fans do not treat this as a once-in-a-lifetime thing. The bricks have been laid. Let's hope they don't fall down."[36]

The fans and the team would enter a new era under new ownership. In August 1979, Hoffberger stunned the city with the announcement that he had sold the Orioles to Edward Bennett Williams. Baltimore civic leaders were shocked. To them, Williams epitomized Washington and its hunger for a major league franchise. These fears were reinforced as the capital city's press jubilantly announced the sale of the "Washington Orioles" and confidently predicted the return of baseball to Robert F. Kennedy Stadium.[37]

Williams attempted to quiet these concerns during a 2 August press conference that announced the sale. He pledged to keep the Orioles in Baltimore, announced that Hoffberger would remain as team president, and promised to keep the club's baseball administration in place. Mayor Schaefer put aside his disappointment, telling reporters he was "pleased" with the sale to Williams and had complete confidence in the new owner's "integrity and honor."[38]

Williams had succeeded where numerous other bidders failed. At least four factors appear to have enabled him to close a deal. First, Williams made his bid in secret, avoiding the publicity that Hoffberger detested. Operating in secret, Williams was able to patiently knit together a deal that satisfied Hoffberger. Williams's pledge to give Baltimore a reasonable chance to support the Orioles was apparently a key assurance. Finally, Williams had his financing in order and could deliver the purchase price as soon as the American League approved a franchise transfer.[39]

Trouble on the Farms

Edward Bennett Williams inherited a top-flight major league team with a growing attendance base. He also bought a minor league system that was dangerously weak. The inability of Orioles management to rebuild the farm system led directly to the team's collapse in the mid-1980s. Without the surplus talent a good minor league operation provides, the Orioles were unable to correct or recover from errors in player selection and from the inevitable loss of key athletes to injury and age.

Under Harry Dalton's leadership, the Orioles maintained one of the best scouting and training operations in the major leagues. Dalton retained most of Jim McLaughlin's ideas and men. By careful attention to the personal needs of his scouts and minor league personnel and by encouraging innovation, Dalton produced a highly motivated minor league system. By introducing a "book" detailing training methods for the entire minor league system, Dalton ensured that players arriving at the major league level were thoroughly schooled in the fundamentals of the game. Finally, by insisting that winning was an essential part of player development at the minor league level, Dalton created a proper psychological attitude among his players while meeting the needs of minor league owners for a product that could attract attendance and create profits. The result was a smoothly functioning organization that produced profitable, winning baseball at all levels of the Orioles system.[40]

The Orioles' minor league system began to decline shortly after Dalton's 1971 departure. Dalton's scouts proved more loyal to the man than to the organization. Within two years, a majority of his best men had left Baltimore and joined Dalton in California. The exodus was probably accelerated by clashes between scouts accustomed to Dalton's smooth handling and their new bosses: Jim McLaughlin and his handpicked assistant, David Ritterpusch. McLaughlin, who returned to direct Orioles farm operations in 1968, felt that Dalton was too easy with scouts. He believed that the scouts had to be held to a stricter accountability by a return to the very carefully constructed system of player assessment and development that he had created and utilized in the 1950s.[41]

Ritterpusch was the type of younger man that McLaughlin instinctively pushed forward. He was energetic, innovative, and educated, characteristics that appealed to the cerebral McLaughlin. Ritterpusch's problem lay precisely in these qualities. He was a Lehigh University graduate, former bank officer, and Orioles administrative aide who had little practical baseball experience. The scouts, McLaughlin recalled, mistrusted Ritterpusch because he wasn't "a baseball man." "[Ritterpusch] wasn't quite able to overcome that, ever. . . . I don't think he exactly knew how. He tried."[42] One scout told a reporter: "I know for a fact of cases where scouts have laughed behind [Ritterpusch's] back, taken his ridiculous forms and thrown them into the wastebasket."[43]

Defections from the scouting staff became so severe that the Orioles had to reorganize their entire minor league operation twice in 1973. The second reorganization in November 1973 was dramatic and revealed how deeply disaffection had crept into the once-proud Orioles player development program. The club announced that three older scouts were "retiring" and that three others were resigning. One of the departing younger scouts told reporters that he had made out a list of thirteen reasons for quitting and that "inadequate pay and lack of communication were right at the top of the list." Much of the departing scouts' criticism was directed at Ritterpusch. An anonymous Orioles official sadly commented: "It's going to show, believe me. Too many good people are leaving and a lot of others feel there's no communication between the Orioles' front office and the scouts in the field." He warned that the minor league system would begin to suffer from a talent shortage within three years.[44]

The scouting drain slowed after the 1973 season. However, the team's overall player development was seriously affected by management's decision to save on scouting costs by joining the Major League Central Scouting Bureau, a consortium of seventeen major league clubs that agreed to pool data on prospects. McLaughlin supported membership in the consortium, believing it was an inexpensive way to increase scouting coverage. He was surprised when Cashen decided to reduce the team's own scouting staff.[45] The reduction in scouting staff, which included the loss of Orioles assistant general manager Don Pries to the scouting bureau, upset one of the best Orioles scouts. Walter Youse, a veteran of nearly twenty years with the Orioles and the club's eastern regional scouting supervisor, abruptly resigned in late November 1974.[46]

At the heart of the Orioles' decision to reduce the scouting staff was the club's major weakness: lack of money. The existing player development system with its heavy reliance on major league subsidization of the minors locked the Orioles into large expenditures. These expenses grew at the same time that other costs, particularly major league salaries, were accelerating. By January 1975 the team had to consider cutting the number of its minor league affiliates. Cashen explained: "Cutting down on our farm clubs has been discussed and it continues [to be] a possibility. We're trying to tighten our belts in some areas but I can't see something like the [major league] player payroll going down. We sort of play brinksmanship—we try to keep the quality up and take a gamble that the expense for high quality will pay off."[47]

The spiraling costs of minor league operations were a general drain on major league operations. In December 1972 Commissioner Kuhn had suggested that the big leagues reduce the overall number of minor league affiliates to cut the drain on their treasuries. The National Association's president, Henry Peters, responded that while the costs of player development were rising the major leagues had no other options: "I don't know of any other concept that can save much money."[48]

Adding to these concerns was the rising cost of free agent amateur talent. By the mid-1960s baseball executives were complaining of a talent shortage. Competition from colleges and other professional sports for top athletic talent probably played a role in this decline. Ironically, baseball officials concluded that the drastic reduction of minor league systems in the 1950s was at the root of their troubles. Without more minor leagues, *The Sporting News* argued, organized baseball would be unable to compete for talent with other sports, especially college programs. Baseball found itself operating in a vicious circle. Large minor leagues were too expensive to maintain. Without expanded minor leagues, the costs of amateur talent rose and the scarcity of top minor league players fueled major league salary increases.[49]

The Orioles were a good example of the problems facing minor league systems. The team had invested in a badly needed minor league training complex in Florida in 1972 while simultaneously revamping its affiliations to adjust for the collapse of one minor league and the move of the former Washington franchise into the territory of another affiliate. Even a well-run and profitable operation like Rochester depended on Orioles subsidies to stay in business. Red Wings general manager Carl Steinfeldt stated that, without financial help, "salaries alone would make it impossible" for Rochester to field a team. The Orioles paid the entire salary of three Rochester ballplayers and picked up the excess over $450 a month on the other twenty Red Wings. In addition, Baltimore covered part of the Red Wings' transportation costs, and of course, scouted, signed, and trained the athletes who performed at Rochester. "We rely on Baltimore," Steinfeldt admitted.[50]

By the end of the 1975 season, Orioles officials were convinced that the team's minor league operations needed a complete overhaul. A key factor influencing Hoffberger's choice of Henry Peters as the club's new general manager was his minor league experience. In the weeks before Peters formally assumed his duties, Cashen, with the incoming general manager's approval, purged the minor league department. Cashen fired the last of the "Dalton Gang," player development director Jack Pastore, and three minor league managers. Peters told reporters, "We have to get some depth in the player development program. . . . You need a strong team inside running the show," and began hiring new men to revamp minor league operations.[51]

The medium-range outlook for Orioles player development was grim. Peters recalled:

> The Rochester club was loaded with major league prospects. However, . . . what we found in the lower leagues where most of the players . . . had been signed after the Orioles joined the Major League Scouting Bureau was that we had practically nothing in the way of prospects. . . . From AA on down about the only players that arrived on the major league scene were Sammy Stewart and Bryn Smith. After we evaluated the system, it was not difficult to decide [that] we would not continue our association with the bureau. . . . It was necessary. . . to try to rebuild our scouting staff.[52]

In rebuilding the Orioles' system, Peters fell back on old friends from his years as general manager of the Kansas City A's. He hired veteran scout Clyde Kluttz to run the minor league operations and another baseball veteran, Tom Giordano, as director of scouting. When Kluttz died in 1979, Giordano succeeded him as director of minor league operations. Ritterpusch was allowed to resign. Jim McLaughlin was excluded from decision making: "I was on a salary . . . a supernumerary," he said.[53]

Since Peters and his associates blamed the weaknesses of the minor league system on the Orioles' decision to join the Major League Scouting Bureau, they dropped the club's affiliation. Baltimore would again rely on expensive, traditional scouting by a large staff. Peters and Kluttz set out to recruit new men to beef up the Orioles' thinned-out scouting ranks.[54]

Reliance on a large scouting staff was a further strain on the club's already limited resources. By 1976, in spite of serious economies, player development was the largest cost in the Orioles' team budget. The club spent $1.5 million for scouting, bonuses, and its farm system in 1975. With the exception of an outstanding club at Rochester, it had little to show for the expense. In order to offset the rising costs of scouting and signing players, the club cut back on its minor league affiliations. Instead of the seven minor league clubs of the Dalton years, only four clubs remained for Peters to operate with. The Orioles attempted to reduce the costs of this skeletal system further by selling the Class A Miami Orioles to local investors at the beginning of 1976.[55]

During the final four years of Jerold Hoffberger's ownership, Peters and his aides had a free hand to revamp the minor league department. The results were disappointing. The club continued to hire and fire managers and scouts as Kluttz and Peters sought the right combination to restock the farm system with top prospects. Baltimore's limited number of good minor league players rose rapidly to the major leagues, denuding the farm system of talent. By 1978 the Orioles' minor league system was reaping the harvest of years of bad selections. For the first time in sixteen years, Orioles farms posted a losing record overall. Rochester, after years as a profitable perpetual contender for the International League championship, started to field losing teams. Conflicts between Orioles management and Rochester Community Baseball surfaced.[56]

A Bull in a China Shop

Edward Bennett Williams's purchase of the Orioles brought hope to the team's battered minor league program. The new owner was in a position to put more money into player development. Rising Orioles attendance helped provide additional money to expand the farm system. In December 1979 Williams, who was attending his first winter meetings as Orioles owner, told a Rochester reporter, "One of the primary things we have to do . . . is to get [the Red Wings] cranked up again. It's a key club for us. We've got to strengthen it." He added, "I believe very strongly in the farm system. That's the way to build. I'm keeping the Orioles's commitment to that."[57] Williams noted that he had already approved a 10 percent increase in the budget for player development.

Williams's words and action were welcome in Rochester. Rochester Community Baseball's problems both off and on the field had mounted since the mid-1970s. The Morris Silver era (1965–74) had been a golden age for Rochester baseball. The club turned a profit every year, and its teams won. Silver, operating through a series of carefully picked young general managers, maintained both the quality of the teams and a good working relationship with the Orioles. Even after Silver's 1974 death, Rochester continued to post winning records and profits through the 1976 season.

The Silver years were never totally placid. Rochester was one of the few stable franchises in the International League. Even with large-scale assistance from the big leagues, minor league baseball solidified its financial position only in the late 1970s. Moreover, the club had some serious clashes with Baltimore management over player assignments. In 1968, for example, Baltimore failed to protect veteran minor league third baseman Steve Demeter from the minor league draft. The Yankees acquired the thirty-three-year-old star, who had been Rochester's best hitter and team leader. Silver said he was "shook up" by the Orioles' action, while the local press condemned Baltimore management.[58]

By and large, however, the relationship between Rochester Community Baseball and the Orioles remained strong. "Baltimore sends us good players [and] doesn't jerk players around like other major league teams," Red Wings general manager Bob Turner stated.[59] The orderly promotion of players, managers, and coaches through the Baltimore minor league system enabled Silver to achieve his two goals: "to win and to put people in the park."[60] When the Orioles briefly were short of AAA-level players, Rochester maintained the working agreement because good players were always somewhere in the system.

With talent available, Rochester's baseball leadership could concentrate its efforts on the chief activity of all minor league clubs, building attendance. In 1971 Rochester general manager Carl Steinfeldt explained: "With so many recreational outlets for people today, the drain on the entertainment dollar is greater than ever. The Red Wing philosophy has always been one of energetic promotions, with the baseball fan first and foremost in mind."[61] By creating a special program for children, offering attractive ticket plans, maximizing media coverage, winning business backing for individual game promotions, improving stadium services and facilities, and having special attractions at the vast majority of home games, the Red Wings set attendance records for the International League on an almost yearly basis.[62]

Rochester's internal problems began to accumulate slowly after Morris Silver's death. For the first time in a decade, the board of Rochester Community Baseball had to take substantial responsibility for Red Wings operations. The new management attempted to follow Silver's administrative style but quickly ran into difficulties. General manager Steinfeldt had resigned in October 1973, and Silver failed to name a successor prior to his death. In October 1974 the board finally settled on a new general manager, Edward Barnkowski. Less than two years later, Red Wings president Vince Stanley forced him out. The same year, manager Joe Altobelli, who had guided a succession of Rochester championship teams, left to accept a position with the San Francisco Giants.[63]

In November 1976 the board chose its new general manager, veteran minor league official Don Labbruzzo. Labbruzzo had been successful in a number of other franchises. Unfortunately, Jim McLaughlin recalled, Labbruzzo also came to his new position with a "chip on his shoulder." "He was like a bull in a china shop. He always felt [that] the majors never paid their fair share, that they had raped the minor leagues clubs. . . . [But] it's not a free market. . . . It never was a free market."[64] President Stanley, whose term of office was ending, gratefully handed over the fullest possible authority to Labbruzzo.[65]

The board's choice of Labbruzzo met with considerable opposition among fans and stockholders, many of whom supported the candidacy of the team's popular business manager, Sam Lippa. Labbruzzo attempted to calm discontent, pledging he would work with Lippa and adding, "If I have a strength, its getting along with people."[66]

In 1976 the Red Wings failed to post a profit for the first time in a decade. The club's loss of $70,772 was due primarily to needed stadium improvements, but it was preceded by a number of years of declining profits. The team's 1976 attendance of 213,003 was its worst in a decade in spite of the Red Wings' championship season. The club raised ticket prices to offset declining attendance. However, Rochester's status as a contender, the key to good attendance, was in peril. The hard-pressed Orioles stripped their weakened minor league organization of its best players.[67]

In 1977 a weak Red Wings team skidded into the International League's second division. The club made a modest $20,264 profit. Stanley bowed out as president and sixty-five-year-old businessman Bill Blackman replaced him. Meanwhile, Labbruzzo managed to alienate both the Rochester community and Orioles management. In November he fired Lippa the day after the club's business manager lost a race for election to the city council. Labbruzzo openly criticized Orioles management for failing to sign a number of free agent players. Adopting a confrontational pose with Baltimore, Labbruzzo warned, "We're looking at what they do very closely," hinting he might shift major league affiliates.[68]

During 1978 spring training Labbruzzo further antagonized Orioles management, laying siege to Clyde Kluttz and demanding that Baltimore acquire more players for his team. "I won't go away," Labbruzzo told reporters; "They know I am here to keep an eye on things." Kluttz warned that he had a "green light" to drop the Orioles' affiliation with Rochester and cautioned Labbruzzo against "tampering" with potential AAA players on other clubs' rosters. A weary Kluttz added, "It's getting to the point where players are no longer all that anxious to go to Rochester." The Rochester *Democrat and Chronicle* commented: "They are on the same team but you'd never know it."[69]

The confrontation continued after the Red Wings posted another sixth-place finish in 1978. Labbruzzo headed down to Baltimore intent on squeezing larger subsidies out of the impoverished Orioles. As usual, he communicated with Baltimore management through the press, telling reporters that the Orioles had to provide the players to turn his club into a contender or pay for their failure. "We don't want to take their word for it. There are financial penalties involved in our proposal. . . . Eighteen years of good teams from

Baltimore doesn't mean much when the last two have been lousy. It's what they can do for us in '79." Labbruzzo's rationale, "They'll have to listen to our demands because we lost money," unnecessarily antagonized a franchise that was itself losing record sums.[70]

In spite of personal friction with the Rochester general manager, Orioles officials were willing to provide some financial support to their hard-pressed affiliate. They rejected Labbruzzo's plan for indemnifying the Red Wings on the basis of the club's position in the final standings. However, they offered to pay a greater share of the salaries of Rochester players, to assume the full costs of the team trainer, and to supply the Red Wings with an additional coach. Labbruzzo heaped praise on Kluttz when the Orioles farm system director told reporters that these concessions "show our desire to stay in Rochester."[71] The clubs signed a three-year renewal of their working agreement.

Labbruzzo next became embroiled in an embarrassing battle with his manager, Frank Robinson. Robinson took charge of the Red Wings at mid-season in 1978 and guided the team to another sixth-place finish. Once the season was over, Labbruzzo and Blackman began searching for a new manager, keeping the press fully informed. The Red Wings then reversed course and indicated Robinson could return. Robinson naturally resented this treatment. He told reporters, "No matter what happens, there's no way I'd come back to Rochester," and signed as an Orioles coach.[72]

The Red Wings board concluded that Labbruzzo was a liability as general manager and dismissed him on 26 February 1979. The board split over Blackman's future. The fissures became so deep that Representative Frank Horton had to step in to negotiate a compromise settlement. Under Horton's plan, Bob Drew replaced the deposed Labbruzzo. Bill Farrell, a local amateur sports promoter, took Blackman's place, while the former president moved up to the largely ceremonial role of board chairman.[73]

Farrell and Drew managed to put some order into the Red Wings' financial position, paring the budget and improving marketing. The Farrell-Drew combination papered over the tension within Rochester Community Baseball and restored cooperation with the Orioles. As a result, the Red Wings finished the 1979 season with a small loss of only $5,000 despite finishing last in the International League with a dismal 53–86 record.[74]

Edward Bennett Williams's promises of an improved minor league system were of critical importance for Rochester Community Baseball. Without a competitive team, Rochester would find it hard to turn a profit or rehabilitate its nearly sixty-year-old stadium. The club waited anxiously to see whether the Orioles would fulfill Williams's pledge.

The Williams Era

12 The Strike

On 22 October 1979 American League owners unanimously approved the sale of the Baltimore baseball franchise to Edward Bennett Williams. Jerold Hoffberger joked, perhaps a bit ruefully, "In all the years I've been in the league, it's the first time I can ever remember a Baltimore resolution being approved by a unanimous vote."[1] The official transfer of ownership took place a week later, at a 1 November stockholders' meeting. Club president Hoffberger announced a $1.5 million profit and a dividend of $7.37 per share and then listened patiently to criticism of the sale from two minority stockholders. Hoffberger and 150 other stockholders went through the formality of a vote approving the sale of the Orioles to EBW, Inc., Williams's holding company. The rest of a largely symbolic meeting went smoothly and Baltimore Baseball, Inc., the last publicly traded franchise in the major leagues, became the sole property of one man.[2] Hoffberger stayed on as club president, telling reporters: "We are just going to try to run the ball club together."[3] He remained with the club through the 1982 season before quietly handing over his office to Williams. Effectively, however, Williams was running the Orioles from the day of purchase.

Enter Mr. Williams

A large, powerfully built man, with enormous drive, Edward Bennett Williams established an eminent position in law and politics through hard work. A graduate of Holy Cross College and Georgetown University Law School, Williams quickly established a reputation as a highly competent trial lawyer. By the 1950s, Williams's list of clients included some of the most famous and infamous names in politics, business, and labor: Joseph McCarthy, Dave Beck, Jimmy Hoffa. The list grew as Williams earned a reputation for successfully defending his clients.

Like many rich and successful men, Williams was attracted by the idea of owning a sports franchise. In 1960 a Williams-led syndicate failed to land an expansion franchise in Washington. In 1961 he helped to smooth the integration of the Washington Redskins, professional football's last segregated franchise. The following year he purchased a small number of Redskins shares from owner George Preston Marshall. Marshall's health failed in late 1963, and two years later, after the death of club president C. Leo DeOrsey, and a series of legal maneuvers, Williams emerged as president of the Redskins.[4]

The manner in which Williams and other minority stockholders acquired control of the Redskins became a subject of controversy and court battles with the Marshall children. Ultimately, however, the courts supported Williams's actions and generally praised his administration of the Marshall estate.[5]

As Redskins president, Williams displayed an intense desire to win and a hands-on management style. His first choice of a coach for the hapless Redskins, Otto Graham, failed to produce a winning team. Williams then turned to the legendary Vince Lombardi. Lombardi fielded a winner in 1969, his first year as head coach, but fell victim to cancer the next year. In 1971 Williams hired another enormously successful coach, George Allen. Allen took Washington to the NFL championship game, the Super Bowl, the following year, although the Redskins lost the championship contest to the Miami Dolphins. Thereafter, until Williams sacked him before the 1978 season, Allen led the Redskins to a series of winning seasons but never repeated his 1972 success.

While deeply involved when the team was losing, Williams was ready to delegate authority to successful coaches. Williams frequently admitted that he made a number of serious mistakes when he intervened in the team's player selection process. He displayed a tendency to acquire name players whenever they became available.[6] The Redskins president participated in the NFL's management council, although, as a minority stockholder, he lacked the influence of many of the league's millionaire owners. He clashed frequently with Commissioner Pete Rozelle and the majority that supported him over an NFL rule prohibiting ownership of other sports franchises.[7]

In baseball, Williams would be an activist owner. "I'll have a direct line to Orioles' offices," he told reporters; "I expect to be very active in the decision making, but I don't intend to interfere in the field managing in any way."[8] The new owner declared his readiness to pour badly needed cash into the team. He added that his pennant-winning team had "to get better" and that "I'm perfectly willing to make reasonable forays into the free agent market, if it will help the club."[9]

Williams's natural bent toward action was reinforced by a 1978 bout with cancer. The disease recurred a number of times in the following years, a stark reminder of his mortality and a spur to action for Williams. In addition, Williams was a naturally competitive individual. He personalized the Orioles' traditional rivalry with the Yankees, whose owner, George Steinbrenner, was one of Williams's former clients. Noting the disparity in markets and income, Williams vowed to beat the Yankees with superior organization.[10]

The Williams-Peters relationship was destined to be marked by conflict. Under Hoffberger, Peters had operated with almost total independence. The general manager insisted on maintaining control of player acquisition and development. Temperamentally cautious, he readily delegated considerable authority to trusted subordinates while restraining the involvement in player selection and minor league operations of activists in the Williams mold like manager Earl Weaver. "I believe in consistency, patience and fairness," Peters told one interviewer; "We don't just bring people in and out. We tinker with the machine but we don't overhaul it."[11] Inevitably, the relationship between the activist owner and his independent and conservative general manager became difficult over time. In 1982, they engaged in a silent power struggle over the selection of a successor to the retiring Weaver. Ultimately, Peters ruled out one of Williams's favorites, Frank Robinson, and placed his candidate, Joe Altobelli, in control of the club. The tall, pleasant Altobelli was a cautious organization man, without Weaver's charisma, lively intelligence, or legendary temper. As long as Peters, his lieutenants, and their methods produced success, Williams limited his active involvement in the daily operations of the ball club or its minor league affiliates, concentrating instead on marketing operations and labor relations issues. Once the team began to decline, the impatient Williams slowly encroached on Peters's preserves.[12] In 1986 he admitted, "I can't let go," explaining that "even if you start out without an ego," the media "make you into a genius or an idiot every morning. Your ego becomes involved for self-protection, for survival."[13]

The first area of Williams's involvement with baseball affairs was labor-management relations, where he established an unusual and mutually advantageous relationship with the players union. Williams recognized that the Orioles' continued profitability was closely linked to composing differences between labor and management. Of equal and more pressing importance, he needed to show a profit in 1980 in order to be able to claim the tax benefits of depreciating the purchase of the club. Immediately after taking control of the Orioles, Williams offered to help fellow owners avoid a crippling players' strike: "I'm hoping with my background and experience I can be helpful. I've negotiated for the biggest union in the country and I've negotiated for management. I'd hate to see a strike."[14] Williams discovered that many owners were not interested in compromise.

Smoldering Resentments

By the winter meetings of 1979, a players' strike loomed. Four years of free agency had created a seller's market in major league baseball. Each year a small number of wealthy owners bid furiously for the skills not simply of the game's best players but for its aging stars and even for some of its more fortunate journeymen. Other players opted to use binding arbitration to increase their incomes. The overall effect of the bidding war and arbitration was to push all players' salaries higher. In 1976, the first year of free agency, the average yearly salary for players was $52,300. By 1980 it had risen to $143,756. The Orioles, without major free agents and ranked eighteenth out of twenty-six clubs in total wage payments, had an average salary of $116,156 in 1980. Teams anxious to retain their best players hastened to sign them to high-paying, multiple-year contracts that frequently included clauses guaranteeing these salaries even if the athlete could no longer perform.[15]

The athletic performance of many of these highly paid players made the rising salary scale even more of a bitter experience for owners and executives. Many players failed to repeat the best-of-their-career performances that won them large pay increases. Others succumbed to injury. Older players frequently faded into retirement, their paths smoothed by guaranteed salaries. Embarrassed, and incapable of controlling their own competitive drives, baseball owners sought to reimpose discipline on the labor market by extracting concessions from the players that would end bidding contests between teams.[16]

During the December 1978 winter meetings Commissioner Kuhn again warned the owners that the continuation of free agency would destroy the game. The wealthy teams, Kuhn prophesied, would soon corner the best talent, saddling smaller markets with perennial second-division teams. The commissioner advised the owners to seek modifications in the rules governing free agency through collective bargaining with the union. Specifically, he proposed that a team signing a free agent player compensate the club losing the athlete with another of approximately equal value.[17]

The Kuhn proposal had two obvious advantages for the owners. First, it would effectively curb, if not end, free agent signings. Wealthy, competitive owners would find free agent players much less attractive if they had to surrender an athlete of equal value. Second, modifying free agency would automatically slow or halt rising salary scales. Marvin Miller rejected the Kuhn proposal, charging that the owners were trying to "turn back the clock," and branded owners' claims that higher salaries would destroy the

game as "hysterical."[18] The union chief pointed out that major league baseball was enjoying both record profits and record attendance. Miller attributed
the game's growing profits and attendance to free agency, claiming that it had
generated enormous public interest in the sport.[19]

Throughout 1978 and 1979 the owners and the union girded themselves
for a major confrontation over a new Basic Agreement. The existing pact
would expire prior to the 1980 season. The union assembled a strike fund.
The owners announced their intention to terminate the Basic Agreement
when it expired, leaving the players without the pact's protection. Kuhn tried
to impose some discipline over the richer owners, fining clubs that expressed
interest in potential free agent players. In November 1979 the owners imposed a gag rule forbidding club officials from discussing labor relations
issues. Violators faced fines of up to $50,000. The Player Relations Commit-
tee became management's designated spokesman as well as its bargaining
agent. Its chief negotiator, forty-nine-year-old Ray Grebey, was a twenty-
eight-year veteran of hardball negotiations with industrial unions. The owners vowed to present a united front, pooling 2 percent of their 1979 home
gate receipts into a strike fund and taking out special strike insurance.[20]

Each side tried to rally public support. In his interviews, Marvin Miller
stressed the rising income of major league baseball. Noting that the teams
grossed $278.7 million in 1978 and paid $76.8 million (27.6 percent) into
salaries, Miller asked, "What happened to the other $200 million?" He
ridiculed Kuhn's claim that a number of teams were on the brink of bankruptcy.[21]

Miller admitted that the union faced an extremely difficult task in trying to
win fan support.[22] Fans generally had little sympathy for the demands of
wealthy players and consequently blamed the union for the strikes that
interrupted their summer entertainment with increasing regularity.

Kuhn utilized the 1979 winter meetings to lay out the owners' case for the
press and public. The commissioner insisted that free agency was a "time
bomb" that would destroy the sport. Labor issues dominated discussion
during the 1979 meetings. The owners indicated that they would like to
adopt a player compensation system similar to that of the National Football
League. The NFL system had effectively restrained salary increases since
the mid-1970s.[23]

The owners found further evidence of the need for compensation in the
wake of their 1979 free agent spending spree. By January 1980 twenty-two
free agent players had won guaranteed contracts amounting to $32 million.
Among the new baseball millionaires was Baltimore's ace relief pitcher Don
Stanhouse, who signed a five-year, $2.1 million guaranteed contract with the
Los Angeles Dodgers.[24]

Edward Bennett Williams's response to Stanhouse's signing and the general escalation of salaries caused by free agency was to insist that he would

resist any temptation to join the bidding war. The Orioles owner gave his opinion on the free agent bidding wars to the press: "It's crazy. It's outrageous. I can't believe it. It's got to come back. It can't work, and in the end, it'll blow up. It's just madness."[25]

Other comments by Williams and general manager Peters underlined their belief that responsibility for baseball's economic woes lay with a minority of irresponsible owners. Peters summarized the club's policy shortly after the 1979 season:

> We have accepted the . . . free agent system. . . . We will draft for the positions that we need. . . . We will make offers commensurate to their abilities. No bidding contests, however.
>
> Our philosophy is to live realistically with what we can afford. . . . We have stuck with it, and so far we feel it has worked for us.
>
> Baseball will be better off when certain owners learn that it's not the worst thing in the world to lose a player to free agency and other owners learn it's not the best thing in the world to sign a free agent.[26]

A few weeks later, Peters commented that the amounts of money being offered to athletes was "scary" and "unbelievable," adding, "I can't fault the players. . . . People giving out the money simply have to show some restraint, some judgement, and they definitely aren't."[27] Williams attempted to play a mediating role between labor and his fellow owners. He had an unusually promising relationship with the union because two Orioles were members of the Players Association's negotiating team, American League player representative Doug DeCinces and club player representative Mark Belanger. Brooks Robinson recalled: "Doug and Belanger enjoyed being part of that [the negotiating team] more than anyone else."[28] Both men were serious about reaching a solution. "What we are trying to do," Belanger explained, "is to avoid a strike any way we can."[29] Williams was in constant contact with both as the strike deadline approached: "There never was a time before—or during—the strike when I couldn't have settled all the issues with them in a few hours," he later claimed.[30]

A Temporary Reprieve

During the winter of 1980 Williams's opportunities for mediation were slim. Long-postponed discussions between the two sides began in earnest in late January when the owners presented their proposals for a new Basic Agreement. The owners' plan called for compensating a team that lost a player to free agency with another major leaguer. Management also wanted to establish specific minimum and maximum salaries for players with less than six years of major league experience, thus limiting the effects of arbitration. As a sweetener, the owners suggested that all players be vested in the pension plan as soon as they began a major league career.[31]

Belanger summed up the initial union reaction: "When I tell the players about the owners' proposals, the first question I get is, 'Are they serious?' "[32] Marvin Miller dismissed the suggested revision of the pension as a "blatant" effort to curry favor with the younger players in the hope of breaking a strike. The union countered with a proposal that would permit the owners to pay financial compensation to teams that lost free agent players.[33]

Talks between the two sides continued into early March 1980 without meaningful progress. Both DeCinces and Belanger echoed Miller in suggesting that the owners were utilizing stalling tactics and unreasonable demands to force a strike. The union leader explained that he had made concessions to "owner hysteria" four years earlier. This time he would seek to broaden the right of free agency to apply to players with four years' major league service.[34] On 4 March the player representatives authorized a strike by a 27–0 vote.

Orioles players solidly backed their union representatives. Peters stressed the club's desire for a negotiated settlement, noting that Williams would be "hit between the eyeballs by a work stoppage."[35] The Orioles owner reached into his vast rhetorical storehouse for some choice hyperbole: "It would be like a nuclear war and cause permanent damage to both sides."[36] Significantly, Williams also publicly complained that he had only "secondhand" information from management's chief negotiator, Ray Grebey.

Faced with a solid union, Grebey dropped one of management's most irritating demands, a stepped maximum salary scale for players with less than six years' major league experience. Both sides dug in over the compensation issue. Peters admitted that the idea of compensation was attractive because it would stanch the flow of Orioles players to other clubs.[37] To further improve management's image Grebey began briefing the press on the PRC's proposals and then called in the Federal Mediation and Conciliation Service to serve as a mediator.[38]

Facing a near-certain strike, the union decided to employ shock tactics to break management's always fragile unity. On 1 April the player representatives instructed union members to refuse to play any further preseason games but to continue working out with their squads in preparation for the regular season. It set 22 May as a strike deadline. The walkout deprived the clubs of a portion of spring training income without significantly affecting the players' financial situation. DeCinces admitted that the move hurt the union's public image but defended it as a necessary reaction to management's negotiating tactics. Peters stated that he was "confused" by the union's action. Williams, who was not, displayed his basic concern when he told reporters: "I'm pleased we are going to open the season on time."[39]

The Player Relations Committee responded to the union's action by instructing its clubs to cut off per diem payments and let the players settle up the remaining portions of their hotel bills. The PRC also instructed the clubs to permit the players to continue their workouts but to refuse to ship any personal effects north with club equipment.[40]

A minority of Orioles players remained in Florida to participate in workouts so listless that manager Weaver canceled them after two days. The players drifted north for opening day while the talks between labor and management continued without concessions. Finally, on 18 April the two sides suspended discussions.

The discussions resumed in New York on 6 May, but remained deadlocked over the compensation issue. Marvin Miller reported that they were making little progress over secondary but important issues like the funding of the pension plan. All signs pointed to a strike.[41]

On 15 May, Miller caught management off guard by suggesting that the free agent compensation issue be tabled for two years while a joint player-owner committee studied it. Under Miller's proposal the existing system would continue to operate until the study group had completed its work. Management rejected this plan the following day. On 18 May, after another fruitless meeting, federal mediator Ken Moffett recessed the discussions for twenty-four hours. When the talks resumed, the two sides failed to make any progress. On 21 May the union instructed its members to walk off the job after the games of 22 May.[42]

Baseball averted the scheduled walkout when management suddenly accepted a modified version of Miller's 15 May proposal. Under terms of the new agreement a four-man committee consisting of two representatives each from the union and the owners would come up with a plan to deal with the free agent issue prior to 1 January 1981. The existing rules governing free agency would continue to operate until February 1981. The owners and players would then be free to protect their respective positions.[43]

Williams and Houston Astros owner John McMullen were instrumental in reversing Grebey's initial decision to reject this modification of Miller's proposal. The Orioles owner had continued to monitor both union and management positions and was convinced that much of the trouble derived from the owners' inflexibility. In one moment of particular frustration, he told manager Weaver that his fellow owners could "foul up a two car funeral."[44] Williams continually prodded an unwilling Grebey to adopt a more conciliatory stance. He was particularly adamant that the PRC utilize Miller's offer to open the way for a settlement of the dispute: "We kept making suggestions at every meeting and each time they got a little more forceful and a little more lengthy. I guess they made an impact or maybe the other owners were getting tired of hearing me."[45]

Round Two

After agreeing to set up a study committee on free agent compensation, negotiators for labor and management worked out the text of a new Basic Agreement with relative ease. On 6 June the owners approved the new agreement. The union followed suit in July. The two sides then appointed representatives to the four-man committee on free agency. Milwaukee's Harry Dalton and the New York Mets' new general manager, Frank Cashen, represented management, and Bob Boone and Sal Bando spoke for the players.[46]

While the committee studied the free agency issue, relations between the union and the owners remained tense. In October 1980 the National Labor Relations Board ruled that the PRC was guilty of unfair labor practices because of its refusal to share financial information with the union. The following month San Diego outfielder Dave Winfield gave a new twist to free agency by announcing that he had a preferred list of clubs for which he would play. The pursuit of Winfield, a superb athlete, set off a bidding war that New York's George Steinbrenner won with the offer of a ten-year, multimillion dollar contract.[47]

The four negotiators failed to resolve differences over free agency before the 1981 deadline. On 19 February 1981 the owners announced that they were unilaterally instituting a compensation plan. Miller responded that management had "decided to instigate a strike."[48] Both sides talked tough and tried with varying success to build support among the press and public. American League player representative Doug DeCinces blamed owners' bad-faith bargaining for the impasse and labeled their free agency actions "ridiculous." George Steinbrenner warned the union to surrender or face a "Waterloo" at the hands of a united and determined band of owners. Commissioner Kuhn lamented the sorry state of baseball's finances to any reporter willing to listen, insisting that the sport had to curb free agency spending or face bankruptcy.[49]

Edward Bennett Williams again offered himself as a potential mediator, telling reporters: "I am confident things can be worked out and I don't intend to stand idly by."[50] Williams, however, was more isolated than he had been nine months earlier. He had alienated a number of big-city owners with proposals for dividing television and box office revenues equally and for a full disclosure of club finances. Phillies president Bill Giles dismissed the television proposal, commenting: "Well, of course, if I were Edward Bennett Williams, I would feel that way, too. But I have a responsibility to the people who invested $30 million in this ball club and we would not have paid so much if we had to share our TV revenue to a greater degree."[51] Moreover, Williams, as a new owner, possessed only limited influence within the baseball fraternity. Finally, Williams's successful efforts to head off a confrontation in 1980 had won him the enmity of a number of owners.[52]

The players reported for spring training on time and discovered that public opinion was decisively against them. On 6 March, Miller tried to conduct an open-air meeting with Chicago White Sox players. Taunting by fans in the bleachers forced him to move the discussion into the clubhouse. Miller's meetings with the twenty-six squads confirmed that the players were united and ready to follow him into a strike.[53]

The union chief made a last effort to avoid a strike by offering new proposals to the owners and requesting the NLRB to intervene, charging that management's negotiating techniques had brought talks to a "ridiculous point."[54] The union stated that the players were willing to accept the concept of compensation but insisted that implementation must not strangle the free agent market.

Management rejected Miller's proposals, appealed for public support, and disciplined waverers in their own ranks. Commissioner Kuhn proclaimed, "The owners are clearly right," and forswore any use of his office to pressure his employers to arrive at a compromise with the union.[55]

On 5 May the PRC announced that it had fined Harry Dalton $50,000 for comments that violated its "discipline code." Dalton had firsthand knowledge of the union's positions because of his role in the abortive negotiations on the free agent issue. He told reporters: "I hope management is really looking for a compromise and not a victory but I'm not certain that's the case. The Players Association is genuinely looking for a compromise, if we'll just give them something they can accept without losing too much face."[56] Informed of the Dalton fine, Marvin Miller commented: "I think I always realized that truth had a price, but I never realized it was that expensive."[57]

Edward Bennett Williams's turn was next. On 21 May, Kuhn summoned the Orioles owner to New York to discuss a 24 March criticism of PRC public relations tactics. Williams had complained that "it is wrong to try to demean the players and the Players Association" and added that the owners should avoid "ugly confrontations" with their employees.[58]

As befitted an owner, Williams was the recipient of soothing reassurances and friendly advice rather than the fines that the PRC imposed on Milwaukee employee Dalton. The Orioles owner was unmollified. The situation continued to deteriorate as the 29 May strike date drew closer. PRC tactics, as Williams warned they would, had infuriated the union's leadership, reinforced the players' belief that once again management was seeking to destroy the Players Association, and consequently solidified support for Miller. *The Sporting News* urged the owners to adopt a more flexible approach on compensation.[59]

Baseball won a brief respite on 27 May. The NLRB, in response to a union appeal, slapped the owners with another unfair labor practices complaint and issued a temporary restraining order to head off the strike. Talks resumed, and the players offered a new plan for a compensation system. Under this proposal each team would designate members of its forty-man roster for inclusion in a pool of players. Teams losing a free agent would be eligible to select one of the athletes from this pool as compensation, purchasing the athlete's contract at a minimal fee of $20,000 to $40,000. Management rejected the union's revised offer.[60]

Four days after the owners' action, a federal judge denied the NLRB's request for an injunction to head off the strike. Judge Henry Worker ruled that "no reasonable cause" existed to support the NLRB's ruling that management had committed unfair labor practices.[61]

Immediately after being informed of the judge's ruling, a group of disappointed union leaders announced that the players would go on strike following the games of 11 June 1981. Labor and management agreed to continue their talks, but federal mediator Ken Moffett remarked that they were "ten miles apart" on the major issues.[62] A long strike loomed.

Both Orioles players and officials were upset by the strike. Union leaders DeCinces and Belanger expressed their disappointment. Manager Weaver admitted he had a "knot in his stomach."[63] Edward Bennett Williams felt "down and depressed," adding, "as for any financial impact, I can't say even if I wanted to because we haven't calculated it. I haven't engaged in the kind of thinking some others have."[64]

Williams acted to maintain his privileged relation with the players. The strike caught the Orioles playing in Seattle. Traveling secretary Phil Itzoe assisted individual players in arranging their return home, explaining: "My reasoning was simple. Someday we're going to have this unfortunate situation behind us and we are going to be operating as a baseball team."[65] The Orioles followed PRC instructions, barring athletes from using club equipment and training facilities, while avoiding actions that could damage the "fine relationship" between Orioles players and management. Peters announced that the club would retain the coaching staff and administrative personnel on full salary. Part-time Memorial Stadium employees were less fortunate. They were furloughed for the duration of the strike. "A lot of little people will get hurt," Peters noted.[66]

After talks with DeCinces, Belanger, and Peters, Williams contacted other owners and arranged a 16 June meeting with Commissioner Kuhn and American League president MacPhail. The Orioles owner wanted a quick settlement and was highly critical both of Ray Grebey's negotiating style and of the lack of information from the PRC.[67]

On 16 June, Williams, together with two other dissenting owners, Steinbrenner and Eddie Chiles of Texas, met with Kuhn and MacPhail. The meeting produced no change in either group's position. The dissident owners reportedly warned Kuhn that his continued inaction could cost him the job of commissioner. The following day the owners' Executive Committee publicly endorsed Grebey while flaying Williams and his allies for breaking ranks.[68]

Williams defiantly replied that he would continue to push for a compromise, adding, "I am not worried a bit about a fine." He would try to form a coalition of dissatisfied owners. When informed that the volatile Steinbrenner had defected to the hardliners, he offered: "Soon they'll be sending Chiles and me to Lower Slobbovia."[69]

Williams's public dissent and private efforts to force a compromise alienated most of the owners and Commissioner Kuhn. However, Williams's efforts succeeded in maintaining good relations with his players, and the display of moderation was well crafted to hold the loyalty of Orioles fans.

Strike talks broke off on 20 June after the owners rejected another compromise offer. The next day, hardline owners forced the cancellation of a meeting at which Williams had hoped to present his position. Looking over the first week of the strike, Moffett warned that both sides appeared ready to play a "long waiting game."[70] He later added: "These are the most bizarre negotiations I've been involved in during twenty-two years as a mediator. The issues are resolvable, but there's no negotiating."[71]

The talks resumed on 24 June and continued into early July without any positive results. Grebey, dismissing Williams and Chiles as a harmless minority of two, insisted that he would maintain an inflexible position with the support of the other twenty-four owners. Departing from one fruitless session, Miller told reporters: "The gap between us is so wide it defies my vocabulary to describe it."[72]

On 5 July the owners' unity once again began to crack. Steinbrenner reversed himself again and suggested the owners seek a compromise. The following day, Williams and the owners of seven other clubs requested a meeting to discuss the twenty-five-day-old work stoppage. The owners failed to settle their differences at their 9 July meeting. The moderates aired their views but remained in a clear minority. A "downcast" Williams hurriedly left the meeting, refusing to attend a PRC-arranged press conference. He told newsmen: "I had an opportunity to express my views. . . . I have learned to . . . lose with grace."[73]

Williams remained in New York to encourage a favorable response to the compromise proposal that federal mediator Moffett laid before the two sides on 9 July. The union responded positively on 10 July, indicating that Moffett's proposal could serve as the basis for a settlement. Grebey's initial reaction was unfavorable, and the following day, he announced that the owners rejected the proposal and were breaking off talks. "Marvin wrote it. It's a setup," he told reporters, effectively ending Moffett's utility as a mediator.[74]

A disgusted Moffett asked Secretary of Labor Raymond Donovan to intervene and reestablish the government's position as an honest broker. By

July the economic effects of a major sports strike were mounting. In addition to the thousands of part-time employees that the clubs laid off, stadium area merchants, newspapers, television networks, airlines, and public transportation all suffered from the lack of baseball. Public pressure for federal action to settle the strike became stronger. The union proposed binding arbitration. The owners immediately rejected this idea. Secretary Donovan then began a series of meetings with individual owners and the player representatives. He invited the two sides to resume talks in Washington on 20 July 1981.[75]

Donovan also arranged a meeting of the PRC with the union leadership on 22 July. The discussions begun at this meeting ended after four days without progress. The players met on 27 July and again offered to compromise on the compensation issue. With the cancellation of the entire season obviously looming, Williams arranged for another owners' meeting for 29 July. The owners met secretly and agreed to abandon their hardline positions. Within forty-eight hours the owners and players settled the strike.[76]

The suddenness of the settlement after a long, bitterly contested strike and the terms of the settlement point to another collapse of owner unity. Williams and his allies remained a minority among the owners but a persistent one that built up pressure for a settlement. The threat of a canceled season combined with the expiration of their strike insurance on 8 August put greater pressure on the majority. Finally, Grebey's management of the issues and his undisguised ambition to succeed Kuhn as commissioner, upset a growing number of the owners. In the end, Kuhn's friend, Lee MacPhail, skillfully isolated the PRC's chief negotiator, opened separate talks with Marvin Miller, and quickly arrived at a settlement. MacPhail recalled: "There was feeling between Miller and Grebey and this was impeding our ability to get things done. And . . . I became the spokesman for our side. . . . But I was doing . . . what our committee, and Grebey was a part of the committee, wanted done. . . . I wasn't running off on my own."[77]

The settlement, Thomas Boswell noted, consisted of a "small step backward" by the players in exchange for a major retreat by management. The players agreed to compensation. However, the compensation agreement, which followed the outlines of the players' 27 May proposal, avoided direct repayment in players to a team losing a free agent. Each team could protect twenty-six of the forty players on its major league roster. The other players entered a pool. A team losing a free agent compensated itself by choosing an athlete from this pool comprised of aging regulars, minor league prospects, substitutes, and marginal players. Moreover, the owners agreed that the players would receive full service credit toward their pensions for the time they were on strike.[78]

The strike had a number of evident winners and losers. The union once again emerged with its unity intact. It had successfully defended free agency from the type of modifications that would significantly brake the upward salary trend. Edward Bennett Williams's major success was psychological. His moderation and search for a compromise reinforced his club's sense of unity, helping pave the way for the team's 1982 and 1983 success. Marvin Miller publicly praised the Orioles owner for his realistic attitudes. On the other hand, Williams had enraged a number of fellow owners. One stated: "The scars that Williams left are very deep . . . and they won't heal easily." Ken Moffett added: "A lot of people don't like to give Williams credit. . . . They think he was trying to do them in, and he was, because he was trying to get this thing settled."[79]

The major losers included the hardline owners, who once again saw their efforts to control Miller and his union reined in from within their own ranks. The owners' effort to stem the rise in player salaries also failed. In 1982 the average salary rose $55,846 over 1981 levels. Salary inflation continued in 1983. The average Orioles salary that year was $305,305, nearly three times its 1980 level; and ten of the twenty-six major league teams had higher average salaries than Baltimore. Moreover, most owners lost money heavily in 1981. Williams acknowledged "tremendous losses" that independent observers put at $1 million and added that "the only thing the strike insurance did was keep our farm system going."[80] Two individuals became the scapegoats for management's debacle. Ray Grebey, who had led the owners into an impasse, was finished as chief labor negotiator for baseball. His hopes of assuming the commissioner's position, pinned to a victory over the union, evaporated with the settlement. The other scapegoat was Commissioner Kuhn. The game's spokesman was virtually invisible during the strike. Kuhn's lack of leadership made him the object of criticism from the press and moderate owners. Williams and a number of other moderates concluded that the sport needed a new activist commissioner.[81]

An Unstable Equilibrium

An uneasy peace reigned over baseball for the following four years. Both sides emerged from the exhausting 1981 strike with powerful motivation to avoid another bruising clash. The desire for moderation was incarnated in the two new chief negotiators, Ken Moffett and Lee MacPhail, who succeeded Marvin Miller and Ray Grebey in the winter of 1983. Miller bowed out with a remarkable record of success. He had built the players union in the face of bitter owner hostility and led it through a series of dramatic confrontations that established its power and won financial security for the average player. The long battle had scarred Miller. At the end of his term, mistrust and hostility characterized labor-management relations.

Miller's last eighteen months were marked by low-level skirmishing with management. The owners wanted to avoid a major confrontation but were clearly disturbed by the continuing rise in player salaries. Their competitive instincts frustrated most efforts to hold the line on pay raises. Miller stymied any collusion. In January 1982 he blocked a California Angels effort to compensate the Yankees for the signing of free agent Reggie Jackson. A few months later, Miller set up a union panel to assist players in their salary arbitration cases. When a committee chaired by Edward Bennett Williams tried to impose a backdoor salary cap by inserting a new rule limiting the ratio of club assets to liabilities, the union filed a grievance.[82]

Owner frustration grew, fueled by rising salaries and the union's ability to employ collective bargaining rules to the players' advantage. Arbitration procedures were a particular source of management discontent. The clubs believed they lost even those cases decided in their favor. In 1983, a typical year, the owners won seventeen arbitration disputes, the players thirteen. The winning players' salaries rose an average of 159 percent. The losing players contented themselves with increases averaging 54 percent.[83]

Baltimore was one of a number of clubs that avoided arbitration as a matter of policy. In addition to the effects arbitration had on club salary scales, Peters believed that it destroyed the type of atmosphere that produced winning teams: "It can have a devastating effect on a player because he has to be present at the hearing and he has to listen to his employer say things the player doesn't want to hear. The process creates an adversary situation."[84]

The clubs attempted to lighten the salary burden by offering the players incentive clauses and bonuses as well as "deferred" salary agreements that stretched out a club's indebtedness to a player beyond the term of his contract. They tried to convince the players to restrain their demands, arguing that the athletes were now "preferred shareholders" with a major interest in the financial health of the game. At the same time, frustrated owners complained that their high-salaried employees were spending increasing amounts of time on the disabled list.[85]

Labor-management relations worsened as the owners became aware of and attempted to deal with extensive player drug use. Player addiction to alcohol and amphetamines had a long history. In the early 1970s the major leagues, with the Orioles taking a leading role, mounted a halfhearted campaign against these forms of addiction in the wake of major scandals in college and professional football. The baseball establishment quickly lost interest.[86]

By the late 1970s baseball was falling into the grip of a new and more threatening form of addiction: expensive "recreational" drugs like cocaine were growing popular in the major leagues and throughout American society. The Orioles, in spite of their reputation as a group of "solid citizens," apparently were part of the trend. According to one former player's sworn testimony, cocaine use was "very prevalent" among the 1979 American League champions.[87]

The problem of drug addiction became a labor-management issue in 1980. Commissioner Bowie Kuhn suspended Texas pitcher Ferguson Jenkins after he was arrested for possession of drugs. The union appealed Kuhn's action. An arbitrator ruled against Kuhn and restored Jenkins to the Rangers' active roster. The decision meant management would have to win the union's assent to implement a serious antidrug program.[88]

Kuhn reacted to the growing prevalence of drug use by setting up an employee assistance program. The commissioner's move met with what he described as widespread indifference on the part of the owners and hostility from the union. In midsummer 1982, as the number of athletes arrested for drug possession rose, Kuhn suggested a program for testing players for drug use. The union responded negatively. Union concern over individual players' rights, dislike and mistrust of the owners and their motives, and fear of negative publicity combined to make negotiations on this issue very difficult.[89]

After Moffett replaced Miller, the new union chief began to discuss cooperative efforts to deal with drug abuse. Pressure for some sort of action grew as the number of drug arrests and investigations of major league players continued to grow. During the early summer of 1983 a Kansas City grand jury indicted four Royals players, including star outfielder Willie Wilson, for drug possession. In July two Orioles players were implicated in drug use. The club maintained a discreet silence since neither player was the subject of legal action. Shortly after the end of the season, the Royals players pleaded guilty to drug possession and were sentenced to jail terms. Kuhn suspended all four.[90]

Progress toward a labor-management agreement on drug abuse came to an abrupt halt on 22 November 1983. The union announced that it had fired Moffett. Marvin Miller returned on an interim basis until the union elected his protégé, attorney Donald Fehr, as its executive director on 8 December 1983. The union put an end to discussions on the drug issue. Moffett expressed "shock" at his dismissal and attributed it to disagreements within the union leadership over how to deal with player drug addiction. Prophetically, he warned the union that more players would be facing trial and jail sentences unless the Players Association acted to deal with drug addiction in its ranks. In the context of the continuing tension between labor and management, Moffett's willingness to cooperate with management on drug-related issues appeared to violate basic Players Association strategy: waiting on the owners to offer a plan and then modifying it through arbitration.[91] Association leaders, and the retired but still-influential Miller, apparently concluded that Moffett was too conciliatory in dealings with the owners and might compromise hard-won rights in future negotiations.

Unfortunately, Moffett was right. While protecting the privacy of individual athletes, the union harmed the interests of its drug-addicted players by refusing to cooperate. It also permitted the owners to seize the public relations high ground and place blame for the sport's drug problems on the union. The sports press joined in the widespread condemnation of Players Association policies, further blackening the union's reputation.[92]

In May 1984 owners and players finally agreed on a drug plan. Under the agreement, the teams would pay the cost of rehabilitation for athletes with addictions. If players with drug problems refused to join a rehabilitation program, the commissioner's office would apply a series of administrative sanctions, which could include suspension. The plan had no provision for mandatory testing, and the union could challenge the commissioner's decisions through the arbitration process. A number of owners complained that the agreement was so heavily weighted in favor of players' rights that it was totally ineffective as a vehicle for deterring drug use. MacPhail, who had negotiated the deal, hoped to strengthen its provisions through further discussions with labor. The agreement, he later explained, was "reasonable for a starter."[93] Drug testing remained another potential flash point in labor-management relations.

In mid-November 1984 MacPhail, Fehr, and their assistants formally opened talks on a new Basic Agreement to succeed the existing pact upon its 1985 expiration. Player benefits, modifications in salary arbitration procedures, and alterations in the free agent system were the major issues. MacPhail signaled management's desire for a compromise by telling the press that neither side could afford a strike. Baseball's new commissioner, Peter Ueberroth, echoed these sentiments, calling on the owners to forge a pact of "unity" with the players and to work out the sport's financial problems.[94]

Management took its usual stance, claiming it faced fiscal disaster as a result of salary inflation and urging the players to cooperate in modifying both free agency and arbitration rules in their own long-term economic interests. The union reacted with customary skepticism.[95]

By May 1985 the two sides appeared to be headed toward another strike despite their stated desire to avoid a costly confrontation. The owners insisted that their payment into the player pension fund be a fixed sum rather than the one-third of national television income the union demanded. They wanted to limit arbitration by excluding players with less than three years' major league service and by adopting a new rule that limited the size of arbitration awards to a maximum of 100 percent of the player's current salary. Management also asked for salary caps. The owners presented the Players Association with financial data purporting to show that in spite of record television income, eighteen teams lost a total of $42 million in 1984 and that the major leagues faced a projected $155 million in losses by 1988.[96]

The union responded that the owners' claims of losses were "voodoo economics." Donald Fehr stressed that franchises were selling for record sums and introduced economist Roger Noll of Stanford to rebut management's specific claims. The union subsequently rejected a management proposal for a salary cap.[97]

Both sides held firm to their positions, and on 6 August 1985 the players again went out on strike. Two days later, they went back to work. Commissioner Ueberroth intervened to mediate a solution that essentially abandoned almost all of the owners' demands in return for four years of labor peace. "Both sides felt the need to go to the brink," *Sports Industry News* commented. "In the end, the owners stepped back first, although the players were more than happy to join them."[98] The owners substantially increased their contribution to the player pension fund, raised the minimum salary, and abandoned their demands for a salary cap and mandatory drug testing. In return, the union accepted a three-year eligibility rule on arbitration rights, written so that it would not affect any current players, agreed to modifications to the free agent selection process rules, and approved lengthening the league championship format from five to seven games.

The 1985 agreement basically put all of baseball's major conflicts on hold for four more years. It failed to deal with the twin roots of owner discontent: the astronomical rise in salaries and the owners' weakening control over the sport. While the owners had only themselves to blame for free agent bidding wars, they were on stronger ground in complaining about arbitration procedures and their effects. Between 1974 and 1985 management won 102 arbitration cases while losing 86. The average player salary rose from $40,839 to $329,408 in the same period. MacPhail, who retired shortly after the signing of the 1985 Basic Agreement, warned owners that they must exercise salary restraint or face the danger of spending the sport into ruin. He noted that baseball teams already owed $45–50 million to retired players, while paying an additional $32 million a year to support the pension fund. In addition, teams were piling up massive long-term obligations. "We must stop daydreaming that one free agent signing will bring a pennant," MacPhail cautioned.[99]

Among the owners who were in the process of learning this hard lesson was Edward Bennett Williams, who had spent millions on free agents to improve his club in the winter of 1984 only to see it play mediocre baseball in 1985. The Williams who had been so active an opponent of a confrontation with the Players Association in 1980 and 1981 was conspicuous by his silence during the labor dispute of 1985.

The unstable equilibrium created by the 1981 strike continued. Increasingly, however, owners ignored legal restraints and practiced collusion in an effort to destroy free agency and impose limits on players' salaries. These actions appeared to lay the groundwork for yet another massive union-management confrontation in 1990.

13 The Best of Times

The Orioles . . . are the
dominant American
League team of our
time. . . . The heart of it,
clearly, is that the Orioles
always cling to and
personify the idea
of a team.
—Roger Angell,
November 1983

On 17 October 1983 a crowd of over 100,000
lined up twenty deep at places along a parade
route that ended in the plaza in front of Baltimore
City Hall. Twenty-five antique cars carrying the
members of the World Series champion Baltimore
Orioles together with their families moved slowly
into the plaza. Master of ceremonies Brooks Robinson introduced each player individually as he
arrived. The team members then walked up the
city hall steps to a portico overlooking the square
that was festooned in black and orange pennants,
streamers, and balloons. Robinson called on the
team owner to say a few words. A beaming Edward Bennett Williams hoisted the championship
trophy before a downtown crowd of 100,000 and
proclaimed "This is yours." The crowd "understandably went nuts."[1]

Between 1980 and 1983 Williams's Orioles were
among the best teams in baseball. Carefully built
by general manager Henry Peters, they embodied
manager Earl Weaver's theory of utilizing strong
pitching, solid defense, and three-run homers to
win consistently. The teams also possessed a remarkable unity and a sort of mystique that created
admiration throughout the major leagues. Yankee
star Graig Nettles commented: "Nobody's going
to beat Baltimore. Baltimore is perfect. Everyone
knows his role and is comfortable and happy in
that role. They get along with their manager . . .
and they've gone out and beaten the hell out of
everybody."[2] The 1980 Orioles won one hundred
games. The 1981 team finished a strike-disrupted
season with the second best record in the Ameri-

can League East. In 1982 the Orioles battled the Milwaukee Brewers until the last day of the season before losing the American League East title. The 1983 team captured the American League East, bested a good Chicago club in the playoffs, and took the World Series in five games.

Washingtonian Williams and the city of Baltimore appeared to have settled down to a durable partnership. The franchise maintained its excellent play, triumphing in a era of major labor difficulties, in spite of a weak minor league system and the retirement of Weaver as manager. Attendance and profits rose in response to Williams's skillful marketing. The franchise's value leapt from $12 million in 1979 to $70 million by 1988.

Marketing a Franchise

Bill Veeck, whose bid for a successful return to the ranks of club owners was a casualty of the spiraling player salaries of the late 1970s, always insisted on the direct link between winning baseball, good marketing, and profitability in managing a baseball franchise.[3] There was no better proof of this link than the Orioles of the early 1980s. Williams, a self-made millionaire, displayed his considerable business acumen in marketing his team, assisted by its status as a consistent contender. He secured favorable television and radio broadcasting contracts, built a large radio network while experimenting with new television technology, and skillfully handled the team's relationship with its Memorial Stadium landlord, the city of Baltimore. Williams built a strong marketing staff, moved his sales operation aggressively into eastern Pennsylvania, Virginia, the Washington area, and even the Carolinas, turning the Orioles into a regional franchise.

Williams inherited a small but experienced public relations staff headed by public relations director Bob Brown, a twenty-year veteran with the club. Brown excelled at handling the press, providing a steady stream of statistical and personal information on the players and publishing highly professional team guides. As was true for most teams, the Orioles made extensive use of their most attractive resource, the players, both in press relations and in off-season ticket sales campaigns.[4]

During the 1960s and 1970s the Orioles were among the most active and innovative teams in the marketing field. In the mid-1960s Baltimore arranged as many as thirty special promotional nights, offering various sorts of free merchandise to ticket purchasers. Hoffberger invited President Jimmy Carter to opening day in Baltimore in an effort to generate press coverage. The team had pioneered the "basebelles" concept. These young women, dressed in shorts and Orioles logo shirts, initially served as ushers and later provided between-innings entertainment for an audience that was still primarily male.[5]

One of the most difficult periods for promoting baseball is the winter. The sport traditionally sought to focus fan attention and build up interest by beginning its preseason training in late winter in Florida. Intense press coverage of the "Grapefruit League" helped spur ticket sales. Ironically, the Messersmith decision, by stimulating fan interest in player signings, provided unexpected and unwanted aid to the owners' ticket sales efforts. The Orioles added a number of ideas to the off-season promotion of baseball. The club hosted annual winter "open houses" and stadium tours for fans. It formed a basketball team comprised of Orioles players to play charity games with local amateur groups. Hoffberger had even purchased time on the broadcast of the 1964 NFL championship game to show support for the Colts, and tactfully remind fans of the availability of Orioles season tickets.[6]

Prior to 1979, however, the Orioles' marketing efforts were marked primarily by their futility. The club failed to attract new fans. In 1965, for example, the team offered thirty separate promotion nights. Its attendance fell from fourth to sixth in the American League.

Under Williams, the team continued utilizing all these marketing techniques. The basebelles, reduced in number, exchanged their tight shorts and shirts for less provocative, more "family-oriented" clothing in response to the growing number of female fans, and they added a new partner, "The Bird" (a man dressed as an oriole), to their between-innings act. The selection of a "Miss Oriole" and her promotional activities pandered to traditional male interests.[7]

Williams brought modern concepts of marketing baseball to the Orioles. He hired attorneys, sales representatives, marketing account executives, and media specialists, and he provided them with new offices and modern equipment, including computers. The team's "front office" swelled from forty to seventy in the first six years of the Williams era. These mostly young new employees mirrored their boss: articulate, ambitious, well-educated, aggressive, skillful at utilizing the media, eager to exploit new technology, and well-versed in public relations. The club experimented with a variety of newsletters; installed "Diamondvision," a costly state-of-the-art scoreboard; formed a television production company; introduced a video yearbook; and lined up corporate support for individual promotions. In 1981 the Orioles opened a baseball store, selling both tickets and baseball memorabilia, in Baltimore's Harbor Place, the showpiece of the city's redevelopment program.[8]

The heart of Williams's marketing effort was his emphasis on broadcasting. He was fortunate to inherit the radio contract with WFBR, a youth-oriented Baltimore station, that Peters had negotiated in 1978. One Washington reporter noted: "The station's aggressive promotion of the Orioles—a promotion that knows no limit and pays no attention to the hour of day—may be the biggest single reason" for the Orioles' booming attendance.[9] Peters was equally pleased, commenting in 1986: "They've done an excellent job for us ... plugging baseball twenty-four hours a day. Doing a good job of producing the games themselves. Then providing [affiliate] coverage ... [and] the fees that they pay."[10]

WFBR built a large radio network for the Orioles: fifty-eight stations in seven states and the District of Columbia by 1986. Simultaneously, the club's two television affiliates, WMAR and Home Team Sports (HTS), were building strong TV networks. By 1986, WMAR had a ten-station network, extending to Florida, for its forty broadcast games. HTS had 260,000 subscribers and seventy affiliates in a seven-state region.[11]

The city supported the club's marketing efforts. Baltimore contributed through its program of continuing improvements to Memorial Stadium: installing new seats and concession stands, improving public transportation services, and assisting in publicizing Orioles baseball. In 1980, for example, Mayor Schaefer declared an "Orioles Magic Week" and gave city employees time off to encourage a massive turnout for a five-game series with the despised New York Yankees. The Orioles Advocates continued to provide willing, free labor for the club's promotional activities. In 1979, shortly after Williams purchased the Orioles, Schaefer and Hoffberger announced the formation of the "Designated Hitters," an unpaid sales force. The Kansas City Royals had pioneered the concept with great success. The Designated Hitters enlisted the talents of successful businessmen to sell season tickets. Membership was by invitation only. Candidates had to pass through a probationary period and qualified for full membership by meeting a sales quota. The club offered members various incentives for exceptional sales performance, such as customized blazers and trips to spring training camp. The Designated Hitters were a major success. They played a key role in the rapid expansion of season tickets sales from 1,623 in 1979, to 5,215 in 1980, and 11,707 in 1985.[12]

The District of Columbia and its highly populous and wealthy suburbs were an especially challenging target for Williams's salesmanship. Democrat Williams enticed Republican President Ronald Reagan to Orioles opening games, as well as to a World Series contest, laying claim to a money-making and prestigious Washington baseball tradition, the presidential opener. An Orioles store, similar to that in Harbor Place, opened in July 1983 in a trendy downtown Washington shopping area, within eyesight of Williams's law office. The Washington operation, linked by computer to the Memorial Stadium ticket office, specialized in group sales and provided special bus service to and from Memorial Stadium.

The Orioles aggressively sought corporate sponsors to pay the costs of individual promotional events and provided special rates and seating for organized groups, such as business, recreational, and church organizations. In the mid-1980s the Orioles were exploiting the popularity of baseball to sell cruises with select team members and a "dream week" in which adults over the age of thirty paid $2,500 to $3,000 to spend a week working out at a simulated baseball training camp. The highlight of the week was the chance for the participants to play a game against a group of retired Orioles stars. Both promotions were highly successful and profitable.[13]

By 1983 the Orioles' marketing campaign was so successful that team officials were entertaining their own dream: 2 million in paid attendance. The team that had never drawn more than 1.2 million in any year prior to 1979 achieved its objective, assisted by a World Series–bound squad. The next two years, the Orioles again passed 2 million in attendance, peaking at 2,132,387 in 1985.[14]

The achievement was remarkable. The Orioles had to overcome fan discontent arising from the players' strike and considerable public mistrust of Williams and his ultimate objectives. Williams aroused Baltimore fans' deepest fears in an August 1980 interview in the *Washington Post*. The Orioles owner proclaimed that the days of a "Ma and Pa" franchise were over. The team was committed to paying the top dollar needed to retain its young stars and compete for free agent talent. Baltimore fans were "on trial," Williams explained: "To have a better team with better players, we must have better revenues. . . . To do this we need great support from Baltimore, not just good support."[15]

Williams's comments were a gratuitous slap in the face of Baltimore fans. The club was advancing toward a new season high in attendance. Making the comments to a Washington newspaper compounded the initial error. The *Sun*'s Bob Maisel probably summed up Baltimore opinion when he called Williams's comment "stupid" and suggested that the owner refrain from involving himself in the operations of his highly successful franchise.[16]

Williams beat a speedy retreat, claiming the interview was a "big blow up" over nothing. He tried to soothe injured local feelings at a 12 November 1980 Salute to the Orioles luncheon. Speaking on a television relay from New York, Williams praised the team's fans for "great support" and vowed, "The time may come when I leave baseball, but baseball will never leave Baltimore."[17] Thereafter, the Orioles owner was extremely positive in his comments about Baltimore. However, the gradual transformation of the team into a regional franchise brought a growing concentration on marketing initiatives aimed at attracting fans from outside Baltimore and reinforced many city fans' mistrust of the Orioles owner. Williams's objective of building a "regional" franchise, meant eliminating references to the "Baltimore" Orioles, including redesigning team uniforms and designating Memorial Stadium and environs as "Birdland" in club publicity.

The Price of Success

Baltimore fans might grumble about regionalization but they joined the outsiders in supporting the team. A major reason for the strong support shown the Orioles after the strike was Williams's success in retaining the nucleus of his young and attractive team. During the winter of 1980, a number of these young stars—including first baseman Eddie Murray, the heart of the offense; right-handed pitcher Dennis Martinez and lefties Mike Flanagan, Scott McGregor, and Tippy Martinez; and second baseman Rich Dauer—were within one or two years of eligibility for free agency. Williams, whose estimated first season profit was $1.5–2 million, was ready to sign these players to long-term contracts at large salary increases. He explained: "I don't think we've gone crazy. I've said all along that my Number One priority was to keep this club intact. I think we've got a good, solid, young team with a good future, and we don't want to lose what we already have."[18]

Peters fully supported the owner's willingness to spend, explaining: "I don't see any merit in offering multi-year contracts too early. But, I feel there's a lot of merit in doing it if you feel certain about a player in their fourth year."[19] Peters stressed the link between winning and turning a profit: "Paying these salaries is necessary if you're going to remain competitive. You can't win without talent, and you can't keep top talent without drawing well, and its tough drawing without winning."[20]

Manager Earl Weaver chimed in: "I know we've got a team to contend with if we stay together."[21] With most of the owner's money committed to retaining these skilled young veterans, reinforcements would be hard to obtain. The club remained willing to enter the free agent market, but escalating salary levels limited its access to that talent pool. In November 1980 Williams broke with the sport's unwritten etiquette to publicly criticize another owner, Atlanta's Ted Turner, for bidding up the prices of free agent players. Ultimately, the Orioles were able to sign a couple of budget-priced hitters to strengthen their bench. Williams ardently pursued Reggie Jackson after the 1981 season, but his eloquence ultimately proved no match for California's larger, long-term contract offer.[22]

In order to support his expanding payroll, the Orioles owner continued to raise ticket prices. By the 1982 season, the Orioles, once the cheapest attraction in the major leagues, had the highest ticket prices in organized baseball. Peters blamed the inflation in ticket prices on "the continuing upward spiral of player salaries, travel expenses and the inflationary effects on costs in general," and he went on to explain, "It is absolutely mandatory that we increase our revenue earning potential for next year. . . . We are grateful for . . . fan support. . . . We don't like to raise prices, but if we are going to remain competitive it is an unfortunate necessity."[23]

Baltimore taxpayers shouldered a large share of the burden for supporting the team. The Orioles won a low stadium rental agreement from the city in the mid-1970s and continued to enjoy this extremely favorable lease agreement through 1984. When the arrangement came up for renewal that year, Williams secured an even better deal that included a larger share of concessions income, a new scoreboard, and further reduced rent. Under a unique arrangement, the Orioles and the city of Baltimore became partners. The team's sales revenues from stadium activities went into a single fund. After the Orioles recovered expenses, the city and club shared evenly in the profits.[24]

The key casualty of the costs of retaining a winning nucleus was a restricted minor league system. Plans to add a fifth team to the Orioles' minor league system were shelved in December 1980 as a result of the cash drain created by signing the team's best players to long-term contracts. Both Williams and Peters were committed to improving the Orioles through minor league development, but the cash flow problems created by large major league salaries delayed expansion of the farm system. Due to the weakness of its farm system, the team lacked a talent surplus that it could use to acquire players at a reasonable price. Even after expanding its minor league system, Baltimore remained short of talent for some years and ultimately had to seek expensive veteran free agents to fill growing gaps on its major league squad.[25]

The continuing inflation of player costs prompted Williams to put forward a plan for revenue sharing modeled on the NFL's highly successful plan for dividing television income. The NFL's decision to pool and share equally television rights income insured that all teams were profitable and could bid on a nearly equal basis for talent. This leveling of income had the added benefit of dampening bidding wars for talent. By equalizing income among its teams, the NFL reduced the economic advantages that, in organized baseball, large population gave to teams in major metropolitan markets.[26] Under Williams's proposal, baseball would go a step further, dividing both its television income and ticket sales. The plan met with fierce resistance from a number of wealthier owners, who succeeded in blocking it.[27]

In spite of this rebuff and the hostility his stand on the strike created, the confident, articulate Williams quickly won the often-grudging respect of his fellow owners. Peters believed that Williams's growing influence was a result of the force of his personality: "Williams . . . has made his living and his mark in life in what he likes to call . . . 'contest living.' He can express himself better on issues. . . . [He] has certain qualities about him that people look to him. . . . He recognizes issues . . . that . . . should be compromised [on]."[28]

Williams allied with a rapidly growing faction of new owners, men like Roy Eisenhardt of Oakland, Peter O'Malley of Los Angeles, and Eddie Chiles of Texas, who were eager to revamp the sport's image and administration. During the 1981 winter meetings he took a leading role in the creation of a twelve-man committee to study restructuring the sport and lay the groundwork for replacing Commissioner Kuhn with a more dynamic executive. To his surprise, Williams won election to baseball's Executive Committee during the same meeting.[29]

While a powerful group of owners remained opposed to Williams's revenue sharing proposal, they agreed with his insistence that the sport had to rein in its spending on free agents. Change would come, Williams predicted, because "we're destroying the competitive balance of the sport as well as its financial health."[30]

Television and the Regional Franchise

As a veteran of NFL management, Williams had a deep appreciation of the importance of television in building a fan base, in generating a secure profit, and in maintaining competitiveness.

Baseball had tended to follow professional football's lead in television marketing but stopped short of pooling its local revenues. The result was a significant imbalance in incomes that tempted owners in large media markets into bidding wars after the Messersmith decision. The size of national TV payments continued to rise. Sponsors and the networks complained about rising costs, but neither wanted to lose the competitive edge that major professional sports provided advertisers and broadcasters. In fact, throughout the 1970s the total volume of sports programming on television increased dramatically. Football, particularly the NFL, was the pacesetter in income hikes. Major league baseball followed closely behind. In 1967 its combined television income was $29.16 million. When Williams took command of the Orioles in 1979, major league baseball's local and national rights payments were $50 million. Then in 1983, in the wake of a massive new NFL contract, the networks offered baseball annual payments of $180 million a year, nearly quadrupling each team's annual national TV income from $1.9 million to $7.7 million.[31]

The growth in local payments was uneven. While national television income continued its steady increase, local payments essentially leveled off during the 1970s. When the first baseball strike threatened in 1972, one local broadcast official faced the prospect of filling his programming gaps with calm: "Baseball was never a great money maker but more of a community image . . . thing. If there were no baseball this year, it wouldn't be a major problem for [local] stations."[32] Even the national networks were unconcerned about the loss of game of the week play. Their major sources of income and audiences were baseball's playoffs and the All-Star Game. ABC president Frederick Pierce remarked a few years later that baseball "is not NFL football" and never would be in terms of ratings, but the network could "reap the benefits" from selling World Series advertising time. Baseball, one broadcasting trade publication explained, was a useful vehicle for reaching male audiences, but this was an "older and downscale" group that typically purchased less than did other segments of the economy.[33]

Baseball executives were worried by developments in another broadcasting technology, cable television. All professional sports fought the introduction of cable television during the 1970s and 1980s. While baseball owners' were ready to sell rights to broadcast games to local cable stations, they worried about the effects of retransmission. The development of commercial satellites during the 1960s permitted well-financed cable companies to create national networks by beaming their programming via satellites to other cable stations. The professional sports leagues became concerned when a number of so-called super stations, such as Atlanta's WTBS, purchased rights to local sports broadcasting and then offered their programming to other cable stations. In effect, these stations had broken the monopoly that each major and minor league team held over its local market, flooding an area with daily broadcasts of one or more rival teams. Owners feared that cable broadcasting would undercut their home attendance.

Commissioner Kuhn led baseball's battle against cable television. Kuhn became a frequent figure at congressional and Federal Communications Commission (FCC) hearings, where he argued that the FCC's existing rules on cable TV deprived the professional sports leagues of the ability to sell their product for top dollar. The FCC took the position that cable stations could broadcast sports events live to any area with the sole restriction that if the home team blacked out the game, cable stations had to avoid broadcasting within a thirty-five-mile radius of the team's city.[34]

Kuhn introduced a complicated plan for cable rights at a 16 April 1975 meeting of the FCC. The baseball plan was strongly reminiscent of its 1950s proposals for regulating commercial television. It would forbid cable broadcasts within a seventy-five-mile zone around major league cities, thirty-five miles around each team's major affiliate station, and twenty miles around all minor league cities. Baseball's arguments for restricting cable broadcasting found little public support. Commenting on the battle over cable television, economist Ira Horowitz told Congress: "The real issue . . . is how the monopoly profits are going to be divided between networks and clubs."[35]

Kuhn's efforts to lobby Congress and the FCC faced significant opposition within his own ranks. George Steinbrenner began to sell part of his highly profitable local broadcast rights to cable shortly after acquiring the New York Yankees. Ignoring protests from both the commissioner and the major networks, the FCC approved Steinbrenner's action.[36]

Kuhn was incapable of disciplining baseball owners. Millionaire broadcaster Ted Turner purchased the Atlanta Braves in 1976 with the evident intent of using baseball broadcasting as a key part of his growing cable empire. By 1979, the New York Mets, San Francisco Giants, and Chicago

Cubs had signed cable agreements. Teams in two other major markets, the Red Sox and Dodgers, were negotiating to sell their games. Kuhn once again appealed to Congress for relief, claiming that baseball faced an oversaturation of broadcasts that would undercut attendance. "Gentlemen, I suggest that you should not wait for the autopsy here. . . . Unless something is done, the autopsy is coming."[37] The leagues must have the right to control their own broadcasting, Kuhn insisted. Turner countered that Kuhn's demand that baseball have the right to limit broadcasting of games "would frankly" put his broadcasting empire "out of business."[38]

The Kuhn-Turner battle over cable broadcasting rights continued throughout the late 1970s and into the 1980s. The two men were frequently paired as witnesses at congressional hearings, much to the chagrin of Kuhn. During the 1982 hearings on cable, Kuhn's irritation showed: "Yes, Mr. Turner is joining me here," the commissioner replied dryly to a questioner, "We are frequently together at these proceedings, I have noticed."[39] In 1985 Turner agreed to compensate his fellow owners for invading their broadcast territories.

Kuhn's campaign to control cable broadcasting was quixotic. Congress, responding to public demand for more sporting events and to the lobbying of the major corporate investors in cable networks, refused to consider tightening the rights of the professional leagues over the airwaves. During the 1970s and 1980s, as in earlier decades, the government limited professional sports' control over broadcasting. In 1973 Congress passed legislation that significantly narrowed broadcasting blackouts of sports events. The same year the FCC investigated the practice of clubs' paying and controlling the announcers for their games, issuing regulations that required the teams to identify their broadcasting employees. At the end of 1973 FCC chairman Dean Burch, a probusiness conservative, warned professional sports owners that his regulatory agency would never permit them to sell "free" events like the World Series or Super Bowl to cable television. Kuhn insisted that such action was "unthinkable" and that baseball simply wanted to prevent cable super stations from saturating the market.[40]

Kuhn's campaign met with further setbacks. In the 1976 Copyright Act, Congress permitted broadcast and retransmission of sports events by cable stations for a minimal fee. The FCC dealt the final blow in a 1981 decision that a cable station owning local rights to a given team's games could broadcast them in whatever markets it wished. Congress has refused to overturn that ruling.[41]

Meanwhile, more baseball owners joined the race to market their product through cable television. Edward Bennett Williams, as befitted a veteran of NFL management, seized upon broadcasting as a critical means of improving club profitability. Anxious to improve his position in the Washington market, he hired Metrosports, Inc., of Rockville, Maryland, to handle the expansion of the team's radio network and monitor the quality of local affiliates' broadcasting. The Orioles were particularly concerned with the performance of the D.C. affiliate, WTOP radio, and Metrosports carefully monitored its game coverage. Williams insisted on telecasting more games into the capital and searched for a "strong local station." However, he was unable to secure a network affiliate and settled instead for renewal of the team's pact with WDCA, an unaffiliated Washington station with a powerful transmitter. The overall effect of the Orioles' media strategy, the *Washington Post* noted, was to "allow us to pretend we have a home team."[42]

The following year Williams ventured into the pay television market, signing an agreement with Super TV, a UHF broadcasting station that scrambled its signals, to televise sixteen 1982 Orioles games. A cable pact followed. In the spring of 1982, Home Team Sports began operations as a regional network with exclusive sports programming. HTS immediately began negotiating for broadcast rights with the Baltimore-Washington area's sports franchises.[43]

Williams was interested. "I think cable is going to be a very big industry," he told an interviewer; "It may even dominate entertainment. And we're exploring it, giving it careful consideration." Williams was concerned about possible "overexposure" and wanted to weigh the effect of cable broadcasts on attendance carefully.[44] A regional sports network like HTS was a new concept in cable broadcasting, and, particularly in its start-up stage, it would be vulnerable to the vagaries of the local economy. Its ability to make and pass on a profit was a major question. The third factor that Orioles officials had to weigh was the slow and uneven progress of cable installation in the Baltimore-Washington market. A number of suburban counties had cable, including Baltimore County and the populous, wealthy Virginia suburbs of Washington; and the city of Baltimore itself was in the last stages of planning for cable operations. However, Washington, where Mayor Marion S. Barry, Jr., presided over a corrupt and inefficient administration, lagged badly behind in this area, as in providing many other services.[45]

At the end of 1983 the Orioles decided to join the general trend by signing with a cable system. At least two factors weighed heavily in the club's decision. The Orioles, as a perennial contender, faced a continuing inflation of its overall team salary level. Moreover, income from local television had flattened out to about $1 million a year. WMAR TV's president Steven Seymour echoed other local broadcasting executives in saying, "We make a profit right now, but I can give you a hundred ways we can invest our money better. [Baseball] is a strong promotion vehicle for us and gives us good community involvement, but it's a fragile thing. If the costs of rights escalates, the club deteriorates or the economy deteriorates, it could turn to a loss."[46]

In June 1983 the Orioles announced agreement with Home Team Sports to broadcast eighty of its 1984 games on cable for rights payments estimated to range between $30,000 and $50,000 per broadcast. The club dropped its broadcasting arrangement with Super TV. Since WMAR was broadcasting slightly more than fifty Orioles games, mostly on the road, HTS would get the pick of Orioles home games. Orioles general counsel Lawrence Lucchino insisted that HTS's "regional bias" would provide the team with "an important source of marketing and promotion." He admitted, however, that the club's cable income would depend on the speed with which local governments authorized the creation of cable systems. Another factor would be the ability of the team's two local broadcasting systems to coexist profitably.[47]

Within a few years, Orioles officials could point to a limited success with cable broadcasting. Attendance levels remained high in spite of the declining competitiveness of the team. WMAR held its audience and sponsors. After some start-up problems, the quality of HTS broadcasting was uniformly very high. However, the growth of cable broadcasting was slow. Many local jurisdictions moved with extreme caution in assigning potentially lucrative cable franchises to rival companies. As a result, the flow of advertising dollars was considerably less than HTS's backers had anticipated. Although HTS officials spoke optimistically about making a profit by 1988, the broadcasting company renegotiated its contracts with all major sports franchises in 1986, reducing the size of its payments. By the late 1980s cable television remained essentially what it had been in the 1970s, a promising source of revenue that had failed to reach its full potential. The Orioles' willingness to continue the experiment indicated that they still believed in the concept of cable television.[48]

The Orioles could afford to be patient with cable TV. By 1985 the club's total local payments from all broadcasting sources were approaching an estimated $4 million. The club also shared in the enormous payoff that baseball received from the 1983 national network contract. The 1983 television deal was the greatest single success of Bowie Kuhn's long reign as commissioner of baseball. The major leagues were the beneficiaries of the rivalry between two of the major networks, ABC and NBC. Baseball carefully built the rivalry and skillfully played the networks off against each other. In 1983 NBC wanted control of the entire baseball package in order to maximize the profits that came from televising baseball's crown jewels: the playoffs, World Series, and All-Star Game. ABC, a network that built its success on heavy sports programming, was unwilling to lose access to these major events. The other major network, CBS, also wanted a share of baseball.[49]

The networks' enthusiasm for baseball was heightened by reports, carefully fed by Kuhn, of a major national deal with a cable network and by a growing realization that baseball's audience had undergone a major generational, social, and sexual metamorphosis during the 1970s and 1980s. Women became a larger part of the audience for baseball. The crowds at stadiums were also markedly younger and more affluent. The audience for baseball on television was also changing to upscale groups who spent on a wide variety of products. As a result, new products joined baseball's traditional advertising mix of beer, oil, cars, and tobacco. Fast food chains, the state lottery, Amtrak, and the dairy industry were among the advertisers buying time on Orioles broadcasts. Advertising rates shot up and so did broadcasting income.[50]

CBS dropped out of the television contract bidding early, but its initial interest, combined with concern that the cable networks might win a major part of the baseball package, fueled competitive fires at NBC and ABC. The two networks engaged in a bidding contest that drove television rights skyward.[51]

The final accord, worked out in the spring of 1983, provided what *Television/Radio Age* labeled an "astronomical jump" in baseball's income. NBC and ABC divided the contract rights. Each network would pay over $500 million for long-term rights to broadcast baseball through 1989. The networks rotated rights to the crown jewels, with one broadcasting the playoffs and the other the World Series each year. They also alternated coverage of the All-Star Game. NBC's package also included the Saturday game of the week, while ABC held rights for a Monday night game and for Sunday broadcasts. In addition, CBS paid out $32 million for a five-year contract for radio rights to a major league game of the week, the playoffs, the World Series, and the All-Star Game. Williams was understandably enthusiastic about the hefty increase in his baseball income. He hailed the new deal as "a tremendous step forward for revenue sharing." The Orioles would continue to operate on a smaller financial base than most of their division rivals, but the club's national television income would enable the team to pay competitive major league salaries and support an expanded minor league system.[52]

Banquo's Ghost

A triumph of the magnitude of the 1983 television agreement should have secured Bowie Kuhn's hold on the commissioner's office for another term. Instead, the commissioner was driven from his job by a small, determined minority of the same conservative owners he had served so faithfully. Williams, initially one of Kuhn's major critics, became one of the commissioner's primary supporters.

Kuhn's position collapsed as a result of his handling of the 1981 strike. The commissioner had abdicated responsibility and never regained his credibility. Kuhn's troubles with Williams were a direct result of surrendering leadership to Ray Grebey and the hardline faction of owners dominating the PRC. According to Kuhn, the Orioles owner flew to New York on the fifth day of the strike, 17 June 1981, to inform the commissioner their "friendship" was at its end. Kuhn professed ignorance over the causes of Williams's action. If so, the commissioner was probably the only interested observer with any doubts.[53] Their conflict escalated as Williams took a leading public role in seeking a compromise solution to the strike while Kuhn stood with the hardliners.

Once the strike was concluded, Kuhn attempted to recapture his position as baseball's official spokesman and chief negotiator. Williams, along with a number of other disgruntled owners, had had enough of Kuhn's brand of leadership. Adding to Williams's discontent was personal pique over Kuhn's handling of the scheduling of the poststrike portion of the 1981 season.

In 1981 the Orioles had put together an unusual early-season winning stretch that left them in first place on the original strike date. By the time the strike actually took place on 11 June, the team had slumped into second place. After the strike, a majority of baseball owners voted for a Kuhn-supported "split season" plan. Under the commissioner's plan the teams with the best prestrike records in each division would contest their respective division titles with the teams that compiled the best poststrike records. The Orioles protested vociferously against this idea, noting that the winners of the "first season" would have little incentive to play competitive baseball in the "second season." Moreover, Orioles officials believed that their team was built for a 162-game season and operated at a disadvantage if the strike-shortened season was further truncated. Kuhn and the defeated conservative owners easily overrode Williams's objections, slapping his wrists for breaking ranks during the strike.[54] Baltimore finished fourth in the "second season" and was eliminated from postseason play and profits, in spite of compiling the second best overall record in the American League East.

In November 1981 Williams took a leading role in organizing a revolt against the commissioner. Nine owners, mostly conservatives, signed a letter calling for Kuhn's ouster and tried to place the issue on the agenda of the December winter meetings. Kuhn's backers rallied to the commissioner and succeeded in beating back this attack. Nevertheless, Kuhn's days as commissioner were clearly numbered.[55]

While opposition to Kuhn hardened among a powerful minority of conservative owners, Williams abandoned his former allies and swung his support to Kuhn. At least two factors motivated Williams's switch. First, the commissioner gave strong backing to television revenue sharing. Kuhn's other opponents, in the main, were enemies of revenue sharing. Moreover, by the spring of 1982, Williams recognized that the other rebellious owners wanted to reduce the already limited powers of the commissioner and replace Kuhn with an even weaker successor. The National League's owners, he commented, "are locked in cement on many ideas. . . . I think it was a long time before any of them had inside plumbing." Baseball, Williams insisted, needed greater centralization as an essential step toward revenue sharing.[56]

At the June 1982 owners' meeting Williams announced his support for Kuhn's reelection bid. After switching sides, Williams became one of Kuhn's strongest public defenders. The hard-pressed Kuhn, in turn, suddenly discovered that "it would be very difficult to have two teams in the Baltimore-Washington area." The commissioner became an "enthusiastic" supporter of Williams's concept of a regional franchise.[57] Williams, however, had acted too late to save Kuhn. He had played a critical role in undermining the commissioner by organizing the initial revolt. Kuhn accepted Williams's assistance, but he never trusted the Orioles owner, resenting Williams's earlier role in organizing the anti-Kuhn cabal.[58]

In November 1982 the anti-Kuhn minority gathered enough support in the National League to defeat Kuhn's bid for reelection. The commissioner fell one vote short of the three-quarters support he needed for another term.[59]

Like Banquo's ghost, the commissioner continued to haunt the major leagues. Undeterred by defeat, and backed by the majority of owners, Kuhn maneuvered for another eight months to retain his position. The conservatives who ousted Kuhn lacked a viable candidate to replace the commissioner. Kuhn's supporters were divided into those favoring a serious search for a replacement and those who wanted to make a further effort to retain the commissioner by having the search committee demonstrate that no suitable alternative existed. As long as Kuhn remained a candidate, a number of potential successors refused to be considered by the search committee, among them the highly regarded president of the Los Angeles Olympic organization committee, Peter Ueberroth.[60]

Ultimately, Kuhn failed to break the solidarity of the minority. On 3 August 1983 he bowed to the inevitable and announced he would not seek a third term as commissioner. Kuhn's withdrawal opened the way for owners favoring basic reform in baseball's organizational and administrative structure to bring forward a strong candidate for commissioner.[61]

Williams had at last found his natural allies: the newer owners who agreed with his views about the need to share revenues, strengthen the administrative powers of the commissioner, and avoid unnecessary confrontation with the union. This group rallied to the support of Ueberroth. Meanwhile, they backed the retention of Kuhn as interim commissioner. In March 1984 the owners agreed to offer the job to the Los Angeles businessman and to continue to employ Kuhn until Ueberroth could wind up his work on the Los Angeles Olympic games that fall. They also agreed that the new commissioner would operate with expanded powers, as "chief executive officer of baseball," and would be elected by a simple majority of owners to a five-year term.[62]

A Championship Season

Thus, a lame duck Commissioner Kuhn presided over the 1983 World Series between the Philadelphia Phillies and his nemesis-turned-mistrusted-ally Williams's Baltimore Orioles. The Orioles' triumph in the series was the greatest success of the Williams era. A team marked less by its stars than by its ability to play the game as a unit climaxed a story that had begun the previous year.

In October 1982 Earl Weaver retired after fifteen successful seasons as Orioles manager. The "Earl of Baltimore" went out in style. He lead the Orioles in a dramatic chase for the American League East title. Surging from behind, the Orioles entered the final series of the season with the division-leading Brewers needing to win all four games in order to wrest the championship from the Milwaukee team. On Friday night, 1 October, Baltimore swept a doubleheader. The next day the Orioles won again, only to bow to the Brewers on the last day of the season.

The defeat seemed to energize both the Orioles and their fans. For a quarter of an hour after the last game ended, a vast Memorial Stadium crowd cheered their heroes, simultaneously bidding a fond farewell to manager Weaver. The demonstration was more the prelude to a new season than the end of the 1982 campaign.

The 1983 Orioles, under new manager Joe Altobelli, opened their season with a disappointing 7–2 loss to Kansas City. The team then put together a rare winning April—the first, in fact, since the 1979 American League championship season. Alternating surges and slumps, the Orioles remained close to or in first place from May to August. Then on 13 August the team began to pull away from its rivals, going 34–10 for the remainder of the season and wrapping up the American League East title on 25 September, appropriately in Milwaukee. Eddie Murray and Cal Ripken, Jr., led the offense, while the pitching staff combined for fifteen shutouts and a 3.63 ERA. Bullpen ace Tippy Martinez had the best year of his career, topping it off with a remarkable 24 August relief stint against Toronto. The diminutive reliever picked off three Blue Jays base runners in succession during a single inning. The Orioles won the game on a dramatic tenth-inning home run by utility infielder Len Sakata.

The Orioles took a tense four-game league championship series from a very good Chicago White Sox team. Their World Series opponents, the Philadelphia Phillies, fell in five games to a combination of good pitching and timely hitting.

On a bright Sunday afternoon in mid-October 1983, left-hander Scott McGregor coolly worked his way through the last part of the Philadelphia Phillies batting order to complete the Orioles's World Series triumph. The team appeared capable of maintaining its dominant position in the American

League East. To an essentially youthful cast that included four top starting pitchers and power-hitting first baseman Eddie Murray, the Orioles farm system had added an outstanding infielder and slugger, Cal Ripken, Jr., the American League's most valuable player for 1983. After two years of financial difficulties caused by the strike and bad weather, the club had posted record revenues, increasing its income by an estimated $4.5 million over 1982's total.[63] The Orioles' future appeared bright. However, looming over the team was the continuing weakness of its farm system. Over the next four years the Orioles dropped out of contention, to the accompaniment of front office confusion and player discontent.

14 The End of an Era

Today, you build a club for the immediate season, not the long-range future. What's that they say? The future is now.
—Henry Peters, October 1984

This is a business. As in every business, you have production and sales. You have to have a product to sell. We can get away with two bad years. We've had them, 1984 and 1985. We can't afford another one.
—Edward Bennett Williams, March 1986

On the evening of 14 June 1985 a near-capacity crowd filled Memorial Stadium waiting for a miracle. The crowd rose to its feet cheering as the short, banty-legged man in the uniform bearing the number 4 strode toward home plate to present the night's lineup card to the umpires. Earl was back. Moments later, Orioles starter Storm Davis pitched himself into a bases loaded situation. The crowd again cheered lustily as Weaver strode to the mound and sternly lectured his young pitcher. Responding to Weaver's talk, Davis worked his way out of trouble. The Orioles rallied to win. Baltimore swept the rest of the series from the lowly Milwaukee Brewers. Many Orioles fans believed that the hoped-for miracle indeed had occurred. Earl Weaver, returned from retirement, had rallied the slumping Orioles and would lead them into contention.

Alas, miracles are always in short supply. Reviving the talent-thinned Orioles required more than Weaver's legendary managerial ability. The day after Milwaukee left Baltimore, the New York Yankees moved into Memorial Stadium and swept a three-game series from the Orioles. A little more than a year later, in the midst of a long losing streak, a discouraged Weaver announced his resignation. In 1986, for the first time in the franchise's history, Baltimore finished last in the American League. A shaken Orioles high command appeared unable to cope with or reverse the team's collapse.

The Big O

As Baltimore prepared for the 1984 defense of its World Series title, Orioles management indulged in a bit of understandable self-congratulation. An essay in the club's 1984 yearbook stressed organization, "the Big O," as the key to nearly thirty years of success: "The players, the managers and general managers . . . and even the owners . . . have changed. . . . The organization's high level of performance . . . and success has remained constant."[1]

The sporting press echoed Orioles management's flattering self-analysis. An article in the *New York Times* entitled "The System, Not the Stars, Keep the Orioles on Top," stressed the role of organization. The Orioles' success was based on careful attention to detail, respectful treatment of players, and an emphasis on stability in place of wholesale change. The *Washington Post*'s Thomas Boswell praised "the sense of moderation, tolerance and decency that runs through the Orioles [organization]," starting with owner Williams, who "bought a team . . . which already embodied many of his values."[2]

Unfortunately, Baltimore baseball had already begun to lose many of the elements of its success. Asked to evaluate the Orioles collapse in 1986, one baseball executive stated that at least three factors were at work. First, the club's "supply lines dried up" as the result of the weakness of its minor league system. The "troops were not coming up from AAA," and the club had to seek replacements at the major league level either through the very difficult path of trading or through the more inviting but perilous route of acquiring expensive free agents. Second, long-dormant but deep differences in values and operational styles between owner Williams and general manager Peters awakened. Under pressure from an owner who demanded immediate success, "Henry had to make some deals that didn't work out." Finally, the team's competitive edge was worn down by success and by the gradual aging of its athletes.[3]

The 1984 season was clearly a major shock to the Orioles high command. Age robbed the club of a number of skilled performers who had provided much of the club's competitive edge. Pitcher Jim Palmer, the articulate perfectionist whose 268 career victories were the most in Orioles history, lost his skills. The club pushed him into retirement in May. Outfielder Al Bumbry, whose disciplined performance and deep involvement in both community affairs and the club's marketing efforts made him a favorite with fans and management, struggled to the end of the season. He had lost the defensive skills that had made him a top major league center fielder. Designated hitter Ken Singleton, once the heart of the offense, barely hit .200 and finished his career on the bench. Eddie Murray and Cal Ripken, Jr., struggled mightily to carry the club's offense. The rest of the team simply didn't hit. The starting pitching was excellent. Nevertheless, the team never challenged the pennant-winning Detroit Tigers and finished with an 85–77 record in fifth place.

By late August 1984 the club owner and general manager were already talking about changes but offered differing prescriptions. Williams talked about complacency and vowed to "shake things up to keep the players motivated. . . . We're going to make changes, a lot of changes, before next season. We really hurt ourselves by keeping the status quo." Williams added that the club needed to take a "long, hard look at our farm system," where talent seemed extremely thin.[4]

Peters, starting from the belief that "top to bottom the pitching is the best in baseball," rejected radical change: "An overhaul? No, we don't need that."[5] The club would seek offensive help but only after a careful evaluation of each current player's performance and prospects.

After late September meetings with his minor league managers, scouts, and administrative personnel and separate discussions with owner Williams, Peters made some significant personnel changes. He placed Singleton, Bumbry, outfielder Benny Ayala, and pitcher Tom Underwood on waivers. The club's minor league system lacked replacements. The Orioles would attempt to rebuild their outfield corps and strengthen their relief pitching through the acquisition of free agent players. Peters defended the work of manager Joe Altobelli, criticizing the players for weakness in baseball fundamentals and for general complacency.[6] Nevertheless, both press criticisms and Williams's comments placed the manager's job in jeopardy. The 1985 team would perform better, or a new field leader would take command.

Rational planning failed to deal successfully with the Orioles' woes. At the 1984 winter meetings owner Williams spent heavily to acquire three free agent players. Center fielder Fred Lynn, rated one of the best at his position; hard-throwing relief pitcher Don Aase; and speedy, line drive–hitting outfielder Lee Lacy joined the Orioles in 1985 after signing long-term contracts worth over $12 million collectively. The Orioles took a major plunge into the free agent market, as Peters put it, "because we had to. . . . We are in the toughest division ever in the history of divisional play and have to stay competitive. . . . Farm systems can't produce every year. All twenty-six teams are after the same things you are and the scouting is much better now, so that you will have your ups and downs. Right now we don't have a great deal on the farm."[7] "I'm comfortable with what we have going into next season," Peters commented after signing the three free agents; "We've gotten Joe Altobelli as many of the horses as we could. . . . Now it's up to him."[8]

The organization's 1984 decisions signaled the end of an era in Baltimore baseball. Columnist Thomas Boswell, who insistently lobbied for a major move into free agency, recognized: "The Orioles as we have known them for the last quarter century—placid, excellent, hermetic, slow to change, tasteful and conservative—are gone." Baltimore had opted for free agent signings that would vastly inflate the team's salary scale. Lynn won a contract that was much greater than those of other athletes at his statistical performance level. Murray and Ripken could expect major salary increases. While the deals offered Aase and Lacy were more modest, they would pull up the salaries of average players. The team surrendered its top minor league draft choices to compensate the clubs that had lost its new players, further weakening its farm system. The acquisition of these expensive new players put tremendous pressure on Altobelli to win and on the team's marketing operation to attract fans. Inevitably, this led to hard lobbying for a new stadium. The Orioles, Boswell concluded, "had little choice," but he was unable to suppress regret for the passing of the old team: "Draw up a profile of a modern major league franchise—free-spending, impatient, controversial, willing to hurt feelings and take wild risks—and the Orioles, once the antithesis of the type, now come close to matching it."[9]

The new-look Orioles failed to justify the expense. The 1985 team hit exceedingly well, with a league-leading 214 home runs, and scored a team record 818 runs. Two of the three free agent players performed up to their previous statistical levels, and pitcher Don Aase, after a rough start, turned in an excellent performance as the team's short reliever. The starting pitching, the traditional strength of Orioles teams, collapsed. Left-hander Mike Flanagan ruptured an Achilles tendon during the winter, missed half the season, and never recovered his form. Scott McGregor lost the pinpoint control that had made him a top pitcher and finished with a 14–14 record. Mike Boddicker, another control specialist, was hampered by injuries and lost seventeen games. Pitcher Storm Davis, the club's brightest prospect, was increasingly erratic and barely posted a winning record. Veteran reliever Tippy Martinez, long the heart of the bullpen, was plagued by injuries that effectively ended his career.

In mid-June, with the team floundering and hopes of a competitive and profitable season vanishing, Williams decided to fire manager Altobelli and replace him with Weaver and his motivational talents. The firing was ineptly handled. Altobelli had to fend off press questions about his future while the owner negotiated with Weaver. Williams and Peters informed the deposed Altobelli only after signing a new manager. Weaver's return was hardly a triumph: the club compiled a .500 record under him and finished in fourth place with an 83–78 record.

After the 1985 season, the team attempted to plug a number of holes through trades for journeymen and by signing a few moderately priced free agents. Once again the minor league system offered little help, and the Orioles added more aging athletes to their major league roster. Peters, admitting that pitching was an "unexpected" problem with the 1985 team, tried to strengthen the relief corps. He and Weaver decided that they would stick with the starters, hoping 1985 had been an off year for an experienced but still young staff.[10]

Weaver conducted a rugged spring training in 1986, hoping that additional work would improve the starters' stamina. By early August the team was in second place, closing on the division-leading Red Sox. Suddenly, the Orioles fell apart, plunging into last place, as weak pitching and erratic hitting turned 1986 into a nightmare for owner, manager, and fans alike. Weaver threw in the towel in early September, announcing he would return to retirement at the end of the season.

Orioles management appeared paralyzed, unable to decide if the sudden collapse was the result of bad morale or an overall decline in player skills. Williams publicly criticized the team's greatest star, Eddie Murray, both for poor play and for exercising a bad influence on other players. Murray, who played despite major injuries, was incensed. Williams's comments poisoned an already unhealthy clubhouse atmosphere.[11] The press joined in the witch-hunt for culprits. Many journalists laid blame for the team's woes on Williams.

By the winter of 1986–87, the club was clearly without options for a quick return to competitiveness. The enormous sums invested in the 1984 free agent signings restricted its ability to bid for top players. In any case, the major league owners had entered into an illegal "gentlemen's agreement" to strangle free agency by refusing to bid for other clubs' available talent. The Orioles' minor league system was short on talent, and the few top prospects were being force-fed toward the major leagues at a pace that might hamper their development. Williams, apparently stung by press criticism of his "meddling" in team affairs, silently retired to the background, leaving Peters to shoulder responsibility. The general manager's choice of a new manager, Cal Ripken, Sr.—a thirty-year veteran of the organization as a player, minor league manager, and coach—reflected his desire to recapture the style and substance of earlier Orioles baseball.[12]

The straightforward Ripken, a no-nonsense believer in hard work, was an admirable choice to preside over the resurrection of Orioles baseball. The only thing he lacked was a club with talent. While the Orioles had a number of good hitters, the team that Ripken inherited was woefully short on defense, pitching, and speed. Throughout the season, the club wavered between efforts to utilize raw talent pushed up through the minor leagues and high-paid but ineffective veteran players. Only a miserable performance by the Cleveland Indians saved the Orioles from a second season in last place. The day after the season ended, Williams moved to assert full control, firing both Peters and farm director Tom Giordano. The rebuilding effort would take place under different leadership.

The Bare Cupboard

At the root of Baltimore's collapse was the decade-long weakness of its farm system. The Orioles had been living on borrowed time since the mid-1970s. After 1983 a combination of injuries, diminishing skills, and inevitable retirements took their toll. The club was unable to fill the growing gaps in its ranks.

The minor league system had produced a few players of unquestionable talent during the Peters years, primary among them shortstop Cal Ripken, Jr., and pitcher Mike Boddicker. Unfortunately, most of the players who arrived from the minors were one-dimensional athletes: power hitters who could neither field nor throw and finesse pitchers without a major league fastball. By 1987 the Orioles were overloaded with youthful designated hitters but short of prospects capable of filling the voids that had opened up in the skill positions of pitcher, infielder, and catcher. The lack of solid defense was a major factor in the demise of Baltimore's pitching staff. Moreover, players with wider natural skills who arrived in 1987 were frequently unschooled in the basics of pitching and defense. Instruction was no longer standardized at the minor league level. Prospects taught to hit, pitch, or field in one manner at the A level found that their AA-level instructors taught another system. Frances Crockett, who served as general manager of the Charlotte Orioles (AA), lamented: "Years ago, everything was the same, the Orioles way," adding that the lack of systematic training left "a lot of talented kids . . . confused."[13] Manager Ripken was forced to teach his young pitchers the techniques that they were supposed to learn in the minor leagues. A "prominent club source" told the *Washington Post*:

> It looks like the priority has been to win at Charlotte and Rochester, not at Baltimore. [Pitchers] come up and . . . they have no idea what it takes to win in the big leagues. Maybe the farm people have been so afraid that they were going to be fired that that was all they cared about. That's a big change. It used to be [that] the goal was to get them ready for Earl. Period. Nothing else mattered. You could throw a no-hitter at AAA and get chewed out. . . . These guys come up now and their mechanics are terrible, and they have no idea how to pitch.[14]

Even before the lack of talent and the poor management in Baltimore's farm system were reflected in problems for the big league Orioles, they were manifested in the minor league affiliates themselves—and, above all, in Rochester. Rochester Community Baseball lagged behind most minor league franchises in the growth of its attendance and profits. A lack of quality players within the Orioles system was a major factor in Rochester's troubles.

The economic position of the minors began to slowly improve in the early 1970s. After over two decades of decline, the number of franchises leveled off. A boom in minor league attendance began in the later part of the 1970s as popular interest in all levels of professional baseball grew. By 1978 the normally cautious *Sporting News* pronounced the minors in "good shape."[15] In 1972 the minors comprised 148 clubs and drew 10,986,628 paying customers. By 1987, 176 "bush league" clubs attracted 20,220,796.[16] Rochester was slow to join in the profit taking.

The period of calm that followed the ouster of Don Labbruzzo was short lived. By 1981 the stockholders of Rochester Community Baseball were engaged in a proxy war for control of the club. The contrast between the 1979 American League champion Orioles and the last place Red Wings was disturbing for both Baltimore and Rochester baseball administrators. During the winter of 1979–80 the Orioles made an effort to build up the Red Wings squad, by trading for players with AAA-level skills and promoting prospects from the AA Charlotte Orioles. The result was to smooth relations between Rochester and its parent club. In early 1980 Red Wings president Farrell commented that even if 1980 was another losing season, Rochester would renew its working agreement with Baltimore. "They've proven themselves to me already. They've made a heck of an effort to turn us around."[17]

The Orioles' efforts to help Rochester paid off in 1980 as the Red Wings qualified for the playoffs with a fourth-place finish and turned a profit of $106,109. The major league club negated some of the benefits of its trades by recalling Rochester stars Mike Boddicker and Floyd Rayford during the International League playoffs. The Red Wings were eliminated in the first round of the tournament. Nevertheless, relations between Rochester and Baltimore were rarely warmer than at the end of the 1980 season. The expected arrival of a number of top prospects from Charlotte for the 1981 season had Rochester fans anticipating a return to pennant contention.[18]

Rochester Community Baseball faced its most serious problems off the playing field. Fifty-year-old Silver Stadium badly needed $2–4 million in structural repairs and a general face-lift. The club could not afford these improvements and had to round up local and state assistance. Farrell hoped to sell the stadium to a private corporation that would carry out renovations with state aid and then lease the park back to the Red Wings.[19]

Another serious problem was the deterioration of the working relationship between Farrell and general manager Bob Drew. During the winter of 1980–81, Drew, demanding greater autonomy, unsuccessfully sought to win the backing of the board of directors of Rochester Community Baseball by offering his resignation. The board supported Farrell. Drew lost both his bid for power and his job.[20]

Farrell maneuvered to take over the general manager's job from the departed Drew and brought in an ally, Walter Lord, as new team president. Farrell's actions crystallized opposition among the stockholders. A group of dissidents demanded the reinstatement of Drew. The club's largest stockholder, Mrs. Anna Silver, widow of Morris Silver, threw her support behind their demands. Silver's stock alone provided the dissidents with a quarter of the proxies needed to oust the sitting board.[21]

The battle over control of the Red Wings halted progress on stadium reconstruction. It also made collaboration between Baltimore and Rochester difficult. Orioles officials maintained a discreet neutrality between the factions but privately expressed concern about the battle's effect on its players, particularly after manager Doc Edwards resigned and Mrs. Silver forced Farrell's ouster. Two relatively inexperienced young administrators, Bob Goughan and Bill Terlecky, took over management of the club. Their authority to correct the team's problems was limited. The dissidents objected to the contract arrangements the board made with the two assistant general managers.[22]

The proxy battle for control of the Red Wings continued into the spring of 1982. An effort by Representative Frank Horton to mediate between the factions failed. The stockholders' meeting of February 1982 ended with a disputed vote tally, and the dissident faction took the board to court. Meanwhile, the Orioles' relationship with the incumbent board soured. New team president Lord began a "dump the Orioles campaign," openly shopping for a new major league affiliation while blaming Baltimore for the poor quality of previous Rochester squads.[23]

The court decided in favor of the dissidents, who elected Anna Silver chairperson of the board and Ray Sorg team president. A number of local businesses rallied to the support of the new board by contributing toward the refurbishing of the stadium. The new management retained the Goughan-Terlecky duo in their front office capacity and enjoyed an extremely successful season. The Red Wings again finished fourth but advanced to the finals of the International League playoffs before falling to the Tidewater Tides. The club's outlook appeared improved. The Orioles had expanded their minor league system from a 1981 low of three teams to five clubs. "We're finished rebuilding," Orioles farm director Tom Giordano announced; "We've turned the corner." Noting a doubling in the minor league budget since Williams took control, Giordano claimed that the Orioles had a surplus of talent at the AAA level from which Rochester could draw. "At this time, at this point, we feel if we have a need at the big league level, we have a [minor league] replacement."[24]

Giordano's predictions of a flourishing farm system were wide of the mark. The 1983 Red Wings finished sixth in the International League. The Orioles purchased the contracts of a number of career minor leaguers to beef up the Red Wings. In 1984 the team fell into the IL cellar, with the worst record (52–88) in Rochester's long history, prompting new calls for breaking the club's working agreement with the Orioles. The franchise managed a small profit of $28,000, but manager Frank Verdi believed the Orioles would have to completely overhaul the team, adding up to eleven "new faces," if Rochester was to contend and continue to turn a profit. "They've got to get us help. Otherwise, you can throw an atom bomb in the park next year, because no one will come out."[25]

Compounding the Red Wings' problems was the lack of a reliable broadcasting voice. Poor play dampened fan interest, and in March 1984 the club gave up its effort to find a Rochester radio station willing to carry Red Wings games. It created a three-station network in neighboring towns that brought a modest $38,000 in rights payments. The three stations, two of which were FM, had signals of varying strength and could cover only parts of the Red Wings' traditional broadcasting territory.[26]

The Orioles promised aid. In view of the general paucity of talent in its farm system, the club's only recourse was to stock the Red Wings with more aging and relatively high-salaried career minor leaguers. Even this talent was in short supply. Thus, Red Wings officials were extremely pleased with the news of the Orioles' 1984 plunge into the high-priced free agent market. The signing of these athletes might force the Orioles to send some promising younger players back to the AAA level.[27]

The Red Wings were not alone in complaining about the quality of Orioles farmhands. As early as 1978 Frances Crockett of the Charlotte Orioles criticized Baltimore's lack of top AA players and "put a hammerlock" on Orioles management to get some talent for her team. By the end of the 1984 season, a powerful voice had been added to those questioning the quality of Baltimore's player development program: that of Edward Bennett Williams.[28]

Williams initially believed that he possessed one of baseball's best farm systems. In 1980 he told one interviewer that the Orioles were getting more quality at a lower cost from a four-team minor league system than the Yankees got from their seven farm teams. The need to hire three high-salaried free agents in 1984 alerted Williams to problems. During the winter of 1985–86, Williams hired thirty-three-year-old Doug Melvin from the New York Yankees to serve as his special assistant. Melvin brought a reputation as a top evaluator of minor league talent. "Fixing the farm system is the Number One thing on my plate," Williams explained. Melvin would provide the owner with the objective evaluation of the farm system that Williams felt he was not receiving from his own organization.[29]

Williams's intrusion into the management of the minor league system met with considerable resentment. Peters, Giordano, and some members of the farm system staff regarded Melvin as a "spy" who coveted the general manager's or farm director's job. One of Peters's friends suggested that the general manager would "walk out" over Williams's intrusion if he were only a bit younger. Another angry and edgy senior employee burst out: "Hell, let him fire me if that's what he wants to do." Manager Weaver rose to the defense of the farms, noting that in 1985 Orioles homegrown rookie pitchers won eleven games, while outfielder and designated hitter Larry Sheets provided seventeen home runs and fifty RBIs.[30]

By mid-1986 Williams was guardedly optimistic about the future of his farm system. The crop of young players at the AAA level appeared better than in past years. At Rochester, manager John Hart skillfully blended a limited number of prospects with career minor leaguers and players demoted from the big leagues to produce respectable teams in both 1986 and 1987. Rochester Community Baseball took an important step forward when it secured the funding needed for a major renovation of Silver Stadium and sold the property to local investors. With stability restored to the Red Wings' board and the team once again competitive, Rochester and Baltimore were able to close ranks and continue their long association. Nevertheless, management of the Orioles' minor league system remained a divisive issue. Rochester Community Baseball prudently avoided any long-term commitments to the Orioles, negotiating a series of one-year contracts. Reinforced by Melvin's analysis of the minor league department, Williams seemed set on major changes. The collapse of the major league team, the weak preparation in basics displayed by many of the players called up to the big leagues, and the clash of personalities between Williams and Peters laid the groundwork for a change in regime.[31]

The Colts Depart

The Orioles' collapse was part of a general pattern of bad news for Baltimore sports fans and for city and state politicians. The club's nosedive into mediocrity began just weeks after the city lost its professional football franchise. Edward Bennett Williams was the primary beneficiary of the distress both politicians and sports fans experienced. The departure of the Colts was the catalyst that drove the state into financing a new stadium for the Orioles.

Robert Irsay's decision to move the Colts to Indianapolis had multiple motives. Certainly the desire for increased profits played a major role. However, Irsay's disagreeable, quixotic personality was another factor. Irsay had worn out his welcome with both the sports fans and political leaders of Maryland. He recognized this and sought refuge and enlarged profits in the Midwest.

Irsay might have recovered from the public relations blunders that marked his first years in Baltimore: the benching of local hero Johnny Unitas and the breakup of the championship teams of the late 1960s. In 1975 the youthful team assembled by general manager Joe Thomas made the first of three consecutive playoff appearances. Baltimore once again was an NFL power.

Irsay, however, sided with coach Ted Marchibroda in a power struggle and fired Thomas. Without the player development talents of Thomas, the Colts quickly fell out of contention again.

Irsay, meanwhile, was demanding major improvements in the Colts' Memorial Stadium lease and in the facility. By early 1979 he was openly discussing franchise relocation with other city governments while seeking a new stadium or a major overhaul of Memorial Stadium.

Baltimore's political and business leaders initially reacted with irritation to Irsay's antics. They were confident he could not move. NFL rules required league approval for any franchise shift, and Commissioner Pete Rozelle was adamantly opposed to Irsay's plans. Moreover, the city was absorbing major losses as a result of the extremely favorable leases it had negotiated with its two professional sports teams. Mayor Schaefer was committed to making improvements to the existing facility and would seek state assistance for a major overhaul, but he opposed building a new stadium.[32]

Irsay's continued maneuvers and the 1979 sale of the Orioles to Washingtonian Williams stimulated fear that the city might lose both its sports franchises. A number of state legislators introduced legislation designed to anchor the two franchises in Baltimore. The proposals were intended primarily to appease Irsay. During the winter of 1979 the General Assembly passed legislation providing $1 million for improvements to Memorial Stadium that were needed immediately. State leaders also discussed a plan that would offer the Colts and Orioles major renovations at Memorial Stadium in exchange for their signatures on long-term leases that would legally bind them to remain in Maryland.[33]

In February 1980 the Hughes administration introduced a bill authorizing $22 million to permit the city to expand Memorial Stadium, add seating and luxury boxes, build new clubhouses and offices for the Orioles and Colts, and increase parking by over 2,000 spaces. In exchange for these improvements, the state demanded fifteen-year leases from both the Colts and the Orioles. The Memorial Stadium Seating and Field Facilities Act passed the two houses of the General Assembly in April, and Governor Hughes signed it into law.[34]

Neither owner leapt at the state's offer. Williams went on record in November 1979, characterizing the offer as "meaningless" and "one-sided." Adding new seats to Memorial Stadium's upper deck would not improve the Orioles' ability to draw fans. Williams instead proposed that the city and state consider building a new stadium for the exclusive use of the Orioles.[35]

On 1 December 1980, speaking at a city hall press conference, Williams reaffirmed his commitment to keep the club in Baltimore and predicted that the city would eventually construct a downtown stadium. He recognized that finding sources of funding would be difficult in view of both the high interest rates then prevailing and the need to round up state and possibly federal money for the project.[36]

Williams's plans found little support among the city's business or political elite. Schaefer went on record as favoring a new stadium at some undefined future date. However, neither the business community nor the usually supportive city council had much use for the idea. A *News American* editorial stated that given "Baltimore's flabby financial muscle," it was "neither the time nor the place" for discussing a new facility.[37]

Both Williams and Irsay declined to sign long-term contracts for the lease of Memorial Stadium. The Colts owner also refused to accept the Memorial Stadium rehabilitation pact offered by the state. Irsay was waiting on the outcome of a major challenge to Rozelle's authority. Oakland Raiders owner Al Davis had moved his team to Los Angeles without NFL approval. Davis's action triggered a welter of suits and countersuits involving both the NFL and the two California cities. If Davis won, Irsay would have a free hand to select a new home for his team from a large list of cities eager for the status and reputed income an NFL franchise brought. While he waited, the Colts owner agreed to a two-year "interim" lease.[38]

Irsay dragged out negotiations with local and state officials over a Memorial Stadium renovation pact for the next two years. Schaefer, alert to the likelihood of the Colts' defection, sought to anchor the team in Baltimore. In February 1983 the mayor decided to separate negotiations over Memorial Stadium. He suggested that the legislature adopt a new $15 million package of improvements, earmarking $7.5 million for improvements desired by each club and tying the offer to agreement by each franchise to sign a six-year-lease on Memorial Stadium. After some intense lobbying by the mayor, the General Assembly approved the Schaefer proposal during its spring session.[39]

The stadium aid debates revealed the depth of the politicians' mistrust and dislike for Irsay. At one point the General Assembly's leaders contemplated offering improvements to Williams alone. The Washington owner reaped the benefits of his cooperation with city leaders. While Williams continued to press for a new facility, he repeatedly reiterated his commitment to remain in the city.[40]

While waiting for final approval of the Memorial Stadium renewal package, the Orioles renewed their lease for one year in March 1983. In January 1984 Williams began negotiations with Schaefer over the terms of a long-term lease. The negotiations were "tough as nails," Schaefer told reporters. Williams sought every possible financial advantage for his club. Eventually, the two sides reached an agreement. Williams signed a three-year Memorial Stadium lease with the option to renew it annually for three more years.[41]

Irsay absconded with Baltimore's football team in the early morning hours of 29 March 1984. The Colts' move followed an appeals court decision upholding Davis's right to transfer his franchise to Los Angeles. The Colts owner selected the best available offer, loaded the team's equipment and records into moving vans, and was on the road to Indianapolis within a matter of hours. Startled Maryland officials, who had been negotiating with Irsay on the evening of the move, awoke to find the city and state without a professional football franchise.[42]

Who Pays? Who Benefits?

The Colts' move, combined with the Orioles' continuing insistence on a new stadium, revived the debate over the value of professional sports to a city, particularly its economic impact. Mayor Schaefer entertained no doubts about the importance of professional teams. In an impassioned April 1984 statement before a U.S. Senate committee considering legislation to halt franchise transfers, he stated:

> A vital part of our community and our economy and our prestige was spirited away under the cover of darkness on a rainy night. . . . The Colts were a vital economic resource. Experts agree that the presence of the Colts generated between $25 to $30 million in economic activity. . . . Their loss leaves an economic void in our hotels, our restaurants. . . . There is a direct relationship of the loss of patronage and harm to the community. Suppliers and concessions, and that intangible but important factor that contributes to local and metropolitan economic development, and of course taxes. . . . It is the equivalent, quite frankly, of losing a major industry.[43]

A majority of American political and business leaders probably shared Schaefer's outlook. They were willing to back up this conviction with tax dollars. By 1987 twenty U.S. and Canadian cities were investing $100 million or more each to refurbish old stadiums or build new ones to hold or attract professional sports franchises. A growing number of Florida communities were financing the construction of extensive training facilities in order to attract or retain an eight-week major league presence during the height of the state's tourist season.[44]

In the midst of this construction boom, a small number of city officials, economists, and irate taxpayers were asking two fundamental questions: who will pay for these new stadiums and who will benefit from them? A growing body of evidence suggested that taxpayers were paying an extremely heavy price to support professional sports while the franchise owners reaped the profits.

Cities seek at least three major benefits from professional sports: the

satisfaction of civic pride, the creation of a positive image of the host community, and economic growth. Major league sports teams clearly provide the two
intangibles, particularly if they win. Whether they spur economic growth or
constitute a parasitic growth on the tax base is a subject of continuing
controversy.

Proponents of stadium spending insist that professional sports produce a
ripple effect in the economy. The spending directly connected with sports
events moves into the community and promotes growth in a variety of local
businesses. The revenues generated by sports move into the city in the form
of salaries paid to athletes and club employees, in services purchased by the
club, and through the taxes the teams collect for the city and state. The sports
dollar when reinvested in other business activities furthers growth in the local
economy. Supporters of this view disagree on the precise "multiplier effect"
of sports spending on the local economy but typically suggest that it is from
two to four times the amount of the money initially spent on this form of
entertainment.[45]

Critics counter that most of the spending on professional sports is in
the form of stadium construction that provides only a temporary economic
stimulus rather than a long-term benefit to the locality. They further note
that this spending is primarily public rather than private investment. The
normal, long-term spending of the professional sports teams goes to businesses that have low growth potential and offer low-paying, part-time service jobs. Food, laundry, and field maintenance are the prime contractors
of professional sports. The taxes sports teams collect at best offset the
local services they receive, including fire, sanitation, police, and public
transportation.[46]

The critics have the best of the argument. In 1979 during the crisis
surrounding the sale of the Orioles, the Baltimore *Sun* and *Evening Sun*
accumulated data on the economic impact of major league baseball. The
Orioles directly participated in the local economy in four ways. The team
paid salaries to its players, administrative personnel, and stadium employees.
It purchased services such as food, laundry, and maintenance, primarily from
local vendors. The team passed on the taxes it collected on ticket and
concessions sales. Finally, the existence of a team in Baltimore created
additional jobs in the local information media.[47]

During the 1978 season the Orioles steadily employed twenty-five athletes
on the parent Baltimore team. All twenty-five had a residence in the Baltimore area. Fourteen players, with a combined income of $1 million, lived in
the area on a yearly basis. The majority, however, lived in the suburbs rather
than the city. The Orioles also employed an administrative staff of thirty, who
received $307,000 in total annual compensation. No data exists on their
domiciles, but in view of the general U.S. pattern of suburban living, many
and quite possibly the majority lived outside Baltimore's city limits. The

team employed approximately 400 part-time workers—grounds crew, ushers, parking attendants, security guards—whom it paid $440,000 for seasonal jobs. Since a number of these employees normally lived close to the stadium, they constituted one of the most direct Orioles investments in the Baltimore city economy.

Work contracted with local service companies was a second way that the club pumped money directly into the local economy. The Orioles' prime contractor was Volume Services, the company that handled stadium concessions. Volume Services reported that it spent approximately $750,000 on supplies, mostly food and containers, and another $750,000 on salaries for between 300 and 500 part-time employees during the course of the 1978 season.

The other major contractor, the team's cleaning service, appropriately named Orioles General Cleaning Services, earned about $150,000 annually from its baseball business. It employed about seventy-five part-time workers at the existing minimum wage of $2.90 to handle Orioles requirements.

The city and state annually put $1.3 million into stadium repairs and renovation. Baltimore's share of this expense was $300,000 per annum. According to city parks director Douglas Tawney, the city spent a total of $1.1 million to provide services for the two major sports franchises in 1978. Entertainment taxes and the city's cut of concessions and parking allowed Baltimore to "break even," Tawney stated.[48]

These figures indicated that the Orioles' spending had a limited impact on Baltimore's economy and that the team received at least equivalent services from the taxpayers. Moreover, the Orioles, like most professional sports teams, enjoyed special concessions from local and state authorities that reduced their financial burdens. These included a growing share of concessions income, free office facilities, and low rent. Hoffberger's financially stretched Orioles of 1978 might have had a claim on special assistance from the city. Williams's Orioles were normally one of the most profitable teams in baseball.

Schaefer and other advocates of stadium construction have argued that professional sports stimulate individual spending that might not otherwise occur. Specifically, Schaefer stated that a new facility located in the Inner Harbor area would bring an additional $25 million into the city economy. The claim is open to question. Money spent on professional sports is by definition "discretionary income." The availability of professional sports simply directs that money into one area of the local economy rather than another.[49]

In exchange for the questionable economic benefits and unquestioned psychological uplift that sports provide, Orioles officials were asking the state to provide a $100 million stadium. The club wanted this facility to increase its profits. New stadiums are expensive to build, costly to maintain, and—as long as they are publicly financed—will constitute a significant drain on taxpayers without providing corresponding benefits to the local economy. Cities that undertake the construction of a new facility are usually influenced by other calculations. Primary among these are intangibles such as civic image and fear that failure to meet the demands of professional sports franchises will cause teams to move. The decision to build two stadiums in the Baltimore Inner Harbor is a case study of noneconomic factors in operation.

Call It Babe Ruth Stadium

In 1983, seeking to associate his major objective with the memory of Baltimore's most illustrious athletic son, Edward Bennett Williams suggested that the city build a baseball park "near the new harbor area and call it Babe Ruth Memorial Stadium—wouldn't that be perfect."[50] The city and state establishment politely ignored Williams. Then Robert Irsay's move changed the entire context of Baltimore's lengthy stadium debate. The city and state had lost a popular institution that provided Baltimore and Maryland with a favorable national image. State politicians began to contemplate the loss of the other major sports franchise and gradually concluded that they had to pay Williams's price to ensure the Orioles' continued presence. They also decided to try to attract a new professional football team. Concerns about prestige drove the political leaders to make the concession that they had avoided for most of the decade: to build a new stadium. In emotional testimony before a 1985 congressional hearing on franchise shifts, Schaefer chastised Governor Hughes and the legislature for failing to "recognize the importance of a franchise in a city until it leaves." He complained that the Colts' move meant the loss to a "city that is struggling like ours" of jobs, tax base, and entertainment, "all the things that keep a city alive."[51]

Schaefer kept up the pressure on the state for a new facility. In addition to his appearances before the U.S. Congress, the mayor appointed a task force to study the issue. To no one's surprise, the mayor's task force issued a report that was highly critical of the existing stadium and recommended the construction of a new facility in downtown Baltimore.[52]

Williams responded to the task force report by indicating his willingness to discuss a long-term lease in a new stadium. "I have no intentions of leaving Baltimore and never have," Williams reiterated, adding that he was ready to consider a long-term lease once he knew what terms the city was offering.[53]

The state's politicians remained divided over the issue of building a new stadium and over the question of its location. Mayor Schaefer emerged as the strongest backer of a new stadium. The mayor, whose plans to run for governor were already well advanced, insisted the new stadium had to be built in downtown Baltimore as part of the reconstruction of the city center. He faced opposition from two sides. State attorney general Stephen Sachs, another unannounced candidate for the Democratic nomination for governor, used the stadium issue to illustrate his claims that the mayor was too tied to Baltimore's local interests to represent the state successfully. Sachs advocated building a new stadium between Washington and Baltimore to complete the transformation of the Orioles into a true regional franchise.[54]

Within the city council, Schaefer faced opposition from the representatives of the Memorial Stadium neighborhood. Area merchants and politicians, concerned about losing income to the downtown business district, wanted the city either to refurbish the existing facility or put the new stadium on Memorial Stadium's site. Many General Assembly delegates from the populous Washington suburbs resisted putting state money into a stadium for Baltimore's team.[55]

While the political battle heated up, Governor Hughes was laying the groundwork for eventual General Assembly approval of a bill authorizing the construction of a new stadium. Following up on Schaefer's initiative, Hughes commissioned a second consultants' study of the stadium question. The governor's consultants' report, released on 26 August 1985, recommended construction of a new multipurpose stadium and the creation of a Maryland Professional Sports Authority to oversee the design, construction, and financing of the new facility. The consultants' report suggested four possible sites: Camden Yards inside Baltimore and three locations situated between Washington and Baltimore. The advantages of a site outside the city were fourfold: easy access from major roadways, extensive parking, an increased ability to attract Washington fans, and considerably lower land costs.[56]

Hughes followed up on the initial report by appointing a sports commission, led by Baltimore attorney Bernard Manekin, to make recommendations on site location. Meanwhile, the governor announced that he would recommend that the General Assembly enact legislation authorizing a Maryland Sports Authority and also setting up a special state lottery to help finance stadium construction.[57]

On 28 January 1986 the Manekin Commission, after receiving yet another consultants' report, announced its recommendations for a site. The commission ranked Lansdowne, located in Baltimore County near Interstate 95 and the Baltimore beltway, as having the best location, land cost, and accessibility. Its second choice was another site outside Baltimore near Baltimore-Washington International Airport. Camden Yards was the third-place choice, primarily because of the cost of acquiring land.[58]

The Manekin Commission's report irritated Baltimore's mayor and a number of the city's most important politicians. An angry Schaefer told reporters that he was drafting a letter of protest to the governor and, criticizing the commission's reasoning, added: "It doesn't take a genius to figure out that if you have 25,000 people coming into an area, the restaurants and businesses would benefit."[59] State Senate president Melvin Steinberg (D.-Baltimore), a Schaefer ally, calmly discounted the political impact of the commission's recommendations, noting that the state's leaders would make their decision based on two critical factors: the "economic impact" and "what site would be in the best interests of the Baltimore Orioles." He added that "you want to have it in metropolitan Baltimore."[60]

Exploiting this opportunity, Edward Bennett Williams pressed for the construction of a baseball-only facility. The Orioles owner gave Manekin a letter that the latter read to a 29 January General Assembly hearing on the proposed Sports Authority. In the letter, Williams indicated his pleasure that a new facility would be built, emphasized his interest in the construction of a facility intended to accommodate baseball alone, and expressed "our willingness to enter into a long-term arrangement for the use of such a stadium, assuming that we can work out satisfactory arrangements." Williams's spokesmen stressed the need for the state's warring politicians to agree on enabling legislation while public and political support for the new stadium existed.[61]

Williams had little influence on the political debate. The battle over a new stadium continued for another eighteen months. Governor Hughes presented his proposal for the creation of a Sports Authority that would possess wide authority over both raising funds and spending them. Under the Hughes plan the Sports Authority would control a state lottery dedicated to funding the new stadium. The body would oversee the actual construction process. Once the stadium was built, the Sports Authority would maintain the facility, utilizing the proceeds from the lottery and admission tax revenues.[62]

Maryland House speaker Benjamin Cardin (D.-Baltimore) spoke for the majority in both houses in rejecting the Hughes plan. Legislators objected to the degree of independence that the Hughes proposal would invest in the Sports Authority. Manekin and other sponsors argued that the Sports Authority needed broad powers to carry out the program of building and administering a new facility. The leaders of the state legislature were particularly insistent on putting a man they trusted at the head of the new authority. Hughes, defending the prerogatives of the executive, declined to name his choice for head of the Sports Authority until the state legislature passed an authorizing bill.[63]

Ultimately, Hughes and the legislature compromised. In order to get a Sports Authority with limited powers, the governor agreed to rule out a number of candidates for chairman prior to passage of the bill. The General Assembly empowered the Sports Authority to determine the site and configuration of a new stadium. However, it required that the Sports Authority return to the General Assembly for authorization prior to entering into a contract to build the new facility.[64]

The Sports Authority, under its new chairman, Herbert Belgrade, a prominent and politically reliable Baltimore attorney, wisely spent the rest of 1986 studying sites and waiting on election returns. Attorney General Sachs, the underdog in the Democratic primary to Mayor Schaefer, continued to exploit the stadium question in his effort to convince Maryland Democrats that Schaefer represented only the interests of the white businessmen of Baltimore. Sachs chose a prominent black Baltimore politician, former Representative Parren Mitchell, as his running mate to underline his charges that Schaefer was insensitive to the needs of most of the citizens of his own city. He portrayed Schaefer's insistence on placing the stadium in downtown Baltimore as another example of the mayor's policies of subordinating state interests to those of the city's business elite.[65]

Schaefer handily won both the Democratic primary and the November 1986 general election. The mayor's victories set the stage for decisive action on the construction of a new stadium. On 6 November 1986, Governor-elect Schaefer called for quick action by the legislature to fund a new stadium. Less than a month later, the Sports Authority delivered its plan. As a Baltimore *Sun* editorial observed, the Sports Authority wanted to build "Schaefer's kind of stadium." Its proposal called for the construction of two separate facilities, one each for football and baseball, in downtown Baltimore, adjacent to the Harbor Place development. Edward Bennett Williams, too, would have his kind of stadium.[66]

Schaefer wasted little time in opening a lobbying campaign for the new facility with the legislature while rallying influential public support for the Sports Authority plan. The Maryland General Assembly, confronted with a powerful, activist governor, initially balked. The legislators refused to raise taxes to pay for the facility as the new governor first proposed. Schaefer learned from this error and by late March 1987 had found a method of financing that both houses could support. The governor dropped his proposal for a ten cents per gallon increase in the state tax on beer and offered a plan for financing the stadium through bond issues and a state lottery.

Schaefer's efforts enjoyed the active assistance of Williams, who testified in support of the bill and lobbied legislators. Williams linked the Orioles' continued profitability, and thus, by inference, their permanence in the Baltimore area, to construction of a new facility. He again pledged to sign a long-term lease agreement. The $200 million stadium proposal faced heated opposition from a loose coalition of groups, including representatives of the suburban Washington counties, the Memorial Stadium neighborhood, and some rural areas. However, Schaefer's political allies moved the bill smoothly through the legislative process and won the approval of both houses in early

April. Schaefer signed the legislation and the plan weathered a court challenge during the summer. In the fall of 1987, Orioles management could look forward to playing baseball in a new facility in 1992.[67]

By the winter of 1987–88, Edward Bennett Williams was in an ironic position. Through hard work and good luck he had secured the construction of a new stadium and built a strong marketing position. However, he was saddled with one of the weakest teams in the major leagues. In order to fully exploit the advantages he enjoyed, Williams had to build a winning baseball team.

Epilogue
The Short Season of
Edward Bennett Williams

I've got the manager of the year on the field and the executive of the year in the front office. What am I going to do?
—Edward Bennett Williams, December 1979

People say I'm a meddler. I call it being a governor. . . . I have a substantial interest in this club, and I'm going to protect it. . . . The team is always on my mind. It nags me all the time. It's distracting. I want to win it all again.
—Edward Bennett Williams, March 1986

On the afternoon of 11 November 1987 Orioles owner Edward Bennett Williams introduced his new management team during a two-hour press conference at Baltimore Memorial Stadium. Roland Hemond, a "little man with Marty Feldman eyes and the energy level of plutonium," took over as team general manager.[1] The charming, talkative Hemond was an aggressive trader with wide major league experience, including a tour working for Bill Veeck. Doug Melvin, the specialist in minor league affairs and Williams protégé, took command of the Orioles farm system. Frank Robinson, an Orioles coach, became Williams's special assistant and, shortly after the beginning of the 1988 season, succeeded Cal Ripken, Sr., as team manager. Another black former sports star, Calvin Hill, recently appointed a member of the team board of directors, assumed the post of vice president for administrative personnel. Quoting Churchill, Williams announced the "end of the beginning" for his team.

What *Washington Post* sportswriter Thomas Boswell called the start of the "Big Ed Era," was destined for a short duration.[2] Within a month Williams entered the hospital for extended cancer treatment. Within ten months, the Orioles owner was dead. Williams's short season of full control of the Orioles, however, marked the beginning of a painful but necessary major restructuring of the club.

Williams had put together a management team that reflected his own impatient disposition. Under Hemond, the Orioles quickly reorganized their pitching staff and acquired a number of new outfielders and infielders. Melvin, who had served as interim general manager, began restructuring the minor league program, firing a number of scouts, managers, and coaches, hiring others, stressing the recruitment of minority players, and shifting the team's AA affiliation. Robinson had a reputation as a good judge of talent. He would get on-the-job training needed to bid for a general manager's position while serving as the owner's extra pair of eyes within the organization. Finally, Williams explained, Hill would monitor "a deadly disease that overtook this organization. Never again will we be guilty of ethnic or gender insensitivity."[3]

Williams's analysis of his organization pointed up weaknesses that included a bad farm system, an unwillingness to make difficult decisions, and racial prejudice. He laid responsibility for these problems at the feet of departed general manager Henry Peters. Williams's comments and judgments were tinged with bitterness that reflected his exasperation with the team's four-year decline. The dignified Peters declined to respond directly to these charges, but his oblique comments indicated that he had been wounded by Williams's statements. Peters was willing to accept a share of the responsibility for the Orioles' decline. "When you lose, the blame is shared. . . . It's partly our fault, partly the players', the scouts', the minor leagues'," he told a reporter near the end of the 1987 season.[4] Peters pointedly reminded questioners that "nonprofessionals," meaning Williams, also had a role in creating the team's poor record.

Williams was on firm ground in pointing to the mediocre quality of the Orioles' player development program. The club's farm system was consistently one of the weakest in baseball throughout Peters's tenure. "I love Hank," one general manager told a *Washington Post* reporter, "but that farm system was terrible. His friend [Giordano] didn't do him any favors."[5] During Peters's tenure no player selected in the first round of the amateur draft made the transition to the big leagues. Williams, however, had contributed to weakening the minor league program by sacrificing top draft choices for aging free agent players.

Much of Williams's pique against Peters was the result of temperamental differences. Once the club began losing, the aggressive Williams was incapable of coexisting with the patient, cautious Peters. Williams wanted immediate change. Peters stressed slow improvement. The club's baseball management split into two warring camps filled with Peters and Williams loyalists. The fruits of impatience were decisions to employ players like the talented but troubled Alan Wiggins, a choice Williams pressed on the reluctant Peters in 1985. Williams paid heavily for that decision, handing over a large guaranteed salary to a player who disrupted club morale. On the other hand, the club clearly needed more than the small, cosmetic personnel changes that Peters introduced in 1985–87. Owner and general manager were unable to cooperate effectively in a crisis, and a separation became inevitable and necessary. Peters commented that he was "relieved at being relieved."[6] He quickly found employment with the wide authority he wanted as president of the Cleveland Indians.

Williams's charges of racial intolerance are harder to evaluate. Peters had a reputation for treating all club employees fairly. He was proud of the club's record on community relations and its treatment of black athletes. However, the Orioles were very short of blacks at all levels of the organization and employed none in the front office. The club's scouting staff apparently searched primarily for blacks who fit a predetermined profile: power hitters. One result of Orioles insensitivity to race issues was low black attendance at a stadium located in the middle of a heavily black neighborhood. Peters admitted that he was "somewhat mystified by it [low attendance]," adding, "Certainly it can't be prejudice. . . . We don't boycott them on coaching or any position. . . . I don't know if it's solely economics."[7]

Williams's new management team tried to field an improved major league squad while restocking the minor league system. The club traded to acquire younger players with some major league experience to fill gaps in its lineup and pitching rotation. "Part of the plan was to find help for 1988," Hemond explained; "We weren't in the position to trade for the future. The future is now. We added some players who are in the good age bracket, the mid-20s. They give us help now, but it also allows our farm system to work in players without rushing them."[8] A more competitive club would help to keep attendance levels high.

Another benefit of a younger club was a reduction in the team's high salary level. The use of young players, trades, and the retirement of a number of highly paid older athletes, together with limits on future long-term contracts, would bring down costs.[9]

Williams's new-look Orioles entered the 1988 season by losing their first twenty-one games, setting a series of negative records that was a source of grave embarrassment to the owner and his management team. Seven of the losses were to Peters's Cleveland Indians. The Orioles were amazingly inept during the first weeks of play, raising comparisons with the 1962 New York Mets and attracting the sort of negative national media attention that rekindled Baltimore's civic inferiority complex. Young players were shuffled between Baltimore and Rochester throughout the year as the Orioles desperately sought help.[10]

On 31 May the seriously ill Williams handed over effective control of decision making to one of his younger law partners, Larry Lucchino. The new team president moved forward with plans for a total overhaul of the team, while a dying Williams opened negotiations for the sale of the Orioles.

Under Lucchino, the club took important steps in the rebuilding process while cutting its financial overhead. The team had spent itself into a corner. Its payroll skyrocketed in 1984 and 1985 as a result of a World Series championship and subsequent long-term signings of free agents and major stars like Eddie Murray. By the end of the 1985 season, the Orioles were carrying the third largest payroll in the major leagues. The subsequent collapse of the team had little effect on its salary scale. In 1987 the Orioles compiled one of the worst won-lost records in club history with the sixth highest payroll in the major leagues. The club's 1988 payroll, an estimated $13.5 million, was still in the top half of baseball's salary scale. In an effort to reduce overhead and to stock talent, the club parted with many of its best and highest-paid veterans during the 1988 season, sending pitcher Mike Boddicker, outfielder Fred Lynn, and pinch hitter deluxe Jim Dwyer to contenders. In December the club traded veteran star Eddie Murray and his $2 million annual contract to Los Angeles for a number of younger players. By reducing the payroll and long-term indebtedness, the Orioles became more attractive to potential buyers.[11]

On 12 August, in the midst of the most dismal season in team history, Williams lost his long and courageous struggle against cancer. Ultimately, the 1988 Orioles finished with a 54–107 record, the worst in the major leagues. In December Williams's widow sold the club to a group of investors led by businessman Eli Jacobs.

Both the Orioles and major league baseball were entering an uncertain era. The political and economic relationships that defined the sport's profitability were in flux. City and state governments continued to meet organized baseball's demands but, in many cases, were growing resentful of the costly outlays required to build new stadiums. Political pressures were growing for another round of expansion. Long-dormant issues of equal treatment exploded upon the sport. Management-labor relations were tense. The television networks and advertisers, dissatisfied with the benefits they received from expensive baseball broadcasting, threatened to cut back their payments. Only the minor leagues appeared to be satisfied with their dependent but profitable relationship with the majors. The manner in which the major leagues dealt with these larger problems, as much as the ability of Orioles management to successfully rebuild the team, would affect the continued profitability of baseball in Baltimore.

They May Not Have the Necessities

No issue loomed larger than baseball's continuing racial discrimination problems. The sport's race relations record again came to the fore in the spring of 1987. Baseball, like U.S. society in general, lost interest in the fate of its black minority in the 1970s. The struggle against the Vietnam War increasingly mobilized white American liberals, while the triumphs of the civil rights movement of the 1960s encouraged the belief that the United States was eliminating discrimination. But the successes of the civil rights movement had been primarily political. Economic discrimination remained rooted in U.S. society, and organized baseball was extremely slow in responding to this problem.

Baseball, while complimenting itself on the success of integration, had maintained barriers against blacks. Minority athletes could perform and win handsome rewards on the playing field but were effectively barred from management positions. Only extreme public pressure dented this color line. In 1974 the owners finally yielded to widespread demands from the press, civil rights advocates, and liberal politicians for a black manager. Cleveland hired Frank Robinson as the major leagues' first black field manager. Subsequently, two other blacks, Larry Doby and Maury Wills, had brief managerial careers, and Robinson went on to manage San Francisco for three and a half years. A small number of blacks held coaching positions.

Until Hank Aaron and Bill Lucas entered the Atlanta front office in 1976, no black held a senior executive position in major league baseball. In their efforts to win front office positions, blacks faced a subtler form of discrimination. Baseball's resistance to their entry into executive offices was not expressed in overtly racist terms. Baseball executives insisted that blacks could join the management team if they were willing to "pay their dues" by working in low-paid minor league positions. Teams hired few blacks for these jobs, however, and fewer still advanced from minor league employment. Blacks were trying to break into an exclusive club. Baseball executives hired and promoted individuals with whom they were comfortable: white ex-ballplayers who shared their background, outlook, and prejudices. Although managers, coaches, and front office personnel circulated easily among the major and minor league teams, few blacks entered into this active employment market.

Commissioner Bowie Kuhn provided little leadership on racial matters. Kuhn did respond to public pressure and the threat of federal legal action in 1974 to prod the owners into hiring a black manager. The commissioner and his employers appear to have correctly judged that public attention would move on to other issues once a black was managing.[12] The teams discovered ways to mute occasional protests over continued segregation in baseball front offices. In 1980 the Boston Red Sox were searching for a new manager. The club, the last team to integrate, traditionally employed few black athletes and kept its front office lily-white. To fend off embarrassing press inquiries, the Red Sox leaked word that Baltimore coach Frank Robinson was one of three finalists for the job. Then Boston hired a white. The Red Sox never bothered to contact either the Orioles or Robinson about his interest or availability. A disgusted Robinson commented: "When you hear you're in the final three and you're not even contacted for an interview, then you know they're not sincere."[13]

Blacks also were stereotyped as players. The success of power-hitting outfielders like Aaron, Robinson, and Willie Mays encouraged scouts to search for this sort of black player while generally ignoring blacks capable of playing skill positions: pitchers, catchers, and middle infielders. Baseball executives turned a blind eye to this sort of discrimination.[14]

In 1987, Kuhn's replacement, Peter Ueberroth, tried to nudge the sport into dismantling its racial barriers. The 1987 season was the fortieth anniversary of Jackie Robinson's integration of the national game at the major league level. Ueberroth called on the owners to honor both Robinson and the concept of racial equality with ceremonies and other symbolic gestures.[15]

Ueberroth's effort received an unexpected boost when the seventy-year-old Dodgers director of player personnel, Al Campanis, a one-time Robinson teammate and friend, went on national television on 7 April 1987. In a few startling minutes, Campanis laid bare the prejudices that underlay baseball's treatment of blacks. Asked why baseball lacked black executives, Campanis responded: "I don't believe it's prejudice. I truly believe that they may not have some of the necessities to be, let's say, a field manager, or perhaps a general manager. . . . I don't say all of them, but how many [black] quarterbacks do you have? How many pitchers do you have that are black? So, it just might be—why are black men . . . not good swimmers? Because they don't have the buoyancy?"[16] "It was," commented the *Washington Post*, "a painful and embarrassing thing to watch."[17] The Dodgers fired Campanis in response to growing public protest.

Prodded by Ueberroth and by the national media, the major league teams began hiring minorities for front office positions. Two teams even offered managerial positions to black coaches. In February 1989, at the urging of incoming commissioner A. Bartlett Giamatti, National League owners appointed Bill White as league president. White, an intelligent, articulate veteran of the black players' struggle for equal treatment in the 1950s and 1960s, took over a position that, despite its strictly limited powers, offered a pulpit for pressing black demands for equal treatment. The central question remained, however: was the owners' action a prelude to the integration of baseball management or simply a public relations gesture like the 1974 hiring of the first black manager?

Edward Bennett Williams had committed his team to a major change in its racial hiring policies. An embarrassed Williams expressed surprise that the Orioles had no blacks in the front office, although he had frequented team headquarters during eight years as owner. He ordered the immediate hiring of three black summer interns. Later, he would hire a black public relations assistant as well as place Robinson and Hill in prominent front office positions. The problem went beyond affirmative action in the front offices. Williams discovered that only 5 percent of the Orioles' minor league players were black. Moreover, the Orioles, and major league teams in general, drew very few black fans to their games. Only 6.8 percent of major league attendance was black, in spite of the sport's relatively low cost and frequent central city location. Black fear of white crowds and knowledge of the sport's racist history and practices effectively discouraged attendance.[18] Organized baseball faced major tasks in recruiting qualified athletes and executives and in breaking down barriers to black attendance and attracting black fans. Based on the sport's past history, blacks were entitled to regard baseball's pledges of action with skepticism.

The Public-Private Partnership

Blacks were not alone in expressing their doubts about major league owners and their professions of goodwill. A small but growing number of taxpayers and public officials at both the state and city level were annoyed by the costs of providing support for professional sports teams and the owners' use of blackmail, in the form of threats of franchise relocation, to extract concessions from government. A few cities resisted. In San Francisco, voters rejected plans to build a stadium in the downtown area. The city government of St. Louis refused to let the owner of the NFL Cardinals play them off against county government. St. Louis lost its football team, and San Francisco apparently would lose its baseball team to a neighboring California city. As long as other city and suburban governments were ready to offer new stadiums and tax breaks to professional sports, municipalities with teams would have to shoulder the heavy costs of new construction or accept the loss of their clubs.

In retrospect, public funding of sports stadiums has proved to be a major error in governmental policy. Cities clearly overestimated the income enhancement potential of professional sports. When combined with the political ambitions of individual city leaders and local pride, this miscalculation encouraged bidding among cities for teams. Stadium construction siphoned tax dollars away from other, more critical public needs. In the 1960s and 1970s, the boom in construction of multipurpose stadiums was frequently linked to the redevelopment of central business districts. By the 1980s, the owners of professional sports teams were demanding separate facilities for each team and increasingly looking to wealthy suburbs as the alternative to playing in the city. The success of Edward Bennett Williams in winning a baseball-only stadium in Baltimore encouraged Redskins owner Jack Kent Cooke, a man whose estimated worth was $700 million, to demand that Washington build his "fans" a new 70,000-seat football-only stadium or see the NFL team relocate to a suburban site. The existing facility, Robert F. Kennedy Stadium, seating over 50,000, was well designed, capable of being easily upgraded, relatively modern, centrally located, serviced by first-class public transportation, and inadequately utilized. Faced with considerable resistance from the press and community, Cooke ultimately scaled down his demands to a piece of well-located public land near the old stadium, together with parking revenues, and offered to build the new facility himself. Mayor Marion S. Barry and other city leaders, with one eye on their objective of attracting a baseball team, agreed in principle to Cooke's plan.[19]

Williams never threatened to relocate his team but consistently drove hard bargains on his Memorial Stadium lease. In the winter of 1987–88 he was playing hardball over the terms of his lease in the new Inner Harbor stadium. The Orioles publicly criticized the Sports Authority's choice of an architectural firm to build the facility, and negotiations for the team's stadium lease became deadlocked. Finally, with angry state legislators threatening to cut off funding for construction, Governor Schaefer sought a meeting with Williams to resolve the issue.[20]

Williams attempted to calm agitated legislators by renewing his Memorial Stadium lease for another two years in April 1988. However, the Orioles owner refused to sign a lease for a new facility under the terms offered by the Sports Authority. He complained that the Authority wanted the Orioles to spend $25 million to erect scoreboards, a television screen, luxury boxes, and concession stands. "I'm a tenant. Whatever they get out of me has to be in rent. They know that. . . . Whoever heard of a tenant paying for where they live? . . . They kept telling me what a great deal it was. If it is, build it. I'm not in the construction business. I've had enough trouble running a baseball team."[21] Williams redefined the nature of tenancy when he added that he wanted the type of profit-sharing lease agreement he enjoyed at Memorial Stadium, explaining: "It makes the city a partner in the operation. . . . This type lease buffers me against hard times and lets them share in the good times."[22]

Compounding state and local concern about the stadium lease was Williams's declining health. After his lengthy cancer treatment in December 1987, Williams revealed that in the event of his death the family would sell the team. The combination of Williams's illness and the lack of a long-term stadium deal made local officials and the Baltimore press nervous. If the team was not anchored in Baltimore by means of a long-term lease at the time of Williams's death, past experience suggested that local interests might lack the organization and capital to purchase it. Another out-of-town owner, perhaps another Irsay, might acquire the team and move the Orioles to a larger, more profitable market area. The presence of a number of wealthy potential bidders in baseball-hungry Washington was particularly troubling.[23]

Fortunately, Williams, with his extraordinary sense of drama, was ready with a final personal coup de théâtre. On 2 May, shortly after the team broke its twenty-one-game losing streak, the Orioles staged Fantastic Fan Night to honor the club's long-suffering followers. A crowd of 50,402 filled Memorial Stadium to hear Governor Schaefer announce agreement on a fifteen-year stadium lease. As the crowd erupted in applause, an emaciated and visibly exhausted Williams basked in a final moment of public adulation.

Under the agreement, the Orioles will pay no rent but share their stadium profits on a 50–50 basis with the Sports Authority. The agreement committed the Orioles to play in Memorial Stadium until the new facility is completed (probably in 1992), specified the number of the new stadium's seats and luxury boxes as well as the size of its cafeterias and public picnic areas, and gave the Orioles a major say in the design.[24]

Williams's skillful handling of the lease agreement had an additional benefit. It isolated the club from sharing the burden of escalating stadium costs, thereby increasing the Orioles' attractiveness to potential bidders. In early September the Sports Authority reported that its initial estimates of construction costs were low by as much as $100 million. Rapidly rising costs of land acquisition in Camden Yards was the main factor in the sudden rise, although its concessions to the Orioles also figured in the Authority's new estimate. An angry Schaefer instructed the Sports Authority to find ways to cut building costs.[25]

Williams's foresight brought immediate benefits to his family. A franchise with a reduced payroll, a highly favorable stadium rental arrangement, and a solid fan base was very attractive to potential buyers. Even before Williams's death, a number of bidders emerged. Two of the groups were Baltimore based: U.S. Fidelity and Guaranty Insurance and a syndicate headed by Jerold Hoffberger. However, Williams avoided making a deal. After his death, Agnes Williams, his widow, sold out to the group headed by New York investor Eli Jacobs for approximately $70 million. While the 6 December 1988 sale left many Baltimore fans concerned about a continuation of outside control of a civic institution, it promised badly needed stability in the team's front office. Williams's longtime lieutenant, club president Lawrence Lucchino, was a minority partner in the Jacobs syndicate. Under Lucchino, the management team Williams created would have the time to carry forward a total restructuring of the Orioles. Moreover, the Jacobs syndicate was keenly aware of local concern that outside ownership portended a franchise move and pledged that the club would remain in Baltimore "into the twenty-second century."[26]

Expansion

The immediate threat of a franchise move disappeared with the stadium agreement and Jacobs purchase. However, baseball's expansion to Washington remained a potential problem for the Orioles. In the late 1980s organized baseball again was discussing expansion. As in the past, baseball appeared to be acting against its will. In 1987 New York Mets general manager Frank

Cashen summarized management's views, telling a Washington reporter: "Until we get our own house straightened out, it would be ludicrous, almost immoral, to consider expansion. We have struggling franchises to stabilize. We have a network contract to negotiate, probably for less money. We have a labor contract that runs out after '89. Player salaries are still escalating."[27]

Although wary of expansion, baseball owners may yet bend to public pressure. In Washington, the representatives of a number of states with major league ambitions formed a group they called the Task Force on the Expansion of Major League Baseball in November 1987. Seventeen senators and representatives from Florida, Colorado, Arizona, Virginia, and New York participated in the group and lobbied baseball intensively. In April 1988 they threatened to introduce legislation revoking baseball's antitrust exemption in an effort to attract the owners' attention and speed action.[28]

Civic leaders from Washington, D.C., hoped to benefit from congressional pressure and secure another major league team. By the mid-1980s, the city's efforts were well organized. The Washington D.C. Baseball Commission actively lobbied the major league owners, while at least three well-financed ownership alternatives existed. Washington's wealth, market size, and political clout obviously made it a legitimate bidder for a new franchise.[29]

Talk of expansion in Washington was likely to send a chill through the front office of the Baltimore Orioles. The team's profit was closely tied to its ability to attract Washington fans. By 1988 nearly one-quarter of Orioles attendance came from the Washington metropolitan area. Moreover, the long-term inability of two franchises to operate profitably on a consistent basis in the wealthy, populous San Francisco Bay area was a pointed warning of the danger of planting a new team, even a National League club, in the Baltimore-Washington market. Washington baseball boosters blithely ignored these realities while Edward Bennett Williams tried to soothe the feelings of Washington fans by publicly renouncing his right to veto expansion to his home city. Williams could make this gesture because owners in both leagues recognized the perils of expansion into the Orioles' market. The Orioles' new owners had to convince Washington leaders that a regional team made more sense than two-club competition in a single geographic market.[30]

The High Cost of Sports Programming

The chances of expansion improved in December 1988. Outgoing commissioner Ueberroth's skillful handling of baseball's latest television contract appeared to remove one barrier to expansion. The sports programming boom of the 1970s that created enormous profits for all sports had leveled off by the early 1980s. Both ABC and NBC encountered growing problems selling advertising time on baseball broadcasts. In 1985 ABC had to drop its World

Series advertising rates to attract sponsors. NBC complained of trouble finding sponsors, especially for its game of the week broadcasts. In the mid-1980s ABC scaled down its Monday night baseball broadcasting. Night baseball had trouble attracting viewers and sponsors even during the television rerun season.[31]

Equally ominous, professional football, the traditional pacesetter in rights payments, was not producing the ratings, income, or sponsors that the networks expected. In 1987 the NFL and the major networks signed a series of new pacts that cut football's TV payments. NFL commissioner Pete Rozelle, probably the most skilled of professional sports negotiators, managed to offset the decline in national network money through cable television deals. The outlook for a profitable renewal of baseball's network pact in 1988 appeared bleak.[32]

For the Orioles, any reduction of national television income would be a serious blow. After reaching 2 million in paid attendance in 1983, 1984, and 1985, home crowds, while still large, gradually declined as the Orioles fielded a series of mediocre teams. Local television income was relatively stable, although cable television finally appeared ready to generate higher profits. The club received a financial setback when a record radio rights deal with station WCBM fell apart. The radio station was unable to meet its payments. In the winter of 1987 the Orioles reclaimed their broadcasting rights and sold them at a substantially lower price to Washington's WTOP radio. WTOP, in turn, sold flagship station rights to Baltimore's WBAL.[33]

On 14 December 1988 Commissioner Ueberroth announced a new television pact that greatly increased baseball's rights payments from the major commercial networks and permitted the sport to establish a pooled national cable arrangement. Under the terms of an exclusive four-year arrangement with CBS, to begin in 1990, the major leagues sold the rights to the All-Star Game, league championship series, and World Series, together with twelve regular-season contests, for $1.1 billion. Sacrificing the venerable, low-rating game of the week, baseball was in a position to sell what amounted to a game of the day package to one of four rival cable sports programming networks for an additional $100 million a year. On 5 January 1989 the major leagues signed a four-year, $400 million accord with the ESPN cable network for the broadcast of 175 games a season.[34]

Under the arrangement, baseball would finally achieve the sort of prime-time national television exposure it had sought since the mid-1960s. As cable service expanded, baseball's rights payments would undoubtedly grow, providing a new source of revenue for owners who continued to face escalating salary demands from players. The sums involved might provide the stimulus needed to restrain the owners from turning 1990 negotiations over the Basic Agreement into another nasty confrontation with the players. Each team's income would increase by approximately $7.5 million under the deal. At the least, the new arrangement encouraged management to proceed with caution rather than permit a strike to consume a major increase in its profits. Unfortunately, money was only part of the mix of issues labor and management faced.

Owners on the Offensive

All of the owners wanted to stem the continuing rise in player salaries, but from their perspective another, equally fundamental, issue was at stake in their relations with the union: control of the sport. For over two decades, the union had steadily circumscribed the owners' power. The owners wanted to halt this trend and perhaps reverse it. The key to dealing effectively with the union was creating discipline among the owners. After the 1985 season, at the urging of Commissioner Ueberroth, the owners closed ranks and began a major offensive against the union. Following a decade of salary inflation caused by their wild spending on free agents and by the effects of salary arbitration, the owners felt they had little to lose. The union's refusal to permit players to submit to random drug testing offered management a club with which to beat the Players Association. Determined to slow salary increases and regain some control over athletes, the owners engaged in a conspiracy to severely restrict free agency. They entered into an unwritten agreement not to bid for any free agent player whom other clubs wanted to retain. In effect, the only players who could enjoy the benefits of free agent status were aging or marginal athletes. When Detroit's star outfielder Kirk Gibson opted for free agency in the winter of 1985, no team bid for his services. Gibson signed with the Tigers. The following year, the Tiger's ace pitcher, Jack Morris, met similar resistance and opted for salary arbitration.

Management vigorously denied that a conspiracy existed. Baltimore's Henry Peters, for example, claimed that neither Gibson nor other free agent players "look like the answer to the problems we have."[35] A few days later, Commissioner Ueberroth told an audience of owners that management was not practicing collusion to stifle free agency but rather responding to the outrageous cost of free agent contracts. "[It's] not conspiracy," he explained, "it's common sense. The pot is dry."[36] George Steinbrenner, whose clubs were loaded with free agent talent, announced that he would decline to bid, relying instead on the Yankees farm system.[37] Edward Bennett Williams, who had spent heavily on free agent talent the previous year, credited Ueberroth with bringing owners to their senses.[38]

Emboldened by this success, the owners announced a number of other policy changes. They vowed to limit long-term contracts to a maximum of three years and to cut back on contract incentives. During the winter of 1985–86, the owners agreed to cut the size of major league squads from twenty-five to twenty-four players. In effect, the owners were terminating the employment of twenty-six major league players. In the long run, club accountants estimated that dropping rosters by one man each would save a total of $10 million in salaries, travel expenses, and related payments per year.[39]

Whatever amount owners ultimately saved by cutting major league rosters, they took a financial bath in 1986. Nineteen of the veterans cut under this decision held guaranteed contracts worth, ironically, $10 million.[40] Moreover, management's display of toughness worsened its already badly strained relationship with the union.

The Players Association found itself under attack on three fronts. Management was openly flaunting the Basic Agreement by practicing collusion to strangle free agency at the same time that it utilized loopholes in the same contract to reduce the number of major league players. Simultaneously, the owners took a tougher stand on drug use, basking in public approbation as they demanded that the players submit to club-administered random testing programs.

Drug use was a major embarrassment for both management and the union. The union was in a particularly difficult position. In defending the privacy rights of the players, it was also damaging the longer-term interests of addicted athletes. Antimanagement feelings among the union leadership appear to have played a significant role in the union's decision to stand firm against any team drug testing plans. In May 1985 a Pittsburgh grand jury indicted a number of drug dealers who specialized in supplying players' habits. By September the press had the names of the players involved in the scandal. The revelations that grew out of the Pittsburgh case involved most major league clubs, including the Orioles, whose free agent right fielder, Lee Lacy, was summoned to testify about his drug use.

Commissioner Ueberroth seized upon the Pittsburgh case to launch a major public relations drive against drug abuse in organized baseball. While badly needed, the Ueberroth approach had overtones of union bashing. During the late summer, the commissioner introduced a mandatory testing plan for all baseball employees, then retreated when the union acted to protect the athletes' constitutional rights to privacy. The Players Association insisted that a drug testing agreement required the players' consent and called for collective bargaining to achieve this end.[41]

The owners canceled the existing drug agreement and announced that they would insert drug testing clauses in each new contract signed with players. The union blocked this move by filing for arbitration. The resourceful Ueberroth managed to blacken the union's image and advance his drug control agenda by summoning all players known to have used drugs for individual meetings. The commissioner announced that he would apply sanctions to each player. *The Sporting News*, while supporting the actions of the owners and the commissioner, admitted that their motives were not "totally pure" and warned that "the drug testing issue promises to keep baseball players and owners at each others' throats throughout the winter, if not beyond."[42]

In February 1986 Ueberroth imposed combinations of fines and community service on all twenty-one players with drug abuse records and insisted that they submit to random drug testing. In addition to disciplining the players, Ueberroth's actions established a precedent for random drug testing, put the commissioner and owners on the high ground, and reinforced public pressure on the union to agree to management's testing plan. The players had little alternative but to accept Ueberroth's sanctions. Contesting the issue in court would expose individual athletes to intense unfavorable media coverage and public condemnation. Marvin Miller damned the players' lack of "guts." The union was prudently silent.[43]

The success of Ueberroth's action emboldened the owners. The cash-short Pittsburgh Pirates filed suit against one of the players involved, out-fielder Dave Parker, to avoid paying $5.3 million in deferred salary that the club still owed him. The Pirates claimed that Parker's use of cocaine seriously effected his performance. The suit, *The Sporting News* commented, had "ugly undertones."[44]

Resisting the pressures exerted by the commissioner, the owners, and a good part of the sporting media, the union held its ground on drug testing issues. At the 1986 winter meetings Ueberroth pronounced baseball "drug free," an optimistic and premature claim. Drug testing likely would be a major and divisive issue when the two sides negotiated a renewal of the Basic Agreement in 1990.

Orioles officials applauded Ueberroth's effort. Peters told reporters, "It's not a program if it doesn't have drug testing."[45] The club, however, took a different tack. The Orioles utilized an unusually good working relationship with player representative Scott McGregor and player agent Ron Shapiro to negotiate individual agreements with a majority of its players permitting random drug testing. The Orioles' accord became a model for a number of teams. It proved to be less than satisfactory from the club's standpoint. Second baseman Alan Wiggins had a history of drug abuse. Asked to evaluate the plan, he stated that it was "not the answer," because the stress on confidentiality would rob the program of its primary tool, "fear" of discovery and punishment. The Orioles apparently arrived at the same conclusions and suspended the program after one year.[46]

The union responded to the owners' offensive with its favorite weapon: arbitration. In February 1986 the union took management to arbitration, claiming the owners had entered into an illegal collusion to kill free agency. The Players Association filed a similar grievance after the owners refused to bid on the 1986 group of free agents. In a separate suit, an impartial arbitrator upheld the union position on drug testing in July 1986.[47]

The Players Association scored a major victory in September 1987 when arbitrator Tom Roberts ruled in favor of the union's contention that the owners had conspired to destroy free agency. Roberts fined the clubs and declared all the players involved in the 1985 case free agents. While a number of the players were by then too old to command serious offers, outfielder Kirk Gibson signed a big new contract with Los Angeles.[48] Bidding for free agents resumed cautiously in the winter of 1987–88, and a number of players switched teams. Hanging over the owners was the probability that the union would win the 1986 free agents' arbitration appeal. This case was more threatening to management because it involved more major stars, including Montreal's Tim Raines and Detroit's Morris. On 31 August 1988, a second independent arbitrator again ruled in favor of the union and criticized management for destroying all vestiges of a free market. The second arbitration decision apparently triggered a salary explosion in the winter of 1988–89, as owners again bid furiously for player talent. The owners exchanged information on their offers in an effort to rein in competitive bidding. The union again filed a grievance. The issue of free agents had triggered the 1981 strike and again appeared to be a major subject for discussion during the talks on a new Basic Agreement.[49]

Management and labor had failed to find a way out of the salary impasse or to find a means of jointly sharing control over the sport. The union refused to relinquish its hard-won gains and utilized arbitration to press for more. Battered by two decades of union success, the owners felt they were being victimized by rules that they could not modify and sought to evade them. Management tactics irritated union leaders and undercut the chances for a negotiated solution. Despite the new television contract, the prospects for labor peace were less than encouraging.

Past, Present, and Future

In the thirty-five years since the major leagues returned to Baltimore, the nature of the baseball business has changed dramatically. A highly conservative, well-entrenched entertainment monopoly during the 1950s, baseball proved incapable of defending its privileges from the encroachments of organized labor or the television industry. Baseball's accommodation with television was eased by the enormous profits broadcasting brought to the sport. The owners have been unable to deal effectively with their organized employees. Between 1966 and 1988 the players won a large share of the profits derived from the exhibition of their talents, together with a major role in regulating the sport.

The owners have successfully established firm control over their player development costs by reducing the size and independence of expensive minor league systems and handing management over to local entrepreneurs. By the 1980s, the minor leagues constituted a source of strength and stability for organized baseball. The minors faced little challenge to their low salary scales from young, ambitious, and insecure players.

The relationship between the major leagues and cities and states that hosted them was much more problematical. While the owners had succeeded in securing public financing of new stadiums in a majority of cases, their tactics, particularly threats of franchise relocation, created local resentment. City, state, and federal officials pressed baseball to add new teams. Commissioner Ueberroth took a public stand against franchise shifts and championed expansion. The owners, however, remained reluctant to assume the economic risks of another expansion.

One factor that almost guaranteed further trouble between baseball and public authority was the sport's disagreeable record in the area of race relations. Baseball's reluctance to open its management structure, combined with its tradition of discouraging black attendance, created powerful resentments among a significant segment of Americans and exposed the sport to steady criticism in the media. Baseball's industriously cultivated public image suffered badly from its racism. Ueberroth sought to counter discrimination with programs of affirmative action in front office hiring. While this move was significant, baseball had yet to confront the practical consequences of policies that promoted segregation in its stadiums. The issue was particularly troubling because a majority of these parks were publicly financed.

Thus, organized baseball entered the last decade of the twentieth century facing serious problems that called for major changes in the structure of a sport that has traditionally been resistant to reform. Baseball, of course, would survive. The question was, in what form?

While baseball wrestled with its larger problems, Orioles fans enjoyed one of the most dramatic and remarkable seasons in the history of baseball. The 1989 Orioles surprised everyone, including club management, by surging back into contention. A young team built on speed and defense seized hold of first place in the American League East in mid-May and held off all challengers for over a hundred days. Ultimately, a veteran and talented Toronto club overtook the Orioles. The young Orioles hung close throughout September, but their challenge fell short in Toronto on the last weekend of the season in two tightly played games. However, the rebuilt Orioles gave a boost to civic pride, provided a spring and summer of fun to a club record 2.5 million fans who crowded Memorial Stadium, and held out the promise of future pennant races. Finally, they constituted posthumous vindication for Edward Bennett Williams, the man who had assembled the team's new management.

Notes

Abbreviations

acc.	accession
D&C	Rochester *Democrat and Chronicle*
FRC	Federal Records Center
House	United States House of Representatives
LC	Library of Congress, Washington, D.C.
MHS	Maryland Historical Society, Baltimore, Md.
NA	National Archives, Washington, D.C.
NBL	National Baseball Library, Cooperstown, N.Y.
NYT	*New York Times*
OH	Oral History
RG	Record Group
SEC	Securities and Exchange Commission, Washington, D.C.
Senate	United States Senate
SI	*Sports Illustrated*
SIN	*Sports Industry News*
TSN	*The Sporting News*
WSJ	*Wall Street Journal*

Introduction

1. House, *Organized Baseball*, pp. 1–2.

2. Ibid., pp. 252–58, 358–59.

3. Ibid., pp. 16, 186–90. Rader, *American Sports*, pp. 117, 346–47. Welch, *Five O'Clock*, p. 88.

4. House, *Organized Baseball*, p. 308. House, *Organized Baseball: Report*, p. 110. *Fortune*, Aug. 1937. See "Baseball's Happy Serfs," *SI*, 5 Mar. 1956, for the players' views.

5. House, *Organized Baseball: Report*, pp. 105–8, 740.

6. The text of the 1946 steering committee report is in ibid., pp. 474–88.

7. Frick, *Games*, pp. 119–21. James, *Historical Baseball Abstract*, p. 148. On the postwar suburbanization of the United States and its impact, see Kenneth Jackson, *Crabgrass Frontier*, pp. 231–45, 272–81.

8. Minutes of the 22 Oct. and 6 Nov. 1951 meetings of the Subcommittee on Monopoly Power, Committee on the Judiciary, "Minutes of Meetings," Celler Papers,

LC. House, *Organized Professional Team Sports* (1957), pp. 1796–97. House, *Organized Baseball*, pp. 474–93. *NYT*, 27 Feb. 1957.

9. MacPhail and Dalton interviews. Reidenbaugh, *The Sporting News*, p. 182.

10. *Newsweek*, 8 June 1953. *TSN*, 10 June 1953.

11. Rader, *American Sports*, pp. 286–87. House, *Organized Baseball*, p. 137.

12. Flemming, *Dizziest Season*, pp. 20, 246. Voigt, *American Baseball*, 2:231. *Broadcasting*, 8 Feb. 1954. Rader, *American Sports*, p. 242.

13. *Broadcasting*, 8 Feb., 12 Apr. 1954. On the failure of the New York Giants to utilize television successfully, see Barber, *1947*, p. 19.

14. Senate, *Broadcasting and Televising Baseball*, pp. 69–96, 167–77. Horowitz, "Sports Broadcasting," p. 279.

15. Horowitz, "Sports Broadcasting," p. 279. Senate, *Broadcasting and Televising Baseball*, p. 145.

16. Medinger to Patterson, 12 Aug. 1952, "Television prior to 1953," Subject Files, NBL. Sisson to Patterson, 13 Aug. 1952, ibid. Lane to Patterson, 20 Aug. 1952, ibid. House, *Organized Baseball*, pp. 97, 280, 971.

17. House, *Organized Baseball*, pp. 97–105, 381–84. *Business Week*, 5 Dec. 1953.

18. *TSN*, 18 Feb. 1953. *Television Age*, Oct. 1953. Horowitz, "Market Entrenchment."

19. *Television Age*, Oct. 1953. Toolson v. New York Yankees 346 US 356 (1953). *Broadcasting*, 18 Jan. 1954. *TSN*, 4 Mar. 1953.

20. House, *Organized Baseball*, pp. 31–33, 76–78.

21. *Broadcasting*, 20 July, 16 Nov. 1953. *TSN*, 25 Nov. 1953.

22. Craig, "Organized Baseball," pp. 2–4, 73. On the decline in entertainment spending, see Sklar, *Movie-Made America*, pp. 272, 274. Kenneth Jackson, *Crabgrass Frontier*, pp. 231–45.

23. Polner, *Branch Rickey*, pp. 89, 124, 221.

24. 1947 press release of the Cincinnati Reds, "Player Development," Subject Files, NBL. House, *Organized Baseball*, pp. 158–59. Voigt, *American Baseball*, 3:95. Polner, *Branch Rickey*, pp. 226–27.

25. House, *Organized Baseball*, pp. 175–84, 444–52.

26. Ibid., pp. 359–60, 760–69, 776–85. Veeck, *Veeck*, p. 51.

27. *Business Week*, 14 Aug. 1954. Voigt, *American Baseball*, 2:147. Seymour, *Baseball*, p. 402.

28. Jerry Jordan, "Long-Range Effect," pp. 53–54, 58. Craig, "Organized Baseball," p. 78.

29. *TSN*, 28 Oct. 1953.

30. Ibid., 17 Feb. 1954. MacPhail interview.

31. Lowenfish, *Imperfect Diamond*, pp. 129–41, 148, 151. Voigt, *American Baseball*, 1:130, 168, 284–87; 2:67–68, 222–23, 225; 3:55, 206. Commissioner's Notes Nos. 76 (18 Aug. 1949) and 114 (21 July 1950), "Players Association," Subject Files, NBL. House, *Organized Baseball*, pp. 1311–20. Rader, *American Sports*, p. 126.

32. House, *Organized Baseball*, pp. 839–50.

33. Ibid., pp. 258–59, 557–75.

34. Gardella v. Chandler 172 F2d 402 (1949). House, *Organized Baseball*, pp. 290, 323. Lowenfish, *Imperfect Diamond*, pp. 155–68.

35. Brosnan, *Pennant Race*, pp. 153–54.

36. House, *Organized Baseball*, pp. 269–77. *NYT*, 2 Feb. 1954. Voigt, *American Baseball*, 3:93. Lowenfish, *Imperfect Diamond*, p. 183. *Newsweek*, 21 Dec. 1953.

37. *NYT*, 22–25, 30 Aug., 1, 26 Sept. 1953. *Sun*, 3 Dec. 1953. Lowenfish, *Imperfect Diamond*, pp. 184–86.

38. House, *Organized Baseball*, p. 125. Lowenfish, "Tale."

39. House, *Organized Baseball*, pp. 88–91, 403–9.

40. Ibid., pp. 535, 1310–11.

41. *TSN*, 27 May, 15 July 1953. Voigt, *American Baseball*, 2:86, 206.

42. *TSN*, 12 Jan. 1955, for Orioles survey. Crepeau, *Baseball*, pp. 112–14, 159. On the persistence of the blue-collar myth, see Leonard Koppett's comments in *TSN*, 28 Sept. 1974.

43. House, *Organized Baseball*, pp. 484–85. Tygiel, *Experiment*, pp. 30, 252, 269, 290. Rader, *American Sports*, p. 242.

44. Scully, "Discrimination," pp. 228–32.

Chapter 1

1. Craig, "Organized Baseball," pp. 292–93. "The St. Louis Browns," *Sport*, Apr. 1951. House, *Organized Baseball*, pp. 95–96.

2. House, *Organized Baseball*, pp. 94–95, 1599.

3. Mead, *Ten Worst Years*, pp. 56–57, 60. Voigt, *American Baseball*, 2:243.

4. Mead, *Ten Worst Years*, pp. 64–65.

5. Craig, "Organized Baseball," pp. 298–99. Mead, *Ten Worst Years*, pp. 33–35. Lowenfish, "Tale." House, *Organized Baseball*, pp. 951–52.

6. Canes, "Social Benefits of Restrictions on Team Quality," p. 97. Lieb, *Baltimore Orioles*, pp. 209–10. Craig, "Organized Baseball," p. 300.

7. Lieb, *Baltimore Orioles*, pp. 210–11. Craig, "Organized Baseball," pp. 300–303. Tygiel, *Experiment*, p. 219.

8. House, *Organized Baseball*, p. 112.

9. Ibid., pp. 80–87, 262, 324, 533–34, 706.

10. Veeck, *Veeck*, p. 153. House, *Organized Baseball*, p. 870.

11. House, *Organized Baseball*, pp. 78–80.

12. Ibid., pp. 544–54, 963.

13. McLaughlin interview. House, *Organized Baseball: Report*, p. 109.

14. Veeck, *Veeck*, pp. 302–3.

15. "Master of the Joyful Illusion," *SI*, 4 July 1960. Veeck, *Veeck*, pp. 302–3.

16. Lieb, *Baltimore Orioles*, p. 213. Veeck, *Veeck*, pp. 229, 302–3.

17. "The St. Louis Browns Stop Singin' the Blues," *Colliers*, 12 Jan. 1952. Veeck, *Veeck*, p. 133. Veeck, *Hustler's Handbook*, p. 27.

18. Veeck, *Veeck*, pp. 224, 228–30, 312.

19. Ibid., pp. 259–60, 281–82, 289.

20. *TSN*, 7 Jan. 1953.

21. Ibid., 21 Jan., 11, 25 Feb. 1953.

22. Ibid., 14 Jan., 11, 25 Feb. 1953. *Television Age*, Oct. 1953. Veeck, *Veeck*, pp. 1, 235. Schaffer to Patterson, 14 Aug. 1952, "Television prior to 1973," Subject Files, NBL.

23. *TSN*, 11 Feb., 11 Mar. 1953. Veeck, *Veeck*, pp. 251–52.

24. *TSN*, 11 Feb., 4 Mar. 1953. Senate, *Professional Baseball*, p. 104. Veeck, *Veeck*, p. 236.

25. Veeck, *Veeck*, p. 307. Lowenfish, "Tale." *TSN*, 11 Mar., 9 Sept. 1953. Sullivan, *Dodgers*, pp. 93, 95–96.

26. *NYT*, 4–7 Mar. 1953. *TSN*, 25 Feb. 1953. Veeck, *Veeck*, p. 290.

27. Beard, *Birds*, p. 163. *Sun*, 3 Jan. 1986. Dunn interview. Veeck, *Veeck*, p. 292.

28. Lieb, *Baltimore Orioles*, p. 174. On D'Alesandro, see *Sun*, 24 Aug. 1987.

29. Veeck, *Veeck*, p. 312. Dunn interview. Clarence Miles's fullest version of the events, in OH 8165, 25 Aug. 1976, MHS, is confused and must be used with care.

30. *News Post*, 13 Mar. 1953. Veeck, *Veeck*, pp. 295–96.

31. St. Louis *Post Dispatch*, 14, 16 Mar. 1953. *Sun*, 16 Mar. 1953. *News Post*, 14 Mar. 1953. *NYT*, 14 Mar. 1953.

32. *Sun*, 17 Mar. 1953. *Evening Sun*, 16 Mar. 1953. *News Post*, 17 Mar. 1953. Veeck, *Veeck*, pp. 294–96, 302.

33. *Evening Sun*, 20 Mar. 1953. *News Post*, 21 Mar. 1953. Parrott, *Lords of Baseball*, p. 6. *TSN*, 25 Mar. 1953.

34. St. Louis *Post Dispatch*, 17 Mar. 1953.

35. Ibid., 17, 18 Mar. 1953.

36. *Evening Sun*, 19 Mar. 1953. *Sun*, 18 Mar. 1953.

37. *TSN*, 25 Mar. 1953.

38. *Sun*, 22, 24, 25 Mar. 1953. *NYT*, 25 Mar. 1953. *News Post*, 19 Mar. 1953. Lieb, *Baltimore Orioles*, p. 176.

39. *Evening Sun*, 5 Apr. 1974. *Sun Magazine*, 7 Oct. 1979. *Sun*, 24 Sept. 1953.

40. *Evening Sun*, 5 Apr. 1974.

41. *TSN*, 4, 22 Apr., 5 Aug., 16 Sept. 1953. *NYT*, 10 Apr. 1953. Veeck, *Veeck*, pp. 311–12.

42. *Sun*, 25 Mar. 1953. Veeck, "Don't Let TV Kill Baseball," *Sport*, June 1953. Veeck, *Veeck*, p. 283.

43. *TSN*, 22 July 1953.

44. Veeck, *Veeck*, p. 312.

45. *TSN*, 29 July 1953.

46. Ibid., 2 Sept. 1953.

47. *Sun*, 16, 17 Sept. 1953.

48. Ibid., 18 Sept. 1953. St. Louis *Post Dispatch*, 23 Sept. 1953. San Antonio *Express*, 23 Sept. 1953.

49. *Sun*, 24 Sept. 1953. *News Post*, 24, 26 Sept. 1953.

50. *News Post*, 24 Sept. 1953. *Sun*, 27 Sept. 1953. St. Louis *Post Dispatch*, 24, 25 Sept. 1953.

51. *Sun*, 28 Sept. 1953.

52. Ibid., 30 Sept., 2 Oct. 1953. "Baltimore's Three Sport Man," *Baltimore*, Aug. 1962. *Business Week*, 17 Oct. 1953. *TSN*, 7 Oct. 1953. *Time*, 12 Oct. 1953. *News American*, 30 Sept. 1953. McLaughlin interview. St. Louis *Post Dispatch*, 23–24 Sept. 1978. Bready, *Home Team*, p. 49.

53. "Back in Big League Baseball," *Baltimore*, Oct. 1953. *TSN*, 7 Oct. 1953.

Chapter 2

1. *Life*, 26 Apr. 1954. Presumably, this was a tongue-in-cheek comment. Baltimore was a pro-secessionist city during the Civil War. On 19 April 1861 the Sixth Massachusetts Regiment attempted to march through the city, setting off bloody riots that the Federal government put down with force. The city remained under Federal occupation for the remainder of the conflict.

2. "A Son of Old Baltimore, the Father of the New," *Baltimore*, July 1982. *Time*, 16 May 1955.

3. MacPhail interview. *Broadcasting*, 23 Nov. 1953.

4. Olson, *Baltimore: The Building of an American City*, pp. 349, 359.

5. Olson, *Baltimore*, pp. 9–10, 22, 53–54.

6. Maryland, *Study of Desegregation*, pp. 1–5. Callcott, *Maryland and America*, pp. 66, 81.

7. *Baltimore*, Jan. 1955. *Time*, 24 Aug. 1981. Maryland, *American City in Transition*, pp. 21–22, 27–28. Callcott, *Maryland and America*, p. 2.

8. Maryland, *Desegregation in Baltimore Schools*, p. 5. Maryland, *American City in Transition*, pp. 90–91. Healy to Lane, 4 Dec. 1950, "Commission on Racial Relations," McKeldin Papers, University of Maryland. Callcott, *Maryland and America*, pp. 8, 27, 45, 56, 145–48, 151. *Saturday Evening Post*, 1 Oct. 1955.

9. *Afro-American*, 28 Mar. 1953. Tygiel, *Experiment*, pp. 219, 313.

10. *Afro-American*, 28 Mar. 1953. Tygiel, *Experiment*, pp. 122, 313.

11. *Afro-American*, 31 Oct. 1953, 13 Mar., 24 Apr. 1954. *NYT*, 8 Apr. 1954. Tygiel, *Experiment*, p. 79. *Newsweek*, 15 Mar. 1954.

12. *Afro-American*, 2 Jan., 6 Feb. 1954. *Sun*, 27 Jan. 1954.

13. *Afro-American*, 22 May, 12, 19 June, 31 July 1954. *Sun*, 2 Dec. 1953. See the comments of Bowie Kuhn, *Hardball*, pp. 116–17.

14. *Sun*, 15 Oct. 1953.

15. McLaughlin and MacPhail interviews.

16. *TSN*, 14 Oct. 1953. *Sun*, 22, 30 Oct. 1953.

17. *Evening Sun*, 1 Oct. 1953. *Sun*, 1, 27 Oct. 1953. Dalton interview.

18. McLaughlin interview. *TSN*, 4 Nov., 9, 16 Dec. 1953, 10 Feb. 1954. *Sun*, 6 Dec. 1953, 25 Jan. 1954.

19. *NYT*, 30 Oct. 1953. *Sun*, 6 Oct., 7, 11, 13 Dec. 1953, 2 Feb. 1954. *Newsweek*, 15 Mar. 1954. "Will Baltimore Be Another Milwaukee?," *Sport*, Mar. 1954.

20. Memorandum from Woods to O'Donnell, 8 Feb. 1954, "Baseball Celebration Committee," Administrative Files, Thomas D'Alesandro, Jr., Files, Baltimore City Archives. D'Alesandro to O'Conor, 18 Feb. 1954, ibid. *Baltimore*, Mar. 1954. *Newsweek*, 15 Mar. 1954. "Back in the Big League," *New Yorker*, 1 May 1954.

21. *Baltimore*, Apr., July 1954. *New Yorker*, 1 May 1954.

22. *TSN*, 31 Mar. 1954. *NYT*, 28 Mar. 1954.

23. *TSN*, 14, 28 Apr., 2 June 1954.

24. Ibid., 16, 30 June 1954. Lieb, *Baltimore Orioles*, pp. 231–32.

25. *Business Week*, 9 Oct. 1954, 5 Oct. 1957. *Baltimore*, Jan. 1955.

26. *Evening Sun*, 27, 28 Aug. 1954.

27. *Sun*, 30 Aug. 1954. *Evening Sun*, 7 Sept. 1954. *NYT*, 15 Sept. 1954.

28. Robinson interview.

29. *Sun*, 16, 17 Sept. 1954. Harwell, *Tuned to Baseball*, pp. 4–5. Honig, *Man in the Dugout*, pp. 129–30.

30. *Sun*, 16 Mar. 1953. *Evening Sun*, 1 Oct. 1953.

31. House, *Organized Baseball*, pp. 865–69. *TSN*, 17 Feb. 1954.

32. McLaughlin interview. *TSN*, 11 Nov. 1953. Beard, *Birds*, p. 169. *NYT*, 7 Nov. 1954. "News for Baltimore: Even Tax Money Can't Buy Pennant," *Baseball Digest*, Mar. 1954.

33. Dalton interview.

34. Ibid. Dunn interview.

35. Dalton interview.

36. *1955 Orioles Yearbook*, p. 6.

37. Dalton and McLaughlin interviews. Kerrane, *Dollar Sign*, p. 124.

38. Honig, *Man in the Dugout*, pp. 140–41. Kerrane, *Dollar Sign*, p. 120. *Sun*, 25 Sept. 1954. *TSN*, 25 May 1955.

39. "Did the Yankees Win the Pennant in the Winter?," *Sport*, Apr. 1955. *NYT*, 19 Nov. 1954.

40. *TSN*, 12 Jan., 16 Feb., 4 May 1955. *Sun*, 11 Feb. 1955.

41. *Afro-American*, 18 June 1955. Bready, *Home Team*, p. 51.

42. *TSN*, 22, 29 June, 10 Aug. 1955. *NYT*, 24 Sept. 1955. Dunn interview.

43. *Sun*, 20, 21 Sept. 1955. *NYT*, 8 Nov. 1955.

44. *Sun*, 18 Nov. 1955. McLaughlin and Dunn interviews.

45. *NYT*, 19 Nov. 1955. *Sun*, 19 Nov., 3 Dec. 1955. *TSN*, 30 Nov. 1955, 18 Apr. 1956.

46. *SI*, 29 July 1957, 14 Apr. 1958. "Richards' DeLuxe Retreads," *Baseball Digest*, Sept. 1957. *1955 Orioles Yearbook*.

47. *Sun*, 23 Nov., 2 Dec. 1957.

48. Senate, *Broadcasting and Televising Baseball*, pp. 1–7, 11–12, 19. Senate, *Organized Professional Team Sports* (1958), p. 264. *TSN*, 2 June 1954. *SI*, 14 Apr. 1958.

49. Dalton and MacPhail interviews. *SI*, 16 Dec. 1957.

50. *Evening Sun*, 29 Nov. 1954.

51. *Sun*, 16 Oct. 1959. Pluto, *Earl*, p. 16. Weaver, *What You Learn*, pp. 101, 105, 109–10. Weaver, *Winning*, pp. 28–30, 34.

52. *Sun*, 16 Oct., 25 Nov. 1959. St. Louis *Post Dispatch*, 24 Sept. 1953. *TSN*, 3 June 1959. *1956 Orioles Yearbook*, p. 2.

53. *NYT*, 6 May 1960. *TSN*, 14 Jan. 1959. Pat Jordan, *Suitors of Spring*, pp. 23–25. Bready, *Home Team*, p. 52.

54. *Sun*, 24 Nov. 1955. *TSN*, 9 Jan. 1957.

55. *TSN*, 13 Feb., 16 Oct. 1957, 18 June 1958, 5 Aug. 1959.

56. Ibid., 20 Jan. 1954, 6 June 1956. *NYT*, 10 Sept. 1958. Senate, *Organized Professional Team Sports* (1958), p. 98. *SI*, 22 Nov. 1954. *Sun*, 7, 8 Dec. 1957.

57. House, *Organized Professional Team Sports* (1957), pp. 1836–38. *NYT*, 7 Dec. 1955.

58. House, *Organized Professional Team Sports* (1957), pp. 188, 191, 208. Lane quoted in "The Rochester Story," *Sport*, July 1957.

59. *TSN*, 30 Jan. 1957. "The Majors and the Minors," *Sport*, June 1957. Horton interview. *SI*, 16 Dec. 1957.

60. San Antonio *Express*, 19 Mar. 1953, 19 Feb. 1954.

61. Ibid., 2, 4 Apr. 1954, 26, 27 Nov., 6, 7, 9 Dec. 1956. *Sun*, 26 Nov. 1956.

62. *Sun*, 12 Nov., 5 Dec. 1957. San Antonio *Express*, 29 Nov., 6, 8 Dec. 1957.

63. *NYT*, 6 Dec. 1957.

64. "A Struggle for Survival: Report of the Minor Leagues to the House of Representatives," 1958, File II: 430: 1, Keating Papers, University of Rochester. Horton interview. *NYT*, 12, 15 Dec. 1957.

65. *NYT*, 15, 16 Jan. 1958. "A Struggle for Survival," File II: 430: 1, Keating Papers.

66. Senate, *Organized Professional Team Sports* (1958), p. 213. Telegram from Keelty to Celler, 23 June 1958, "HR 10378–85(2)," Legislative Files, Celler Papers, LC.

67. Horton interview.

68. *NYT*, 6 July 1956. Obojski, *Bush League*, pp. 28–29.

69. Horton interview. *Sun*, 7 Nov. 1958.

70. House, *Organized Professional Team Sports* (1957), pp. 1836–38. Letter from Earl Mann, 12 Mar. 1959, "Sports Monopoly, Dec. 1958– ," FRC acc. no. 70A 3434, Records of the Senate Judiciary Committee, RG 46, NA. Giles to Mann, 3 Apr. 1959, ibid. Cooke to Mann, 10 Apr. 1959, ibid. Harwell, *Tuned to Baseball*, p. 51.

71. Butler to Frick, 25 July 1960, "Realignment," Subject Files, NBL. *TSN*, 1 July 1959. *NYT*, 11 July 1959. Stevens to Kefauver, 21 Jan. 1959, "Sports Monopoly, Dec. 1958– ," FRC acc. no. 70A 3434, Records of the Senate Judiciary Committee, RG 46, NA. Horton interview.

72. "Stabilization of the Minor Leagues," undated memorandum, "Player Development," Subject Files, NBL. *TSN*, 16 Mar. 1960. *D&C*, 31 July 1960. Horton interview.

73. Kahn, *Good Enough to Dream*, p. 139. Kerrane, *Dollar Sign*, pp. 149, 199.

Chapter 3

1. Dunn interview.

2. *TSN*, 27 Aug. 1957. "Baltimore's Bonus Baby Blues," *Saturday Evening Post*, 9 Aug. 1958.

3. *Sun*, 25 Nov. 1956. *TSN*, 5 Oct. 1956. *NYT*, 16 Oct. 1956. Dunn and McLaughlin interviews.

4. *Sun*, 29, 30 Oct., 1 Nov. 1958. *NYT*, 1, 11 Nov. 1958. MacPhail interview.

5. *Sun*, 6, 9, 11 Nov. 1958. MacPhail interview.

6. MacPhail and Dunn interviews. *Sun*, 9 Dec. 1959.

7. *Sun*, 25 June 1956. *Evening Sun*, 14 Dec. 1959. Veeck, *Veeck*, pp. 324, 327.

8. *TSN*, 27 Feb. 1957.

9. *Sun*, 2 Dec. 1957. *TSN*, 12 Jan. 1955. Memorandum of conversation between Frick and Rickey, 23 Nov. 1959, "Memorandums," Baseball Correspondence, Rickey Papers, LC.

10. *Sun*, 6, 26 Nov., 13 Dec. 1959.

11. Dunn interview.

12. *Sun*, 10, 12, 24, 25 Nov., 4 Dec. 1958.

13. *Broadcasting*, 30 Aug. 1954, 22 Aug. 1955. Callcott, *Maryland and America*, p. 68. Horowitz, "Market Entrenchment."

14. *Broadcasting*, 3 Jan. 1955, 25 Feb. 1957. *NYT*, 3 July 1956. *Television Age*, Mar. 1956, 25 Mar. 1957.

15. *Television Age*, Mar. 1956. *NYT*, 29 Nov. 1955, 11 Oct. 1960. House, *Organized Professional Team Sports* (1957), pp. 102–3. Senate, *Organized Professional Team Sports* (1958), pp. 95–97, 113–19, 158. Hansen to Porter, 5 Mar. 1958, "Sports Monopoly, April 1959," FRC acc. no. 70A 3434, Records of the Senate Judiciary Committee, RG 46, NA. Fellows to Kefauver, 1 July 1958, "Sports Monopoly, Against," ibid. Voigt, *American Baseball*, 3:107. Kahn, *Good Enough to Dream*, p. 120.

16. *NYT*, 5 Jan., 19 Nov. 1954. *Television Age*, Oct. 1954. *Broadcasting*, 8 Feb. 1954, 7 Mar. 1955. Harwell, *Tuned to Baseball*, pp. 66–68.

17. Dunn interview.

18. *Television Age*, 25 Mar. 1957, 24 Mar. 1958. *Sun*, 18 Nov. 1958.

19. *Television Age*, 22 Apr. 1957, 24 Mar. 1958.

20. MacPhail interview.

21. *Television Age*, 6 Apr. 1959, 20 Mar. 1960.

22. Memorandum from Frick to major league clubs, 17 Feb. 1956, "Public Relations," Subject Files, NBL. *TSN*, 11 Apr., 18 July 1956.

23. MacPhail interview.

24. *Sun*, 21 Nov. 1956. *1960 Orioles Yearbook*, p. 16. Press release of Orioles Advocates, 12 July 1960, "Baseball," Grady-Goodman Files, Baltimore City Archives. Barrett to Grady, 10 May 1961, ibid. Memorandum to Orioles Advocates, 12 Aug. 1960, ibid.

25. Tygiel, *Experiment*, pp. 285–92, 299.

26. Ibid., pp. 258, 287.

27. *Afro-American*, 21 May 1955. Tygiel, *Experiment*, p. 336.

28. *Afro-American*, 25 June, 17 Dec. 1955, 21 Apr., 2 June 1956. Mann, *Decline and Fall*, pp. 181–82.

29. *Afro-American*, 8 Sept. 1956.

30. Ibid., 11 Jan., 12, 19 Apr. 1958, 15 July 1961. *Baltimore*, Mar. 1958. On Richards's treatment of Doby, see Moore, *Pride*, pp. 115–16.

31. *Afro-American*, 2 July 1955.

32. Ibid., 6 Apr., 1 June, 20 July 1957, 14 June 1958.

33. *U.S. News and World Report*, 5 Dec. 1958. "When a Negro Moves Next Door," *Saturday Evening Post*, 4 Apr. 1959. Walsh and Fox, *Maryland*, pp. 827–28. Callcott, *Maryland and America*, p. 58. *Time*, 11 Oct. 1954.

34. Tygiel, *Experiment*, pp. 311–20. *TSN*, 25 Mar. 1959. "The Negro in Baseball," *SI*, 21 Mar. 1960.

35. *TSN*, 4 Feb., 18 Mar., 13 May 1959.

36. *NYT*, 19 Feb. 1961. *TSN*, 5 Apr. 1961.

37. "Spring Training Unsegregated—Almost," *Sport*, Apr. 1962. *TSN*, 15 Feb. 1961. *NYT*, 19 Feb. 1961. *Afro-American*, 18, 25 Mar., 12 Aug. 1961.

38. *Afro-American*, 17 June, 13 Nov. 1961, 7 July 1962. MacPhail interview. See Tygiel, *Experiment*, pp. 129, 130–31, on intimidation of black fans. See also, "Where Are the Black Fans?," *NYT Magazine*, 17 May 1987.

39. A copy of the 12 Nov. 1953 agreement is in SEC Files, SEC 0-637-2.

40. Armstrong to D'Alesandro, 25 Apr. 1950, "Orioles Baseball Team," Thomas

D'Alesandro, Jr., Files, Baltimore City Archives. *Sun*, 18, 19 Oct. 1953, 19 Feb. 1954. *Baltimore*, May 1953.

41. Tawney to Wilson, 19 Sept. 1957, "Memorial Stadium," Department of Parks and Recreation, Thomas D'Alesandro, Jr., Files, Baltimore City Archives. *Sun*, 19 Mar. 1954. *News Post*, 15 Apr. 1954. *Evening Sun*, 9 June 1954.

42. *Sun*, 13 Dec. 1956.

43. *U.S. News and World Report*, 8 Apr. 1958.

44. Dunn and Dalton interviews. *TSN*, 19 Jan. 1955.

45. Dunn interview. *Sun*, 28 July 1957.

46. Dunn interview.

47. *TSN*, 7 Aug. 1957. *Evening Sun*, 29 July 1957. *Sun*, 3 Aug., 18 Sept. 1957.

48. *American City*, Nov. 1957. *NYT*, 3 Jan. 1958.

49. *American City*, Jan. 1958.

50. *Baltimore*, July 1958, Dec. 1958, Mar. 1959.

51. *Sun*, 9 July 1958.

52. *Evening Sun*, 21 Mar., 25 May, 1 June 1960. *Sun*, 8 Apr., 30 May, 4 June 1960. MacPhail to Grady, 16 June 1960, "Memorial Stadium," Department of Parks and Recreation, Grady-Goodman Files, Baltimore City Archives.

53. Press release of Mayor Grady, 28 Aug. 1960, "Memorial Stadium," Department of Parks and Recreation, Grady-Goodman Files, Baltimore City Archives. Boucher to Grady, 6 Oct. 1960, ibid. *TSN*, 24 Nov. 1962.

54. *D&C*, 10 Dec. 1960. Senate, *Organized Professional Team Sports* (1959), p. 66.

55. MacPhail interview.

56. "The Rochester Story," *Sport*, July 1957. Horton interview.

57. *D&C*, 22 Sept., 2 Oct. 1960.

58. Ibid., 30 Aug., 2 Oct. 1960. MacPhail and McLaughlin interviews.

59. *D&C*, 2, 18 Oct. 1960.

60. Ibid., 15 Sept., 3, 4 Oct. 1960. MacPhail and Horton interviews.

61. *D&C*, 12 Jan. 1961. McLaughlin and MacPhail interviews.

62. McLaughlin interview.

63. Kerrane, *Dollar Sign*, p. 121.

64. *Sun*, 22 Dec., 15 Nov. 1959.

65. Ibid., 20 Nov. 1960. *1960 Orioles Yearbook*.

66. *TSN*, 12 Oct., 21 Dec. 1960. *NYT*, 2 Oct. 1960.

Chapter 4

1. Marazzi and Fiorito, *Aaron to Zipfel*, pp. 243–44. *Sun*, 15 Dec. 1960.

2. House, *Organized Baseball*, pp. 410–12.

3. *TSN*, 7 Oct. 1953.

4. Ibid., 2 Feb. 1955. On Arnold Johnson and the Yankees, see House, *Organized Professional Team Sports* (1957), pp. 2082–95, 2136–42.

5. *Sun*, 17 Jan. 1954. *TSN*, 16 Feb. 1955, 7 Mar. 1956.

6. *Business Week*, 8 June 1957. "Alas Poor Giants," *SI*, 20 May 1957.

7. *TSN*, 9 Jan. 1957. *SI*, 10 June 1957. House, *Organized Professional Team Sports*

(1957), pp. 1850, 1860–65. For a contrasting view and defense of O'Malley's motivations, see Sullivan, *Dodgers*.

8. House, *Organized Professional Team Sports* (1957), pp. 1359–60, 1365, 1369–70, 1940–42. "The Business," *Baseball Digest*, Dec. 1957–Jan. 1958.

9. *NYT*, 14 Nov. 1958. "National League Lost to New York Forever," *Baseball Digest*, Dec. 1957–Jan. 1958, pp. 22–24.

10. *TSN*, 22 May 1957. House, *Organized Professional Team Sports* (1957), pp. 127, 129, 131. Senate, *Organized Professional Team Sports* (1958), pp. 169–70. *NYT*, 4 Jan., 13 Apr. 1958.

11. Polner, *Branch Rickey*, pp. 252–54. "Is a Third Major League in the Cards?," *Sport*, Mar. 1959.

12. Senate, *Organized Professional Team Sports* (1960), p. 170. *NYT*, 2 July 1959.

13. *NYT*, 10 July 1959. Senate, *Organized Professional Team Sports* (1959), pp. 73–79, 88–89, 170–71. *TSN*, 5 Aug. 1958, 1 July 1959.

14. President's report to the members of the Continental League, 13 Nov. 1959, "Meeting," Baseball Correspondence, Rickey Papers, LC. Memorandum of conversation between Frick and Rickey, 23 Nov. 1959, "Memorandums," ibid. Memorandum of conversation between Rickey and Rand, 26 Feb. 1960, ibid. Continental League press release, 8 Dec. 1959, "Continental League," Subject Files, Mann Papers, LC. "Memorandum on Expansion," undated, ibid. Senate, *Organized Professional Team Sports* (1959), pp. 123, 126. Senate, *Organized Professional Team Sports* (1960), pp. 74–77. *TSN*, 18 May 1960. Rickey to Dixon, 26 July 1960, "S 168 Correspondence," FRC acc. no. 70A 3434, Records of the Senate Antitrust Subcommittee, RG 46, NA.

15. *TSN*, 31 Oct. 1956, 7 Oct. 1959. Senate, *Organized Professional Team Sports* (1959), pp. 87–90, 180. Senate, *Organized Professional Team Sports* (1958), pp. 78–79, 85–87, 90–95. *NYT*, 28 July 1959.

16. Senate, *Organized Professional Team Sports* (1958), p. 171. Memorandum of conversation between Rickey and Paul, 18 Oct. 1959, "Memorandums," Baseball Correspondence, Rickey Papers, LC. *TSN*, 28 Oct. 1959. "Cal Griffith Is No Walter O'Malley," *Sport*, Jan. 1960.

17. *SI*, 1 Sept. 1958. *U.S. News and World Report*, 18 Apr. 1958. *NYT*, 16 Oct. 1959. *TSN*, 28 Oct. 1959.

18. Continental League press release, 15 Apr. 1960, "Western Carolina League," Baseball Correspondence, Rickey Papers, LC. *NYT*, 30 Jan. 1960. Notes of conversations with Horton and Frick, undated, File II: 430: 1, Keating Papers, University of Rochester. Senate, *Organized Professional Team Sports* (1960), pp. 14–33, 64–73.

19. *NYT*, 7, 29 June 1960. Frick to Hart, 7 June 1960, "Baseball," Hart Papers, University of Michigan. Undated strategy paper, "Wires to Washington," Continental League, Rickey Papers, LC. Butler to Rickey, 5 July 1960, "Senate Correspondence," ibid.

20. Frick, *Games*, pp. 128–29.

21. *NYT*, 19, 21 July, 3 Aug. 1960. Memorandum of conversation between Rickey and O'Malley, 22 July 1960, "Memorandums," Baseball Correspondence, Rickey Papers, LC.

22. *NYT*, 31 Aug., 11, 27 Oct. 1960. Continental League press release, 1 Nov. 1960, "Continental League," Subject Files, Mann Papers, LC.

23. *NYT*, 14 Aug. 1960. *TSN*, 2 Nov. 1960. Memorandum of conversation between Rickey and Greenberg, 23 Nov. 1960, "Memorandums," Baseball Correspondence, Rickey Papers, LC. Veeck, *Veeck*, p. 372. In a discussion with Rickey, Webb stated that in the event of Griffith's move to Minnesota, Baltimore would shift its franchise to the nation's capital. MacPhail denied that any such suggestion was made by the Orioles. Most likely it represented a bit of wishful thinking on Webb's part that went to the heart of the region's marketing problem: two teams located so close to each other in a limited market simply could not make baseball profitable. Memorandum of conversation between Webb and Rickey, 25 Oct. 1960, "Memorandums," Baseball Correspondence, Rickey Papers, LC. MacPhail interview.

24. *TSN*, 2, 30 Nov. 1960. *NYT*, 16, 23 Nov., 7, 8 Dec. 1960. Memorandum of conversation between Webb and Rickey, 25 Oct. 1960, "Memorandums," Baseball Correspondence, Rickey Papers, LC. Rickey to Spink, 29 Nov. 1960, "The Sporting News," ibid.

25. *NYT*, 18 Nov. 1960. Veeck, *Veeck*, pp. 372–76.

26. *Sun*, 15, 28 Nov. 1960.

27. Dunn interview.

28. *TSN*, 1 Feb., 19 Apr. 1961.

29. Ibid., 20 Jan. 1960, 11 Jan., 1 Mar. 1961.

30. *Baltimore*, Apr. 1961.

31. MacPhail interview. *TSN*, 6 Sept. 1961. *Sun*, 24, 25 Aug. 1961. *Afro-American*, 9 Sept. 1961.

32. *TSN*, 20 Sept., 1 Nov. 1961. *Sun* 2, 26, 28 Sept., 6 Oct. 1961.

33. Veeck, *Veeck*, p. 237. Koppett, *Thinking Man's Guide*, p. 88. Veeck, *Hustler's Handbook*, p. 55. Weaver is quoted in Boswell, *Life*, pp. 151, 154.

34. Veeck, *Veeck*, p. 237.

35. *Sun*, 7, 11 Oct. 1961. *TSN*, 18 Apr. 1962.

36. *Sun*, 3 Nov. 1961.

37. Ibid., 22 Aug., 21 Nov., 12 Dec. 1961. *TSN*, 10 Jan. 1962. MacPhail quoted in *Sun*, 6 Dec. 1961.

38. Dunn interview. *TSN*, 15 Nov. 1961. *Sun*, 17 Nov. 1961.

39. *TSN*, 3 Jan., 14 Feb. 1962.

40. Ibid., 4, 11, 25 Aug. 1962. On Gentile and his managers, see Herzog, *White Rat*, pp. 60–61.

41. *TSN*, 1, 22 Sept., 29 Dec. 1962.

42. *Sun*, 3, 20 Oct. 1962. *TSN*, 13 Oct. 1962.

43. *TSN*, 20 Oct. 1962, 2 Mar. 1963.

44. *Sun*, 11 Jan. 1963.

45. *TSN*, 26 Jan. 1963. When questioned, Brooks Robinson had a hard time remembering this incident. He commented that it was typical of his relationship with every general manager during a twenty-three-year career: "They just wore you down," he said, with tactics like the ones MacPhail employed. Robinson interview.

46. *TSN*, 26 Jan. 1963. *Baseball Digest*, Apr. 1963. Veeck, *Hustler's Handbook*, pp. 119, 144.

47. *Sun*, 7, 14 Dec. 1962. "New Look of the 1963 Orioles," *Baltimore*, Mar. 1963.

48. *TSN*, 6, 12 July 1963. "Brooks Robinson Untroubled Oriole," *Sport*, Oct. 1963.

49. *Sun*, 30 Sept. 1963.

50. *TSN*, 12 Oct. 1963. *D&C*, 3 Mar. 1964. *NYT*, 20 Nov. 1963.

51. *SI*, 10 Sept. 1962.

52. "The Dying American League," *SI*, 9 Sept. 1963.

53. Ibid. "Whatever Happened to Baseball?," *SI*, 27 Aug. 1962. Voigt, *American Baseball*, 2:296; 3:xviii, 318. See James, *Historical Baseball Abstract*, pp. 159–60, 231–33, 250–51, on changes in the rules.

54. "The Dying American League," *SI*, 9 Sept. 1963.

55. *TSN*, 14 Sept. 1963. Bready, *Home Team*, pp. 51, 61. Quirk and El Hodiri, "Economic Theory of a Professional Sports League," pp. 46–47, 54–55.

56. "The American League Is Dying," *Look*, 17 Feb. 1959.

57. *Sun*, 20 Nov. 1959, 27, 28 Nov. 1961. Davis, "Self-Regulation in Baseball," p. 365.

58. *Sun*, 30 Nov. 1961. *NYT*, 1 Dec. 1961.

59. *TSN*, 21 July 1962.

60. *Sun*, 25, 27 Nov. 1962.

61. Ibid., 15 Dec. 1962. *TSN*, 8 Dec. 1962, 16 Mar. 1963.

62. *TSN*, 10 Aug. 1963, 22 Aug. 1964. Davis, "Self-Regulation in Baseball," p. 367.

63. *Sun* 31 Oct. 1964. MacPhail interview.

64. MacPhail interview.

65. *TSN*, 19 Dec. 1964. *NYT*, 3 Dec. 1964, 28 Feb. 1965.

66. *Sun*, 4 Dec. 1964.

67. Ibid., 11 June 1965.

68. Ibid., 14 Sept. 1965. *TSN*, 3 July 1965. The other major effect of the draft was to change the nature of scouting. Prior to 1965, the classic scout had to be equally skilled in finding and in signing prospects. He operated in an intensely competitive situation. Rival scouts were almost always present to bid for the services of a particularly attractive prospect. After baseball enacted the draft rule, scouts became "investment analysts" with little personal contact with prospects because the chances their team would get the rights to negotiate with an individual prospect were limited. Responsibility for signing drafted prospects increasingly passed to farm directors and general managers. Kerrane, *Dollar Sign*, p. 19.

Chapter 5

1. *TSN*, 24 Oct. 1964, 6 Feb. 1965. *Sun*, 21 Nov. 1964.

2. "Is the Yankee Dynasty Dead?," *Sport*, June 1963. Golenbock, *Dynasty*, pp. 236, 276–78. Veeck, *Hustler's Handbook*, p. 136. Voigt, *American Baseball*, 3:173. MacPhail interview.

3. *TSN*, 9 May 1962. "Is the American League *That* Bad?," *Sport*, Mar. 1964. "The Decline and Fall of a Dynasty," *SI*, 21 June 1965.

4. Mann, *Decline and Fall*, p. 139.

5. *TSN*, 29 Aug., 24 Oct. 1964. Veeck, *Hustler's Handbook*, pp. 340–44. *NYT Magazine*, 20 Dec. 1964. "The Big Sellout," *SI*, 24 Aug. 1964. "A Sad Day for Baseball," ibid., 21 Sept. 1964. "Is Television Taking Over Baseball?," *Sport*, Dec. 1964.

6. *SI*, 24 May 1965.

7. Iglehardt letter, *SI*, 2 Aug. 1965. Dunn interview.

8. Dunn interview. *Sun*, 19 Sept. 1964.

9. Dunn interview.

10. "Baltimore's Three Sport Man," *Baltimore*, Aug. 1962. Mr. Kreiger did not respond to my request for an interview.

11. *NYT*, 4 Nov. 1964. *Sun*, 4 Nov. 1964. *TSN*, 6 Feb. 1965.

12. Senate, *Professional Sports Antitrust Bill, 1965*, pp. 1–2, 6–14, 111, 150–61.

13. *Sun*, 30 Mar. 1965.

14. Ibid., 2, 14 Dec. 1963. *TSN*, 25 Jan. 1964.

15. Hoffberger quoted in Beard, *Birds*, p. 131.

16. Dunn interview. *TSN*, 16 Nov. 1963.

17. *D&C*, 5 Nov. 1963. *Sun*, 9, 14, 15 Dec. 1963. Dunn interview.

18. *Sun*, 5, 11 Nov. 1963. Baltimore Baseball Club, Form 10-K, 1964, SEC Files.

19. Iglehardt letter, *SI*, 2 Aug. 1965.

20. *Sun*, 27, 28 May 1965. Beard, *Birds*, pp. 171–72.

21. *Sun*, 27 May, 12 June 1965. *NYT*, 12 June 1965. Hoffberger quoted in *Sun*, 12 June 1965.

22. Hoffberger quoted in Beard, *Birds*, p. 131.

23. MacPhail interview.

24. Horton interview. *D&C*, 7, 13, 20, 25 Mar., 14 May, 1, 2 June 1961.

25. *D&C*, 8, 12, 25 Sept., 18 Nov. 1961.

26. Ibid., 1 Nov. 1961.

27. Ibid., 6 Nov. 1961.

28. Ibid., 16 Apr., 9 May 1961, 25 Mar. 1962.

29. Ibid., 25 Oct. 1961.

30. Ibid., 29 Jan., 4, 6 May 1961. Senzel, *Cold War*, pp. 23, 190.

31. *D&C*, 26 Oct., 8 Dec. 1961, 6 Mar. 1962.

32. Ibid., 27 July, 15, 26, 28, 30 Nov. 1962.

33. Obojski, *Bush League*, pp. 30–31.

34. Lyttle, *Minors*, pp. 9–10. Kahn, *Good Enough to Dream*, pp. 78–79. *D&C*, 31 Oct. 1962.

35. *D&C*, 30 Mar. 1961, 31 Oct. 1962. Even millionaire Jack Kent Cooke of unaffiliated Toronto was unable to compete after 1960. Without an affiliation, Cooke could not acquire enough quality AAA-level players. On the declining profitability of nonaffiliated Toronto, see Cooke to Davis, 16 Mar. 1960, "Montreal," Baseball Correspondence, Rickey Papers, LC, and Cooke comments, Minutes of 25 Apr. 1960 meeting of Continental League, "Meeting—4/25/60," ibid.

36. *D&C*, 17 Nov. 1961, 3 Apr., 31 Oct., 14 Nov. 1962. *Sun*, 21 Oct. 1962.

37. *D&C*, 19 Oct., 7, 22 Nov. 1962.

38. Ibid., 31 Mar. 1963, 24 Mar., 8 Apr. 1965.

39. Silver quoted in ibid., 24 Oct. 1962.

40. *Sun*, 25 Sept. 1963, 13 Sept. 1964. *D&C*, 17, 27, 28 Sept. 1964.

41. *D&C*, 2 Mar. 1961.

42. Horton interview.

43. *D&C*, 20 Nov., 2, 3, 5 Dec. 1963.

44. Ibid., 4, 8 Dec. 1963; quotes from Frick and Silver in 8 Dec. issue.

45. Richardson quoted in ibid., 8 Nov. 1964. *TSN*, 24 Apr. 1965.

46. *D&C*, 17 Sept., 9, 13, 14 Nov. 1965. *TSN*, 20 Nov. 1965.

47. *D&C*, 19, 21, 24 Nov., 9 Dec. 1965. Devine quoted in ibid., 6 Dec. 1966.

48. Horton interview.

49. *Sun*, 28 Aug., 12 Dec. 1964. *TSN*, 16 Jan. 1965.

50. Dalton interview.

51. Interview with Veeck, *U.S. News and World Report*, 12 Aug. 1963. Veeck, *Hustler's Handbook*, pp. 328–33, 340–44.

52. "The Baseball Establishment," *Esquire*, Aug. 1964. Interview with Veeck, *U.S. News and World Report*, 12 Aug. 1963.

53. Veeck, *Veeck*, pp. 101–2.

54. Veeck quoted in Kahn, *Season in the Sun*, p. 130.

55. See the comments of Maisel in *Sun*, 16 Oct. 1965.

56. Dalton interview.

57. Ibid.

58. *Sun*, 16 Oct. 1965. *TSN*, 30 Oct. 1965.

59. MacPhail interview.

60. *NYT*, 6, 8 Nov. 1964. *TSN*, 27 Mar. 1965. "Slow Search for Another Frick," *SI*, 2 Aug. 1965.

61. *Sun*, 13, 19, 21 Oct. 1965.

62. *NYT*, 18 Nov. 1965. *TSN*, 6 Nov. 1965.

63. MacPhail interview.

64. *Sun*, 18, 19 Nov. 1965.

65. Ibid., 20 Nov., 8, 11 Dec. 1965.

Chapter 6

1. Dalton interview.

2. *SI*, 18 Apr. 1966. Beard, *Birds*, pp. 35–36, 38.

3. *SI*, 18 Apr. 1966.

4. *TSN*, 23 July 1966. *Sun*, 21 Aug. 1966. Beard, *Birds*, p. 82.

5. Dalton quoted in *Sun*, 29 Aug. 1966. Ibid., 4, 22 Aug. 1966.

6. *SI*, 26 Sept. 1966.

7. Daley quoted in *NYT*, 10 Oct. 1966. "Battle for a Shot at the Birds," *SI*, 3 Oct. 1966.

8. *D&C*, 29 Sept. 1966. *Sun*, 17, 20 Sept. 1966. Frank Robinson, *My Life*, p. 202.

9. *NYT*, 10 Oct. 1966.

10. "Those Happy Birds," *SI*, 17 Oct. 1966.

11. *NYT*, 21 Oct. 1966. *Sun*, 30 Sept. 1966.

12. *Time*, 30 Sept. 1966. *TSN*, 25 Dec. 1965.

13. *TSN*, 3 Aug. 1963.

14. Quote from Dolson, *Beating the Bushes*, pp. 110–11. *Afro-American*, 4 Aug. 1962. On life in the minor leagues, see Flood, *The Way It Is*, p. 58; Frank Robinson, *My Life*, pp. 46, 52–53; and Tygiel, *Experiment*, pp. 252–53.

15. Tygiel, *Experiment*, p. 253. Dolson, *Beating the Bushes*, p. 100.

16. Scully, "Discrimination," p. 222. Tygiel, *Experiment*, p. 305. Rader, *American Sports*, p. 334. Rosenblatt, "Negroes in Baseball."

17. *NYT*, 30 May 1962, 27 Feb. 1966. *Afro-American*, 30 Apr. 1966. Tygiel, *Experiment*, p. 339.

18. "Get With It, Baseball," *Sport*, June 1968. *TSN*, 22 Aug. 1970. Former Orioles manager Earl Weaver commented that the lack of a black manager before 1974 was "slightly ridiculous," adding, "It was also right in line with the forward thinking that had always been prominent in the upper echelons of baseball." Weaver, *What You Learn*, p. 156.

19. Scully, "Discrimination," p. 236. *Afro-American*, 14 Apr. 1962, 11 Apr. 1964, 20 Mar., 25 Sept. 1965. The edition of 25 Sept. 1965 contains an interview with MacPhail.

20. *Sun*, 12 Sept. 1965. *Afro-American*, 25 Sept. 1965, 19 Feb. 1966.

21. *Afro-American*, 5 Feb. 1966. Frank Robinson, *My Life*, pp. 104, 169. Frank Robinson, *Extra Innings*, p. 57.

22. Frank Robinson, *My Life*, p. 16.

23. Beard, *Birds*, p. 17. Frank Robinson, *My Life*, p. 215. Frank Robinson gives a slightly different version that apparently compresses two separate experiences into a single episode in *Extra Innings*, pp. 59–60.

24. *Afro-American*, 23 Feb. 1963. Frank Robinson, *My Life*, pp. 176–77.

25. Walsh and Fox, *Maryland*, p. 866. *Newsweek*, 6 June 1966. Meier and Rudwick, *CORE*, pp. 359, 377, 383–85, 409–10, 420.

26. Olson, *Baltimore*, p. 23.

27. Ibid., pp. 23, 53–54, 57. Olson, *Baltimore: The Building of an American City*, p. 377. Meyer, *Maryland*, pp. 5–6.

28. Olson, *Baltimore*, p. 26. Olson, *Baltimore: The Building of an American City*, p. 364. Meyer, *Maryland*, p. 162. On the political elite's commitment to the redevelopment of the business sector, see "Baltimore Might Make It," *New Republic*, 9 Apr. 1966; *Time*, 4 Feb. 1966; and "How Baltimore Fends Off Riots," *Reader's Digest*, Mar. 1968. On the persistence of residential segregation in Baltimore, see *Washington Post*, 1 June 1987.

29. *Newsweek*, 6 June 1966. Notes for McKeldin's Use, [June 1966], "White House Conference—Response from Baltimore," Series III, McKeldin Papers, University of Maryland.

30. *Time*, 10 June 1966. *Newsweek*, 6 June, 8 Aug. 1966. *Afro-American*, 6 Aug. 1966. Jackson (of NAACP) to Brewster, 9 June 1966, "Civil Rights, Jan.–July 1966," Brewster Papers, University of Maryland.

31. Callcott, *Maryland and America*, pp. 70–71. McCurdy to Brewster, 22 June 1966, "Civil Rights, Jan.–July 1966," Brewster Papers, University of Maryland. Manekin to Brewster, 26 July 1966, "Civil Rights, Aug.–Dec. 1966," ibid.

32. McKeldin quoted in *NYT*, 5 Oct. 1966.

33. *Afro-American*, 1, 15 Oct. 1966. "A Wink at a Homely Girl," *SI*, 10 Oct. 1966.

34. *Sun*, 26 Jan. 1966.

35. Frank Robinson, *My Life*, p. 215.

36. McKissick to McKeldin, 4 Oct. 1966, "CORE Target City," McKeldin Files, Baltimore City Archives. Frank Robinson, *My Life*, p. 216.

37. Fox and Walsh, *Maryland*, p. 872. Callcott, *Maryland and America*, pp. 70–71. Brewster to Zeltzer, 2 Apr. 1968, "Baltimore," Brewster Papers, University of Maryland.

38. Fox and Walsh, *Maryland*, pp. 868–71, 876–77. "A Son of Old Baltimore, the Father of the New," *Baltimore*, July 1982.

39. *Afro-American*, 17 June 1967. *Sport*, Nov. 1968. "High Flight for An Oriole," *SI*, 3 Feb. 1969. Frank Robinson, *Extra Innings*, p. 63, noted Brooks Robinson's role in creating a good relationship between black and white athletes on the Orioles team but also stressed the limits of social contacts between the races.

40. *Sun*, 3 Nov. 1966.

41. Ibid., 22 Feb., 18 Oct. 1966. *TSN*, 7 Jan. 1967. *NYT*, 29 Jan. 1967.

42. *TSN*, 28 Jan., 18 Mar. 1967. *Sun*, 27 Nov. 1966, 28 Feb. 1967. *NYT*, 29 Nov. 1966. Okrent, *Nine Innings*, p. 130.

43. *TSN*, 25 Feb., 4 Mar. 1967. *Sun*, 2 Feb., 19, 30 Mar. 1967.

44. *TSN*, 8 Apr. 1967. "Sore Arms and No Cigarettes," *SI*, 10 Apr. 1967.

45. Dalton quoted in *Sun*, 28 Oct. 1966. Ibid., 20 Oct. 1966.

46. *TSN*, 19 Aug. 1967.

47. *Sun*, 26 Jan., 22, 24 Feb. 1968

48. *TSN*, 2 Sept., 14 Oct. 1967. *Sun*, 24, 29, 30 Sept. 1967. Weaver, *Strategy*, pp. 118–19. Weaver, *What You Learn*, p. 139. Pluto, *Earl*, p. 52.

49. *Sun*, 7 Aug. 1966. Okrent, *Nine Innings*, p. 19. Falkner, *Short Season*, p. 91.

50. Robinson quoted in Pluto, *Earl*, p. 52.

51. *Sun*, 4 Oct. 1967, 12 July 1968.

52. *TSN*, 21 Oct. 1967. *Sun*, 14 Dec. 1967, 10 Jan., 30 Mar., 12 July 1968. Weaver, *What You Learn*, pp. 141–42. Brooks Robinson, *Third Base*, pp. 161–63.

53. Weaver, *Winning*, p. 64. Weaver, *What You Learn*, p. 146.

54. "Armageddon for a Pennant Race," *SI*, 5 Aug. 1968. *TSN*, 10 Aug. 1968.

55. Napp quoted in *Sun*, 3 Sept. 1968. Weaver's habit of antagonizing umpires worried a number of Baltimore executives; see the comments of Jim Russo in Boswell, *Life*, p. 151.

56. *TSN*, 19 Feb. 1966.

57. House, *Telecasting of Professional Sports*, pp. 64–65. Memorandum by Dwight Davis, 12 Feb. 1960, "Television," Baseball Correspondence, Rickey Papers, LC. *Broadcasting*, 6 Mar. 1961.

58. *Congressional Quarterly Almanac*, vol. 17, 1961, p. 502. Horowitz, "Market Entrenchment."

59. *Television Age*, 5 Mar. 1962, 4 Mar. 1963, 2 Mar. 1964. A copy of the 1963 agreement between the Orioles and National Brewery is in SEC Files, SEC 0-637-2.

60. *TSN*, 7 Sept. 1963. *Broadcasting*, 4 Mar. 1963.

61. *TSN*, 7 Sept. 1963. Senate, *Professional Sports Antitrust Bill, 1965*, pp. 9–11, 33–34.

62. *Television Age*, 2 Sept. 1963.

63. Ibid. *TSN*, 15 Feb. 1964.

64. *NYT*, 12 Feb. 1964. Draft letter, Frick to Fetzer, n.d., with attachments, "Television prior to 1973," Subject Files, NBL.

65. *NYT*, 12 Feb., 21 Apr. 1964. *Television Age*, 2 Mar. 1964.

66. *NYT*, 19 July, 7 Nov. 1964. *TSN*, 3 Oct., 21 Nov. 1964. Senate, *Professional Sports Antitrust Bill, 1965*, pp. 26–29, 62–64.

67. *NYT*, 26 Nov., 16 Dec. 1964. Detroit Tigers press release, 15 Dec. 1964. "Television prior to 1973," Subject Files, NBL.

68. Senate, *Professional Sports Antitrust Bill, 1965*, pp. 89–90. *TSN*, 6 Feb. 1965. *Television Age*, 15 Feb. 1965.

69. *TSN*, 18 Sept. 1965. *NYT*, 11, 16 Oct. 1965, 28 Feb. 1966.

70. *Sun*, 22 Oct. 1965. Kuhn, *Hardball*, p. 267. *Broadcasting*, 28 Feb. 1966.

71. *TSN*, 9 Mar. 1968. *Broadcasting*, 19 Feb. 1968.

72. *Sun*, 20 Nov. 1965. Lane quoted in *Newsweek*, 26 Apr. 1965.

73. *Sun*, 29 Nov. 1966. *Broadcasting*, 20 Feb. 1967.

Chapter 7

1. Angell, *Summer Game*, p. 241.

2. Robinson interview.

3. *TSN*, 31 July 1965, 4 Feb. 1967.

4. Ibid., 1 June 1968. *Sun*, 24 Dec. 1967, 22 Feb. 1969. Baltimore Baseball Club, Form 10-K, 1967, SEC Files.

5. *NYT*, 8 Aug. 1968.

6. Ibid., 29 May, 11 July 1968. *TSN*, 15 June 1968.

7. "Welcome Angels, Welcome Senators," *Sport*, May 1961. *TSN*, 18 Jan., 10 May 1961, 10 Jan., 1 Sept., 6 Oct. 1962, 26 Oct. 1963.

8. "Keep the Athletics in Kansas City," *Sport*, Oct. 1962. Clark, *Champagne*, pp. 15, 37.

9. *TSN*, 27 July, 3 Aug. 1963, 11 Jan. 1964.

10. "Bravura Battle for the Braves," *SI*, 2 Nov. 1964.

11. "Era of the Carpetbagger in Baseball," *Sport*, Oct. 1964. Senate, *Professional Sports Antitrust Bill, 1965*, pp. 39–41, 101–6. *TSN*, 5 June 1965, 30 Apr. 1966.

12. *NYT*, 20, 25 Oct., 5 Nov., 3 Dec. 1967.

13. Cashen quoted in *Sun*, 16 Nov. 1967. See also ibid., 17, 20 Oct. 1967. Parrott, *Lords of Baseball*, p. 9.

14. *TSN*, 23 Dec. 1967, 31 Aug. 1968. "Three Danger Points of Expansion," *Sport*, Feb. 1968. Veeck, "My Plan to Remodel the Majors," ibid., May 1968. *D&C*, 12 Dec. 1968.

15. *TSN*, 10 Feb. 1968.

16. Dalton quoted in *Sun*, 16 Oct. 1968. On the Orioles' draft preparations, see ibid., 11 Jan., 29 Sept., 9, 13 Oct. 1968, and Weaver, *Winning*, p. 71.

17. Hoffberger quoted in *D&C*, 9 Dec. 1968. *NYT*, 7, 10 Dec. 1968. *TSN*, 4 Jan. 1969. Kuhn, *Hardball*, pp. 29–31.

18. *NYT*, 8, 22 Dec. 1968, 7 Jan., 5, 10 Feb. 1969. Kuhn, *Hardball*, pp. 31–35, 60, 66. *TSN*, 22 Feb. 1969.

19. Senate, *Organized Professional Team Sports* (1958), p. 50.

20. *NYT*, 4 Oct. 1958, 23 Feb. 1969. Orioles official quoted in *Sun*, 22 Nov. 1958.

21. *NYT*, 3 Dec. 1958.

22. Ibid., 25 Mar., 6 Dec. 1959. Lowenfish, *Imperfect Diamond*, pp. 190–91.

23. Senate, *Professional Sports Antitrust Bill, 1964*, pp. 38–42. Lowenfish, *Imperfect Diamond*, p. 191.

24. Voigt, *American Baseball*, 3:208. *NYT*, 5 Dec. 1957.

25. *NYT*, 3 Feb., 5 Dec. 1957. *TSN*, 15 Feb. 1964. Veeck, *Hustler's Handbook*, pp. 157–58. *Saturday Evening Post*, 30 May 1964.

26. Lardner quoted in Flemming, *Dizziest Season*, p. 107. *Sun*, 24 Feb. 1966.

27. *NYT*, 28 Jan. 1966. Lowenfish, *Imperfect Diamond*, p. 200.

28. *NYT*, 6 Mar. 1966. Lowenfish, *Imperfect Diamond*, pp. 196–97.

29. *NYT*, 3 Apr. 1966. *TSN*, 28 May 1966. Lowenfish, *Imperfect Diamond*, p. 199.

30. *NYT*, 3 Apr. 1966.

31. Ibid., 4 May 1966. Voigt, *American Baseball*, 3:270.

32. *NYT*, 7 June 1966.

33. Ibid., 12 July, 26 Aug. 1966.

34. Robinson interview. *TSN*, 10 Sept. 1966. Scoville, "Labor Relations in Sports," p. 193.

35. Miller quoted in Parrott, *Lords of Baseball*, p. 17.

36. *NYT*, 1 Dec. 1966, 2, 11 Aug. 1967. *TSN*, 9 Sept. 1967. Davis, "Self-Regulation in Baseball," p. 380.

37. Miller quoted in *NYT*, 12 Feb. 1967. *TSN*, 10 June 1967.

38. Richards quoted in *NYT*, 1 Dec. 1967. Ibid., 2 Dec. 1967.

39. Ibid., 21, 27 Jan., 22 Feb. 1968. *Sun*, 2 Mar. 1968. Voigt, *American Baseball*, 3:210–11. A copy of the first Basic Agreement is in "Players Association," Subject Files, NBL.

40. Robinson interview.

41. *NYT*, 1 Aug. 1967, 19 Mar. 1968. *TSN*, 17 Aug. 1968. *D&C*, 8 Dec. 1967.

42. *NYT*, 13 Sept. 1968.

43. Robinson interview.

44. Beard, *Birds*, pp. 127–28.

45. Brooks Robinson, *Third Base*, p. 155–57. Frank Robinson, *My Life*, p. 177.

46. *TSN*, 31 Dec. 1966. *Sun*, 6 Mar. 1967.

47. *TSN*, 29 July 1967.

48. Robinson interview. Beard, *Birds*, p. 18. Frank Robinson *My Life*, pp. 139, 173. See also Frank Robinson, *Extra Innings*, pp. 57–58.

49. *Sun*, 28 Feb. 1967.

50. Robinson interview. *Sun*, 8 Aug. 1966, 5 Nov. 1968.

51. *NYT*, 6 Dec. 1968.

52. Ibid., 18, 20 Sept. 1968. *TSN*, 5 Oct. 1968. Miller and Dalton quoted in *Sun*, 12 Dec. 1968.

53. *NYT*, 18 Dec. 1968.

54. *Sun*, 5 Dec. 1968, 8 Jan. 1969. *NYT*, 2, 4 Feb. 1969.

55. *NYT*, 5, 7, 18 Feb. 1969.

56. Ibid., 12, 13, 18, 20 Feb. 1969. Flood, *The Way It Is*, p. 50.

57. *NYT*, 5 Feb. 1969.

58. *Broadcasting*, 17 Feb. 1969.

59. *NYT*, 15, 21 Feb. 1969. *U.S. News and World Report*, 17 Feb. 1969.

60. *Look*, 18 Feb. 1969.

61. *Sun*, 19 Feb. 1969.

62. Ibid., 22 Feb. 1969.

63. Ibid., 20 Feb. 1969.

64. Ibid., 28 Jan., 19–21 Feb. 1969. Hardin lost his starting job in 1969 and finished out his career as a long reliever and spot starter, positions that were not highly paid.

65. *NYT*, 22, 23, 25, 26 Feb. 1969.

66. *TSN*, 15 Mar. 1969. *U.S. News and World Report*, 10 Mar. 1969. *Time*, 28 Feb. 1969. Hoffberger quoted in *Sun*, 27 Feb. 1969.

67. Olson, *Baltimore: The Building of an American City*, pp. 382–84.

68. D'Alesandro quoted in "Winning Is a Many-Splendored Thing," *Nation's Business*, Dec. 1971.

69. Boucher quoted in ibid.

70. Ibid.

71. Boucher to D'Alesandro, 28 June 1961, "B," Thomas D'Alesandro, Jr., Papers, MHS. *Baltimore*, Aug. 1961. On Baltimore's successful urban renewal, see *Business Week*, 15 Feb. 1969, 30 Mar. 1963, and Olson, *Baltimore*, p. 49

72. Olson, *Baltimore: The Building of an American City*, pp. 358–59.

73. Meyer, *Maryland*, p. 139. Olson, *Baltimore*, pp. 68–69.

74. "Baltimore Might Make It," *New Republic*, 9 Apr. 1966.

75. Olson, *Baltimore*, pp. 34, 51. *Business Week*, 15 Feb. 1969. Olson, *Baltimore: The Building of an American City*, p. 362.

76. Minutes of a meeting of the "Hospitality and Transportation Committee," 16 Sept. 1971, "World Series (2)," Thomas D'Alesandro III Files, Baltimore City Archives. Memorandum from Eddinger to D'Alesandro, 16 Sept. 1971, "World Series (3)," ibid.

77. Schaefer's comments are reported in a press release by the Charles Center–Inner Harbor Management, Inc., 7 Oct. 1971, "World Series (2)," Thomas D'Alesandro III Files, Baltimore City Archives. The Washington press has traditionally enjoyed poking fun at Bawlmerese. For a selection of local pronunciations, see Washington *Star*, 19 Sept. 1976.

78. Olson, *Baltimore*, p. 15.

79. *Sun*, 5 Nov. 1987. Olson, *Baltimore: The Building of an American City*, p. 365.

80. *Sun*, 26 Sept. 1969.

81. Angell, *Summer Game*, p. 206.

82. Dalton quoted in *Sun*, 16 Oct. 1970. Ibid., 19 Oct. 1969.

83. *SI*, 13 Apr. 1970.

84. *Sun*, 6 Nov. 1969.

85. "Watch Out! There Are More En Route," *SI*, 31 Aug. 1970. *Sun*, 16 Oct., 2 Dec. 1970.

86. *D&C*, 18 Oct. 1971.

87. Dalton interview.

Chapter 8

1. House, *Inquiry into Professional Sports, Hearings*, 1:423–55, 524–49. Kuhn, *Hardball*, pp. 93–98. *TSN*, 2 Jan., 4 Sept. 1971, 15 Jan. 1972. On the Senators' attendance problems, see James, *Historical Baseball Abstract*, p. 234, and "Destiny's Whipping Boys," *SI*, 5 Apr. 1965.

2. "Bait That Caught the Texas Rangers," *Business Week*, 1 Apr. 1972.

3. *TSN*, 9 Oct. 1971. See the comments of Red Smith, *NYT*, 31 Mar. 1972.

4. Cashen quoted in *Sun*, 23 Sept. 1971. Kuhn, *Hardball*, p. 96.

5. Baltimore Baseball Club, Annual Report, 1970, SEC Files.

6. Baltimore Baseball Club, Form 10-K, 1971 and 1974, SEC Files.

7. *TSN*, 26 Feb., 18 Nov. 1972. Kuhn, *Hardball*, pp. 190–91.

8. Kuhn, *Hardball*, pp. 99–100. Sisk to Celler, 4 Nov. 1971, "Sports," General Office Files, Celler Papers, LC. *Business Week*, 2 June 1973. *NYT*, 2 Dec. 1971.

9. "What's Happened to Baseball?," *Saturday Review*, 14 Sept. 1968. *Newsweek*, 16 Dec. 1968. On the Hoffberger committee's report, *NYT*, 7 Dec. 1969. "Baseball in the 70s," *Sport*, Feb. 1970. "A Strange Business, Baseball," *NYT Magazine*, 2 Sept. 1973.

10. *NYT*, 25 May, 14 Aug. 1969. *TSN*, 30 Aug. 1969. Kuhn, *Hardball*, pp. 37–67.

11. Dalton interview. *Sun*, 7, 28 Oct., 4, 8 Nov. 1971. *TSN*, 13 Nov. 1971.

12. *Sun*, 31 Oct. 1971. *TSN*, 2 Nov. 1971.

13. *Sun*, 19 Nov. 1971.

14. Weaver quoted in *TSN*, 18 Dec. 1971.

15. Weaver quoted in *Sun*, 3 Dec. 1971. See the comments of Frank Lane, ibid., 23 May 1972.

16. Martin quoted in *D&C*, 29 Mar. 1972. *Sun*, 3 Dec. 1971, 24 Feb. 1972.

17. Flood, "My Rebellion," *SI*, 1 Feb. 1972. Flood, *The Way It Is*, pp. 229–36.

18. *NYT*, 31 Dec. 1969, 17 Jan. 1970.

19. Ibid., 18 Jan. 1970.

20. *TSN*, 17 Jan. 1970.

21. Ibid., 24 Jan. 1970. *NYT*, 18 Jan. 1970.

22. *NYT*, 24 Sept., 17 Dec. 1969. *TSN*, 3 Jan. 1970.

23. *NYT*, 25, 28 Jan., 15 Mar., 25 May 1970. A copy of the 1970 Basic Agreement is in "Players Association," Subject Files, NBL.

24. *NYT*, 15 Dec. 1969. For a summary of Kuhn's 1969 meeting with the Players Association, see Flood, *The Way It Is*, pp. 219–27, and *TSN*, 25 Apr., 13 June 1970.

25. *NYT*, 21, 22, 27 May, 4, 6, 11 June, 13 Aug. 1970.

26. Ibid., 28 May, 14 June, 14 July 1970. *TSN*, 20 June, 29 Aug. 1970.

27. *NYT*, 1–5, 8 Oct. 1970.

28. *NYT*, 8 Apr., 20 Oct. 1971. Flood v. Kuhn 316 F Supp 271.

29. *TSN*, 24 July, 20 Nov. 1971. *Sport*, Aug. 1971. *NYT*, 6 July 1971.

30. *Washington Post*, 26 Feb. 1972. *Sun*, 2, 11 Mar. 1972. *NYT*, 28 Mar. 1971.

31. Dalton interview.

32. Ibid. Kuhn, *Hardball*, pp. 104–5. Rader, *American Sports*, p. 349. *Washington Post*, 23 Mar. 1972.

33. *NYT*, 22, 26 Feb. 1972. *Sun*, 24, 25 Feb. 1972.

34. *NYT*, 10 Mar. 1972.

35. *Sun*, 27 Mar. 1972.

36. Cashen quoted in ibid., 17 Mar. 1972.

37. Hoffberger quoted in ibid., 27 Mar. 1972. *Washington Post*, 27 Mar. 1972.

38. *Washington Post*, 1 Apr. 1972.

39. *D&C*, 2 Apr. 1972.

40. *Sun*, 2 Apr. 1972.

41. Ibid., 1, 2 Apr. 1972.

42. Ibid., 2 Apr. 1972.

43. Maisel quoted in *Sun*, 2 Apr. 1972. Veeck, "The High Price of a Home Run," *Tropic*, 2 Apr. 1972. Cincinnati Reds press release, 6 Apr. 1972, "Players Association," Subject Files, NBL.

44. *Sun*, 1 Apr. 1972. *NYT*, 30 Mar., 2, 3, 9 Apr. 1972.

45. *NYT*, 3–5, 8–9 Apr. 1972. *Washington Post*, 4 Apr. 1972. *TSN*, 29 Apr. 1972.

46. Weaver and Cashen quoted in *Sun*, 5 Apr. 1972. *Washington Post*, 5 Apr. 1972.

47. Miller quoted in *TSN*, 27 Apr. 1972. *NYT*, 5–6 Apr. 1972.

48. *Sun*, 6, 8 Apr. 1972. Cashen quoted in 8 Apr. edition. *NYT*, 5 Apr. 1972.

49. Robinson interview. Robinson quoted in *NYT*, 6 Apr. 1972. *Sun*, 8, 9 Apr. 1972.

50. *NYT*, 11, 12, 14 Apr. 1972. *Washington Post*, 12 Apr. 1972.

51. *NYT*, 21 May 1972.

52. Baltimore Baseball Club, Form 10-K, 1973, SEC Files. *TSN*, 4 Nov. 1972. *Sun*, 1 June 1972. *NYT*, 18 May 1972. "And So They Played Baseball," *SI*, 24 Apr. 1972. "Funny Kind of a Race," ibid., 25 Sept. 1972.

53. Weaver quoted in *Sun*, 1 Dec. 1972. Weaver quickly regretted making the remark. Weaver, *What You Learn*, p. 205. On the Orioles' search for help, see *TSN*, 1 July 1972; *NYT*, 15 Oct. 1972; and *Sun*, 19, 24 Oct. 1972.

54. Flood v. Kuhn, 407 US 258, 282–83, testimony and exhibits. *NYT*, 20 June 1972.

55. *Washington Post*, 20 June 1972. *NYT*, 8 July, 11 Aug. 1972. *TSN*, 1, 22 Apr., 23 Sept. 1972.

56. Dalton interview.

57. *Newsweek*, 3 July 1972.

58. *NYT*, 22 June 1972. *TSN*, 8 July 1972.

59. *NYT*, 30 Nov., 12 Dec. 1972.

60. Ibid., 1–2, 8 Dec. 1972.

61. Ibid., 1, 8 Dec. 1972. *TSN*, 6 Jan. 1973.

62. *Sun*, 9 Feb. 1973.

Chapter 9

1. Robinson quoted in *Sun*, 6 Feb. 1973. *Time*, 5 Mar. 1973.

2. *NYT*, 8, 9, 12 Feb. 1973.

3. Cashen quoted in ibid., 9 Feb. 1973. Robinson comments in *Sun*, 9 Feb. 1973.

4. Robinson quoted in *NYT*, 10 Feb. 1973.

5. Ibid., 10, 13 Feb. 1973.

6. *Sun*, 17 Feb. 1973.

7. *NYT*, 26 Feb. 1973. *Washington Post*, 26 Feb. 1973.

8. Scully, "Binding Salary Arbitration." Voigt, *American Baseball*, 3:212. See the comments of Peter Seitz, *NYT*, 2 Aug. 1974.

9. *Sun*, 17 Apr. 1973. *TSN*, 19 May, 3 Nov. 1973.

10. Weaver, *What You Learn*, pp. 204–17. "Birds Bug Off Towards a Title," *SI*, 3 Sept. 1973.

11. *TSN*, 17 Nov. 1973. *Sun*, 1 Dec. 1973.

12. *TSN*, 1, 8 Dec. 1973. *Sun*, 18 Nov. 1973. Bready, *Home Team*, p. 88.

13. *NYT*, 4 Jan. 1974.

14. Cashen quoted in ibid., 5 Jan. 1974.

15. Ibid., 1 Feb. 1974. *Sun*, 22, 24 Feb. 1974.

16. *TSN*, 16 Mar. 1974. McNally quoted in *Sun*, 27 Mar. 1972. See also ibid., 21 Mar. 1974.

17. *Sun*, 9 Mar. 1974. *TSN*, 27 July 1974.

18. *TSN*, 19 Oct. 1974

19. *Sun*, 27 Sept. 1974.

20. Ibid. *D&C*, 13 Nov. 1974.

21. *TSN*, 16 Nov., 21, 28 Dec. 1974.

22. Baltimore Baseball Club, Annual Report, 1975, SEC Files.

23. *Sun*, 20 Jan. 1988.

24. On Schaefer, see *Baltimore*, Sept. 1983, and *Washington Post*, 18 Mar., 2 June 1986, 12 Apr. 1987.

25. Olson, *Baltimore*, p. 26. *Time*, 24 Aug. 1981. Meyer, *Maryland*, pp. 152–54.

26. *Nation*, 21 Dec. 1970. *Sun*, 20 Jan. 1987.

27. Interview with Thomas D'Alesandro III, 17 June 1976, OH 8119, MHS. Olson, *Baltimore: The Building of an American City*, pp. 373–74. On Schaefer and Reagan, see *New Republic*, 18 Oct. 1982.

28. Callcott, *Maryland and America*, pp. 276–87.

29. *Sun*, 20 Jan. 1987.

30. *New Yorker*, 28 Oct. 1972.

31. Olson, *Baltimore*, pp. 54, 64. *Sun*, 4–5 Apr. 1988.

32. *Baltimore*, Sept. 1983. *Ebony*, Dec. 1981 (includes Mitchell quote).

33. Olson, *Baltimore*, p. 33. Walsh and Fox, *Maryland*, p. 899. Olson, *Baltimore: The Building of an American City*, pp. 352–53, 366–67.

34. *TSN*, 28 Apr. 1973.

35. Boswell, *Life*, p. 146. *Washington Post*, 10 Sept. 1987.

36. Dunn interview.

37. *NYT*, 5 July 1964. Reidenbaugh, *The Sporting News*, pp. 214–15. Kahn, *Season in the Sun*, pp. 61–62. "The Ball Park Becomes a Palace," *Fortune*, Mar. 1973.

38. Grady memorandum for Mayor Cutrer of Houston, Texas, ca. 1961, "Memorial Stadium," Department of Parks and Recreation, Grady-Goodman Files, Baltimore City Archives. *Evening Sun*, 3 Apr. 1963, 28 Dec. 1966. Baltimore, *Capital Improvement Program, 1965–1970*, pp. 104–5. *TSN*, 8 Feb. 1964. *Sun*, 9 Dec. 1965. On the city's utilization of sports to attract business, see *Nation's Business*, Dec. 1971.

39. *Sun*, 18 Sept. 1965.

40. *Evening Sun*, 4 Oct. 1967.

41. *Sun*, 23 Oct. 1967.

42. "Report to the Comptroller by the Department of Parks and Recreation on

Stadium Deficiencies and 'Optimum Requirements,' " 19 Jan. 1968, "Memorial Stadium," Vertical Files, Enoch Pratt Free Library, Baltimore. *News American*, 22 Dec. 1967, 21 Jan. 1968.

43. *News American*, 10 Dec. 1967.

44. *Sun*, 9 July 1969. *TSN*, 26 July 1969.

45. *Sun*, 17 Sept. 1970.

46. Dalton interview. D'Alesandro to Kuhn, 22 June 1970, "Football," Thomas D'Alesandro III Files, Baltimore City Archives. Memorandum from Eddinger to Kane, 15 Sept. 1971, "World Series," ibid. Memorandum from Eddinger to D'Alesandro, 16 Sept. 1971, ibid. Cashen to Eddinger, 19 Oct. 1971, ibid. *Sun*, 17 Sept., 1 Oct., 17 Nov. 1970. *TSN*, 28 Aug. 1971. The baseball club was concerned that a football game, especially one played in poor weather, would have a serious effect on the playing field on the eve of a championship series and possible World Series. The city's contract with the Orioles stated that it would attempt to prevent any use of the stadium by a football team within thirty-six hours of a scheduled Orioles game. The Monday night game fell less than thirty-six hours prior to the Orioles next scheduled home game. In ruling in favor of the Colts, the court imposed certain restrictions in order to keep the field in good shape.

47. *Sun*, 27 Mar. 1971.

48. *News American*, 7 Mar. 1971. *Sun*, 4 Apr. 1971. House Resolution [HR] 84, 5 Mar. 1971, Maryland, *Journal of Proceedings*, House, 1971, p. 657.

49. *Sun*, 4 Apr. 1971.

50. Ibid., 4 Nov. 1971, 29 Mar. 1972.

51. Maryland, *Journal of Proceedings*, House, 1972, pp. 1793, 1820, 1939, 2506, 2601. Ibid., Senate, 1972, pp. 1384–85, 2029–31, 2111–13, 2200, 2233, 2455. *Sun*, 29 Mar., 6 May 1972. Chapter 178, "Maryland Sports Complex Authority," *Laws of Maryland*, 1972, pp. 480–92.

52. *TSN*, 29 Jan. 1972. *Sun*, 13 Aug. 1972.

53. Maryland Sports Complex Authority, "Report to the Governor, Mayor of Baltimore and General Assembly," 15 Nov. 1972, "Sports Complex Authority," Maryland State Archives, Annapolis. Maryland Sports Complex Authority, "Feasibility Study, Stage I," 10 Jan. 1973, ibid.

54. "Feasibility Study, Stage I," ibid.

55. Ibid.

56. Maryland Sports Complex Authority, "Final Report, Feasibility Study" 21 Feb. 1973, ibid. *Sun*, 25 Mar. 1973.

57. House Bill [HB] 236, 11 Jan. 1973, Maryland, *Journal of Proceedings*, House, 1973, p. 157. HB 474, 25 Jan. 1973, ibid., p. 280. Baltimore, *Baltimore's Development Program as Recommended by the Planning Commission, Feb. 23, 1973*. *TSN*, 20 Jan. 1973. Interview with Robert Irsay, *Baltimore*, Nov. 1972. *Sun*, 13 Aug. 1972.

58. *Sun*, 18 Feb., 9 Apr. 1973. *TSN*, 28 Apr. 1973.

59. *Sun*, 2 Dec. 1973.

60. *TSN*, 26 Jan. 1974. *Sun*, 2 Dec. 1973, 28 Feb., 16 Mar. 1974.

61. Hoffberger quoted in *Sun*, 2 Mar. 1974. See also Kreiger comments, *NYT*, 11 Oct. 1974.

62. "Why Those WFL Owners Expect to Score a Profit," *Fortune*, Sept. 1974. Leonard Koppett column, *TSN*, 4 May 1974. "A Strange Business, Baseball," *NYT*

Magazine, 2 Sept. 1973. Markham and Teplitz, *Baseball Economics*, pp. 17–23, a study done for the major leagues, claims that profit in baseball is marginal at best. For a contrasting view, see Noll, *Sports Business*, pp. 18–22, 164–65, and Voigt, *American Baseball*, 3:80. Representatives of labor and management discuss the issue of profitability and its impact in House, *Inquiry into Professional Sports, Hearings*, 1:45–46, 126–39, 246–49; 2:115–19, 130, 164–84, 257–58, 372–73, 416, 453–54. On this topic, see also *Sun*, 7 July 1974. On the whole, I am inclined to see three factors motivating owners of franchises: ego gratification, a belief that the owner's particular business skills will result in a steady profit, and the security of a large profit when selling out. See the discussion in *Forbes*, 29 Oct. 1979.

63. On National Brewery's troubles, see *News American*, 6, 27 Oct. 1974; *Washington Post*, 16 Feb. 1975; and *Sun*, 7 Jan., 1 Nov. 1975.

64. *Sun*, 14 July 1974.

65. Baltimore Baseball Club, Annual Report, 1974, SEC Files. *TSN*, 3 Feb. 1973, 2 Feb., 19 Oct. 1974.

66. *Washington Post*, 16 Feb. 1975.

67. Dalton interview. *TSN*, 30 Nov. 1974. *Washington Post*, 16 Feb. 1975.

68. *Sun*, 30 Sept. 1972. Kuhn, *Hardball*, pp. 101–3. *Business Week*, 2 June 1976.

69. *Sun*, 7 Apr. 1974.

70. Ibid., 29 July, 8 Aug. 1974. *TSN*, 27 Apr. 1974.

71. *TSN*, 17 Aug. 1974. *Washington Post*, 16 Mar. 1972. *Sun*, 7 Apr. 1974.

72. *Sun*, 11 Oct. 1974.

73. Ibid.

74. *NYT*, 11 Oct. 1974.

75. *Sun*, 11, 13 Oct. 1974.

76. *NYT*, 17 Oct. 1974. *Sun*, 18 Oct. 1974.

77. *Sun*, 25 Oct., 8 Nov. 1974. *NYT*, 27 Oct. 1974.

78. On the vote, the turnout, and the reaction of Maryland officials, see *Sun*, 6, 7 Nov. 1974. On the efforts to sell the team, see *Sun*, 14, 15, 22 Nov. 1974; *NYT*, 15 Nov. 1974; and *TSN*, 23 Nov. 1974.

79. *Sun*, 1, 7 Dec. 1974. *NYT*, 7, 8 Dec. 1974.

80. *NYT*, 14 Dec. 1974. *TSN*, 4 Jan. 1974. *Sun*, 8 Dec. 1973, 28 Mar. 1975.

81. HR 29, 5 Feb. 1975, Maryland, *Journal of Proceedings*, House, 1975, p. 533. Senate Resolution [SR] 32, 5 Feb. 1975, ibid., Senate, 1972, p. 491. *NYT*, 24 Jan. 1975. *Sun*, 28 Jan., 6, 8 Feb. 1975.

82. *Sun*, 30 Jan., 11 Feb. 1975. *Washington Post*, 8, 9 Feb. 1975. *TSN*, 13 Feb. 1975. On Lerner and other Washington developers with ambitions to own a franchise, see "The Making of Washington," *Washingtonian*, Nov. 1987

83. *Washington Post*, 12 Feb. 1975. *Sun*, 18, 28 Feb. 1975.

84. *Washington Post*, 21 Feb. 1975.

85. Hoffberger quoted in *TSN*, 14 Feb. 1975. *Sun*, 28 Feb. 1975. *Washington Post*, 27 Feb. 1975. Kuhn, *Hardball*, pp. 100–101.

86. *Sun*, 8, 20 Feb. 1975. *Washington Post*, 15, 16 Feb. 1975. Veeck, *Veeck*, p. 371.

87. *Washington Post*, 2 Mar. 1975.

88. HB 1341, 3 Mar. 1975, Maryland, *Journal of Proceedings*, House, 1975, pp. 1277–78, 2257, 2488–90, 2551–54, 2931. *Washington Post*, 4, 6 Mar. 1975.

89. *Washington Post*, 26 Mar., 5, 7 Apr. 1975. *Sun*, 3, 5 Apr. 1975.

90. *NYT*, 7 May 1975.

91. *Sun*, 15 May 1975.

92. Orioles press release, 9 June 1975, "Orioles," Subject Files, NBL. Veeck quoted in *NYT*, 8 Apr. 1973, 11 June 1975. *TSN*, 28 June 1975. The *Sun*'s Bob Maisel, who had unusual access to Orioles management, wrote some years later: "I always thought Hoffberger became very leery of his [Veeck's] history of acquiring a franchise, pumping it up with promotions (something at which he was an absolute genius), then selling out for a profit, after which the new organization would fall on leaner times" (*Sun*, 3 Jan. 1986). This is probably as good an analysis of Hoffberger's motives as we are likely to get. Mr. Hoffberger declined to be interviewed for this book.

Chapter 10

1. Baltimore Baseball Club, Annual Report, 1975, SEC Files. *Sun*, 1 Oct. 1975, 17 Jan. 1976. Baltimore Orioles press release, 16 Jan. 1976. "Orioles," Subject Files, NBL.

2. *Sun*, 22 Oct., 1, 4 Nov. 1975.

3. Ibid., 18 July 1975.

4. Ibid., 17, 18 July 1975. *NYT*, 17, 18 July 1975. *TSN*, 15 Nov. 1975. Kuhn, *Hardball*, pp. 144–53. Clark, *Champagne*, pp. 365–66.

5. Peters interview. Weaver, *What You Learn*, p. 233.

6. *NYT*, 16 Dec. 1974. *Sun*, 19 Dec. 1974. *TSN*, 4 Jan. 1975. Clark, *Champagne*, pp. 197–98.

7. *TSN*, 15 Jan. 1975. See also *Washington Post*, 1 Jan. 1975, and *NYT*, 2 Jan. 1975.

8. *NYT*, 3 Jan. 1975

9. Ibid., 12, 14 Jan. 1975.

10. Ibid., 3 Jan. 1975. Voigt, *American Baseball*, 3:213.

11. *Sun*, 7 Mar. 1975. Lowenfish, *Imperfect Diamond*, p. 219. Robinson interview.

12. *SI*, 11 Mar. 1974. *NYT*, 11 Apr. 1972. Scoville, "Labor Relations in Sports," p. 215.

13. *TSN*, 22 Mar. 1975.

14. Ibid., 29 Mar. 1975. *NYT*, 15 Nov. 1975. Information supplied by John Gaherin on player salaries, Note in files, 2 Apr. 1975, "Salaries, 1974–1980," Subject Files, NBL. *U.S. News and World Report*, 24 Mar. 1975. Kuhn, *Hardball*, pp. 155–56.

15. *NYT*, 15 July, 6, 13 Aug. 1975.

16. Ibid., 24 Oct. 1975.

17. Ibid., 15, 22 Nov. 1975.

18. Kuhn, *Hardball*, pp. 157–59. Weaver, *What You Learn*, p. 225. Lowenfish, *Imperfect Diamond*, p. 20.

19. *NYT*, 24 Dec. 1975. *Washington Post*, 24 Dec. 1975. House, *Inquiry into Professional Sports, Hearings*, 1:391–92.

20. *Sun*, 24 Dec. 1975.

21. Ibid.

22. Ibid.

23. Ibid.

24. *Washington Post,* 23 Dec. 1975. *NYT,* 9 Jan., 5, 6 Feb. 1976.

25. Peters quoted in *Sun,* 7 Jan. 1976. *TSN,* 21 Feb. 1976. *NYT,* 21 Feb. 1976.

26. *NYT,* 16 Jan., 13 Feb. 1976. *Sun,* 26 Jan. 1976. *TSN,* 31 Jan. 1976.

27. Peters interview. *NYT,* 1 Feb. 1976. *Sun,* 30 Jan., 17 Feb. 1976.

28. *NYT,* 24 Feb. 1976. *Sun,* 27 Feb. 1976.

29. *NYT,* 27 Feb. 1976. Veeck, *Veeck,* pp. 402–3.

30. *NYT,* 19 Feb., 5, 7, 9 Mar. 1976. *Washington Post,* 4 Mar. 1976.

31. *Sun,* 11 Mar. 1976. *NYT,* 12 Mar. 1976.

32. *TSN,* 13 Mar. 1976. *NYT,* 11, 16, 17 Mar. 1976. *Washington Post,* 16, 17 Mar. 1976. *Sun,* 16 Mar. 1976.

33. *NYT,* 21 Jan., 15, 18 Mar. 1976. Kuhn, *Hardball,* pp. 161–62.

34. *NYT,* 18 Mar. 1976. *Sun,* 18 Mar. 1976. Kuhn, *Hardball,* pp. 163–64.

35. *NYT,* 20, 26 Mar., 20 Apr., 11 May, 13, 20 July 1976. House, *Inquiry into Professional Sports, Hearings,* 1:41, 54–57, 368–73, 380. House, *Inquiry into Professional Sports, Final Report,* pp. 31–33. Kuhn, *Hardball,* p. 166.

36. *Sun,* 19, 20 Mar. 1976.

37. Dalton interview. House, *Inquiry into Professional Sports, Hearings,* 1:70–73. *NYT,* 27 Jan. 1977. *TSN,* 12 Feb. 1977.

38. House, *Inquiry into Professional Sports, Hearings,* 1:282–83, 287–88, 290. *TSN,* 27 Mar. 1976. *Sun,* 27 Mar. 1976.

39. *TSN,* 17 Jan. 1976. *Sun,* 5 Feb., 6 Mar. 1976.

40. *Sun,* 14 Feb., 17 Mar. 1976. *TSN,* 28 Feb., 3, 27 Mar. 1976. *NYT,* 28 Mar. 1976. Weaver, *What You Learn,* p. 235.

41. *TSN,* 17 Apr. 1976. *Sun,* 23 Apr. 1976. Reggie Jackson, *Reggie,* pp. 104–5. Falkner, *Short Season,* pp. 229–30.

42. *Sun,* 4, 6 Apr. 1976. *TSN,* 22 Apr. 1976.

43. Peters interview. *Sun,* 6, 7 Apr. 1976.

44. Palmer quoted in *Sun,* 15 Apr. 1976. Ibid., 25, 26, 28 Apr. 1976. *TSN,* 24 Apr., 1 May 1976.

45. *Sun,* 1, 2 May 1976.

46. Ibid., 2, 3, 6 May 1976. *TSN,* 29 May 1976.

47. *Sun,* 2, 7, 11 May 1976.

48. Ibid., 10–12, 15, 16, 19 June 1976. Pluto, *Earl,* 176–77. Weaver, *What You Learn,* p. 237.

49. House, *Inquiry into Professional Sports, Hearings,* 1:58, 66–68. *NYT,* 16, 17, 19, 20 June 1976. Kuhn, *Hardball,* pp. 173–82.

50. Hoffberger quoted in *Sun,* 19 June 1976. *NYT,* 18, 20, 26 June 1976. House, *Inquiry into Professional Sports, Hearings,* 1:293–97, 366–68. *TSN,* 3 July 1976.

51. *Sun,* 19 June 1976. *TSN,* 28 Aug. 1976. Reggie Jackson, *Reggie,* pp. 104, 108, 111–12. Linn, *Steinbrenner's Yankees,* p. 23.

52. *SI,* 26 July 1976.

53. *Washington Post,* 28 Aug. 1976. *TSN,* 11 Sept. 1976. Jackson quoted in "Hitting a Million," *SI,* 30 Aug. 1976.

54. *Sun,* 24 June, 16 Sept., 6 Oct. 1976. *Washington Post,* 19 Aug. 1976. *TSN,* 18 Sept. 1976.

55. *D&C,* 3 Nov. 1976.

56. Peters interview. *NYT*, 5 Nov. 1976. *Sun*, 5 Nov. 1976. Orioles press release, 8 Nov. 1976, "Orioles," Subject Files, NBL.

57. Walker quoted in *Sun*, 18 Nov. 1976.

58. Peters quoted in ibid.

59. Ibid., 10, 26, 27 Nov. 1976. *TSN*, 6 Nov. 1976.

60. Kuhn, *Hardball*, pp. 188–97. *TSN*, 27 Nov. 1976. *Sun*, 10 Apr. 1976.

61. All quotes from *SI*, 13 Dec. 1976. *Washington Post*, 5 Dec. 1976. *Sun*, 2, 12 Dec. 1976. *TSN*, 18 Dec. 1976.

62. Peters quoted in *Sun*, 2 Dec. 1976.

63. Peters quoted in *TSN*, 11 Dec. 1976, 29 Jan., 26 Feb. 1977. *Sun*, 12 Jan., 24 Feb. 1977.

64. Peters quoted in *NYT*, 6 Apr. 1977. Orioles press releases, 4 Nov. 1976, 14 Jan. 1977, "Orioles," Subject Files, NBL. *Sun*, 18, 24 Jan., 9 Mar. 1977. *TSN*, 5 Mar. 1977. Baltimore Baseball Club, Annual Report, 1976, and Annual Report, 1977, both SEC Files. Since the club sold players after the 31 October end of its 1976 fiscal year, the transaction was in the 1977 report. The sale was large enough to cover the losses the Orioles experienced in both years.

65. *Sun*, 20 Jan. 1977.

66. Hoffberger quoted in ibid., 8 Mar. 1977.

67. Kuhn, *Hardball*, p. 210. *Sun*, 25 Mar. 1977.

Chapter 11

1. Palmer quoted in *Sun*, 1 Mar. 1977. Ibid., 1 Dec. 1976.

2. Hoffberger quoted in ibid., 8 Dec. 1976. Ibid., 10, 11 Dec. 1976, 24 Mar. 1977. *TSN*, 25 Dec. 1976, 1 Jan. 1977.

3. *D&C*, 29 Mar. 1977. In explaining the Orioles' opposition to a National League team in Washington, Peters stated simply, "It's an overlapping TV market" (*Sun*, 25 Mar. 1977). While Hoffberger denied charges that he had undercut Washington's bid, he had used MacPhail's good offices to effectively defeat Kuhn's plans for putting an American League franchise in the nation's capital; see Kuhn, *Hardball*, pp. 192–94. Walter O'Malley complained that "every time the question [of a National League franchise in Washington] is raised, he [Hoffberger] hits the roof" (*Sun*, 25 Mar. 1977).

4. *Washington Post*, 29 Mar. 1977. *Sun*, 29 Mar. 1977. *TSN*, 16 Apr. 1977.

5. *U.S. News and World Report*, 17 Sept. 1977.

6. Baltimore Baseball Club, Annual Report, 1977, SEC Files. *Sun*, 4 Mar. 1977. *TSN*, 23 Apr. 1977.

7. *D&C*, 13 Apr. 1977.

8. *Sun*, 28 Oct. 1977.

9. Baltimore Baseball Club, Annual Report, 1977, SEC Files. *Sun*, 28 Oct. 1977.

10. Orioles press release, 26 Oct. 1978, "Orioles," Subject Files, NBL. *Sun*, 8 Nov. 1977.

11. Harazin quoted in *Sun*, 2 Dec. 1977. *Washington Post*, 3 Dec. 1977. See also Thomas and Jolson, "Components of Demand for Major League Baseball."

12. Peters interview. See also *TSN*, 25 Feb. 1978.

13. *Sun*, 27 Sept., 18 Oct. 1978. Orioles press releases, 26 Oct., 22 Dec. 1978, "Orioles," Subject Files, NBL.

14. *NYT*, 1 May 1978. *Sun*, 7 May 1978, 21 Jan. 1979. Hoffberger quoted in *Sun*, 28 Sept. 1978. In October 1979, Hoffberger denied reports that he was under family pressure to sell the team, calling them "absolute garbage" (*Sun*, 3 Oct. 1979).

15. *Sun*, 28 Sept. 1978. Kuhn, *Hardball*, pp. 4, 229–30.

16. Hoffberger quoted in *Sun*, 8, 28 Dec. 1978.

17. *U.S. News and World Report*, 20 Oct. 1975. *Newsweek*, 15 Jan. 1979 (including quote).

18. *Time*, 24 Aug. 1981. *Newsweek*, 26 July 1982. See also *Esquire*, Oct. 1984.

19. *Time*, 24 Aug. 1981. *Sun*, 14 Feb. 1979. On Rouse, see *Washington Post*, 24 Mar. 1988, and "Captain Enterprise," *Baltimore*, Apr. 1987.

20. *Sun*, 9 June 1976, 7 Nov. 1978.

21. On the formation of the Baltimore groups, see *Sun*, 1, 7, 11, 12, 14 Jan. 1979. On the city's inferiority complex regarding Washington, see "Is Washington Taking Over Baltimore?," *Baltimore*, Dec. 1979.

22. *Sun*, 21, 23, 27 Jan. 1979. *Evening Sun*, 26 Jan. 1979.

23. *Evening Sun*, 26 Jan. 1979. *Sun*, 5 Feb. 1979.

24. *Sun*, 26, 28 Jan. 1979.

25. Ibid., 1 Feb. 1979.

26. Ibid., 6 Feb. 1979.

27. Ibid.

28. *News American*, 6 Feb. 1979.

29. *Sun*, 6, 7, 9 Feb. 1979.

30. Ibid., 8 Feb. 1979.

31. Ibid.

32. Ibid., 11 Feb. 1979.

33. Ibid., 11, 14 Feb. 1979.

34. Ibid., 11 Feb. 1979. Maryland, *Journal of Proceedings*, House, 1979, pp. 929–30, 2226, 2347, 2408, 2510.

35. *Sun*, 5 Mar., 10 May 1979.

36. Ibid., 27 Sept. 1979.

37. Ibid., 2 Aug. 1979. *Washington Post*, 3 Aug. 1979.

38. *Sun*, 3 Aug. 1979. *Washington Post*, 3 Aug. 1979.

39. *Sun*, 1, 2 Aug. 1979. *TSN*, 18 Aug. 1979.

40. *Sun*, 25 Feb. 1979. *TSN*, 7 Feb. 1970.

41. McLaughlin interview. *Sun*, 9 Feb. 1973, 8 Feb. 1979.

42. McLaughlin interview.

43. Scout quoted in *D&C*, 28 Nov. 1973. *Sun*, 9 Feb. 1973.

44. *D&C*, 28 Nov. 1973.

45. McLaughlin interview.

46. *Sun*, 6 Aug., 1 Dec. 1974. *NYT*, 6 Aug. 1974.

47. Cashen quoted in *Sun*, 14 Jan. 1975. House, *Inquiry into Professional Sports, Hearings*, 1:319.

48. Peters to National Association Clubs, 15 Dec. 1971, "Player Development,"

Subject Files, NBL. *D&C*, 26 Oct. 1972. "Down in the Minors," *New Yorker*, 6 Oct. 1975. Obojski, *Bush League*, pp. 55–57.

49. *TSN*, 20 Apr. 1968, 29 Nov., 13 Dec. 1979. House, *Inquiry into Professional Sports, Hearings*, 1:43, 254–55. Voigt, *American Baseball*, 3:118.

50. Steinfeldt quoted in *D&C*, 3 Dec. 1972. *TSN*, 19 Feb. 1972.

51. *Sun*, 12 July, 24 Nov. 1975. *TSN*, 20 Dec. 1975.

52. Peters interview. *Sun*, 13 Dec. 1975.

53. *Sun*, 8 Jan., 10, 15 Feb. 1976. Orioles press release, 6 Feb. 1976, "Orioles," Subject Files, NBL. McLaughlin interview.

54. Peters interview. Kerrane, *Dollar Sign*, p. 27.

55. *Sun*, 17 Jan. 1976. *NYT*, 31 Jan. 1976.

56. *D&C*, 5 Apr., 22 Oct. 1977. *TSN*, 17 Dec. 1977, 7 Jan., 1 Apr. 1978. *Sun*, 8 Jan. 1976. Orioles press releases, 5 Mar., 12 Nov. 1976, 19 Jan. 1977, "Orioles," Subject Files, NBL.

57. Williams quoted in *D&C*, 6 Dec. 1979.

58. Ibid., 3, 4 Dec. 1968.

59. Ibid., 5 Nov. 1968.

60. Silver quoted ibid., 15 Nov. 1976. Ibid., 12 Nov. 1968, 1 Oct. 1969, 22 Nov. 1977.

61. Steinfeldt quoted in ibid., 22 Nov. 1971.

62. National Association of Professional Baseball Clubs press release, 8 Apr. 1971, "Rochester Red Wings," Subject Files, NBL. Obojski, *Bush League*, pp. 124–30. *D&C*, 3 Dec. 1972, 11 Apr. 1973.

63. *D&C*, 2 Oct. 1973, 5 Oct. 1974, 27 Nov. 1975, 1 Sept. 1976.

64. McLaughlin interview.

65. *D&C*, 17 Nov. 1976.

66. Ibid.

67. Ibid., 24 Nov. 1976, 13 Apr. 1977.

68. Ibid., 4, 9, 10 Nov., 2 Dec. 1977.

69. Ibid., 2 Apr. 1978.

70. Ibid., 22 Sept. 1978.

71. Ibid., 29 Sept. 1978.

72. Robinson quoted in ibid., 9 Nov. 1978. Ibid., 19 Oct., 8 Nov. 1978. *TSN*, 2 Dec. 1978. For Frank Robinson's reflections on the situation, see *Extra Innings*, pp. 161–63.

73. *NYT*, 28 Feb. 1979. *D&C*, 6 Nov. 1978, 27 Feb., 14, 16, 20 Mar., 8 Apr. 1979.

74. *D&C*, 2 Sept., 29 Nov., 5 Dec. 1979.

Chapter 12

1. *Sun*, 23 Oct. 1979

2. Baltimore Baseball Club, Annual Report, 1979, SEC Files. *Sun*, 2 Nov. 1979.

3. *Sun*, 28 Sept. 1979.

4. See Pack, *Williams for the Defense*, pp. 73–81, for details.

5. See ibid., pp. 83–84, for judgment of Williams. "A Legal Eagle and His Boy Scout," *SI*, 25 July 1966.

6. Pack, *Williams for the Defense*, pp. 86–87, 90–98.

7. Harris, *League*, pp. 205–7, 296, 306–8, 336.

8. *Sun*, 3 Oct. 1979.

9. Ibid., 23 Oct. 1979.

10. *TSN*, 5 Jan. 1980.

11. *Washington Post*, 16 Oct. 1983.

12. *TSN*, 18 Aug. 1979, 30 May 1981. "The Peters Principle," *Baltimore*, Apr. 1984. On Altobelli, see "He's Managing Quite Well, Thank You," *SI*, 16 May 1983.

13. *Sun*, 3 Mar. 1986. Commenting on his relationship with his "Baseball people," Williams added that it would not be prudent for them to ignore his suggestions: "I don't tell them what to do, but I do make suggestions. And I wouldn't think it would be prudent to ignore them." Falkner, *Short Season*, p. 88.

14. Williams quoted in *D&C*, 6 Dec. 1979. *Sun*, 9 Mar. 1980.

15. *NYT*, 23 Jan. 1978, 11 Feb., 13 Mar. 1979. *SI*, 22 June 1981. *U.S. News and World Report*, 9 Apr. 1984. "Moneyball," *Across the Board*, Sept. 1981, pp. 12–21.

16. *NYT*, 19 June 1978. *TSN*, 15 July 1978.

17. *NYT*, 5 Dec. 1978.

18. Ibid.

19. Ibid., 18 Nov. 1978.

20. Ibid., 7 May 1978, 31 Aug., 14, 27 Nov., 2 Dec. 1979. *Sun*, 26 Nov. 1978. *Washington Post*, 24 June 1981.

21. *NYT*, 12 Jan. 1979.

22. Ibid., 21 Feb., 16 Apr. 1979. See also Miller's comments in "Whither Opening Day, 1980?," *SI*, 3 Mar. 1980.

23. *NYT*, 4, 7 Dec. 1979.

24. Ibid., 6 Jan. 1980.

25. *TSN*, 5 Jan. 1980.

26. *Sun*, 23 Oct. 1979.

27. Ibid., 17 Nov. 1979.

28. Robinson interview.

29. Belanger quoted in *NYT*, 29 May 1981. For an evaluation of the role played by Belanger and DeCinces during the strike, see *News American*, 10 Aug. 1981. Belanger did not respond to my request for an interview.

30. "How Edward Bennett Williams Plans to Save Baseball," *Baltimore*, Apr. 1982.

31. *NYT*, 24 Jan. 1980.

32. Ibid.

33. Miller quoted in ibid., 27 Feb. 1980. Ibid., 28 Feb. 1980.

34. *Sun*, 4 Mar. 1980. Miller's views are presented in "Whither Opening Day, 1980?," *SI*, 3 Mar. 1980.

35. *Sun*, 6 Mar. 1980.

36. Ibid., 9 Mar. 1980.

37. Player Relations Committee press release, 18 Mar. 1980, "Players Association," Subject Files, NBL. *NYT*, 19, 23 Mar. 1980. *Sun*, 20 Mar. 1980.

38. *NYT*, 20, 28 Mar. 1980.

39. *Sun*, 2 Apr. 1980.

40. Ibid., 3 Apr. 1980.

41. *NYT*, 7, 11 May 1980. *Sun*, 10 May 1980.

42. *NYT*, 16, 17, 19, 22 May 1980.

43. Voigt, *American Baseball*, 3:337.

44. Williams quoted in Weaver, *What You Learn*, p. 298. *Washington Post*, 23 May 1980. *NYT*, 24 May 1980.

45. *Sun*, 24 May 1980.

46. *NYT*, 6 June, 8, 10 July 1980.

47. Ibid., 30 Oct., 11, 13 Nov. 1980. *SI*, 5 Jan. 1981.

48. *NYT*, 20 Feb. 1981.

49. Player Relations Committee press release, 29 Dec. 1980, "Players Association," Subject Files, NBL. *NYT*, 19, 20, 26 Feb. 1981. On Kuhn's exposition of the owners' position, see *Dun's Review*, Mar. 1981.

50. *Sun*, 1 Mar. 1981.

51. *U.S. News and World Report*, 12 Apr. 1982.

52. Kuhn, *Hardball*, p. 339.

53. *NYT*, 7, 9 Mar. 1981.

54. Ibid., 11 Mar., 8 Apr. 1981.

55. Ibid., 24, 30 Apr. 1981.

56. Ibid., 6 May 1980.

57. Ibid., 8 May 1981.

58. Ibid., 22 May 1981.

59. Ibid., 14 May 1981. *Sun*, 21 May 1981. *Washington Post*, 24 May 1981. *TSN*, 16, 23 May 1981.

60. *NYT*, 8, 14, 27, 28 May, 7 June 1981.

61. Ibid., 11 June 1981.

62. *Washington Post*, 12 June 1981.

63. *Sun*, 11 June 1981.

64. Ibid., 13 June 1981.

65. *TSN*, 4 July 1981.

66. *Sun*, 12, 13 June 1981. Peters quoted in 13 June edition.

67. Ibid., 15 June 1981.

68. *NYT*, 17 June 1981. *Sun*, 17, 18 June 1981. Kuhn, *Hardball*, pp. 352–53.

69. *Sun*, 19 June 1981.

70. *NYT*, 20, 22 June 1981. Moffett quoted in 22 June edition. *Sun*, 21, 22 June 1981.

71. *SI*, 22 June 1981.

72. *NYT*, 25 June, 2 July 1981. Miller quoted in 2 July edition. *Washington Post*, 28 June 1981.

73. *NYT*, 6, 7 July 1981. *Sun*, 8, 10 July 1981. Williams quoted in 10 July edition. *Washington Post*, 6 July 1981.

74. *NYT*, 10–12 July 1981. *Sun*, 11 July 1981.

75. See *Washington Post*, 12, 17–18 July 1981. *NYT*, 13, 20 June, 1 Aug. 1981, for the economic impact of the strike.

76. *NYT*, 23 July 1981. *Sun*, 28, 30 July 1981. *Washington Post*, 25, 28 July 1981.

77. MacPhail interview. *Sun*, 5 Aug. 1981. *SI*, 10 Aug. 1981. Kuhn, *Hardball*, pp. 357–58. *TSN*, 12 Sept. 1981.

78. *Washington Post*, 2 Aug. 1981.

79. Moffett quoted in *Sun*, 5 Aug. 1981. *NYT*, 16 Aug. 1981, 4 Apr., 16 Sept. 1983.

80. Kuhn, *Hardball*, p. 341. *NYT*, 19 Dec. 1982, 15 Jan. 1984. *Sun*, 1 Aug. 1981. *TSN*, 24 Oct. 1981.

81. Kuhn, *Hardball*, pp. 360–61, 363.

82. *NYT*, 6, 22 Jan., 6 Feb., 10 Mar. 1982.

83. Ibid., 21 Feb. 1983.

84. *Sun*, 2 Feb. 1983

85. *NYT*, 5, 16 Aug. 1981. Bowie Kuhn interview, *Sport*, Sept. 1983.

86. *NYT*, 19, 28 Feb. 1971. *TSN*, 20 Mar. 1971. *Sun*, 2, 6 Mar. 1971. Dolson, *Beating the Bushes*, pp. 114, 119, 122. Kahn, *Season in the Sun*, p. 104. Voigt, *American Baseball*, 3:260–61. Welch, *Five O'Clock*, pp. 16, 34, 40, 304.

87. *Washington Post*, 2 Mar. 1984. *NYT*, 3 Mar. 1984.

88. *Sun*, 23 Sept. 1980. *NYT*, 27 Sept. 1980. Kuhn, *Hardball*, pp. 302–9.

89. Kuhn, *Hardball*, p. 307.

90. *Washington Post*, 9 July 1982, 16 July 1983. *NYT*, 16, 17 July 1983.

91. *NYT*, 23–24, 30 Nov., 9 Dec. 1983.

92. Ibid., 23 Feb. 1984. For fan attitudes, see results of polling in *Washington Post*, 30 Oct. 1985.

93. *NYT*, 24, 27 May, 29 June 1984.

94. Ibid., 15 Nov., 4 Dec. 1984.

95. Ibid., 2 Dec. 1984.

96. *Washington Post*, 17 May 1985.

97. Ibid., 18, 21 May 1985.

98. See the analysis in *SIN*, 7 Aug. 1985.

99. *SI*, 4 Mar. 1982. MacPhail's letter to the owners is quoted and summarized in *USA Today*, 15 Nov. 1985.

Chapter 13

1. Baltimore *Sun*, *Championship Season*, p. 91.

2. Nettles, *Balls*, p. 223.

3. See Veeck, *Hustler's Handbook*, pp. 19–21, for his best exposition of the relationship.

4. *TSN*, 20 July 1974. *Sun*, 22 Feb. 1977, 30 Nov. 1979.

5. Orioles Information Guide, "The Road to Birdland," 1972, "Baltimore Orioles, Misc.," Subject Files, NBL. *Sun*, 7 Mar. 1977. *TSN*, 6 Feb. 1965. Bready, *Home Team*, p. 65. On the use of sex to promote baseball in Baltimore, see Pat Jordan, *Suitors of Spring*, pp. 97–98.

6. *Sun*, 16 Jan. 1966, 14 Jan. 1968, 21 Jan. 1972. *TSN*, 9 Jan. 1965. See Kahn, *Good Enough to Dream*, p. 89, on spring training. Lowenfish, *Imperfect Diamond*, p. 23.

7. "Bird Man of the Orioles," *Washington Post Magazine*, 1 Apr. 1984. On the trend toward "family" entertainment in baseball's marketing, see *USA Today*, 11 Apr. 1986,

and Okrent, *Nine Innings*, p. 57. On the growing emphasis on marketing, see "Grand New Game," *SI*, 11 Aug. 1975.

8. Orioles press releases, 15 Feb. 1980, 11 Mar. 1981. *1986 Orioles Scorecard*, pp. 12, 39. "Orioles Magicgram," Spring 1986, provides information on promotions and is the first of a series of experiments with a newsletter for fans. For the transformation in marketing under Williams, see *Washington Post*, 15 Feb. 1985, and *TSN*, 29 Oct. 1984. On the trend to corporate involvement in marketing throughout baseball, see *WSJ*, 7 May 1986.

9. Washington *Star*, 21 Mar. 1980.

10. Peters interview. See also the comments of Okrent in *Nine Innings*, p. 58.

11. *1986 Orioles Yearbook*, p. 47.

12. *NYT*, 14 Aug. 1980. Baltimore, *Annual Report of the City of Baltimore*, 1978, p. 11. On the Orioles Advocates, see *1986 Orioles Scorecard*, p. 47, and Peters interview. *Sun*, 30 Nov. 1979, 25 Mar. 1981. On the Designated Hitters, see Orioles press release, 29 Nov. 1979, "Orioles," Subject Files, NBL, and *1986 Orioles Scorecard*, p. 48.

13. *Washington Post*, 24 Feb. 1985. *TSN*, 16 Dec. 1985. *Sun*, 3, 4 Feb. 1986.

14. *Sun*, 6 Apr. 1983,

15. *Washington Post*, 6 Aug. 1980.

16. *Sun*, 7 Aug. 1980. See also, *TSN*, 30 Aug. 1980.

17. *Sun*, 7 Aug., 13 Nov. 1980. Williams quoted in 13 Nov. edition.

18. *NYT*, 27 Dec. 1980.

19. *Sun*, 7 Oct. 1980.

20. Ibid., 10 Feb. 1981.

21. *TSN*, 15 Nov. 1980.

22. *Sun*, 21 Nov. 1980, 6 Nov. 1981. Reggie Jackson, *Reggie*, pp. 295–96.

23. Orioles press release, 12 Dec. 1980, "Orioles," Subject Files, NBL.

24. *Washington Post*, 2 Feb. 1984.

25. *TSN*, 13 Dec. 1980. See also the comments of Jim Palmer in an interview published in *Sport*, Apr. 1983.

26. Harris, *League*, pp. 5–6, 11–17, 279–80, 479, 491–95.

27. "Is There a Ceiling?," *SI*, 5 Jan. 1981. *TSN*, 24 Jan. 1981.

28. Peters interview.

29. *SI*, 12 Apr. 1982. *NYT*, 11, 12 Dec. 1981, 19 May, 18 June 1982. *TSN*, 26 Dec. 1981. See also interview with Roy Eisenhardt, *Sport*, May 1983.

30. *Dun's Review*, Mar. 1981.

31. *Television Age*, 1 Aug. 1966, 30 Jan. 1967. *Broadcasting*, 20 Feb. 1967. "It's a Sport, It's Money, It's TV," *SI*, 25 Apr. 1966. *NYT*, 8 Apr. 1983.

32. *Broadcasting*, 10 Apr. 1972.

33. Ibid., 6 Nov. 1972, 13 Mar. 1978. Pierce quoted in 13 Mar. issue. See *Television/Radio Age*, 4 Feb. 1974, on baseball's audience.

34. *Broadcasting*, 3 Apr. 1972, 20 May 1974, 30 June 1975.

35. House, *Inquiry into Professional Sports, Hearings*, 2:122.

36. *Broadcasting*, 24 June, 25 Sept. 1974, 21 Apr. 1975.

37. House, *Communications Act of 1979*, p. 160. *TSN*, 16 June 1979.

38. House, *Communications Act of 1979*, p. 288.

39. House, *Cable Copyright Legislation*, p. 1412.

40. Ibid., pp. 127–30, 655, 658. House, *Communications Act of 1979*, pp. 158–62, 222–23, 231–32. *TSN*, 31 Mar. 1979. *Broadcasting*, 4 June, 17 Sept., 12 Nov. 1973. *NYT*, 26 Oct. 1974.

41. *TSN*, 9 Aug. 1980. Kuhn, *Hardball*, pp. 289–90.

42. *Sun*, 1 Mar. 1981. *Washington Post*, 13, 27 Aug. 1982.

43. *Television/Radio Age*, 28 Feb. 1983. *Sun*, 22 Mar. 1982.

44. *Sun*, 23 Mar. 1982.

45. Ibid.

46. Ibid. See *Television/Radio Age*, 28 Feb. 1983, for an overview of local broadcasting.

47. Lucchino quoted in *Washington Post*, 18 June 1983. *Television/Radio Age*, 20 Feb. 1984. *Sun* 13, Mar. 1986.

48. *Washington Post*, 18 Apr. 1986.

49. Kuhn, *Hardball*, p. 288. See *Sun*, 8 Mar. 1985, on Orioles local rights.

50. *NYT*, 13 Apr. 1983. *Broadcasting*, 10 Mar. 1975. *Television/Radio Age*, 2 Feb. 1976, 12 Feb. 1979, 22 Feb. 1981.

51. *NYT*, 2, 5 Mar. 1983.

52. *Television/Radio Age*, 20 Feb. 1984. Williams quoted in *Sun*, 12 Mar. 1983.

53. Kuhn, *Hardball*, pp. 3–5.

54. *Sun*, 3 Aug. 1981. Kuhn, *Hardball*, pp. 360–61, 363.

55. Kuhn, *Hardball*, pp. 7–11.

56. Williams quoted in *SI*, 12 Apr. 1982. Kuhn, *Hardball*, p. 376. *NYT*, 18 June 1982.

57. Kuhn interview in *Sport*, Sept. 1983.

58. *NYT*, 19 Aug. 1982. Kuhn, *Hardball*, pp. 10, 366–67, 425.

59. *NYT*, 2 Nov. 1982.

60. Ibid., 2 June 1983.

61. Ibid., 14, 15, 18 June 1982, 31 July, 4 Aug. 1983.

62. Ibid., 9 Dec. 1983, 1, 4 Mar. 1984.

63. Ibid., 14 Nov. 1983.

Chapter 14

1. *1984 Orioles Yearbook*, pp. 45–46.

2. *NYT*, 1 Apr. 1984. Boswell, *Time*, pp. 23–35, 62–63, 65, 76.

3. Confidential interview.

4. *Sun*, 24 Aug. 1984.

5. Ibid.

6. Ibid., 21 Sept. 1984. *Washington Post*, 23 Sept. 1984.

7. *TSN*, 18 Feb. 1985.

8. *Sun*, 13 Dec. 1984.

9. *Washington Post*, 1 Feb. 1985.

10. Ibid., 12 Dec. 1985. *Sun*, 29 Jan. 1986. On the aging of the Orioles teams, see also comments in James, *James Baseball Abstract*, 1988, pp. 104–6.

11. *USA Today*, 22 Aug. 1986. *Washington Post*, 25 Aug. 1986. *Sun*, 26 Aug. 1986.

12. *Washington Post*, 20 Feb., 15 Mar. 1987.

13. *Sun*, 27 Mar. 1988. For another essentially negative evaluation of the minor league system, see Frank Robinson, *Extra Innings*, pp. 162–63, 185–86.

14. *Washington Post*, 3 July 1987.

15. *TSN*, 25 Mar. 1978.

16. Data on minor league attendance from a letter of Sal Artiaga, administrator of the National Association, *Baseball America*, 10 Apr. 1988.

17. *D&C*, 7, 8 Dec. 1979, 11 Apr. 1980. Farrell quoted in 11 Apr. edition. *TSN*, 26 Jan. 1980.

18. *D&C*, 5, 7 Sept., 14 Oct., 9 Dec. 1980.

19. Ibid., 28 Sept., 17, 18 Nov. 13, Dec. 1980. Rochester *Times Union*, 17 Mar. 1981.

20. *D&C*, 6 Nov. 1980, 16 Apr. 1981. Rochester *Times Union*, 9 Apr., 9 May 1981. *TSN*, 13 June 1981.

21. *D&C*, 11 July, 17, 25, 29 Sept., 15 Oct. 1981.

22. Rochester *Times Union*, 15 Oct. 1981. *D&C*, 14, 16 Oct., 19 Nov., 4, 11 Dec. 1981.

23. Horton interview. *D&C*, 22 May 1982.

24. *D&C*, 8 Sept., 19 Dec. 1982, 18 Mar. 1983. Giordano quoted in 18 Mar. edition.

25. Press clipping, Sept. 1984, "Rochester," Subject Files, NBL. *D&C*, 1, 2 Dec. 1984. Verdi quoted in 2 Dec. edition.

26. Rochester *Times Union*, 1 Apr. 1982. *D&C*, 7 Mar. 1984.

27. *D&C*, 7, 9 Dec. 1984, 7 Apr. 1985.

28. On Crockett, see *SI*, 26 Apr. 1982.

29. *Washington Post*, 6 Aug. 1980, 16 Feb., 13 Mar. 1986. Williams quoted in 13 Mar. edition.

30. Ibid., 13 Mar. 1986. *Sun*, 27 Mar. 1988.

31. *Sun*, 24 July 1986, 31 July 1987. *Washington Post*, 3 July 1987. *TSN*, 23 June 1986.

32. *Sun*, 28 Jan., 20 Dec. 1979. See *Evening Sun*, 2 Sept. 1977, on stadium losses. Baltimore, *Capital Improvement Program, 1965–1970*, p. 27.

33. Maryland, *Journal of Proceedings*, House, 1979, pp. 586, 2108, 2261, 2681, 3384, 3576, 3613, 3639. Ibid., Senate, 1979, pp. 482, 2834, 2942, 3279. *Sun*, 1 Nov. 1979.

34. Maryland, *Journal of Proceedings*, House, 1980, pp. 1900–1901, 1993, 2125, 3289–90. Ibid., Senate, 1980, pp. 2412, 3507, 3523, 3685. *Laws of Maryland*, 1980, pp. 1903–6.

35. Maryland, *Journal of Proceedings*, House, 1980, pp. 204, 445. *Sun*, 1 Nov. 1979. *News American*, 19 Dec. 1979.

36. *Sun*, 2 Dec. 1980.

37. *News American*, 8 Feb. 1981. *Sun*, 2 Mar. 1981.

38. See Harris, *League*, pp. 209–10, 265–66, 363–69, 495–500, 548–54, for details. *News American*, 23 Nov. 1981.

39. Maryland, *Journal of Proceedings*, House, 1983, pp. 1027–28, 1933, 2048–49, 2460. Ibid., Senate, 1980, pp. 720, 2099, 2142–45, 2357–58. *Laws of Maryland*, 1983, p. 1507. *Sun*, 11 Feb., 8 Mar., 1 Apr. 1983. *Washington Post*, 11 Feb. 1983.

40. *Sun*, 12, 17 Mar. 1983. *Washington Post*, 17 Mar. 1983.

41. *Washington Post*, 31 Jan. 1984.

42. See Harris, *League*, pp. 561–67, for details.

43. Senate, *Community Protection Act*, pp. 36, 38.

44. *WSJ*, 20 Mar. 1987. "The New Arenas Debate," *Insight*, 21 Sept. 1987.

45. Senate, *Community Protection Act*, pp. 36–40. *Sun*, 31 Jan. 1978. *Evening Sun*, 31 Jan. 1978.

46. *WSJ*, 20 Mar. 1987. *Insight*, 21 Sept. 1987.

47. The information that follows was compiled from *Sun*, 31 Jan. 1978; *Evening Sun*, 31 Jan. 1987; and Baltimore Baseball Club, Annual Report, 1978. A check of Orioles media guides indicated that only three of fourteen Orioles residing in Maryland on a yearly basis lived in the city of Baltimore. Two significant changes in the pattern described in the text have taken place since 1978. The club is paying its athletes much larger salaries and has doubled the size of its administrative staff. In addition, with the opening of a baseball store subsidiary in Harbor Place, the Orioles have created a few additional jobs for the local economy and also contribute directly to the city's economy through rent payments, taxes, and the purchase of local services.

48. *Sun*, 31 Mar. 1979. Senate, *Community Protection Act*, p. 40. It is not clear if Tawney included sanitation, police, fire, and public transportation in his estimate.

49. Senate, *Community Protection Act*, pp. 36–40. *WSJ*, 20 Mar. 1987. Schaefer was certainly correct in suggesting that locating the new stadium in Harbor Place would create a greater direct impact on the city economy than building it in a Baltimore County site. However, the location of Memorial Stadium, even in the days when the team was drawing 2 million fans a year, had relatively little visible effect on the neighborhood economy.

50. *NYT*, 23 Oct. 1983.

51. Senate, *Community Protection Act of 1985*, pp. 130–32. See also "Behind the Battle Over Baltimore's Sports Future," *Baltimore*, Nov. 1984.

52. *Sun*, 11 Jan., 27 Feb. 1985.

53. *Washington Post*, 23 Jan. 1985.

54. Ibid., 26, 28 Aug., 27 Oct. 1985.

55. *Sun*, 30 Aug. 1985. *Washington Post*, 16 Oct. 1985.

56. *Sun*, 27 Aug. 1985. *SIN*, 4 Sept. 1985.

57. *SIN*, 30 Oct. 1985, 8 Jan. 1986.

58. *Sun*, 29 Jan. 1986.

59. *Washington Post*, 29 Jan. 1986.

60. *Sun*, 29 Jan. 1986.

61. Ibid., 25 Jan. 1986. *Washington Post*, 26, 30 Jan. 1986. Williams letter quoted in 30 Jan. edition.

62. *Washington Post*, 30 Jan. 1986.

63. Ibid. *Sun*, 20 Mar. 1986, 15 Jan. 1987.

64. *Sun*, 21, 26 Mar. 1986. *Washington Post*, 3 Apr. 1986. *SIN*, 9 Apr. 1986.

65. *Washington Post*, 24 Mar., 3 June 1986.

66. *Sun*, 6 Nov., 5 Dec. 1986.

67. Ibid., 12 Dec. 1986, 27 Feb., 5, 10 Mar. 1987. *Washington Post*, 25 Feb., 5 Mar., 2, 5 Apr. 1987.

Epilogue

1. Tim Kurkjian's description of Hemond in *Sun*, 1 Apr. 1988.
2. *Washington Post*, 11 Nov. 1987.
3. Ibid.
4. Peters quoted in *Sun*, 3 Oct. 1987. Ibid., 8 Nov. 1987. *Washington Post*, 3 Nov. 1987, 3 Mar. 1988.
5. *Washington Post*, 6 Oct. 1987. For Peters's views, see *Sun*, 3 Oct. 1987. See also comments in Frank Robinson, *Extra Innings*, pp. 254–55.
6. See Boswell's comments in *Washington Post*, 6 Oct. 1987. Peters's remarks in *Sun*, 3 Oct. 1987.
7. Peters interview. *NYT*, 15 Feb. 1984. In a 31 Oct. 1980 interview in the *Sun*, Peters stated that the team was unable to find black prospects. Frank Robinson, *Extra Innings*, p. 129, notes that until 1987 Orioles scouting forms included a box for race, suggesting that it was a factor in scouting evaluations. Robinson also noted that the Orioles' one black coach was repeatedly passed over for promotion (ibid., pp. 2–3).
8. *Sun*, 1 Apr. 1988.
9. *USA Today*, 1 Apr. 1988.
10. *Sun*, 20 Apr. 1988.
11. *TSN*, 16 Dec. 1985. *NYT*, 12 Apr. 1987. *USA Today*, 19 Nov. 1986.
12. *Sun*, 9 July 1974. *NYT*, 27 July, 18 Aug. 1974. Kuhn, *Hardball*, pp. 109–25. For some statistical data on the lack of black mobility in both major and minor leagues and commentary, see Frank Robinson, *Extra Innings*, pp. 68, 113, 170–71.
13. *D&C*, 11 Nov. 1980. See the comments of Frank Robinson, *Extra Innings*, pp. 172–73.
14. Baseball officials have heatedly denied this charge since it was first made over twenty years ago. Recently, the sport's defenders have cited the large number of black or racially mixed shortstops playing at the major league level as proof that segregation by position does not exist. Two points need to be made in response. First, baseball teams will utilize an exceptionally talented player such as St. Louis's Ozzie Smith at a skill position. Second, in recent years the Dominican Republic has been producing a remarkable number of very talented black or racially mixed shortstops. However, the overall statistics continue to show a marked tendency to hand the so-called thinking positions to white players. A 1988 study by Northeastern University's Center for the Study of Sports in Society noted white domination of these positions. Blacks constituted 6 percent of all major league pitchers, 4 percent of catchers, 18 percent of second basemen, 29 percent of shortstops, and 15 percent of third basemen. Overall, 78 percent of all blacks play in either the outfield or at first base. Marginal or journeyman black players continued to have significantly shorter careers than comparable white athletes. *CSSS Digest*, Oct. 1988. Interestingly, these figures have remained constant over more than twenty years. Cf. Rosenblatt, "Negroes in Baseball," for 1967 statistics and Rader, *American Sports*, p. 334, for 1976 figures. See also the comments in Frank Robinson, *Extra Innings*, p. 9.
15. *Washington Post*, 6 Apr. 1987.
16. Ibid., 9 Apr. 1987.
17. Ibid., 10 Apr. 1987.
18. "Where Are the Black Fans?," *NYT Magazine*, 17 May 1987. *Sun*, 1 July 1987.

Washington Post, 22 July 1987. *Washington Post*, 23 Nov. 1988. Cf. the data in *CSSS Digest*, Oct. 1988.

19. *WSJ*, 20 Mar. 1987. *Insight*, 21 Sept. 1987. *NYT*, 9 Sept. 1986. *Sun*, 12 June, 2 Sept. 1987. *Washington Post*, 23 Mar., 4 Sept. 1987.

20. *Sun*, 26 Jan. 1988.

21. *Washington Post*, 5 Apr. 1988.

22. Ibid.

23. *Sun*, 27 Jan., 3, 7, 15 Mar. 1988. *Washington Post*, 13 Mar. 1988.

24. *Sun*, 3 May 1988. *Washington Post*, 6 May 1988.

25. *Washington Post*, 31 Aug. 1988. *Sun*, 1, 16 Sept. 1988.

26. *Sun*, 7 Dec. 1988.

27. *Washington Post*, 24 Feb. 1987.

28. Ibid., 15 Apr. 1988.

29. Ibid., 24 July, 1 Dec. 1985.

30. House, *Inquiry into Professional Sports, Hearings*, 1:76. *SIN*, 13 Nov. 1985. *TSN*, 25 Nov. 1985. For Williams's comment on baseball in Washington, see *Washington Post*, 11 Dec. 1985.

31. *SIN*, 30 Oct. 1985, 12 Mar. 1986. *TSN*, 10 Feb. 1986.

32. *Washington Post*, 15 Nov. 1985, 13 Mar. 1987. *TSN*, 13 Oct. 1986, 30 Mar. 1987.

33. *Sun*, 6 June, 25 July 1986, 23, 28 Oct., 5 Nov. 1987.

34. Ibid., 15 Dec. 1988. See *Washington Post*, 16, 21 Dec. 1988, 6 Jan. 1989, for analyses of the two deals' impact.

35. *TSN*, 9 Dec. 1985.

36. *Washington Post*, 11 Dec. 1985.

37. *USA Today*, 9 Dec. 1985.

38. *Washington Post*, 15 Dec. 1985.

39. *TSN*, 20, 27 Jan. 1986.

40. *USA Today*, 11 Apr. 1986.

41. *Washington Post*, 27 Sept. 1985. *SIN*, 2 Oct. 1985.

42. *SIN*, 23 Oct., 20 Nov., 4 Dec. 1985. *TSN*, 9 Dec. 1985.

43. *Washington Post*, 1 Mar. 1986. *Sun*, 1, 9 Mar. 1986.

44. *Washington Post*, 22 Apr. 1986. *TSN*, 5 May 1986. In December 1988 the Pirates and Parker agreed to an out-of-court settlement that reportedly reduced the club's indebtedness to Parker.

45. *Washington Post*, 3 Mar. 1986.

46. The Orioles' program is outlined in *Washington Post*, 30 Jan. 1986, and *Sun*, 31 Jan. 1986.

47. *Washington Post*, 1 Feb. 1986, 5 Mar. 1987.

48. *NYT*, 22 Sept. 1987. See also comments on the balance of power between players and management in *Baseball America*, 25 Mar. 1988.

49. *Washington Post*, 1 Sept. 1988.

Bibliography

Manuscript Collections

Baltimore City Archives, Baltimore, Md.
    Files of Thomas D'Alesandro, Jr., 1947–59
    Files of Harold Grady, 1959–63 (Grady-Goodman Files)
    Files of Theodore McKeldin, 1963–67
    Files of Thomas D'Alesandro III, 1967–71
Library of Congress, Manuscript Division, Washington, D.C.
    Papers of Emanuel Celler
    Papers of Arthur Mann
    Papers of Branch Rickey
McKeldin Library, University of Maryland, College Park, Md.
    Papers of Daniel J. Brewster
    Papers of Theodore McKeldin
Maryland Historical Society, Baltimore, Md.
    Papers of Thomas D'Alesandro, Jr., 1940–69
    Oral History Interviews:
        Thomas D'Alesandro, Jr.
        Thomas D'Alesandro III
        Clarence Miles
Maryland State Archives, Annapolis, Md.
    Records of the Maryland Sports Complex Authority
National Archives, Washington, D.C.
    Record Group 46: Records of the U.S. Senate, Files of the Antitrust
        Subcommittee, Judiciary Committee
National Baseball Library, Cooperstown, N.Y.
    Subject Files
Securities and Exchange Commission, Washington, D.C.
    Reports filed by Baltimore Baseball, Inc., 1954–79
University of Michigan Historical Collections, Ann Arbor, Mich.
    Papers of Philip A. Hart
University of Rochester Library, Rochester, N.Y.
    Papers of Kenneth B. Keating

Interviews

Harry Dalton, 24 Nov. 1986
Jack C. Dunn III, 5 June 1986
Hon. Frank C. Horton, 2 Dec. 1986
James McLaughlin, 9 Aug. 1986
Lee MacPhail, 15 Oct. 1986
Henry J. Peters, 10 June 1986
Brooks Robinson, 15 Apr. 1987

All interviews were conducted by the author.

Public Documents

Baltimore
Annual Report of the City of Baltimore. Baltimore, 1972–84.
Commission on City Plan. *Capital Improvement Program for Baltimore (April 1947).* Baltimore, 1947.
Department of Planning. *Baltimore's Development Program.* Baltimore, 1977.
_____. *Baltimore's Development Program: An Overview.* Baltimore, 1977.
_____. *The Use of Leisure Time.* Baltimore, 1967.
_____. Planning Commission. *Baltimore's Development Program as Recommended by the Planning Commission, February 23, 1973.* Baltimore, 1973.
_____. *Recommended Capital Improvement Program, 1965–1970.* Baltimore, 1964.

Maryland
Journal of the Proceedings of the House of Delegates of Maryland. Annapolis, 1971–85.
Journal of the Proceedings of the Senate of Maryland. Annapolis, 1971–85.
Laws of Maryland. Annapolis, 1972–85.
Maryland Commission on Interracial Problems and Relations. *An American City in Transition.* Baltimore, 1955.
_____. *Desegregation in the Baltimore City Schools.* Baltimore, 1955.
_____. *The Report of a Study of Desegregation in the Baltimore City Schools.* Baltimore, 1956.

United States
U.S. Congress. House. Committee on Education and Labor. *Labor Reform Act of 1977. Part 2. Hearings before the Subcommittee on Labor-Management Relations, 95th Congress, 1st Session, on HR 8410.* Washington, D.C., 1978.
_____. Committee on Interstate and Foreign Commerce. *The Communications Act of 1979. Hearings before the Subcommittee on Communications, 96th Congress, 1st Session, on HR 3333.* Washington, D.C., 1979.
_____. Committee on the Judiciary. *Cable Copyright Legislation. Hearing before the*

Subcommittee on Telecommunications, Consumer Protection, and Finance. 97th Cong., 2nd sess. Washington, D.C., 1982.

———. *Copyright/Cable Television. Hearings before the Subcommittee on Courts, Civil Liberties, and the Administration of Justice. Part 1.* 97th Cong., 1st and 2nd sess. Washington, D.C., 1982.

———. *Copyright Issues: Cable Television and Performance Rights. Hearings before the Subcommittee on Courts, Civil Liberties, and the Administration of Justice.* 96th Cong., 1st sess. Washington, D.C., 1980.

———. *Organized Baseball. Report of the Subcommittee on Study of Monopoly Power Pursuant to H. Res. 95.* 82nd Cong., 1st sess. Washington, D.C., 1952.

———. *Organized Professional Team Sports. Hearings before the Antitrust Subcommittee. Part 2.* 85th Cong., 1st sess. Washington, D.C., 1957.

———. *Study of Monopoly Power. Hearings before the Subcommittee on Study of Monopoly Power. Part 6: Organized Baseball.* 82nd Cong., 1st sess. Washington, D.C., 1952.

———. *Telecasting of Professional Sports Contests. Hearing before the Antitrust Subcommittee (Subcommittee No. 5) of the Committee on the Judiciary.* 87th Cong., 1st sess. Washington, D.C., 1961.

———. Select Committee on Professional Sports. *Inquiry into Professional Sports. Final Report.* Washington, D.C., 1977.

———. *Inquiry into Professional Sports. Hearings.* 94th Cong., 2nd sess. Washington, D.C., 1976.

U.S. Congress. Senate. Committee on Commerce, Science, and Transportation. *Amendments to the Communications Act of 1934. Part 3. Hearings before the Subcommittee on Communications.* 96th Cong., 1st sess. Washington, D.C., 1979.

———. *Professional Sports Community Protection Act of 1985. Hearings.* 99th Cong., 1st sess. Washington, D.C., 1985.

———. *Professional Sports Team Community Protection Act. Hearings.* 98th Cong., 2nd sess. Washington, D.C., 1984.

———. Committee on Interstate and Foreign Commerce. *Broadcasting and Televising Baseball Games. Hearings.* 83rd Cong., 1st sess. Washington, D.C., 1953.

———. Committee on the Judiciary. *Cable Copyright and Signal Carriage Act of 1982. Joint Hearing before the Committee on Commerce, Science, and Transportation and the Committee on the Judiciary.* 97th Cong., 2nd sess. Washington, D.C., 1983.

———. *The Industrial Reorganization Act. Hearings before the Subcommittee on Antitrust and Monopoly. Part 4A: American Ground Transportation.* 93rd Cong., 2nd sess. Washington, D.C., 1974.

———. *Organized Professional Team Sports. Hearings before the Subcommittee on Antitrust and Monopoly.* 85th Cong., 2nd sess. Washington, D.C., 1958.

———. *Organized Professional Team Sports. Hearings before the Subcommittee on Antitrust and Monopoly.* 86th Cong., 1st sess. Washington, D.C., 1959.

———. *Organized Professional Team Sports, 1960. Hearings before the Subcommittee on Antitrust and Monopoly.* 86th Cong., 2nd sess. Washington, D.C., 1960.

———. *Professional Sports Antitrust Bill, 1964. Hearings before the Subcommittee on Antitrust and Monopoly.* 88th Cong., 2nd sess. Washington, D.C., 1964.

———. *Professional Sports Antitrust Bill, 1965. Hearings before the Subcommittee on*

Antitrust and Monopoly. 89th Cong., 1st sess. Washington, D.C., 1965.
————. *Professional Sports Antitrust Immunity. Hearings*. 99th Cong., 1st sess. Washington, D.C., 1986.
————. *Subjecting Professional Baseball Clubs to Antitrust Laws. Hearings*. 83rd Cong., 2nd sess. Washington, D.C., 1954.

Legal Records

Flood v. Kuhn 407 US 258, 282–83. (316 F Supp 271.)
Gardella v. Chandler 172 F2d 402.
Kansas City Royals Baseball Club v. Major League Baseball Players Association 532 F2d 615 (409 F Supp 233).
Kuhn v. Finley 569 F2d 527.
Radovich v. the National Football League 352 US 445.
Toolson v. New York Yankees 346 US 356.

Baltimore Orioles Publications

Media guides, 1972–88
Newsletters, 1985–87
Yearbooks, 1954–86

Periodicals

Across the Board
American City
Baltimore
Baseball America
Baseball Digest
Broadcasting
Business Week
Colliers
Dun's Review
Ebony
Esquire
Forbes
Fortune
Harper's
Inside Sports
Life
Look
Maclean's
Nation
National Review

Nation's Business
New Leader
New Republic
Newsweek
New Yorker
Reader's Digest
Reporter
Saturday Evening Post
Saturday Review
Sport
Sports Illustrated
Sports Industry News
Television Age
Television Quarterly
Television/Radio Age
Time
Tropic
U.S. News and World Report
Washingtonian
Washington Monthly

Newspapers

Baltimore *Afro-American*
Baltimore *Evening Sun*
Baltimore *News American*
Baltimore *News Post*
Baltimore *Sun*
New York Times
Rochester *Democrat and Chronicle*
Rochester *Times Union*
St. Louis *Post Dispatch*
San Antonio *Express*
The Sporting News
USA Today
Wall Street Journal
Washington Post
Washington *Star*
Washington Times

Secondary Materials

Adreano, Ralph. *No Joy in Mudville*. New York, 1965.
Alexander, Charles. *Ty Cobb*. New York, 1984.
American League of Professional Baseball Clubs. *American League 1988 Red Book*.
    New York, 1988.

Angell, Roger. *Five Seasons*. New York, 1977.
————. *Late Innings*. New York, 1982.
————. *The Summer Game*. New York, 1972.
Baltimore *Sun*. *A Championship Season*. Indianapolis, Ind., 1983.
Barber, Red. *1947—When All Hell Broke Loose in Baseball*. New York, 1982.
Beard, Gordon. *Birds on the Wing*. New York, 1967.
Beirne, Francis. *The Amiable Baltimoreans*. Baltimore, 1984.
Boswell, Thomas. *How Life Imitates the World Series*. New York, 1982.
————. *Why Time Begins on Opening Day*. New York, 1984.
Bouton, Jim. *Ball Four*. New York, 1970.
Bready, James H. *The Home Team*. Baltimore, 1984.
Breslin, Jimmy. *Can't Anybody Here Play This Game?* New York, 1963.
Briley, Ron. "Amity Is the Key to Success: Baseball and the Cold War." *Baseball History* 1 (Fall 1986): 4–19.
Brooks, Neal H., and Eric G. Rockel. *A History of Baltimore County*. Towson, Md., 1979.
Brosnan, Jim. *The Long Season*. New York, 1960.
————. *Pennant Race*. New York, 1962.
Callcott, George H. *Maryland and America, 1940 to 1980*. Baltimore, 1985.
Canes, Michael. "The Social Benefits of Restrictions on Team Quality." In *Government and the Sports Business*, edited by Roger Noll, pp. 81–114. Washington, D.C., 1974.
Chandler, Alfred, Jr. *The Visible Hand*. Boston, 1977.
Clark, Tom. *Champagne and Boloney*. New York, 1976.
Congressional Quarterly Almanac, 1961. Washington, D.C., 1962.
Cook, Earnshaw, with Wendell Garner. *Percentage Baseball*. Cambridge, Mass., 1966.
Cosell, Howard. *I Never Played the Game*. New York, 1985.
Craig, Peter S. "Organized Baseball: An Industry Study of a $100 Million Spectator Sport." Honors thesis, Oberlin College, 1950.
Creamer, Robert W. *Stengel*. New York, 1984.
Crepeau. Richard. *Baseball: America's Diamond Mind, 1919–1941*. Orlando, 1980.
Davids, L. Robert, ed. *Insider's Baseball*. New York, 1983.
Davis, Lance E. "Self-Regulation in Baseball, 1909–1971." In *Government and the Sports Business*, edited by Roger Noll, pp. 349–86. Washington, D.C., 1974.
Dolson, Frank. *Beating the Bushes*. South Bend, Ind., 1982.
Dorer, Skip, and Wayne Kaiser. *In the O Zone*. Baltimore, 1980.
Durso, Joseph. *The All American Dollar*. Boston, 1971.
————. *Baseball and the American Dream*. St. Louis, 1986.
Enright, Tim, ed. *Trade Him!* Chicago, 1976.
Falkner, David. *The Short Season*. New York, 1986.
Flemming, G. H. *The Dizziest Season*. New York, 1984.
Flood, Curt, with Richard Carter. *The Way It Is*. New York, 1971.
Frick, Ford. *Games, Asterisks and People*. New York, 1973.
Gammons, Peter. *Beyond the Sixth Game*. Boston, 1985.
Garrow, David J. *Bearing the Cross*. New York, 1986.
Garvey, Edward. "From Chattel to Employee: The Athlete's Quest for Freedom and

Dignity." *Annals of the American Academy of Political and Social Science* 445 (Sept. 1979): 91–101.

Golenbock, Peter. *Bums: An Oral History of the Brooklyn Dodgers.* New York, 1984.

———. *Dynasty: The New York Yankees, 1949–1964.* Englewood Cliffs, N.J., 1975.

Grebey, C. Raymond, Jr. "Another Look at Baseball's Salary Arbitration." *The Arbitration Journal* 38 (Dec. 1983): 24–30.

Gregory, Paul M. *The Baseball Player.* Washington, D.C., 1956.

Gunther, Marc. *Basepaths.* New York, 1984.

Hall, James R., and William Spellman. "Professional Baseball: The Reserve Clause and Salary Structure." *Industrial Relations* 22 (Winter 1983): 1–19.

Harris, David. *The League.* New York, 1986.

Harwell, Ernie. *Tuned to Baseball.* South Bend, Ind., 1985.

Herzog, Whitey, and Kevin Harrigan. *White Rat.* New York, 1987.

Holohan, William L. "The Long Run Effects of Abolishing the Baseball Player Reserve System." *Journal of Legal Studies* 7 (Jan. 1978): 129–37.

Honig, Donald. *The Man in the Dugout.* Chicago, 1977.

Horowitz, Ira. "Market Entrenchment and the Sports Broadcasting Act." *American Behavioral Scientist* 21 (Jan.–Feb. 1978): 415–30.

———. "Sports Broadcasting." In *Government and the Sports Business,* edited by Roger Noll, pp. 275–324. Washington, D.C., 1974.

Jackson, Kenneth T. *Crabgrass Frontier.* New York, 1985.

Jackson, Reggie, and Mike Lupica. *Reggie.* New York, 1984.

James, Bill. *The Bill James Baseball Abstract* (published annually). New York, 1983–88.

———. *The Bill James Historical Baseball Abstract.* New York, 1986.

Johnson, Arthur T. "Congress and Professional Sports: 1951–1978." *Annals of the American Academy of Political and Social Science* 445 (Sept. 1979): 102–15.

Jordan, Jerry. "The Long-Range Effect of Television and Other Factors on Sports Attendance." ca. 1950. Study for Television Manufacturers Association

Jordan, Pat. *The Suitors of Spring.* New York, 1973.

Kahn, Roger. *The Boys of Summer.* New York, 1972.

———. *Good Enough to Dream.* New York, 1985.

———. *A Season in the Sun.* New York, 1977.

Kerrane, Kevin. *Dollar Sign on the Muscle.* New York, 1984.

Koppett, Leonard. *A Thinking Man's Guide to Baseball.* New York, 1967.

Kuhn, Bowie. *Hardball.* New York, 1987.

Lee, Brian E. "A Survey of Professional Team Sport Player Control Mechanisms under Antitrust and Labor Law Principles: Peace At Last." *Valparaiso University Law Review* 11 (Fall 1976): 373–434.

Levine, Peter. *A. G. Spalding and the Rise of Baseball.* New York, 1985.

Lieb, Frederick G. *The Baltimore Orioles.* New York, 1955.

Linn, Ed. *Steinbrenner's Yankees.* New York, 1982.

Lowenfish, Lee. "A Tale of Many Cities: The Westward Expansion of Major League Baseball in the 1950s." *Journal of the West* 17 (July 1978): 71–82.

Lowenfish, Lee, and Tony Lupien. *The Imperfect Diamond.* New York, 1980.

Lyttle, Richard. *A Year in the Minors.* New York, 1975.

McCormick, Robert. "Baseball's Third Strike: The Triumph of Collective Bargaining in Professional Baseball." *Vanderbilt Law Review* 35 (Oct. 1982): 1131–69.

Mann, Jack. *Decline and Fall of the New York Yankees*. New York, 1967.

Mantle, Mickey, and Herb Gluck. *The Mick*. New York, 1985.

Marazzi, Rich, and Len Fiorito. *Aaron to Zipfel*. New York, 1985.

Markham, Jesse, and Paul Teplitz. *Baseball Economics and Public Policy*. New York, 1981.

Mead, William B., and Harold Rosenthal. *The Ten Worst Years of Baseball*. New York, 1982.

Meier, August, and Elliott Rudwick. *CORE*. New York, 1973.

Meyer, Eugene. *Maryland: Lost and Found*. Baltimore, 1986.

Michener, James A. *Sports in America*. New York, 1976.

Miller, Marvin. "Arbitration of Baseball Salaries: Impartial Adjudication in Place of Management Fiat." *The Arbitration Journal* 38 (Dec. 1983): 31–35.

Moore, Joseph T. *Pride Against Prejudice*. New York, 1988.

Mortimer, Jeffery T. "The Development of Organized Baseball's Government." Senior thesis, Bard College, 1967.

Mosedale, John. *The Greatest of All: The 1927 New York Yankees*. New York, 1974.

Nettles, Graig, and Peter Golenbock. *Balls*. New York, 1984.

Noll, Roger, ed. *Government and the Sports Business*. Washington, D.C., 1974.

Obojski, Robert. *Bush League: A History of Minor League Baseball*. New York, 1975.

Okner, Benjamin. "Subsidies of Stadiums and Arenas." In *Government and the Sports Business*, edited by Roger Noll, pp. 325–48. Washington, D.C., 1974.

Okrent, Daniel. *Nine Innings*. New York, 1985.

Olson, Sherry. *Baltimore*. Cambridge, Mass., 1976.

———. *Baltimore: The Building of An American City*. Baltimore, 1980.

Pack, Robert. *Edward Bennett Williams for the Defense*. New York, 1983.

Parrott, Harold. *The Lords of Baseball*. New York, 1976.

Pluto, Terry. *The Earl of Baltimore*. Piscataway, N.J., 1982.

Pluto, Terry, and Jeffrey Neuman, eds. *A Baseball Winter*. New York, 1986.

Polner, Murray. *Branch Rickey*. New York, 1982.

Quirk, James, and Mohamed El Hodiri. "The Economic Theory of a Professional Sports League." In *Government and the Sports Business*, edited by Roger Noll, pp. 33–80. Washington, D.C., 1974.

Rader, Benjamin. *American Sports*. Englewood Cliffs, N.J., 1983.

———. *In Its Own Image*. New York, 1984.

Reichler, Joseph L. *The Baseball Trade Register*. New York, 1984.

Reidenbaugh, Lowell. *The Sporting News: The First Hundred Years*. St. Louis, 1985.

Remington, John L. *The Red Wings*. Rochester, N.Y., 1969.

Renchler, Joseph, ed. *The Baseball Encyclopedia*. 6th ed. New York, 1985.

Riess, Steven. "Baseball Myths, Baseball Reality and the Social Foundations of Baseball in Progressive America." *Stadion* 3 (1977): 273–311.

Robinson, Brooks, with Jack Tobin. *Third Base Is My Home*. Waco, Tex., 1974.

Robinson, Frank, with Dave Anderson. *Frank*. New York, 1976.

Robinson, Frank, with Al Silverman. *My Life Is Baseball*. New York, 1968.

Robinson, Frank, with Berry Stainback. *Extra Innings*. New York, 1988.

Rodin, Donald. "Baseball and the Quest for National Dignity in Meiji Japan." *American Historical Review* 85 (June 1980): 511–34.

Rogosin, Donn. *Invisible Men.* New York, 1983.

Rosenblatt, Aaron. "Negroes in Baseball: The Failure of Success." *Transaction* 4 (Sept. 1967): 51–53.

Rosenthal, Harold. *The Ten Best Years of Baseball.* New York, 1979.

Schneider, Russell. *Frank Robinson: The Making of a Manager.* New York, 1976.

Scoville, James. "Labor Relations in Sports." In *Government and the Sports Business,* edited by Roger Noll, pp. 185–220. Washington, D.C., 1974.

Scully, Gerald. "Binding Salary Arbitration in Major League Baseball." *American Behavioral Scientist* 21 (Jan.–Feb. 1978): 431–50.

_____. *The Business of Major League Baseball.* Chicago, 1989.

_____. "Discrimination: The Case of Baseball." In *Government and the Sports Business,* edited by Roger Noll, pp. 221–74. Washington, D.C., 1974.

Senzel, Howard. *Baseball and the Cold War.* New York, 1977.

Seymour, Harold. *Baseball: The Golden Age.* New York, 1971.

Sklar, Robert. *Movie-Made America.* New York, 1975.

Sullivan, Neil J. *The Dodgers Move West.* New York, 1987.

Thomas, Susan, and Marvin Jolson. "Components of Demand for Major League Baseball." *University of Michigan Business Review* 31 (May 1979): 1–6.

Thorn, John, and Peter Palmer. *The Hidden Game of Baseball.* New York, 1984.

Tygiel, Jules. *Baseball's Great Experiment.* New York, 1983.

_____. "Playing by the Book: Baseball History in the 1980s." *Baseball History* 1 (Winter 1986): 6–17.

Veeck, Bill, and Ed Linn. *The Hustler's Handbook.* New York, 1965.

_____. *Veeck—As in Wreck.* New York, 1962.

Voigt, David. *American Baseball.* 3 vols. University Park, Pa., 1983.

_____. "A Century of Baseball Strife." *Baseball Historical Review,* 1981, pp. 11–15.

Walsh, Richard, and William Lloyd Fox, eds. *Maryland: A History, 1632–1974.* Baltimore, 1974.

Weaver, Earl, and Terry Pluto. *Weaver on Strategy.* New York, 1984.

Weaver, Earl, and John Sammis. *Winning.* New York, 1972.

Weaver, Earl, and Berry Stainback. *It's What You Learn After You Know It All That Counts.* New York, 1982.

Welch, Bob, and George Vecsey. *Five O'Clock Comes Early.* New York, 1982.

Whitfield, Shelby. *Kiss It Goodbye.* New York, 1973.

Wills, Garry. *Nixon Agonistes.* Boston, 1970.

Zanger, Jack. *The Brooks Robinson Story.* New York, 1967.

Index